UNIX®
Relational Database Management

UNIX®
Relational Database Management

Application Development
in the
UNIX Environment

Rod Manis
Evan Schaffer
Robert Jørgensen

PRENTICE HALL
Englewood Cliffs, New Jersey 07632

Library of Congress Cataloging-in-Publication Number 87-36103

Cover design: Lundgren Graphics, Inc.
Manufacturing buyer: Mary Ann Gloriande

This book was typeset by the authors. UNIX programs formatted the text and printed the final copy. We acknowledge the special assistance of Barbara Wright, who is responsible for the description of ve in Chapter 5.

Prentice Hall Software Series
Brian W. Kernighan, Advisor

The publisher offers discount on this book when ordered
in bulk quantities. For more information, write:

Special Sales/College Marketing
College Technical and Reference Division
Prentice Hall
Englewood Cliffs, New Jersey 07632

Printed in the United States of America

10   9   8   7   6   5   4   3   2   1

ISBN 0-13-938622-X

PRENTICE-HALL INTERNATIONAL (UK) LIMITED, *London*
PRENTICE-HALL OF AUSTRALIA PTY. LIMITED, *Sydney*
PRENTICE-HALL CANADA INC., *Toronto*
PRENTICE-HALL HISPANOAMERICANA, S.A., *Mexico*
PRENTICE-HALL OF INDIA PRIVATE LIMITED, *New Delhi*
PRENTICE-HALL OF JAPAN, INC., *Tokyo*
SIMON & SCHUSTER ASIA PTE. LTD., *Singapore*
EDITORA PRENTICE-HALL DO BRASIL, LTDA., *Rio de Janeiro*

This book is dedicated to the people who have made
/rdb
possible

Thomas Arnow
Robert Berkley
Andy Chang
Michael J. Defazio
Steve Eberhart
Keith Eisenstark
Raymond Eisenstark
David Fiedler
Tom Johnson
Ray Jones
Brian Kernighan
Paul S. Kleppner
Mark Krieger
Gig Graham
William Hamilton
Joel Harrison
Beth Harsaghy
Chris Lynch
John Mashey
Marc Meyer
Phoebe Miller
Eli Nielsen
Fred Pack
Durk Pearson
Ron Posner
Pat Rafter
William Robinson
Pat Sarma
David Schmidt
Tom Slezak
William P. Spencer
Shawn Steel
Ed Taylor
Roy Takai
Zhang Yuchao
Richard Vento
Peter Vizel
Jerry Walker
Colin Watanabee
Barbara Wright
Myron Zimmerman

Contents

Preface

This book shows you how to develop software applications in a UNIX environment, in a small fraction of the time and effort needed with other systems. The UNIX environment is so different that it makes possible a new approach to computing.

There are many books available on writing C programs, administering a UNIX system, and specific software like spreadsheets and word processors. But this book tells you how to put them all together. System integration is the hardest part of software development. Therefore, we have filled this book with examples, solutions, source code, tricks, hints, and useable theory to help you.

Each of the authors has over 20 years of experience in computing in which we have had to put together an enormous number of applications on many different systems for a wide range of users. We have tried to put as much of what we have learned into this book as possible.

We emphasize database management because almost all applications require data to be entered, manipulated, searched, or reported. By learning simple database operations, you can approach any application with a powerful tool kit.

Model Business System

We have even included, as an example to get you started, a model business system with general ledger, tax, accounts receivable and payable, inventory, payroll, and operations. Included is a tutorial, manual pages, and source code of the UNIX shell scripts. They show you how to use the system, and also how to manage a business with a computer.

New Approach to Relational Database Management

Most books on relational database theory take a very mathematical approach and use a difficult language. They talk of relations, tuples, attributes, degrees, cardinality, and normalization. We've translated these terms into familiar words like tables, rows, and columns. We also show a new approach to normalizing tables which anyone can understand. We have tried to make relational database theory accessible to everyone.

The UNIX System

The UNIX system, of course, is among the greatest software tools available. It is portable, multi-user, and multi-tasking. It runs on hundreds of computers, from the IBM PC/XT to the Cray 2. It has been adopted as the standard operating system by the U.S. federal government (POSNIX), and many corporations and universities. But the most important features of the UNIX system are the UNIX shell, the software tools, and the *pipe and filter* approach.

To get the full power of the UNIX system, one must relearn and rethink how to do software development. Most software people are not aware of what they can do with the UNIX system. They use the same approach that they learned on other systems. It is as if they had a Porsche, and hitched a horse to it, not knowing that they could start its engine and roar away. In this book we will teach you how to drive, but you may have to give up your attachment to old fashioned horse and buggy styles of programming.

UNIX Shell is the Best Fourth Generation Programming Language

It is the UNIX shell that makes it possible to do applications in a small fraction of the code and time it takes in third generation languages. In the shell you process whole files at a time, instead of only a line at a time. And, a line of code in the UNIX shell is one or more programs, which do more than pages of instructions in a 3GL. Applications can be developed in hours and days, rather than months and years with traditional systems. Most of the other 4GLs available today look more like COBOL or RPG, the most tedious of the third generation languages.

Flat File Database

There are two approaches to database management. Traditionally, a large database management program had to be written to run on the old mainframe and mini computer operating systems which provided only a minimum of assistance. Therefore, all of the functions needed had to be coded. Each system had its own language and data formats. They seldom talked to each other. It was hard to pass data from one to the other. It took a lot of work to learn and code them. Then when you moved to another system, you had to learn a new language and figure out how to transfer and convert your data and rewrite your programs.

UNIX solved most of these problems by providing a huge set of tools and facilities and the ability to link them together with pipes and shell programs. Therefore, the burden on a database manager is significantly reduced. To take advantage of the UNIX environment, *flat file* database management systems were developed, including **/rdb** (pronounced slash-r-d-b) from Robinson Schaffer Wright, **Prelude** from VenturCom, **Unity** from AT&T, among others. These database managers work with UNIX and keep their data in flat ASCII UNIX files. You can mix UNIX and database commands in the same shell scripts and pipe commands. Therefore, you do not lose the power of UNIX by going into the database program. You use your UNIX knowledge, and/or learn UNIX skills once. Then you can move to most computers without having to learn *yet another system and language*.

/rdb Relational Database Management System for UNIX

We use **/rdb** for the examples in this book because it is so simple to learn and use, and does not get in the way of your understanding the principles of UNIX database management and applications development. It makes a good teaching aid. Examples with **/rdb** show you how to do basic tasks, without having to spend time learning complex systems. So even if you choose other software packages, you have learned the principles in the easiest way. You can then focus on the more cumbersome syntax of other software packages. **/rdb** is also one of the least expensive of the database managers and is available on any UNIX computer.

At the end of this book is a manual of the **/rdb** commands including examples of their use, and the source code of all of the UNIX shell programs. They will give you many ideas about how to handle specific problems in more detail than is appropriate for the tutorial part of this book.

UNIX and DOS

There is a joke going around that in the future there will be only two operating systems, *UNIX running DOS* and *DOS running UNIX*. It has already happened. The latest UNIX operating systems run DOS applications. And you can get the MKS Toolkit of over 100 UNIX commands, including the latest UNIX korn shell, vi, awk, grep, etc., to run on your DOS. **\rdb** (pronounced backslash-r-d-b), is the DOS version of */rdb.* Therefore, most of the programs described in this book will also run on DOS (MS-DOS, PC-DOS, OS/2) with the MKS Toolkit and **\rdb.** See the tear out card in this book, which offers a discount on these packages.

Since UNIX and DOS run on most of the world's computers, you can develop an application on one computer and run it on many others. You can also network computers together and run the same programs on each, transferring data in a standard format. It is an old dream come true. But there are lots of details to make it all work, which is what this book is about.

Macintosh

We see no conflict between the UNIX/DOS approach and the Macintosh approach. In an integrated computing environment, we'll be able to 'point and click' on, for example, a shell script, or any arbitrary collection of commands. The concept of relations as flat files and relational operators as programs is the common ground.

Required Knowledge

You should know how to log on to UNIX, to use its commands, to use a text editor like **vi.** You should be aware of the method of using UNIX programs, often piped together, to get things done without having to write C or other language programs. You do not have to know how to program, although it helps.

There are many introductory books on UNIX and a few books on advanced UNIX and shell programming: *The UNIX*^{TM} *Shell Programming Language* by Rod Manis and Marc H. Meyer [Manis 1986]. For more advanced UNIX, you should read Stephen Prata's *Advanced UNIX*^{TM} *- A Programmer's Guide* [Prata 1985], and Brian Kernighan and Rob Pike's book *The UNIX*^{TM} *Programming Environment* [Kernighan 1984], and the new Kernighan book on **awk.** See the bibliography for more complete citations.

This book starts where those leave off, and covers the details of putting together real applications with databases. One or more of these books should be read because they teach the UNIX and shell programming basics that we build upon. We assume that basic knowledge so that we can focus on application development. But even if you are new to UNIX, you should try to get started. If you get stuck, you can look up ideas in the other books and in your system's UNIX documentation.

To help overcome the old beliefs, we show how to develop and use software applications in the UNIX environment, covering all of the important tasks of programming and setting up computer systems to do real work for users. A beginner will learn the

basics of database design and fourth generation programming. Experienced programmers will learn how to work in this new environment. Many UNIX gurus
understand in principle that UNIX is a far better environment, but need to know
more of the details of how to handle certain problems.

Computer Revolution

This book aims at nothing less than a revolution in computing! It challenges some of
the most encrusted assumptions and proposes a simple, elegant approach which
solves many of the major problems in computing today.

1. Data should be kept in flat ASCII tables (files), not binary, so that we can
    always see what we are doing, and do not have to depend upon some special
    program to decode our data for us.

2. Programming should be done in a fourth generation programming language,
    the most powerful of which is the UNIX shell, not in lower level languages,
    except in extreme cases.

3. Programs should be small and should pass data on to other programs.
    Software prisons, or large programs with self-contained environments, must be
    avoided because they require learning and they make extracting data difficult.

4. All programs should be integrated with a common interface with both users
    and data. All of our tools should look more or less the same for quick learning
    and easy use.

5. We should build software and systems to meet interface standards so that we
    can share software and stop dreaming that any individual or company can do it
    all from scratch.

6. We should use networks to tie together computers and software so that simple
    tables of data can be passed from one to another.

7. Industrial strength artificial intelligence and expert systems will have to be
    developed in the same environment previously described, and not in toy
    languages like LISP and PROLOG.

8. The UNIX system embodies the most advanced facilities for implementing
    these principles.

Rod Manis
Evan Schaffer
Robert Jørgensen

Foreword

I stumbled into using UNIX in late 1978, in a Bio-Medical Research environment. The machine was a PDP 11-34 running V6 UNIX, with custom automated micros-copy gear used for image processing of mammalian cells. In those days there was the Kernighan and Ritchie C book and the UNIX manuals themselves; nothing more. Two degrees in computer science prepared me to tackle UNIX but I was still perhaps understandably shy about investigating all of the 100+ tools, including such strange ones as **awk**, **lex**, and **yacc**.

I quickly discovered that the use of the UNIX tools freed me from the great bulk of the drudgery of supporting real end users on a computer system. I could string tools together quickly instead of writing small *one shot* programs to do the myriad of data manipulation tasks that characterize real life in the scientific computing world. In the course of my work I acquired a relational database package, but found that it did not mesh well with the UNIX tool-kit philosophy. Like the mammoth database sys-tems I had previously used on large IBM systems, one had to *drop into* the database package, where a whole new command language applied and the UNIX tools could only be reached with extreme difficulty, if at all.

By 1983 I had added an early 16-bit microprocessor-based UNIX timesharing sys-tem running V7 UNIX to my computer shop. I had a growing number of users who were doing general purpose data processing and needed a variety of tools to handle their needs. I was fortunate enough to be in attendance at the Usenix conference where Rod Manis first described his **/rdb** database, that existed as a set of UNIX filters. As he presented his paper I realized, along with numerous other members of the audience, that Rod had grasped and implemented the central abstraction I had been toying with but never formalized: a UNIX database should use ASCII files and operate at the shell level as a series of filters. This simple but brilliant insight of Rod's, brought about by his mastery of a UNIX tool (**awk**) that I had ignored to that point, provided my researchers with the single most powerful tool I have been able to acquire to this date. Along with many others who remained after his talk to discuss his ideas, I was one of the first users of the **/rdb** package. The medical research environment is characterized by chronic lack of funding for computing equipment and scarcity of programming expertise. Without mega-funding, I had no choice but to find ways to let end users solve their own problems as much as possi-ble, without making them all *programmers*.

To my mind, the power of this tool is the freedom it gives to the end users. For the first time I could sit down with a novice and create a working sample database using real data in a matter of minutes. Queries could be demonstrated and stored in *user-friendly* shell scripts. Within hours the end users were fully capable of creating their own databases. Their creativity was amazing: One researcher who had had a single Fortran class eight years earlier wrote a two-page shell script using **/rdb** filters to completely computerize her laboratory data processing and analysis. Other users discovered that the innocent-appearing simple report writer was in reality a powerful meta-tool that allowed them to write shell scripts that wrote shell scripts, yielding in effect a *two-dimensional* program. By word of mouth it was demanded to be bought for at least a dozen other machines at this site. The database for the world's largest melanoma (skin cancer) epidemiology study runs on **/rdb,** as do many other applications.

I have found this abstraction of a database (regular ASCII files, filter programs, normal file access) to serve well for moderate size databases and the frequency of update and query that are common in the scientific research fields. Like most UNIX utilities and indeed UNIX itself, it is always possible to write a single-point solution that would be faster. I have found, however, that the ability to apply the full power of the UNIX toolkit to *database problems* far outweighs any speed penalties that I might be paying on the current generation of super-micros and super-minis. Even in situations where a "TRADITIONAL DATABA$E" is required, the rapid prototyping of the **/rdb** approach is often used to provide the early insights into the proper way to tackle problems requiring exceptional speed or size. I find that writing a custom program to manipulate or calculate data is virtually unnecessary, since such problems can nearly always be solved with the **/rdb** database and regular UNIX filters.

A completely unexpected benefit of this tool-kit approach to databases has been the education of users, many of whom have had no prior computer training or exposure. The early confidence gained in putting up their own simple databases often led to users taking the plunge and developing more complex shell scripts using those tools. In numerous cases, their continued interest led to them delving into **awk** and writing custom front or back end programs. A few adventurous souls then began writing C code in the awk scripts, as well as learning to use **lex,** which after all is merely a C program-generator cleverly (?) disguised as a lexical-analyzer. The net result is that I have had several novice users bootstrap themselves up to be excellent applications programmers in C in an amazingly short time, all due to the good first experience with the database tools!

The evolution of personal computers into machines with sufficient power to run UNIX well (IBM AT, Mac II, etc.) puts the ability to use the UNIX tool-kit philosophy into the reach of every research lab and small business. A book like this is as much a guide to using UNIX itself and the UNIX philosophy of problem solving as it is to being a guide to a specific database. The authors have quietly effected a revolution in the use of databases as a problem-solving tool that is as startling in its clarity and simplicity as the development of the spreadsheet program.

Tom Slezak
Computer Scientist, UNIX Support
Lawrence Livermore National Laboratory

1. Introduction

There are two fundamental ideas in this book that are necessary for application development in a UNIX environment. One is the relational model which allows you to see all applications as simple operations on tables. The other is the idea of using UNIX tools to pass data through pipelines and filter programs, instead of traditional programming. These are the ideas that this book seeks to teach.

1.1 Overview: Relational Database and UNIX

First we will introduce you to tables. All information can be entered into and manipulated in tables. This is the fundamental idea of relational databases. After covering the basic operations, you'll see simple database design principles. Then you will learn how to use UNIX tools. You will also be introduced to advanced database problems and solutions, and to logic programming, PROLOG, and artificial intelligence. A model business operation and accounting system tutorial and manual is included as a case study. Finally, manual pages, with shell source code to help you get started, are appended. Are you ready for all of this?

1.2 Operating Systems that Support UNIX Style Environments

By UNIX environment we mean file redirection, pipes, and UNIX style tools like **awk, grep, sed,** etc. This environment can be on a computer running the UNIX operating system, or other operating systems such as MS-DOS, PC-DOS, or OS/2 with UNIX tools added.

1.3 Applications Development

When people use a computer in their work, they usually need to have it programmed for their particular application. They might be scientists studying the data from their experiments, or entry clerks taking orders or reservations, or business people managing their businesses, or accountants preparing financial statements and tax forms, or lawyers doing research and preparing briefs, or any of the myriad users of computers. Some users can develop their own applications. UNIX tools makes this possible with their easy-to-use facilities. But most users need computer professionals to set up the applications for them. In this case, UNIX power eases the job of the developers and extends what they can do.

1.4 Databases

Almost all applications require some form of database. A database management system is a computer program that maintains data and performs many tasks such as easing the input and validation of data, the finding of data, the computations and transformations of the data, the reporting, and so forth.

1.5 UNIX Environment

The UNIX system is not just an operating system. It has hundreds of programs which work together to do most of the common computer jobs. UNIX tools provide an entire support environment for software application development and operation. It does so much of the work, that the jobs of both the developer and the user are enormously simplified. But since this environment is new to the computer profession, it is seldom used to its maximum potential. Often, developers don't know how to do on the UNIX system many of the things they are used to doing on other systems. Frequently, developers do things in the UNIX environment in difficult or slow ways that could be done much better if they knew how. We show you how to do the important tasks of setting up and running software applications.

1.6 Fourth Generation Programming Language

The first generation programming languages were the zeros and ones of the early computers. The second generation was assembly languages in which one line of code equaled one computer instruction. The third generation was programming languages like Fortran, COBOL, PL/I, C, Basic, and LISP. These have dominated computing for the last 30 years. They require programmers. Fourth generation programming systems do not require third generation programming. They allow nonprogrammers to set up applications, or significantly reduce the time it takes programmers to develop an application. The UNIX shell programming language and **/rdb** type database packages are excellent examples of fourth generation programming systems. The fifth generation will include artificial intelligence, natural language processing, and graphics to make a smart interaction with users. This is still a few years away, but fourth generation is here today.

1.7 UNIX Shell Programming

The UNIX system has a programming language called the shell programming language. The shell is the program in UNIX that talks to users and runs programs. However, it also has a full language with flow control statements. It is a string oriented language that descends from the Snobol language. It is ideal for a fourth generation application language.

1. Shell programming is easy to learn. You begin by simply typing commands.

2. It is powerful. Each command can execute one or more programs. This is much higher level than the lines of code in a third generation programming language.

3. With shell programming it is easy to automate your work. You can put your commands in files and call them by name to save typing and remembering.

4. It is easy to set up large systems and to call programs from menus.

5. Shell programming is worth learning. UNIX runs on over 150 different computers, from over 80 different computer companies around the world. Knowing the shell means being able to move from computer to computer and being able to talk to them all without starting over to learn another language. One can also get very good. It is hard to be proficient when one must keep starting over to learn new languages every few years.

6. There are now several books on shell programming, including *The UNIX Shell Programming Language* (Manis & Meyer, 1986, Howard Sams).

7. Shell programming makes possible fast prototyping. One can quickly set up an application for the user to see. One can continually improve on the system with easy edits of programs, files, menus, screens, and so on.

1.8 Assemble Software Modules

Traditionally, each time software developers start a new project they start from scratch. They write new database programs, new sort programs, new user interface programs, and so on. In this table, everything is written again for each project.

TABLE 1. Software Application Projects

Project	DB	Menu	Sort	Backup	Dataacq	Testing
payroll	x	x				x
order	x	x		x	x	x
lease	x	x				x
labauto	x		x	x	x	x
library	x	x	x	x		x

This is tremendously wasteful. Each project should simply assemble software programs. We should look at software development from a different direction by shifting our focus from projects to interchangeable program subsystems. A project should be seen as the assembly of software modules.

The UNIX system has most of the needed programs already. Only missing ones should be written. Professionals who have been working in the UNIX environment for years usually have several programs that they have written. Packages are available that extend UNIX to cover needed areas.

1.9 Fast Prototyping

The UNIX system also makes possible an old computer science dream: fast prototyping. A prototype is a model. It can be put together quickly and can demonstrate the way the system looks and works. Users and developers can use it to communicate with each other. In the construction industry the architect usually builds (or has built) a model of the building that is being designed. Then the buyer can look at it and say, *Well, I like this and this, but can you change that?* The architect can modify the model and come back to the buyer for another review.

In electronics, the design engineer has a breadboard upon which to build a prototype. The breadboard has many small holes for inserting wires and chip pins. When finished, it is a mass of wires, resisters, computer, memory, other chips, and switches. With luck it works and does the job. It cannot be used in a real application because it falls apart too easily and is not economical to manufacture. But it is excellent for testing and demonstrating the new device. Most importantly, when errors are discovered, changes are quick and easy. When the marketing department insists that another feature be added or simplified, it is easy. When the cost is too high, cheaper versions can be developed. When it heats up too fast, cooling fans can be added and/or parts can be moved farther apart. When a race condition, or noise is discovered, it can be corrected. Only when the prototype has been thoroughly tested should the product be assembled and sold.

In UNIX environments, software modules can also be quickly assembled to show how the application will look and perform. Top menus can be set up quickly, the database can be created and filled with a few sample records of data, a few reports can be laid out, a few calculations can be programmed or simulated. In a few days or weeks, the developer can show the user what the system will look like.

There is an old rule in software development. The users can never tell you what they want when you are designing the program, but they can always tell you that what you have delivered to them is **not** what they want. It seems that users start thinking about the software only when they get to see and work with it. Then they are full of suggestions that are very difficult to implement. In a UNIX environment, the developer can welcome these ideas, because change is so easy. A few days or weeks later, the user can see a modified prototype. The user and the developer can repeat this refinement process over and over again.

2. Tables: Where to store information

2.1 A World of Tables

The central idea of relational databases is that all information can be put into tables and can be manipulated by a few simple operations. This is a revolutionary idea and takes some thinking to understand. It means that all of our information needs can be handled in a simple way. All information, data, knowledge, facts, or whatever you call it, can be put into tables. For example, a table named *expenses* might look like this:

```
Date     Amount   Account   Description
------   ------   -------   ---------------------------
850125    67.00      4120    plane ticket
850126    12.00      4120    meal with client
850127   150.00      4120    hotel bill
```

At the top of the table are the column names. The dashed line makes it easier to read. Each row of the table holds information about a particular expense item.

We see information in tables every day — train schedules, scientific data, phone books, restaurant menus, price lists, catalogs, math tables, conversion tables, accounting and financial reports, tax forms, and so on. We all understand tables: we know how to fill them in and how to look up information in them. Tables and our operations on tables are independent of the information they contain. The purpose of this book is to help you to think about your information problems in terms of tables and operations on tables.

In accounting, information is collected in journals, then manipulated to create financial statements which you can look at to see the state of the business. Scientists have instruments in their labs that collect data and store it in their computers. Statistical programs compress masses of data into simple tables and graphs for the scientist to look at to see responses of systems to various inputs and to discover causal relationships. Employee information is stored in tables and can be extracted to print pay checks, make phone books, and so on.

2.2 Files

When we take these abstract ideas to the UNIX system we find a very friendly environment for storing tables and manipulating them. Computers store tables in files that live on hard disks. They have names by which they can be called up. Tables can be created with a text editor, with UNIX commands, from other tables, or with many of the forms packages available.

There are only three rules for creating a table in the UNIX and **/rdb** environment:

1. A tab is inserted between each column.

2. On the first line of the table, each column is given a name.

3. The second line of the table has lines of dashes for each column, showing the width of the column.

This is much easier for the user than systems that require the overhead of setting up schema and special files. Once tables are created, they can be manipulated by UNIX and **/rdb.** You should use the **ve** forms editor to initially create tables and enter data from your terminal, avoiding potential problems caused by (among other things) the wrong number of tabs.

2.3 Column

When we try to look up information in a table, we usually find that there is a lot more information there than we want. We have to find the single fact we want from all the rest. Often, there are more columns than we need. Therefore, we want to reduce the table to only those columns we need. When we look at a table with our eyes, we try to ignore the extra columns. Or we use our fingers to scan down the column we want.

When using the computer we have a command called **column,** which is a program that inputs one table and outputs another table that has only the columns you specify. For example consider our *expenses* table. One can project some of the columns of a table by typing this simple command, which says to project columns *Amount* and *Description* from the input *expenses* table:

```
$ column Amount Description < expenses
Amount  Description
------  --------------------------
 67.00  plane ticket
 12.00  meal with client
150.00  hotel bill
```

Note that now we have a new, smaller table with only the two columns we want to see. For another example, you might project just the names and phone numbers from the employee table to make a phone book. In other words, the company phone book is a projection of the name and phone columns of the employee table.

2.4 Row

The most common operation is to search the table for a specific piece of information. We want to know when the next plane leaves, the price of the scallops on the menu, the degrees Centigrade for 72 degrees Fahrenheit, the ball player with the highest batting average, the grade for a class on a report card, the amount spent on phone calls by the company last year, and so on. Each search requires that we select just one, or a few, rows from a table.

On the computer, you can select only the rows desired with the **row** command. Here we select all rows in the *expenses* table in which *Amount* is greater than 50:

```
$ row 'Amount > 50' < expenses
  Date   Amount   Account   Description
 ------   ------   -------   ---------------------------
850125    67.00      4120    plane ticket
850127   150.00      4120    hotel bill
```

With one simple operation you can select information from any table containing any data.

2.5 Column and Row

Often you want to find one or a few rows and see only a few columns. On UNIX you can put these two commands together. The UNIX pipe symbol (|) means to take the table that is output from the **column** command on the left and input it into the **row** command on the right.

```
$ column Amount Description < expenses | row 'Amount > 50'
Amount   Description
------   ---------------------------
 67.00   plane ticket
150.00   hotel bill
```

Since the output of one program can be piped into the input of another, you can create report programs with one or a few lines of commands and pipes. For example, you can project some columns of a table with the **column** command, pipe the output to a **row** program which will select certain rows, pipe that output to a **sort-table** program which sorts it, then on to a **jointable** to pick up other columns from another table. All of this can be done by typing one line on your terminal. Or this line can be typed into a shell program file with a text editor, and given a name, like **weeklyreport**. Then, by simply typing **weeklyreport**, the report can be produced when you wish. Several reports can be invoked by a higher level shell script. This is called **shell programming.** These reports, and other programs, can be placed in a menu and selected with a few keystrokes, or if you have a terminal with a mouse, by pointing and clicking. Therefore, you can automate whole operations in hours and days, rather than the months and years that it takes on other systems.

2.6 Shell Programming and Flat ASCII Files

The key to this approach is shell programming and flat ASCII files. *Flat* means there is no structure to them. UNIX thinks of them as a stream of characters. ASCII is a standard code for converting characters to numbers for storage in the computer. The files have variable length records and fields. This is a break from the IBM tradition of structured binary files with fixed length records and fields. Breaking with this old tradition is an essential part of the UNIX revolution.

2.7 Lists

In addition to the table format shown previously, **/rdb** also has a list format for data that is hard to fit into a table, such as mailing lists:

```
$ cat maillist

Number    1
Name      Rambo
Company   One Man Army
Street    123 Mac Attack
City      Anywhere
State     Thirdworld
ZIP       30000
Phone     (111) 222-3333

Number    2
Name      Chuck
Company   ...
```

Note that the list format begins with a blank line, unlike the table format, and that a single tab separates the field name from the data for each field. You can use the UNIX **vi** text editor or the **/rdb ve** form editor to initially create tables, and to enter and edit data in a table. You can convert from table to list and from list to table format easily with the **tabletolist** and **listtotable** commands.

3. Query and Report: How to get data out

In the last chapter you were introduced to tables and lists. You also saw some simple operations on tables. Now let's look in more detail at operations on tables.

Whatever your computer application is, you always want to put data into the computer, manipulate it, and get information out. Basically, you will want to enter your data into the computer in an easy way and then be able to ask questions or *query* your data, sending data and reports to your screen and your printer. You will also want to compute new data and transform your data in many ways. This chapter shows you how to get information out. This is done to motivate you to learn more. When you see what you can get, you will be more interested in finding out how to put the information in and how to manipulate it.

This chapter covers the basic query commands. Later chapters go into detail on subjects such as designing databases, report writing, data entry, UNIX utilities, other database models, and so on. As you look through these examples, you will see how powerful a relational system can be. You can get your data out in a multitude of ways to meet almost any need.

A few examples will make it easy to understand. You can start by simply typing your data into a table using a text editor. Any text editor will do. Screen editors like **vi** and **EMACS** are much easier to use than line oriented editors like **ed**. You can also enter your data with several **/rdb** programs, the **ve** screen forms entry package, or by any program that outputs flat UNIX files. A table is saved in a file and has a name. For example, the file **expenses** might look like this:

```
$ cat expenses
Date       Amount    Account    Description
-------    -------   -------    ------------------------------------
830102       5.00    lunch      lunch with boss, discussed new project
830103      14.23    phone      called vendor about late order
830104      76.00    plane      flew to la to meet with new client
etc.
```

The dollar sign ($) is the UNIX prompt, meaning: **enter your next command.** The **cat** command is the UNIX command that simply sends the input file to the standard output, which in this case is the computer terminal screen.

A table is a normal UNIX ASCII file with a single tab between each column. The names of the columns must be at the top of the table so that the **/rdb** commands will know which columns you are referring to when you issue commands. The second line of the table should be dashes (minus signs, not underscores). If you need more blank space between columns than the tabs provide, you can insert all the space you wish. The key thing to remember is that the **/rdb** programs must see only one tab between each column. Otherwise they (and your output) will get confused. If you

9

ever get a messed-up output, you can use the many UNIX commands to see the tabs in the table and make sure that they are all there. Helpful commands are the **see** command, or the **vi** editor **:set list** or **:l** colon commands, or the UNIX **od -c**, or, if you have the Berkeley enhancements, the **see** or **cat -v** commands.

```
$ see < expenses
Date      ^IAmount    ^IAccount    ^IDescription
------    ^I-------   ^I-------    ^I-----------------------------
830102  ^I 5.00    ^Ilunch    ^Ilunch with boss, discussed new project
830103  ^I14.23    ^Iphone    ^Icalled vendor about late order
830104  ^I76.00    ^Iplane    ^Iflew to la to meet with new client
```

After you enter your table with the editor, you have several powerful **/rdb** programs to manipulate the table or *query the database*.

3.1 column

If you wish to see a table with only the columns **Account** and **Amount** in that order, type:

```
$ column Account Amount < expenses
```

and the computer will display on the screen a new table:

```
Account   Amount
-------   -------
.lunch      5.00
phone      14.23
plane      76.00
```

You can see that **column** allows you to specify a new table with the columns you want, in the order you want them in. The first dollar sign ($) is the UNIX shell prompt. The rest of the line you type. Note that the left arrow (<, or less-than sign) means to take the input from the file named **expenses**. This is called the UNIX **file redirection** mechanism. The input to the program, instead of coming from your terminal, will come from a file. A right arrow (>, or greater-than sign) means to put the output into a file. Therefore, you can specify both the input and output files (including printers and CRT terminals) in a simple manner. This is one of the great benefits of the UNIX system, and has been added to the DOS system. Also note that we are taking data from the file and not changing the data in the file. This protects your original table from accidents.

If you wish, you can call the **column** command **project,** which is relational database literature name for the same program.

3.2 row

You may want to find all expenses over $10. You would use the **row** command this way:

```
$ row 'Amount > 10' < expenses
   Date   Amount   Account   Description
  ------- -------  -------   ---------------------------------
  810103  14.23    phone     called vendor about late order
  830104  76.00    plane     flew to la to meet with new client
```

Here you get all the columns, but only the rows that match your logical condition, amount greater than ten, *Amount > 10*. For another example, you might create an *inventory* table that looks like this:

```
$ cat inventory
   Item   Onhand      Cost    Value    Description
  ------- -------   -------  -------   ---------------
        1       3         5        0   rubber gloves
        2     100         1        0   test tubes
        3       5         8        0   clamps
        4      23         2        0   plates
        5      99         3        0   cleaning cloth
        6      89        18        0   bunsen burners
        7       5       175        0   scales
```

If you wished to find all items you were low on, you could ask for all items with less than 10 on hand. You would type:

```
$ row 'Onhand < 10' < inventory
   Item   Onhand      Cost    Value    Description
  ------- -------   -------  -------   ---------------
        1       3         5        0   rubber gloves
        3       5         8        0   clamps
        7       5       175        0   scales
```

If you prefer, you can use the name **select** instead of **row.** The relational database term is *select.* However, the Korn shell has a **select** command, so in the future we will need to use **column** and **row.** We give the same program two names with the UNIX **ln** command.

3.3 Quotes

Note that the single quote (') was put before and after the conditional expression in the previous **row** command. This protects the expression from the UNIX shell. The shell is the program within the UNIX system that reads the commands you type and executes them. Without the single quote, the shell would see the left arrow (<) and think we were inputting a table named *10*. The single quote is also needed to put the whole expression together as one argument for the **row** command. If you need to quote something within the expression, use the double quote ("). For example, if you had a column name with special characters (including spaces) in it, you must put it in double quotes.

```
$ row '"Net Pay" == "Gross-Pay"' < payroll
```

A column name consists of upper and lower case letters, numbers, and the underscore character (_). Therefore, if you put special characters and spaces in column names, you will have to keep putting the double quotes around them every time you refer to them. (This is true of C language versions of **column** and **row.** For shell script versions, and in **rdb** only a single-word, made up of upper and lower case letters and numbers, is a valid column name, because it is passed to **awk** directly. Therefore, it is safest to stick with single word column names).

Also note that we used a double equals '==' instead of just one '='. This comes from the C language and the **awk** program, that the **row** and **compute** commands use. The rule is to use the single equal to mean, *assign the value on the right of the equal sign, to the variable on the left.* Use the double equal (==) to mean *logically equal,* as we used it in the **row** command. Another way to remember this, is that you usually use the logical equal (==) in **row** commands, and the assignment equal (=) in **compute** commands. Why not use just one? In advanced usage, you will find that you need both in **row** and **compute** for very powerful commands.

3.4 compute

compute allows you to calculate one column as a function of other columns, and/or constants. For example, you could calculate the *Value* column in your *inventory* table as *Onhand* times *Cost* with this command:

```
$ compute 'Value = Onhand * Cost' < inventory
   Item    Onhand     Cost     Value  Description
 -------   -------   -------   -------  ---------------
      1         3        5        15  rubber gloves
      2       100        1       100  test tubes
      3         5        8        40  clamps
      4        23        2        46  plates
      5        99        3       297  cleaning cloth
      6        89       18      1602  bunsen burners
      7         5      175       875  scales
```

For a fancier example, add $5 to the *Cost* of item 4 only, and recompute the *Value* column:

```
$ compute 'if (Item == 4)
           Cost += 5; Value = Onhand * Cost' < inventory
   Item    Onhand     Cost     Value  Description
 -------   -------   -------   -------  ---------------
      1         3        5        15  rubber gloves
      2       100        1       100  test tubes
      3         5        8        40  clamps
      4        23        7       161  plates
      5        99        3       297  cleaning cloth
      6        89       18      1602  bunsen burners
      7         5      175       875  scales
```

Note that the *Cost* of item 4 is now 7 (2+5). Also note that you can write commands down the page. From the line on which you open the single quote, until you enter the closing single quote the shell will keep reading lines. You can do lots of powerful calculations with **compute**. See the /**rdb** manual pages for **compute**. If you really love power, read the **awk** tutorial in your UNIX documentation.

3.5 justify

Often when you type in a table, or for other reasons, the columns containing numbers might be left justified.

```
$ cat < inventory
Item      Onhand    Cost      Value     Description
-------   -------   -------   -------   ----------------
1         3         5         15        rubber gloves
2         100       1         100       test tubes
3         5         8         40        clamps
4         23        7         161       plates
5         99        3         297       cleaning cloth
6         89        18        1602      bunsen burners
7         5         175       875       scales
```

In this *inventory* table, you may not like looking at number columns left justified. It is not the way we usually see numbers in tables. But it is an easy way to enter data into a table with a text editor because we do not have to space over to line up our numbers. To make our table a lot prettier, the **justify** command is available. It right justifies numbers and left justifies character strings. It also blank fills the character columns, so that they can be placed in any order and the columns to their right will still line up.

For example, it might be easier to enter the *inventory* table as shown previously. Then the **justify** command can be used to right justify the numerical columns:

```
$ justify Onhand Value Cost < inventory
Item      Onhand    Cost      Value   Description
-------   -------   -------   -------   ----------------
1              3         5        15   rubber gloves
2            100         1       100   test tubes
3              5         8        40   clamps
4             23         2        51   plates
5             99         3       297   cleaning cloth
6             89        18      1602   bunsen burners
7              5       175       875   scales
```

Note that only the columns selected were justified, including their column headings. *Item* was not selected and was not justified. Now if we project the columns in *inventory* in a different order, the columns will line up correctly:

```
$ column Description Item Onhand Cost Value < inventory
Description        Item    Onhand     Cost    Value
----------------   -------   -------   -------   -------
rubber gloves         1         3         5        15
test tubes            2       100         1       100
clamps                3         5         8        40
plates                4        23         2        51
cleaning cloth        5        99         3       297
bunsen burners        6        89        18      1602
scales                7         5       175       875
```

3.6 total

Often you will wish to total columns of a table. Simply type:

```
$ total < inventory
   Item    Onhand     Cost    Value    Description
 -------   -------   -------  -------  ----------------
     28       324      212     2980
```

Note that we have totaled the *Item, Onhand* and *Cost* columns. Summing these columns does not make much sense, but **total,** in this automatic or default mode, will operate on all numeric columns. Naming specific columns will result in your getting only those columns totaled.

The *-l* option will let you see the whole table. (The *l* in *-l* is the letter *ell*, not the number one.)

```
$ total -l Value < inventory
   Item    Onhand     Cost    Value   Description
 -------   -------   -------  -------  ----------------
      1         3        5       15    rubber gloves
      2       100        1      100    test tubes
      3         5        8       40    clamps
      4        23        2       51    plates
      5        99        3      297    cleaning cloth
      6        89       18     1602    bunsen burners
      7         5      175      875    scales
 -------   -------   -------  -------  ----------------
                              2980
```

3.7 subtotal

To subtotal, enter the break column first, followed by the columns to be subtotaled. The break column is the column watched by the program. If, on a new row, the value in the break column is the same as the previous value in that break column (same Account number), the values in the other columns are added. But if the value in the break column changes (breaks), then a line is drawn and the subtotals of the other columns are printed. As long as the value in the break column remains the same row after row, the values in the selected columns are accumulated. When the break column's value changes, the subtotal is printed and a new subtotal is started.

For example, we might have the following *ledger* table:

```
$ cat ledger
Account     Date     Debit    Credit
-------   -------   -------   -------
101        820102    25000
101        820103              5000
101        820104             15000
130        820104    30000
150.1      820103    10000
211.1      820104             15000
211.1      820102             25000
211.1      820103              5000
```

In this example *Account* is the break column and *Debit* and *Credit* are to be summed. (This is done to *foot* the ledger at the end of an accounting period.)

```
$ subtotal -l Account Debit Credit < ledger
Account   Date       Debit    Credit
-------   -------    -------  -------
101.0     820102     25000
101.0     820103               5000
101.0     820104              15000
-------   -------    -------  -------
101.0                25000    20000

130.0     820104     30000
-------   -------    -------  -------
130.0                30000        0

150.1     820103     10000
-------   -------    -------  -------
150.1                10000        0

211.1     820104              15000
211.1     820102              25000
211.1     820103               5000
-------   -------    -------  -------
211.1                    0    45000
```

Debit and *Credit* are named on the command line, so only they are totaled and not the *Date* column, which would be useless to total. Note that the value in the break column is carried down to identify the subtotal. The *Account* values are not subtotaled. That would also be meaningless.

The *-l* tells subtotal to output the whole table, not just the subtotals. Without the *-l*, we would get only the subtotals:

```
$ subtotal Account Debit Credit < ledger
Account       Date      Debit    Credit
-------      -------    -------  -------
101.0                   25000    20000
130.0                   30000        0
150.1                   10000        0
211.1                       0    45000
```

3.8 Pipes

Pipes (|) are a UNIX shell mechanism which sends the output of one program to the input of another program. This allows you to perform a series of operations on a table. You now can begin to see the real power of this system. In a single line we can produce a report. If you wished to select only rows where *Value* was greater than 100, but wanted to see only the *Description* and *Value* columns sorted in alphabetical order, you could pipe the **row** command's output into the **column** command which would be piped into the **sorttable** command like this:

```
$ row 'Value > 100' <inventory |
> column Description Value |
> sorttable
Description          Value
---------------      -------
bunsen burners        1602
cleaning cloth         297
scales                 875
```

Note the pipe symbol (|) which means that the output from the program to the left becomes the input to the program on the right, or below. As with quotes, the shell will keep accepting lines ending with pipes. Therefore, you can write long pipe programs down the page, which is easier to read and debug. The **sorttable** program, without any columns named, will default to sorting on the first and subsequent columns.

Here is a warning about UNIX. Never use the same file as input and output in one command or pipe. If you want to save the output that normally comes to your terminal screen in a file, use > *tmp*. The *tmp* file name is a common name for a file that has only temporary use. It should always be ok to remove it later.

```
$ sorttable < inventory > tmp
```

You can then move *tmp* to inventory:

```
$ mv tmp inventory
```

Now your *inventory* table is sorted. If you type:

```
$ sorttable < inventory > inventory
```

your *inventory* table will be zeroed out (have zero characters or lines in it). The reason is that the UNIX shell, in opening the inventory file for output, zeros the file's size. Then, when the **sorttable** program (or any UNIX program) reads it in, it gets *end-of-file* on the first read. It closes the file, empty! Your data just went *poof!* You'll get the same disastrous effect if you pipe the output through several programs and then try to write it into the original input file. Do not do it! Also, get in the habit of looking at your *tmp* file before moving it onto your original good data. You may have made an error and be moving or copying bad data onto good. Finally, be careful not to type ''> `file`'' when you mean ''< `file`''. The first will wipe out the file, rather than reading it.

3.9 Syntax: How to enter commands right

In the manual you will see the commands and their syntax (called SYNOPSIS). Syntax is the rules for forming a correct command. Semantics is what the resulting command will do. Computer programmers are familiar with this way of expressing the syntax rules. If you are not, read this chapter. We will start with simple syntax and go to complex. The simplest syntax is a command with no options:

```
$ commands
```

You just type **commands** and you get all of the commands' descriptions and their syntax rules. Most commands require an input table. For example:

```
$ column < table
```

You will substitute the name of your table for the *table* in the syntax rule. But you type the **column <** exactly as specified. If you have a table named *inventory,* you would type:

```
$ column < inventory
```

Many commands allow you to input *tableorlist*. This means they can handle both table and list formatted files.

```
$ column < tableorlist
```

Options are placed in brackets ([ ]) because you do not have to type them unless you want them.

```
$ justify [ column ... ] < table
```

The brackets here mean that you can optionally name columns to be justified. The three dots (...) mean that you can have many column names. But since there are brackets around the *column ...,* you can also leave them out. In which case, all the columns would be justified. Note that there are no brackets around the < *table*. This part is not optional. You must have it to tell the UNIX shell which file to open for input.

You should know that whenever you see '<table' you can also use a pipe to input a table into the command:

```
$ cat table | justify
```

would have the same effect as:

```
$ justify < table
```

If you see a vertical bar (|) within brackets, it means *or*, not a pipe. Other commands give lists of options in brackets.

```
$ jointable [ -a[n] -n - ] [ -j[n] column ] table1 [ table2 ]
```

This means that each option may or may not be selected. Note that there are brackets within brackets. This means that if you chose the *-a*, for example, you have the further option of adding a number *n* to specify which table number. The brackets around the *-j column* mean that the two strings go together, as well as being optional. The *column* should be replaced by the name of one of the columns in one of the tables. Finally, the second table is in brackets, meaning it is optional. But the manual page goes on to explain that if it is not there, and the - option is not chosen, then the **jointable** command will get its second table from the standard in.

The most complex syntax is for **compute.** It can only be hinted at with the rule:

```
$ compute 'column = expression' < table
```

expression can be quite complex. You must look at the manual pages for **compute** and **awk** to get an idea of all of the things you can do.

3.10 UNIX Shell Scripts

You can also put commands (including pipes) into a file and execute the file by simply typing its name. These new commands are called *views* in the database literature because they give you a particular *view* of your data. Use a text editor to type the commands into a file, just as you would at the screen. Use a name for the file that you will remember and that reminds you of what you are trying to do with the series of commands, like **weeklyreport**. After leaving the text editor, type:

```
$ chmod +x weeklyreport
```

This UNIX command makes the file executable. **chmod** means *change mode*. Whenever you want the series of commands that make up **weeklyreport,** just type:

```
$ weeklyreport
```

You can also use this new program in other UNIX shell script files. If you want the new program to be available to others, put it in */usr/lbin,* (Bell Labs standard), or */usr/local/bin,* (Berkeley standard), or some other *bin* that is in the path of your users.

Suppose that at the end of each day, after making changes and updates to your *inventory* file, you wanted to fix up the file. If you wanted to recompute the *Value* column, right justify the number columns and left justify (blank fill the character columns); you could pipe together **compute** and **justify**. But since you will need to perform these functions often, you could create a program. The commands to fix up a table could be saved in a file with an easy-to-remember name. For example, the **fix** command could look like this:

```
$ cat fix
# fix is a little routine to compute
# and right justify the number columns
compute 'Value = Onhand * Cost' < inventory | justify
$
```

Remember to type:

```
$ chmod +x fix
```

to make it executable. If you don't, you'll see ''Permission denied'' when you type the name of the file. To run **fix** just type its name.

```
$ fix
```

```
  Item    Onhand      Cost    Value   Description
-------   -------   -------   ------- ----------------
      1         3         5        15   rubber gloves
      2       100         1       100   test tubes
      3         5         8        40   clamps
      4        23         2        46   plates
      5        99         3       297   cleaning cloth
      6        89        18      1602   bunsen burners
      7         5       175       875   scales
```

You can see how easy it is to write programs in the UNIX environment. This is called *shell programming.* **/rdb** is an extension to the UNIX system that adds database commands to the UNIX commands.

3.11 Report Writing: How to get reports from your data

As with querying, report writing is also very easy. In fact, any query can be printed as a report by directing its output to your printer. Likewise, any report can be a query by directing it to your terminal (which is usually the default anyway).

In addition, a very powerful program named **report** can easily be used to produce reports, form letters, mailing lists, invoices, packing slips, purchase orders, and so on. Just lay out the format of the report in a file using your text editor. Put angle brackets (< >) around the column names of the data you wish to insert into the report. For example: <Column>. Save the form file with some name. Let's use *form*. Then type:

```
$ report form < table
```

In this case you will get a report for each of the rows in the table, with the information inserted where you placed the angle brackets. You can even invoke UNIX commands from within the form with <*! command !*> and the output of the command will print at that place on the form. If you want to put a little table in the middle of your form you could call a UNIX, **/rdb,** or shell program. You can even call the report program to create a report within your report.

Getting dizzy? This is the kind of *levels of power* that UNIX is so good at. With most systems you are limited to the functions the developers have programmed into the system. With UNIX and **/rdb** you are limited only by your own imagination.

There are UNIX commands that will help. **pr** will set up your output with head lines, and it will break on, and number, pages. **nroff** and **troff** will format your text and data for attractive printouts. For example, if you have a file called *maillist* that looks like this:

```
$ cat maillist
Name      Ronald McDonald
Company   McDonald's
Street    123 Mac Attack
City      Memphis
State     TENN
ZIP       30000
Phone     (111) 222-3333
```

```
Name      Chiquita Banana
Company   United Brands
Street    Uno Avenido de la Reforma
City      San Jose
State     Costa Rica
ZIP       123456789
Phone     1234
```

You would use an editor to develop a form like the following:

```
$ cat form
<Name>
<Company>
<Street>
< City >, <State>  <ZIP>

Hi <  Name >:

The date and time is <!date!>

We are also sending this letter to:

<!column Name City < maillist|row 'Name!="<Name>"'|justify!>
Bye <! echo <Name> !>
```

Note that we have used all three types of inserts: regular, command, and command insert. There is a *<Name>* and *<Company>* for each field we want from the *maillist* inserted into our letter. Also, there is a *<!date!>* command for the date, and a shell program to search for all rows in the *maillist* that do not (!) equal the name of the person to which we are sending this letter.

Now with these two files ready, you only need to type:

```
$ report form < maillist
```

and Unix will respond with:

```
Ronald McDonald
McDonald's
123 Mac Attack
Memphis, TENN  30000

Hi Ronald McDonald:

The date and time is Wed Oct 19 01:58:19 EDT 1983


We are also sending this letter to:

Name              City
---------------   -------
Chiquita Banana   San Jose

Bye Ronald McDonald
```

```
Chiquita Banana
United Brands
Uno Avenido de la Reforma
San Jose, Costa Rica  123456789

Hi Chiquita Banana:

The date and time is Wed Oct 19 01:58:40 EDT 1983

We are also sending this letter to:

Name            City
---------------  -------
Ronald McDonald  Memphis

Bye Chiquita Banana
```

3.12 Conclusion

In school you learned how to add, subtract, multiply, and divide. With those simple operations you can do all arithmetic. By combining them in various ways we have gone to the moon and decoded DNA. These four operations work on numbers. A relational database gives you a simple set of operations on *information*. With **column, row, join,** and so on you can do enormously powerful things, but you will have to start thinking about what you want in terms of these operations.

Just as the **add** does not care if it is adding apples or space shuttles, **column** does not care what the information in the tables is. Therefore, these commands can manipulate any data. This is an incredibly powerful idea that will take some time to get used to. These relational operations are a well thought out, pretty complete set of all of the things you will want to do with your data. It is up to your imagination to discover all of the powerful, yet quick and easy tricks you can do with these extensions of UNIX.

4. Data Entry: How to put data in

You have seen how to access your data, now we have to think of how to get your data into the data tables. This is the real work of any database system, so there are many tools to make data entry as easy as possible.

4.1 ve

ve was created to serve as the principal data entry and data editing system for **/rdb** databases. It has much the same interface as the UNIX text and program editor **vi**. We wrote it that way so as to minimize the amount of user training required to bring a new data entry person up to speed and to minimize the amount of confusion that could be caused by switching back and forth between the UNIX text editor **vi** and the **/rdb** forms editor **ve**. Like the **vi** text editor, **ve** is a very powerful editor. Unlike **vi**, however, **ve** edits data in **forms** rather than in the free-form manner of **vi** and **ve** has optional features you can invoke to check the validity of your entries as you enter data, create an audit trail of your entries (or changes), automatically number your rows, and much, much more. **ve** also allows you to create **/rdb** tables directly from the forms editor and has a built in help facility so that you can review any of its features or commands in the middle of your editing session.

Please note that **ve** is called a *forms editor*. This means that you, the user, have control over the way your screen looks and the placement of the various fields that you will enter data into on the screen. The form definition of your **ve** screen is defined by a *screen file* or *screen template* that you create. To create a *screen file* use any text editor to set up a one screen form that consists of the labels you want to have on the screen to prompt you for each column and the other text or symbols you want on the screen to identify the row. This procedure is called *painting the screen*. The labels on your screen are to be followed by the actual names of your columns, enclosed in angle brackets *<columnname>*. This is much the same format that you use to create a **report** template. For example, if you want to create a telephone list form for data entry, you might create a screen form that looks like this:

```
               ***Black Book****
       Name <Name    >     Phone <Number>
            Street <Street        >
City <City      >    State <State> Zip <Zip      >
```

The column names must be butted up against the left angle bracket. You can have spaces **after** the column name. Because **ve** is designed to handle variable length columns (and rows) you don't need to be concerned if the space you leave between the angle brackets in your form isn't enough to record all the data you plan to put into any particular column. **ve** will allow you to enter data in columns of variable length, even if you exceed the space available between the brackets on your screen, by shifting the *window* containing your data if you key in more data than you have space for on the screen. **ve** also provides a scroll left or right command and a zoom command so that you can see the full text of any column for which there is insufficient space on the screen to display.

Once you have created the *screen form*, you then create the table by invoking **ve.** If you tell **ve** to check the validity of your entries as you enter data into your table (with the **-v** switch), then **ve** will prompt you for validation constraints when you create your table. You can then set limits on column size, eligible characters to be keyed in, and table lookups in other tables to cross-check the validity of your entry. These validation constraints can always be modified later, so you do not have to get it perfect the first time.

ve also supports multi-user data entry or editing of the same table. It provides record locking features that will allow you to avoid the problems that could be caused by having two or more users attempting to edit the same row at the same time. With **ve**'s multi-user record locking, only one user has access to a row at a time. Subsequent requests for a row in use are inhibited, and a message is displayed.

This is a brief and general introduction to forms editing with **ve.** We have omitted a discussion of the special data security features provided with **ve**, issues such as protected fields in **ve**, instructions for optional cursor positioning, a **ve** command summary, a discussion of the default list screen format, and more. You will want to review the next chapter and the manual section on **ve** in your **/rdb Manual** for complete details of this very important program.

The remainder of this chapter on data entry is concerned with methods for data entry into **/rdb** tables *other* than **ve.**

4.2 Text Editor or Word Processor

Another simple way to start a data table is to use a text editor or word processor. Type the column head lines and dash lines and the first few rows of your table. Then save it, leave the editor and try some of the query programs to see if you have set it up correctly. See the section on *Rules for Table and List File Set up* later in this chapter for details.

This approach is good for starting your databases and for small databases, but at some point a database may get too large for text editors. Then special purpose programs are needed. Each has its advantages and disadvantages.

4.3 Enter

The **enter** program is good for typing in a lot of data. For example, you or your operators might have to enter card files, or mailing lists, or other bulk data. You may not have time to train them to use a word processor. With the **entry** program, they just type *enter* and the name of the file. The program then prompts them for each column of each row, which they type in. Each new row is simply appended to the table. It lets them go back to an earlier column if they make a mistake, but there is no validation or browsing of the table. It requires the lowest skill level and is the quickest to learn. That's it.

4.4 Update

The **update** program lets you browse through a table file of any size, find a record with fast access methods if you wish, edit the record found with any text editor you like, and return the record to the file where it came from, or append the record to the end of the file if it is too big to fit back in where it came from.

4.5 Programs and Other Formats

Another great thing about UNIX and **/rdb** is the ease of converting data files into different formats. The **/rdb** table and list formats can be converted to and from all of the other database and word processor formats with simple shell, **awk, sed,** and other UNIX program tools. Therefore, you can use other programs, instruments, computers, tapes, floppies, networks, barcode readers, natural speech recognizers, expert systems, deep space probes, and more to get your data, then simply transform it into **/rdb** table and list format and use its commands to do whatever processing you want. There are, therefore, a multitude of ways to get your data in. After processing, you can transform it again and send it back out.

4.6 Rules for Table and List File Setup

If you use **ve** to create and enter your tables you won't have to worry a lot about these rules. But if you don't use **ve** you'll need more detail about setting up a data file. Your data is kept in files which can have either of two formats: table or list.

4.6.1 Table.

A table looks like this:

```
$ cat table
Name      Title       Wage
-------   -------     -------
Mary      Pres.        4.98
Shawn     V.P.         2.98
```

To repeat, there are only three rules for making tables that the **/rdb** programs can understand. The rules are:

1. Insert a single tab between each column.

2. Put a column name, in the first line of the table, at the head of each column. Be sure there is a tab between each column name.

3. Put a dashed line as the second line of each table above each column. There must also be a tab between each column's dashes.

It is best if the dashed line is as wide as the widest string in each column, but it is not necessary. The **justify** command will set it to that width for you, if you wish.

Remember to use the dash or minus character (-), not the underline character (_).

In addition, there are several suggestions for making your tables pretty and for handling special problems. However, the programs only require that you follow these three rules in order to work.

4.6.2 List.

In addition to table format there is also list format, which looks like this:

```
Name    Mary
Title   Pres.
Wage    4.98

Name    Shawn
Title   V.P.
Wage    2.94
```

The rules for lists are similar to those for tables.

1. The first character of a list-formatted file must be a newline. A *newline* character is what you get when you hit your *RETURN* key. It appears on the screen as a blank line. Be careful that there are no unseen spaces or tabs in this first line that would also look like a blank line, but would confuse the programs into thinking they are looking at a table-formatted file. The programs use this first character to decide the format of the file so they can handle both list and table-formatted files.

2. The file has exactly two columns. There must be a tab between the column name (i.e. Name) and the value (Mary).

3. Each row (or record, corresponding to a row in a table) must be separated from the next row by a newline character. It looks like a blank line on the screen. (Note the blank line between Wage (for Mary) and Name (for Shawn) in the list example). There must also be a blank line at the end of the list file. Remember that a blank line has no characters in it. The programs can detect these two newline characters in a row. That is how they know that the end of the row (record) has been reached.

4.7 Tab Problems

The use of tabs to separate columns in **/rdb** has many advantages, but they create a few problems. The advantages include:

1. Ease of input. When you press the tab key, the cursor jumps to the next column. This is very natural to typists.

2. Tabs look nicer in tables then printable characters. They line up columns and are a natural separator.

3. UNIX utilities like **awk, sort**, and others, know about tabs and handle them correctly.

4. File compression. No extra characters are needed to fill out the table (unless the table is justified).

5. No schema or other special file must be created and maintained to tell the programs where data fields start and end, as is true with most other database management systems. COBOL programs are even worse. They have the exact length of each field and record defined at the beginning of their code. This creates extreme inflexibility. If you need to change any of your data, such as making a string longer or adding a column, a COBOL program would have to be modified by a programmer and recompiled. The output of one COBOL program is unacceptable as input to another COBOL program unless the fields and their widths are exactly the same.

Some of the problems and their solutions are:

4.8 Seeing the Tabs

You can see the effect of the tab, but not the tab character itself. So, if you make an input error, how do you know? Using **ve** takes care of the the tabs problem. You can also use the **check** program. It is especially important for large files. It will report any lines that don't have the same number of columns (tabs) as the head line. It will also display the line to simplify finding where the missing or extra tabs are located within the row. In the **vi** editor (also **ex** and **ed**) you can type *:l* for a line or *:1,$l* for a table and see a *^I* for every tab on the line or in the table respectively. When you type the *:* in the **vi** editor, the cursor will jump to the bottom of the screen. Then type the *l* (that is the letter, not the number one). The *:1,$l* tells the editor to list all of the lines from line number one (1) to the end of the file ($). Or type *:set list* to get the special characters, tabs and line ends displayed at all times.

Outside the editor you can also use the **see** command or **od -c table** to see the special characters in the file. The **see** command turns tab characters into *^I*. Out will come a strange looking table showing each character including nonprinting characters converted so that they can be seen. **od** means *octal dump*, but the *-c* option means to convert the bytes of the file into their ASCII character representation. A tab is printed as: \t, as in the C programming language.

4.9 Table Width Problems

Your screen is usually 80 characters wide. What if a table is wider than that?

1. Use **ve** to view your table. If a field is wider than the screen, you can shift the field left and right. The default screen format tries to make a multiple column list of each field of a record.

2. Use the list format when you create your table. See the manual pages for **listtotable** and **tabletolist** commands.

3. You might decide simply to live with letting a long row in a table **wrap around** to the next line on the screen.

4. Break the table into two or more smaller tables. You may join them back with the **jointable** command if you occasionally need to.

5. A table created by **jointable,** in a pipe, can be up to the maximum character width that your available computer memory will hold. If no human has to see the table, who cares?

6. You can, if you wish, project only the columns you want to look at from your big table.

7. You can get a wider terminal (some are 132 characters wide instead of the standard 80) and/or printer (some allow compressed print).

8. If all this fails to satisfy you: *Life is hell. What can we tell you?*

4.10 Special Characters

You can use special characters in the column names (in the header lines), but it is best not to. If you do, you will need to put double quotes (") around the names when you type them at the terminal to protect them from the UNIX shell. The rules for quotes, on UNIX shell command lines, are: single quotes ('...') absolutely protect everything enclosed and double quotes ("...") protect every character except the dollar sign ($).

Therefore, put single quotes around the whole string you are passing to **row, compute** and **validate**. Use double quotes around column names that contain special characters including spaces. For a complex example:

```
$ compute '"Item#" == 15 { len = length ("col 1") }' < table
```

Note that *Item#* has a special character in it, and that *col 1* has a space in it. All of these must be double quoted ("). Also, the entire command must be single quoted (').

4.11 Data Validation: How to get data right

Data can be easily validated in many ways. **ve** allows you to specify validation constraints at data entry time, checking each entry as it's made to make sure it passes tests on what's allowed and what isn't. There is also a **validate** command which allows you to specify the conditions that are invalid, and the error message that should print out when the invalid data is found. The **validate** command is like the **row** and **compute** commands. They all pass their instructions on to **awk**, which does all of the hard work. First a simple example. If you had an inventory table like this:

```
$ cat inventory
Item#   Onhand   Cost   Value   Description
-----   ------   ----   -----   --------------
    1        3     50     150   rubber gloves
    2      100      X     500   test tubes
    3       -5     80    -400   clamps
    4       23     19     437   plates
    5      -99     24   -2376   cleaning cloth
    6       89    147   13083   bunsen burners
    7        5    175     875   scales
```

There are several invalid values that have gotten into your table. You might want to check that no *Onhand* item is less than zero. You can type this command:

```
$ validate 'Onhand < 0 {
                print "negative Onhand in line " NR
                }' < inventory
Item#   Onhand   Cost   Value   Description
-----   ------   ----   -----   --------------
1            3   50       150   rubber gloves
2          100   X        500   test tubes
3           -5   80      -400   clamps
negative Onhand in line 3
4           23   19       437   plates
negative Onhand in line 5
5          -99   24     -2376   cleaning cloth
6           89   147    13083   bunsen burners
7            5   175      875   scales
```

You can also put the command into a file and call it something like *checkinventory*. It would then be a shell program that can be run regularly. See the **validate** command in the manual for more examples and information.

5. ve Form and Screen Database Editor

ve is a database table editor designed for any computer which runs the UNIX operating system. Most UNIX users will find that editing with **ve** comes quickly and naturally to them. Users who are familiar with the *vi* text editor will enjoy the added advantage of understanding **ve**'s mode of operation and will already know most of the **ve** commands. Because **ve** uses the same file structure as the database management system **/rdb**, it is an ideal method of inputting data for **/rdb**'s programs.

This chapter describes in detail how to set up a **ve** (and/or **/rdb**) database table, how to use the optional features to tailor **ve** to your application, what the commands are and what they mean, and other considerations which will help you in both designing and using your database.

5.1 File Structure

Tables used by **ve** are flat ASCII text files in which individual lines are *rows*; the components of each line, or the *columns* in each row, are identified by the placement of a designated character between columns. As such, rows and columns can be of variable length, and the size of your table is determined only by the length of your rows, not by unflexible preset length restrictions.

5.1.1 What are Rows and Columns?

A *row* is defined as all the data associated with a particular entity or transaction, a line or row in a table, or a tuple, or a record in a file. A *column* is defined as a subset or portion of a row, a column within a row or line, or an attribute of a tuple.

For example, a row in a personnel table would typically consist of all the items of information associated with an individual; these items or columns or columns might include the name of the individual, his/her social security number, the date he/she was employed, salary, and so on. In an accounting table a row would typically consist of a complete transaction, and the columns in such a row might be the invoice number, the name of the customer, the item and quantity purchased, and the amount paid.

5.1.2 The Column Separation Character (TAB).

A specific character, (TAB unless user specifies another), separates the columns or columns in each line or row. Since the column separation character is **ve**'s way of figuring out where one column ends and another begins, it cannot be used in the data itself. As rows are modified and added to the table with **ve**, this character is automatically inserted between columns.

5.1.3 Column Names.

ve keeps track of the data in each column by associating it with the *name* of the column.

How does **ve** name each column?

It doesn't need to because you name the columns when you create your table. When naming your columns, you must be sure to use a unique name for each column so that **ve** knows which is which, and that the column names do not contain the column separation character. Try to keep your column names short and simple. For example, the names of the columns in the personnel table previously mentioned might be *Employee, Snumber, Date,* and *Salary*.

How does **ve** remember the names of the columns?

Each time you call up **ve** with the name of a table, **ve** looks for the column names in the *header rows*.

5.1.4 Header Rows.

For every **ve** table, two special rows are necessary to describe the columns which comprise each row. These rows are called header rows, and they will usually be the first two rows of your **ve** table, although they can be stored in a separate *header file*.

There is one column in each header row for each column. In the first header row, these columns are the names of the columns. Each column in the second header row is a series of dashes (-).

For example, the header rows for an address book table with one column each for name, street address, city, state, zip code, and phone number might look like this:

```
Name       Street    City     State     Zip      Phone
----       ------    ----     -----     ---      -----
```

5.2 The Command Line

The files **ve** uses and the way it displays and formats your data are all determined by entering a single command line at your prompt. The syntax for the **ve** command line is:

> **ve** [*table* [**-s** [*file*] **-h** [*file*] **-a** [*file*] **-v** [*file*] **-n**[*n*] **-fc** **-mc** **-i**]] [**-b**]

Dashes which are followed by a single letter are called *switches* (**-s, -h, -a, -v, -n, -m, -i, -b**). Each switch tells **ve** to perform a specific job when it is invoked.

Words, symbols, and letters which directly follow each switch, when substituted for file names, numbers, and characters, further define how **ve** should do the job indicated by the switch. The word *table* shows where you would type in the name of your table; the *file* words show where you would substitute the names of any files you might use. The 'n' symbol shows where you would substitute a number, and the *c' (as in* **-fc** or **-mc**) shows where you would put a letter or *c*haracter.

The brackets ([ ]) are used to indicate items on the command line which are *optional,* and should not be used in an actual command line. You will notice that with the exception of the word **ve**, everything on the command line is optional. In fact, the command

```
$ ve
```

is a perfectly valid **ve** command which displays the on-line help file index.

Each option applies to the item which immediately precedes it, and can be used *only* if that item is specified. For example, the syntax

$$\textbf{-s}\ [\textit{file}]$$
$$|\ \ \ |\ \ \ |$$
$$|<\!\!-\!\!-\!\!-\!\!-$$

means that *file* may be specified if and only if **-s** precedes it. If we apply the rule to the whole (optional) set of options, it is clear that all of the switches, with the exception of the **-b** switch, may be specified only if *table* has been specified:

$$\textit{table}\ [\textbf{-s}\ [\textit{file}]\ \textbf{-h}\ [\textit{file}]\ \textbf{-a}\ [\textit{file}]\ \textbf{-v}\ [\textit{file}]\ \textbf{-n}[n]\ \textbf{-fc}\ \textbf{-mc}\ \textbf{-i}]$$
$$|\qquad\quad|\qquad\qquad\qquad\qquad\qquad\qquad\qquad\qquad\quad|$$
$$|<\!\!-$$

All options must follow the name of the table when it is specified.

5.2.1 File Options (-s, -h, -a, -v).

The first four switches in the command line apply to files which, with the exception of the screen file, follow the **ve** file structure as described in section on File Structure. They enable the user to define how the screen displays the data (**-s**), to separate the header lines from the data rows (**-h**), to keep track of each modification made to the table (**-a**), and to impose various restrictions on the data as it is entered (**-v**). Each of these switches can be used with the name of a file.

For example, the command

```
$ ve blackbook -s display
```

means *edit the blackbook table and use the screen display described in the file named display.* If we're also keeping track of each **ve** session in a file named *history*, then the command:

```
$ ve blackbook -s display -a history
```

means *edit the table named blackbook using the screen display described in the file named display and list all modifications made to blackbook in the audit file named history.*

5.2.1.1 File creation.

How do we use the file options if the files, or even the table, don't exist? One way is to create each desired file with any text editor and type in the appropriate header rows. This method can be confusing and prone to errors, especially for tables with many columns.

The best and simplest way is to let **ve** create, format and store the header rows in the desired files. This can (and should) be done in a single **ve** command, so that all files are created and initialized at the same time. The following table shows the conditions under which **ve** can create each type of file:

TABLE 2. ve File Creation

ve Will Create	When
the table	there is a screen or a header file
the header file	there is a screen file and no table
the audit file	there is a screen or a table or a header file
the validation file	there is a screen or a table or a header file
the screen file	never — the user must do this

By examining this table, it is apparent that the only file **ve** really needs in order to create all of the other files, including the table, is a screen file. The preferred method for initializing a **ve** table (starting up from scratch with no files), is

1. Create a screen file, making sure to include all of the column names you want to be part of your table.

2. On the **ve** command line, type in

    a. the name of your table

    b. the **-s** switch with the name of the screen file you've just created.

    c. the file option switch followed by a name for each file you wish **ve** to create.

5.2.1.2 Example.

For example, let's say we want to create a table named *blackbook*. Also, we want to impose certain limitations on how the data is entered in some of the columns, and put these limitations in a validation file called *limits*. Finally, we want to keep track of each **ve** editing session in an audit file named *history*. So far, none of these files exists.

The first thing we do is create a screen file which we name *display*. In the *display* file, we include all of the column names we want in our *blackbook* table. When we finish making our screen file, and type in the command

```
$ ve blackbook -s display -v limits -a history
```

the following steps are performed:

1. **ve** looks in the *blackbook* file for the header rows. But *blackbook* doesn't exist, so **ve** creates it.

2. **ve** then reads the screen file we have created named *display*. It creates the header rows from the column names in the screen file, and puts them in the new *blackbook* table.

3. **ve** creates an audit file named *history* and uses the header rows to create the audit file header rows, which it puts in *history*.

4. **ve** creates a validation file named *limits* and uses the column names in the first header row to create the rows in *limits*.

When **ve** is finished making all the new files, it draws your screen according to the *display* screen file, and puts you in **ve** edit mode, exactly as if the files had already existed before issuing the **ve** command.

5.2.1.3 Using the ve file-naming scheme.

Typing in the **ve** command line can be time consuming and tedious when using the file option switches, especially if you are using any of the other switches as well. **ve** has a built-in method of naming optional files associated with a table. When you take advantage of this feature, the command line is greatly simplified.

Whenever a **ve** command is issued with the name of a table, **ve** looks for files with names that begin with the name of the table and end with each of the four file option switches. These files are called default files, or files which are used by **ve** in the absence of specified files. For example, consider the table named *blackbook*:

TABLE 3. ve File Switches

File Switch	File Type	File **ve** Looks for (Default)
-s	screen	*blackbook-s*
-h	header	*blackbook-h*
-a	audit	*blackbook-a*
-v	validation	*blackbook-v*

If any of the default files exist, **ve** automatically includes them in the command line.

For example, if the file *blackbook-s* exists, then **ve** translates the command

```
$ ve blackbook
```

to mean *ve blackbook -s blackbook-s* Or, if all four default files exist, then **ve** translates the command

```
$ ve blackbook
```

to mean *ve blackbook -s blackbook-s -h blackbook-h -a blackbook-a -v blackbook-v.*

Specifying a file option switch with a file name overrides **ve**'s inclusion of the existing default file in the command line. As a corollary to this, files which are to be included in the **ve** editing session which do *not* have default names must *always* be typed in the command line, following the appropriate file option switch. For example, suppose all four default files previously listed exist, but you want to use a screen file named *myscreen* instead of the default screen file named *blackbook-s*. **ve** will translate the command

```
$ ve blackbook -s myscreen
```

to mean *ve blackbook -s myscreen -h blackbook-h -a blackbook-a -v blackbook-v*.

Creating files from scratch also becomes much easier when using the default **ve** file names. The same rules apply for creating files, but the names of the files do not need to be typed in. Let's assume that we are starting out fresh with no files. We want to start a new table named *blackbook*, with a validation file and an audit file. If we create a screen file and name it *blackbook-s* (or create a header file named *blackbook-h*), then the command line

```
$ ve blackbook -v -a
```

is all that is necessary to create the table named *blackbook*, the validation file named *blackbook-v*, and the audit file named *blackbook-a*.

5.2.2 Automatic Row Numbering (-n).

The **-n** switch tells **ve** to give each row a unique numerical identifier automatically as it is written. **ve** looks for and stores this number in the first column of each row.

If you are initializing a new table and you use the **-n** switch, you must reserve the first column for this number. Of course, you may name the column anything you like — it just has to be there. **ve** will start the row numbering at 1.

If your table already exists, **ve** figures out what to number new rows by scanning the first column of each row in the table and adding 1 to the largest number it finds.

The *n* option to the **-n** switch, when substituted with a number, tells **ve** to start new rows with that number. If the number you specify is less than the greatest numbered row in your table, **ve** simply ignores your request, since it would mean duplicating existing row numbers.

Once the **-n** switch has been specified in the command line for a particular table, it is not necessary on subsequent calls to **ve** to include **-n** in the command line (unless you are resetting the number with the *n* option), since **ve** keeps track of the largest numbered row. The command

```
$ ve blackbook -n2001
```

is an example of using the **-n** switch to invoke automatic row numbering beginning with 2001. When you are editing a table which uses automatic row numbering, and the first column is displayed on the screen, you will notice that your cursor will never land on it. This is **ve**'s way of making sure that you don't mess it up by putting a different number there.

5.2.3 Field Separator Specification (-f).

Normally, **ve** uses the TAB character to separate columns because TABs are not likely to be part of the data. The column separator can be respecified, however, by using the **-f** option to **ve**, along with the desired column separation character. The character must be nonblank and cannot be a dash (-).

For example, if we want our columns to be separated by a colon (:) we could use the command:

```
$ ve blackbook -f:
```

ve knows how to initialize the table and any of the optional files used with the table with the specified column separator.

5.2.4 Start-up Mode Specification (-m).

The **-m** switch tells **ve** to enter the editing session in a particular mode. This mode is specified by a character which must follow the **-m** switch, and can be *i* for insert mode, / for search mode, or *n* for next mode. **ve** will return to this mode whenever a row is written. If, for example, we want **ve** to start up in the insert mode, we would use the command:

```
$ ve blackbook -mi
```

5.2.5 Initialization Option (-i).

ve creates and maintains an index of the rows in your table. During **ve** edit sessions, this index keeps track of which rows are being accessed by other users and which rows have been deleted. When the table is quiet, **ve** uses the index to clean up the table by removing the deleted rows and putting the updated rows in order. The index is also used to store the last automatic row number (if applicable) and the column separation used by your table.

If your table has been modified using a method other than **ve**, the index must be recreated. This is done with the **-i** switch, which means *i*nitialize the table. It is not necessary to use the **-i** option when you are creating the table.

5.2.6 Bright Option (-b).

If your terminal has different intensities, **ve** can take advantage of this capability when displaying the column names, screen file text, and key words in the on-line help files, by making them brighter than other text on the screen. It does this by reading a file named */etc/termcap* which describes the capabilites of each type of ter-minal your system uses. If there is no description for your terminal, or if it does not have highlighting capability, all text will be displayed at normal intensity.

If column highlighting screws up your screen (perhaps the description is wrong or your terminal type is set incorrectly) or you simply don't want columns and key words highlighted, you can refrain from using this feature by omitting the **-b** switch on your command line. The command:

```
$ ve -b
```

means *give me the ve on-line help files, and try to highlight portions of my screen.*

5.3 The Screen File

A screen file is an ordinary text file, which can be created with any editor. It visually describes the way the data are displayed during a **ve** edit session. If there is no screen file, **ve** displays your column names in fields on the screen, with the corresponding data adjacent to the name.

So why bother to create a screen file? Most importantly, using a screen file allows you to take advantage of **ve**'s security features. Secondly, it is the simplest and most accurate way to create your table, since you don't have to bother creating header rows. Finally, it allows you to label or not label your columns, to make your screen display match specific hard copy forms, to arrange the order and/or placement of your column names to accommodate the size of data in the column, and determine on which column your cursor will land each time a row is displayed.

5.3.1 Screen File Format.

Basically, the screen file should be formatted to look the way you want **ve** to display your data. Use the following guidelines when creating a screen file:

1. For each column, indicate the beginning and ending positions for data display in the screen file with the '<' and '>' angle brackets, respectively. Both brackets must appear on the same line. Type the name of the column between the brackets. If **ve** identifies text surrounded by < >'s to be a valid column name, then data in that column will be displayed between the brackets, and the brackets themselves will become blank.

2. If you are using the screen file to create a table, consult the guidelines in the section on *Field names,* or the chapter on Entry, for naming columns. Keep in mind that the names of all columns must be included in the screen file, and that their top-to-bottom, left-to-right order on the screen will determine the order in which **ve** arranges your data. (This consideration is usually important only when you are planning to use automatic row numbering or an audit file with your table. In that case, the uppermost, leftmost column name will be assumed to be the name of the number column.)

    If your table already exists, you must be sure that the column names in the screen file are identical to those listed in the first header row of the table.

3. The entire screen file should be no longer than 23 lines and no wider than 80 characters, since this is the most information that standard screens accommodate (the 24th line is reserved by **ve** for data entry messages).

    For example, the screen file for the address book table might look like this:

In this example, the only text which will appear on the screen other than actual data is the *Black Book* title line. You may add labels to indicate the kind of data each column represents:

```
┌─────────────────────────────────────────────────────────────────┐
│                       *** Black Book ***                          │
│                                                                   │
│        Name:  <Name                 >   number:  <Phone        >  │
│     Address:  <Street               >                             │
│  City/State/Zip:  <City             >       /  <State> /  <Zip >  │
└─────────────────────────────────────────────────────────────────┘
```

5.3.2 Denying/Limiting Field Access.

Once a table has been created, a screen file can be used to selectively protect specific columns by denying or limiting access to those columns. When you **ve** a table with a screen file, *only* the data for columns which are named in the screen file will be displayed. Thus, the simple omission of the names of confidential columns in the screen file protects those columns from being displayed. Data in columns not named in the screen file are also excluded from searching. This is called a *view*. This feature comes in handy when you want to use **ve** to edit a specific subset of columns and do not need to see the entire row.

By limiting access, we mean simply disallowing modification of designated columns. In the screen file, column names preceded by an exclamation point (!) indicate to **ve** that they cannot be modified.

To illustrate the security features, let's use the *personnel* table previously mentioned. For the sake of this example, we'll add two columns for the name of the person to contact in an emergency, and the phone number of that person. The header rows for such a table might look like this:

```
Employee        Snumber Date    Salary  Emergency      Phone
--------        ------- ----    ------  ---------      -----
```

Let's assume that this table exists, and we simply want to update it. We want to be able to search for employees by their name or their social security number, but we don't want these columns modified. Also, because the salary column is highly confidential, we don't want it displayed at all. Our screen file might look like this:

```
┌─────────────────────────────────────────────────────────────────┐
│            Company X-Y-Z Employee Information Card                │
│        ─────────────────────────────────────────────             │
│                                                                   │
│          Employee   !<Employee        >                           │
│     Social Security  !<Snumber         >   Date employed  <Date >│
│                                                                   │
│  In case of emergency  <Emergency      >       Number  <Phone  > │
└─────────────────────────────────────────────────────────────────┘
```

5.3.3 Setting the Cursor.

Unless you are searching for a particular pattern, **ve** will position the cursor at the uppermost, leftmost column name on the screen.

The column name on which your cursor automatically lands can be changed by preceding the desired column name with an asterisk (*). For example, if we were updating the emergency name and phone number columns in the *personnel* table, we could make the cursor land automatically on the emergency column as each row is displayed, by changing the last line of the screen file to look like this:

| In case of emergency   *<Emergency   >   number   <Phone   > |

5.4 The Header File

Normally, the header rows are the first two rows in your table. If you don't want your data to contain the header rows, they can be stored in the optional header file. Header rows and data rows may be separated *only* for the tables themselves — associated validation and audit files must contain their own header rows.

5.5 The Audit File

An audit file is a **ve** file in which each row marks a specific modification to your table.

If you are using an audit file, then each time you add a new row or delete a row or change a column in a row in your table, **ve** adds a row to the audit file, indicating the date, time, and type of modification that was made. When you modify or delete a row, it is copied into the audit file before it is modified or removed in your table.

5.5.1 Why Use an Audit File?

In some applications, it may be desirable to be able to track transactions over time. For example, in an equipment inventory table, the audit file can be used to trace the maintenance history and disposition of specific items. Or, in a customer credit table, the audit file can give you customer account histories and show you which customers spend a lot of money, which customers are always late paying bills, how to effectively direct your sales pitch to customers by examining the items they purchase, and so on. In a sales inventory table, the audit file can show you which items move fast, which items are dogs, and how often each item needs to be reordered to keep sufficient stock on hand.

The audit file can also be used to recreate your table as it existed at some prior date.

5.5.2 Audit File Structure.

The audit file is a standard **ve** table in its own right. The first column of each row in the audit file contains the date and time a table's row was modified. The second column contains a single letter which indicates the type of modification performed on the table row: **a** for appending a new row, **c** for changing columns in an existing row, and **d** for deleting a row. There is also one column in each audit row for every column in a table row. For example, consider the header rows for a table of credit customer accounts:

```
Number   Name     Credit   Debit
------   ----     ------   -----
```

The header rows for the audit file would look like this:

```
YYMMDDhhmmss   ?         Number   Name     Credit   Debit
------------   -         ------   ----     ------   -----
```

The first two column names are *YYMMDDhhmmss* (YY for year, MM for month, DD for day, hh for hour, mm for minute and ss for second) and '?' (for the transaction letter column).

5.5.3 Unique Identifiers.

Each time a customer makes a payment or purchase, his/her row is updated to reflect the current transaction. We don't need to keep track of the date because the audit file will do that for us.

What if there are two customers named John Doe? How do we keep their rows straight? We keep track of the identity of our customers by assigning each one a unique number. When you are using an audit file, **ve** automatically invokes row numbering (described in section on *Automatic row numbering*).

5.6 The Validation File

A validation file describes column-by-column requirements that data must meet as it is entered in the table. There are three different kinds of tests which you may force your data to pass before allowing it to become part of your table: character range specification, column length restriction, and table look-up.

5.6.1 Validation File Format.

The validation file is a regular **ve** table. The header rows look like this:

```
Name          Characters  Length    Table
----          ----------  ------    -----
```

For each column in your table which must pass one or more validation test, there is a row in the validation file. The first column of each row in the validation file contains the name of the table column.

5.6.2 Validation File Creation.

ve can create your validation file, but you must supply the validation parameters. To make this task easier, **ve** calls on itself to edit the validation file, before opening up and displaying your table.

If you don't want to make a column pass validation tests, simply delete the row which contains the column name from the validation file. When you are finished editing your validation file with **ve**, your table will be displayed on the screen, and the validation parameters will take effect immediately.

5.6.3 Character Range Specification.

This validation option allows you to specify exactly which characters are acceptable (or not acceptable) in a named column. For example, the *Snumber* column of the personnel table should be comprised of numbers and dashes. The *Employee* column can be letters (upper case and lower case), dashes, periods, commas and blanks. The *Zip* column of the *blackbook* table must be numbers only.

ve allows you to specify these parameters in terms of ranges, or as single characters, in the second column of your validation file. A range is defined as a low limit character and a high limit character separated by a dash (-). When more than one character or range of characters is specified, they are separated by a comma (,). Using these examples, the character specifications for *Snumber* is `0-9,-`; for *Employee* is `A-Z,a-z, ,-,,,.`; for *Zip* is `0-9`.

Let's say we have a column which can contain anything except upper case letters:

`a-z,0-9,?, ,,,.,:,;,!,=,+,<,>,[,],(,),*,&,^,%,$,#,@,{,},|,~,`,-`

The '!' symbol, when it precedes a range or character, means *not this range*, or *not this character*. Sometimes, as in the example above, the '!' can greatly simplify the parameter list: `!A-Z`. The '!' can also be used to exclude specific members of a range. For example, one way to specify all numbers except *8* is: `0,1,2,3,4,5,6,7,9`. A simpler way is: `0-9,!8`, or `0-7,9`.

5.6.4 Field Length Restrictions.

ve looks at the third column of the validation file to see if you want to impose column length limits. These limits are used for several reasons. For example, we know that zip codes should be exactly five numbers long. We know that social security numbers are exactly 11 digits and dashes. Data entered in these columns which are not the proper length would render them meaningless.

Also, it is sometimes the case that other limits indicate the necessity for a column length restriction. If, for example, we use the *blackbook* table to produce labels, then we should restrict the length of the columns in the table to conform to the size of the labels.

Another use of column length might apply when you want to force a column to contain data, but you don't care (or don't know) what the length should be. For example, in the *Date* column of the personnel table, you might require that something be entered, but it might be of indeterminate length (October 1981, 10/1/81, 10/81, and so on).

Four specifications describe how **ve** should pass data for the column length test:

TABLE 4. Validation of Column Length

=*n*	the column length must be exactly equal to n.
<*n*	the column length must be less than n.
>*n*	the column length must be greater than n.
!	the column can be blank (length 0).

Using these examples, the column length for *Zip* column in the *blackbook* table is =*5*, which means *exactly equal to five characters*. If the size of our labels is 32 characters, then the column length for the *Name* and *Street* columns of the *blackbook* table is <*33*, which means *less than 33 characters*. The column length for the *Date* column of the personnel table might be >*0*, which means *there must be at least one character in this column*.

When more than one of these specifications is used, they are separated by a comma (,). The *!* column length specification, when used in conjunction with other specifications, tells **ve** to ignore other length specifications if the column is blank. For example, if you specify the *Zip* column length previously mentioned to be *!,=5*, then **ve** will allow you to skip over that column — however, if you enter any data in this column, **ve** will force you to make them exactly five characters long.

You can also indicate column length ranges by using the < and > specifications together. (In fact, another way of saying *!,=5* is *!,<6,>4*.) In the personnel table, the least number of characters needed to specify *Date* is four (1/82); the greatest number is 18 (September 11, 1949). You may wish to place an upper limit on this column simply to preclude the user from typing in something like: *gosh, I don't know, I guess Bud joined the firm round about September, a few years back, because I first met him at the company's Labor Day barbeque.* In any case, the specification is *>3,<19*, which means any data in this column must have more than three characters and less than 19 characters.

5.6.5 Look-up Tables.

The fourth column in the validation file is for the name of a look-up table. If you use table look-up validation on a particular column, then each time you enter data in that column, **ve** compares it with data in the table. **ve** makes this comparison based on how you specify the name of the table: if it is preceded by *!*, then it passes the table look-up test only if it is *not* in the table; otherwise, it passes only if it *is* in the table.

ve updates all look-up tables created from a table as you change, delete, and add data to columns in that table. As such, you need to create each table only once. As long as you use **ve** to maintain your table, your look-up tables will be current.

5.6.5.1 Table creation.

The **vindex*** command is used to create look-up tables. To use **vindex** to create a new look-up table (or overwrite an existing one), you must specify the name of the

---

* There is a more complete description of the **vindex** command in the **/rdb** manual.

table and the names of the columns in the table you want to index.*

For example, if we want to create look-up tables for the *Snumber* and the *Employee* columns of the personnel table, we would use the command:

```
$ vindex personnel Employee Snumber
```

5.6.5.1.1 Files.

vindex creates two auxiliary files for each look-up table, using the naming convention *column_name-A* and *column_name-B*. If the name of the column you are **vindex**ing is longer than 14 characters, it will be truncated to 14 characters before the *-A* and *-B* extensions are appended to the resulting auxiliary files. Special characters which may be part of the column name are omitted, and spaces are converted to '_'. In the validation file, the look-up table is referred to without the extensions, as in **Snumber.**

5.6.5.1.2 Decode columns.

An optional feature when creating and using look-up tables is the *cross-indexing* capability. When you are creating a table for a column in a table, you can select a second column which should be displayed when your data matches a pattern in the table. The displayed data is called a *decode* column. The decode column must also be in the table and, because each indexed or key column can have only one associated decode column, **vindex** assumes that data in the key column is unique. Similarly, when **ve** is used to update tables which contain decode columns, the contents of the key column must be unique.

For example, consider the following *states* table:

```
$ cat states
State   Name
-----   ----
NY      New York
CA      California
MA      Massachusetts
NJ      New Jersey
```

In each row of the *states* table, the *State* column contains a standard state abbreviation, and the *Name* column contains the name of the state, which corresponds to the abbreviation. To create a look-up table on the *State* column and cross-index the *Name* column, we use the command:

```
$ vindex states State : Name
```

The colon (:) character in this command is used to indicate that the following column name *Name* is a *decode* column for the column name preceding the colon (*State*).

---

*   Of course, column names which contain blanks must be surrounded by double quotes (").

5.6.5.2 Unique columns.

We can use the *Snumber* table, created in the section on *Table creation* to illustrate the use of look-up tables to enforce *unique* column entries. In order to make sure that we don't enter duplicate employee rows, we can make **ve** check each social security number as it is entered against a table of those already in the table by specifying the name of the look-up table in the fourth column of the validation row for *Snumber,* using the '!' symbol:

```
Name          Characters   Length        Table
----          ----------   ------        -----
Snumber       0-9,-          !,=11       !Snumber
```

In this case, the column passes the test if **ve** does *not* find an identical social security number in the table. When we are editing the *personnel* table using **ve**, each time we add a new social security number **ve** will look it up in the table. If it's already there, **ve** will complain; otherwise, **ve** will add the new number to the table.

5.6.5.3 Field inclusion.

We can use the *blackbook* table to show how table validation can be used to make sure that the data we enter in the *state* column are *included* in a table which lists all of the standard state abbreviations. We can use the table created from *states.*

By specifying the name of the table in the *blackbook* validation file, each time we enter a state abbreviation in the *blackbook* table, **ve** will look it up in the table. If it's there, **ve** will print the name of the state next to the abbreviation.

```
Name          Characters   Length        Table
----          ----------   ------        -----
st            A-Z            =2           State
```

5.7 Commands

All **ve** commands are described in detail in the following sections; a quick command reference list is provided both in the **ve** Manual and in the first on-line help page. **ve**'s command language is very much like the command language used by the **vi** UNIX editor, in that both editors use regular letters and symbols as commands. As such, the keys you hit are interpreted either as commands to **ve** or as text that is being entered into your table depending on the *mode* **ve** is in when you type them. **ve** has two modes: *insert* mode and *command* mode, discussed in the section on *Inserting text.*

Because **ve** is essentially a *visual* experience, no amount of documentation will help you understand it better than simply sitting down at a terminal, creating a **ve** table, and experimenting with it.

5.7.1 Displaying Your Data.

There are two basic methods for displaying data on your screen. One way is to display it sequentially, or as it appears in the table. The other way is to look for specific rows by searching the table.

5.7.1.1 Sequential display (n,-).

The **n** (or *next*) command displays the row in the table which immediately follows the one currently displayed. If **n** is the first command you give **ve**, then it begins at the first row in your table. The **-** displays the row in the table which immediately precedes the one currently displayed. If **-** is the first command you give **ve**, then it begins at the last row in your table. Both sequential display commands will wrap around to the beginning/end of your table after the last/first row has been displayed.

5.7.1.2 Searching (/).

When you use the / (slash) command, **ve** will scan your table row by row, looking for the pattern you specify. It can repeat a search without making you retype the pattern or character. If you have denied access to some columns by excluding their names from your screen file, **ve** will omit these columns in its search.

The / command will begin its search at the position of your cursor in the row and is complete when the pattern you specify is found or when the entire table has been examined. For example, to search for *John Doe* in your *blackbook* table, you would use the command /*John Doe*. In order for you to see what you are typing, **ve** provides the last line of your screen to display the pattern as you type it in. You can use your erase character to edit this line. When you are done typing in the pattern, hit the **ESC** key or **RETURN** key to let **ve** know you are done. If *John Doe* is a pattern in your table, then the row which contains *John Doe* will be displayed on the screen if it is available.

Because **ve** remembers your search pattern, you need only type / and hit **ESC** or **RETURN**, to repeat your search of a specified pattern. Each time you specify a new search pattern **ve** forgets the previous one.

5.7.1.2.1 Getting the right row.

Normally, the only requirement **ve** enforces when trying to match a search pattern to data is that the entire pattern be contained in a single column, regardless of which column it is or its position in the column.

5.7.1.2.2 Position matching (^,$).

Sometimes a search pattern will match data in many rows when you are looking for a specific row. Choosing a search pattern which is unique to the row you want displayed will speed up the search process considerably. If this is not possible, you can limit the way **ve** searches by forcing the pattern to match the beginning or end of a column, and/or by specifying a particular column to which **ve** should limit the search.

The character '^', when it is the first character of a search pattern, tells **ve** that the pattern following it must match data at the beginning of a column. The character '$', when it is the last character of a search pattern, tells **ve** that the pattern preceding it must match data at the end of a column.

If you are searching for the '^' character in the first position of your pattern, or the '$' character in the last position of your pattern, you must precede these characters with a backslash (\). Next are screen displays of two rows in the *personnel* table:

```
┌─────────────────────────────────────────────────────────────┐
│          Company X-Y-Z Employee Information Card            │
│          ───────────────────────────────────────            │
│                                                              │
│       Employee    Custard, John                              │
│   Social Security 705-34-1977     Date employed    1977-85  │
│                                                              │
│ In case of emergency  Joan Cumberland      number   555-1234│
└─────────────────────────────────────────────────────────────┘
```

```
┌─────────────────────────────────────────────────────────────┐
│          Company X-Y-Z Employee Information Card            │
│          ───────────────────────────────────────            │
│                                                              │
│       Employee    Cumberland, Joan                           │
│   Social Security 190-00-2185     Date employed    1977     │
│                                                              │
│ In case of emergency  John Custard         number   555-1234│
└─────────────────────────────────────────────────────────────┘
```

By examining the two rows above you can see that in order to find the right row the first time using a regular search command, you almost have to know the social security number of the employee. If you are searching for '*Cumberland*' or '*Joan*' you may have to look at John's row before finding Joan's. If you know that Joan was employed in 1977, you might hit John's social security number and employment date before getting to Joan's row.

You could search for '*Cumberland, Joan*' and hope that the name is spelled correctly, the comma has been inserted, and that there is exactly one space between the first and last name. Also, the longer your search pattern, the more time it takes to type and the more typos you are likely to make.

If you specify your search pattern to be '*^Cum*' then only the first column in Joan's row will match, and that is where your cursor will land. You must specify at least the first three letters of the name to distinguish between *Cu*mberland and *Cu*stard.

If you are searching for Joan's employment date, the command '*/^1977*' might find the employment date in John's row first. You could match the end of the column with '*/77$*', but this also matches the end of John's social security number. The only way to be sure to get Joan's row by searching for the date is '*/^1977$*'; this pattern tells **ve** to search for columns in which the data exactly matches the pattern *1977* from beginning to end.

5.7.1.2.3 Search column selection (m,M).

Another way to limit your search is to make **ve** search only one column in each row by using the **m** command. When you *mark* a column to be searched, **ve** doesn't bother trying to match your search pattern with data in other columns. As such, the search results are more likely to yield the desired row on the first try.

For example, if we use the **m** key to mark the *Employee* column, then the *'/Cum'* or *'/Joa'* search command will yield only Joan's row.

To use the **m** command, simply position your cursor at the column you want to search and hit **m**. Subsequent searches will be limited to data in that column only. Hitting the **m** key on a different column changes the search column to that column.

If you have marked a search column and you want to go back to searching all of the columns in each row, hit the **M** key to *unmark* your columns.

5.7.2 Moving Around (RETURN,TAB,B,l,SPACE,h,k,j,ˆ,$,G,H,L,w,b,e,<,>,f,F,;).

TABLE 5. Movement Commands in **ve**

Key	Scroll	Count	Target	Action
RETURN **TAB**	no	yes	no	The **RETURN** and **TAB** keys will move you to the next column in top-to-bottom, left-to-right order on your screen. The **RETURN** key also works in insert mode.
B	no	yes	yes	The **B** command will move you to the next column in bottom-to-top, right-to-left order on your screen.
l, SPACE	yes	yes	yes	The **l** key and the **SPACE** bar are interchangeable commands which move right in the column by characters.
h	yes	yes	yes	The **h** command moves left by characters.
k, j	no	yes	no	The **k** and **j** keys move up and down the screen by columns.
ˆ, $	yes	no	yes	The ˆ and **$** keys move to the beginning and end of the column.
G	no	yes	no	The **G** command moves to the last row in your table. When you precede the **G** command with a count, **ve** displays the row in the *count* position in the table. For example, *100G* means *display the 100th row.*
H, L	no	no	no	The **H** key moves to the beginning of the first column on the screen; the **L** key moves to the the beginning of the last column on the screen.
w, b, e	yes	yes	yes	The **w** key moves right one words; the **b** command moves right one word; the **e** command moves to the end of words.
<, >	yes	no	no	The **>** command scrolls continuously through the column, left to right, until it reaches the end. The **<** command scrolls continuously through the column, right to left, until it reaches the beginning.
f, F, ;	yes	yes	yes	The **f** command looks left to right from your cursor for the character you specify; the **F** command looks looks right to left from your cursor for the specified character. The key you hit immediately after typing **f** or **F** is assumed to be the character you are looking for. When **ve** finds the character, your cursor moves to its position in the column. The **;** command repeats your last **f** or **F** request.

Movement commands move your cursor to a desired column or character on the screen. Sometimes, the columns on your screen will not be long enough for the data they contain. It may look as though data is missing, but this is not the case: **ve** displays as much data as your screen allows. Many movement commands will scroll left and right through the data, allowing you to see the entire contents of columns which are too long for the screen space allowed.

Some movement commands allow you to specify how many times **ve** should repeat the command before repositioning the cursor. Counts are used with commands by typing in a number before hitting the command key. For example, to move to the fourth character in the column, moving left to right, use the command *4l*. The command *2b* will move your position in the column two words to the left of your current cursor position.

When **ve** beeps or flashes at you instead of moving, it means that the command is inappropriate or that your cursor is already at your destination.

5.7.3 Inserting Text (a,A,i,I,o,O,c,C,s,r,R).

There are several commands which will put **ve** in insert mode, and they are all pretty much the same. Some commands destroy existing text (indicated by *); others simply add to it.

TABLE 6. Insert Commands

Command	means
a	append text to the right of the cursor
A	append text at the end of the column
i	insert text to the left of the cursor
I	insert text at the beginning of the column
o*	open the column and insert text at the beginning
O	open a blank row
c*target*	change the text between the cursor and *target*
C*	change text from the cursor to the end of the column
s*	substitute the character at the cursor for text
R*	replace (overwrite) text character by character

Because most **ve** commands are ordinary characters, how does **ve** know when you are typing in a command, and when you are actually trying to enter text? More importantly, how do you know?

When you type one of the insert commands listed above, **ve** switches from *command* mode to *insert* mode. When you are in insert mode, everything you type will be considered text and will be displayed on your screen. You know when you're in insert mode because the `<Insert/append mode>` message will be printed at the bottom of your screen. If you don't see that message, then you are in command mode.

The only way to get out of insert mode is to hit the **ESC** key, at which point **ve** erases the `<Insert/append mode>` message at the bottom of the screen and returns to command mode.

The **C**, **c**, and **s** commands mark your text with a '$' symbol to show you the text that will be changed. The '$' disappears as you type over it, or when you hit **ESC**.

The **r** or *replace* command is the only command which substitutes text without entering insert mode. To use the **r** command, position your cursor at the character in the column you wish to change, type **r** and the character to replace it. The **r** command can be used with counts. For example, to replace the next 4 characters with the letter 'x', use the command *4rx*.

5.7.4 Deleting Text (dd,D,x,d).

The delete commands let you delete entire rows and columns, partial columns, or characters from your table. The **x** command also knows about counts.

TABLE 7. Delete Commands

Command	means
dd	delete the entire row
D	delete text from the cursor to the end of the column
x	delete the character(s) at the cursor
d*target*	delete text from the cursor to *target*

5.7.5 Targets (c,d,^,$,b,e,w,f,F,;).

The insert command **c** and the delete command **d** require that you specify a *target*. A target is as it implies — an object for the command being executed. Commands which can be used as targets are listed in the section on *Moving Around*. The following table shows sample **d** and **c** commands and what they mean when used with different targets.

TABLE 8. Change Commands

Command	means
3dw	delete the next three words
de	delete to the end of the word
c2f*g*	change the text to the second *g* found moving right
c^	change the text to the beginning of the column
c$	change the text to the end of the column
d;	delete text to character specified by last **f** or **F** command

All targets assume that the delete or change action begins from the position of the cursor. Counts must be specified before the actual target — for example, the command *3dw* and *d3w* are identical.

5.7.6 Time Savers (y,Y,p,P,u).

Sometimes accidents will happen when you are editing — you will hit the wrong key, or decide that you really don't like a modification. You may even delete an entire row and then realize it shouldn't have been deleted. Or perhaps you are entering rows which are almost identical and you are tired of typing in the same strings over and over again. **ve** has a number of commands that help you to efficiently deal with a change of mind after a change of text, mistakes and repetitive data entry. These commands are known as *yank*, *put* and *undo* commands.

5.7.6.1 Yanking and putting (y,Y,p,P).

Yank commands are used to copy data from the row displayed on the screen into a special buffer. *Put* commands are used to put the yanked data from the buffer into the row on the screen.

Yanking data does not alter the row from which it is copied. Generally, once data has been yanked, it can be put indefinitely without having to yank it again. Because **ve** remembers only the text last yanked for each column displayed, yanking data from the same column in another row overwrites previously yanked data in that column with the text that is currently displayed. When entire rows are yanked or deleted, all yanked columns are overwritten with the text in the displayed row.

Selected columns are yanked with the **y** command. To use it, position your cursor on the column you want to yank and hit the **y** key. Different columns may be yanked from different rows.

All columns on the screen can be yanked with the **Y** command, and it works by hitting the **Y** key from any position on the screen.

Putting data replaces the data in the row or column being displayed with the data last yanked by a **y**, **Y**, or **dd** command. Data can be put only in columns from which it was yanked. For example, you can't yank text from a *phone number* column and put it in a *customer name* column.

The **p** command replaces the data in the column at which your cursor is positioned with data that has previously been yanked from that column.

The **P** command replaces the data in all columns currently displayed with data that has previously been yanked from each column. Since **ve** considers deleted rows to be yanked text, using the **P** command after mistakenly deleting a row will restore it.

5.7.6.2 Undo (u).

ve remembers the data in the last column modified prior to the last command which modified it, and can restore the data to that state by hitting the **u** key. The **u** command works only for undoing modifications made to the row currently being displayed.

5.7.7 For Your Information (v,t,S,z,#).

The **v** command displays the validation requirements for the column on which your cursor is positioned.

The **t** command prints the validation table for the column upon which your cursor is positioned (if such a table exists and is specified in the validation file).

If your data display gets messed up, use the **S** command to redraw your screen.

The **z** command will draw a window under the column your cursor is on and display the contents of the column in the window. This command comes in handy when the data for a particular column does not fit in the screen space allowed. The next command you hit will erase the window.

The **#** command will display the list of topics in the on-line **ve** help files available for perusal. The on-line **ve** help files are a condensed version of the *ve Tutorial* which provides a handy quick-reference guide for you during **ve** edit sessions.

To read one of the help files, position your cursor at the '==>' which precedes the desired topic by using the **j** or **RETURN** key to move down the list and the − and **k** keys to move up the list. Then, hit any other key (except **q**) to select the topic. The information available on that topic will be displayed, a file (or page) at a time. The **j** and **RETURN** keys will display successive pages, and the − and **k** keys will display previous pages. Any other key (except the **q** key) will display the table of contents. When you are finished with the help files, hit **q** to return to your data display.

5.7.8 Writing Rows (W,ZZ).

Whenever you change the data by adding or changing a row or column, you must use a **W** or **ZZ** *write* command to make your changes and/or additions part of your table. When you use the **W** or **ZZ** command, **ve** rechecks the data to make sure that all validation tests have been passed.

When you are using the **W** command and the data does not pass your validation tests, **ve** will complain and refuse to write your row in the table. In this case, your cursor will land on the column which contains the bad data and you can fix it. If there are no tests, or when the data passes your tests, **ve** will write your row in the table, and await your next command.

The **ZZ** command is a quick way to exit from **ve**. If the row currently displayed on the screen has been added or modified and it passes your validation tests (if any), **ve** will put it in the table before quitting.

If your data has been changed and you attempt to display a different row with a **q, n,
-, O,** /, or **?** command before using the **W** command, **ve** will warn you that the row
has not yet been written. If you ignore this warning and repeat your command, **ve**
will assume that you really don't want the new row (or the changed version of the
row) to be part of the table and execute your command.

5.7.9 Getting Back to UNIX (q,ZZ,%,!).

There are two kinds of commands which will get you back to UNIX: *shell* commands (**!,%**) and *quit* commands (**q,ZZ**). Shell commands let you talk to a new
UNIX shell while your **ve** process is suspended in the background, waiting for you to
return. Quit commands end the **ve** process and return you to your UNIX shell.

5.7.9.1 Shell commands (%,!).

The **%** command displays a **%** symbol at the bottom of your screen and puts **ve** on
hold. When you see your login prompt appear at the bottom of the screen, UNIX is
ready for your command. To resume your conversation with **ve**, hit CTRL-d (your
EOF character). If you are not familiar with UNIX processes and shells, remember
that it is easy to get carried away with UNIX and forget that **ve** is still patiently waiting for your return. You will know something odd is happening when you try to log
out and UNIX answers, `not login shell`. You must first return to **ve** and give it
a proper *quit* command. If UNIX still complains, it means that you have repeated
the **%** command a succession of times, and you will have to repeat the EOF-q
sequence until you can log out.

The **!** command, when followed with a UNIX command, will execute the UNIX
command and return immediately to **ve**. In order for you to read the results of your
UNIX command, the message `[Hit RETURN to continue]` will appear and **ve**
will wait for your response before redrawing your screen.

If you wish to repeat a **!** command, all you need to type is **!!**, because **ve** remembers
your last (**!**) shell command.

5.7.9.2 Quit commands (q,ZZ).

When you are finished using **ve**, you can use the **q** or **ZZ** command to exit. The only
difference between the **q** and **ZZ** commands is that **q** will complain if the row on the
screen has not been written after a modification has been made. (A second **q** command will simply exit without writing the row.)

The **ZZ** command will automatically write your row before exiting **ve**.

5.7.10 Colon Commands (next,open,help,write,shell,!,!!,quit).

People who are accustomed to using the UNIX editor *vi* are already familiar with *colon* commands, and that is the only reason **ve** provides them.

People who are not familiar with the *vi* editor don't need to learn colon commands because they have one-key command counterparts which do exactly the same thing.

The following table shows the colon command, the **ve** command counterpart and the section in which the command is described.

TABLE 9. Colon Commands

Command	Same as	Section
:n[*ext*]	**n**	Sequential display
:o[*pen*]	**O**	Inserting text
:h[*elp*]	**#**	For your information
:w[*rite*]	**W**	Writing rows
:s[*hell*]	**%**	Shell commands
:!*command*	**!**	Shell commands
:!!	**n**	Shell commands
:q[*uit*]	**q**	Quit commands

Colon commands are always preceded by a colon (**:**). When the colon key is hit, it appears at the bottom of the screen and the remainder of the command appears after the colon as you type it in. You must type in at least the first letter of the colon command for it to work. Letters enclosed in square brackets ([ ]) show how much of the command you don't need to type. You must end colon commands with RETURN or ESC to let **ve** know you are done.

5.7.11 Macros (CTRL-a - CTRL-z).

A *macro* command is defined as one or more **ve** commands mapped to a single CTRL key. Any **ve** command can be used to define a macro. Each time the CTRL key is hit, the command or sequence of commands defined for that CTRL key will be executed.

Macro commands can be used to simplify an often-repeated sequence of commands into a single keystroke. Because CTRL keys are nonprintable characters and cannot be confused with potential data (unlike regular **ve** commands), they work from both command mode and insert mode. The mode from which the user executes the macro is restored after successful completion of all the commands which define it. It is even possible to design a set of macro commands which will make **ve** appear to be a single-mode editor. This might be desirable for beginning users who find two edit modes confusing. For example, it can be make to look more like the EMACS editor.

A maximum of 23 macro commands may be defined for the CTRL-a through CTRL-z keys.* If your erase character, or your interrupt character, is a CTRL key in this range, then it is excluded from the list of CTRL keys available for macros. Macro commands which include a second macro in their list of commands will replace whatever commands follow the second macro in the list with the list of commands in the second macro. Imbedding macros in macros is confusing and it is not recommended.

Macro definitions are stored in a **ve** table named *.verc*.** If you want to define your own macros, this file must be in your home directory where it can be shared by all **ve** tables in your account. If you don't have your own *.verc* file, **ve** will use its own.

```
CTRL key    command
--------    -------
a           #
d           ddn
o           O
q           ZZ
r           S
s           %
t           t
w           W
```

The first two rows in your *.verc* file *must* be header rows, and the column separation character *must* be TABs. The first column in the *.verc* file contains the letter which is hit simultaneously with the CTRL key to make the CTRL key code. The second column in the *.verc* file is the **ve** command or commands which are executed when the CTRL key is hit. Four nonprintable commands which you may want to use in your macros are TAB, ESC, RETURN and *backspace*. They should be indicated by \t, \e, \n and \b, respectively.

For example, let's say we're editing the *blackbook* table and we forgot to type in the area codes for local phone numbers with *429* prefixes. If we *mark* the phone column using the **m** command, and the macro

```
p       /^429\I(408)\W
```

is a row in our *.verc* file, then every time we hit CTRL-p, **ve** will find rows in which the first three characters of the phone column are *429*. **ve** will then insert *(408)* at the beginning of the column and write the row. A simpler command which scrolls forth and back through the leftmost column on the last line of screen columns each time CTRL-s is hit:

```
s       L       ><
```

---

*   *CTRL-m, CTRL-j,* and *CTRL-i* are reserved by **ve**.

** If your terminal has function keys which use the same CTRL keys defined in your *.verc* file, you may also use the appropriate function key to execute your macro command.

This is a fairly silly example, but it illustrates how to create more complicated macros. Remember that your macros will apply to all **ve** tables in your account.

5.8 Multi-User Considerations

ve is a *multi-user* table editor. This means that any number of users can be entering and/or editing data in the same table at the same time. When a row is displayed on your screen, it belongs to you until you release it by moving to another row, writing the row, or deleting it. That means that anyone else who may be using the table at the same time will be prevented from viewing or editing that row until you are finished with it.

Because **ve** knows which rows are in use at any given time, you will sometimes see the message

```
other match(es) currently in use
```

when you search for a pattern in a row which belongs to someone else. This is to let you know that the pattern is in your table, but the row which contains the pattern simply isn't available.

When you use a sequential display command (**n**, **-**), **ve** will skip over rows which belong to other users until it finds a free one. When **ve** has to skip over rows, it will let you know how many. Similarly, the **G** command will let you know that it can't land on a specified row because either it is currently in use or it has been deleted during the edit session.

5.9 /rdb Compatability

If you are planning to use **/rdb** with **ve**, take the following precautions when setting up your tables and avoid trouble later on.

Because **/rdb** expects that the header rows are part of the table, it is best not to use the **ve -h** option which stores header rows in a separate file. Otherwise, you will have to join the header and data files each time you use **/rdb**.

In **/rdb** tables, the column separation character *must* be a TAB. If you use a different column separation character, it must be changed to TAB before using **/rdb** on your table.

Because many **/rdb** commands use table column names as command line arguments, care must be taken to exclude symbols and/or words which have special meaning to the shell from your column names. Specifically, stay away from the /, # and *!* characters. If column names can be confused with shell commands (ie., *date*, *who*) remember to protect them from shell intrepretation by enclosing them in quotes (") when you use them as arguments to **/rdb** commands.

When using **ve** in a shell script, care must be taken not to access the original file until **ve** is done with it. You can check for this by testing for the existence of a *data+lck* file. If *data+lck* exists, then wait until it disappears before using the *data* table.

5.10 Limits

ve imposes limits on the maximum number of columns and the maximum number of characters in each row. On most installations, the maximum number of columns is 66 and the maximum row length is 4096 bytes.

If you need more than 66 columns in a row, we recommend that you create two separate tables, each with a common column, and use the **/rdb jointable** command to merge the two tables after data entry has been completed.

If you use the look-up table validation feature, you should be aware that a 64 byte limit is imposed by truncation for key and decode lengths.

6. Database Design: How to set it up

When you try to design your first database, you are likely to be quite confused. Which data go into which tables? Can you have just one big table? Should you have lots of little tables? How do you find out? It turns out that there is a simple way to decide how to lay out your database. Once you learn it, any application will be easy. This chapter will show you how.

6.1 One-to-one Relationships in One Table

When you look at your data, you will notice that some information has what we call a one-to-one relationship. For example, each person has a first name, a last name, a birthdate, a sex, an ID number, and so on. All of these items of information can be put into one table. Here is such a table that is called *employee:*

```
$ cat employee
Id   First    Last    Birth    Sex
--   -----    ----    -----    ---
1    Howard   Ho      450503   Male
2    Jane     Dobbs   540129   Female
```

The rule then is put all one-to-one relationships into a single table. Another example is *department:*

```
$ cat department
Dept   Name    Head    Address
----   ----    ----    -------
1      act     Jones   Basement
2      sales   White   4th Floor
```

6.2 One-to-many Relationships in Two Tables

Another relationship is one-to-many. People have a one-to-many relationship with their children. A person can have from zero to many children. Relational database theory insists that one-to-many relationships cannot be put into one table, but require two. In addition to the *employee* table, you will need a *child* table:

```
$ cat child
Parent   Name
------   -----
1        Sally
1        Lynn
```

Note that Howard Ho (Id 1) has two children Sally and Lynn. However, Jane Dobbs

(Id 2) has no children, because her Id (Parent) number is not in the *child* table. To put this information back together, use the *jointable* command:

```
$ jointable employee child
Id   First   Last   Birth   Sex    Name
--   -----   ----   -----   ---    -----
1    Howard  Ho     450503  Male   Sally
1    Howard  Ho     450503  Male   Lynn
```

Here we have the two tables, *employee* and *child,* joined together on the *employee Id* and the *child Parent* key columns. These connect the two tables for the **jointable** command. Note that since Howard Ho has two children, he has two rows in the table. Also note that Sally Dobbs was not included in the table because she has no children. There is a simple way to diagram or graph this database structure.

Figure 1. One-to-Many Relationship

employee		child
Id	---ID--->	Parent
First		Name
Last		
Birth		
Sex		

A box represents a table with the name on top and a list of the columns, or fields, inside. The arrow shows the one-to-many relationship by pointing at the table which has the *many* rows. The arrow is labeled by the key column that can be used to join the tables together.

You can also begin to see why we need to keep these kind of data in separate tables. We need information on employees, even when they have no children. Of course, we could include Sally Dobbs and leave her children column empty, but that will complicate processing. More seriously, we have all of the information on Howard Ho repeated for each child. This not only wastes space, but requires that when we update the table we have to find every entry for Howard Ho and correctly make the update. The extra time and effort, plus the risk of errors, make the single table approach unacceptable. Therefore, we must keep one-to-many relationships in separate tables and join them together only when needed.

6.3 Many-to-many Relationships in Three Tables

There are also several many-to-many relationships. For example, students take zero to many courses and courses have zero to many students. This relationship requires three tables.

Figure 2. Many-to-Many Relationship

student		student.course		course
Student	--Student-->	Student	<--Course--	Course
First		Course		Credit
Last				Room
Year				Day
				Time

First we need a *student* table:

```
$ cat student
Student   First   Last   Year
-------   -----   ----   ----
      1   Jim     Clark     2
      2   Mary    Witte     1
```

We also need a *course* table:

```
$ cat course
Course   Credit   Room   Day   Time
------   ------   ----   ----  ----
art-1a        3   RB-8   MWF   10am
chem-1        4   HA-18  TTh   2pm
```

To connect these two tables, a third table is needed that we will call *course.student*

```
$ cat course.student
Course   Student
------   -------
art-1a        1
chem-1        1
chem-1        2
```

We can join these tables together with two **jointable** commands. First let's see individual joins.

```
$ jointable course course.student
Course   Credit   Room   Day   Time   Student
------   ------   ----   ----  ----   -------
art-1a        3   RB-8   MWF   10am         1
chem-1        4   HA-18  TTh   2pm          1
chem-1        4   HA-18  TTh   2pm          2
$ jointable -j Student student course.student
Student   First   Last   Year   Course
-------   -----   ----   ----   ------
      1   Jim     Clark     2   art-1a
      1   Jim     Clark     2   chem-1
      2   Mary    Witte     1   chem-1
```

All together now:

```
$ jointable -j Student student course.student |
> jointable -j Course - course
Student   First   Last   Year   Course   Credit   Room   Day   Time
-------   -----   ----   ----   ------   ------   ----   ----  ----
      1   Jim     Clark     2   art-1a        3   RB-8   MWF   10am
      1   Jim     Clark     2   chem-1        4   HA-18  TTh   2pm
      2   Mary    Witte     1   chem-1        4   HA-18  TTh   2pm
```

So we can bring it all together when we want to see it, but we keep many-to-many relationships in three separate tables.

6.4 Planning

When you look at your application, look for the kind of relationships that you have and group your data accordingly. Continuing the college example above, we will also need tables for instructors, rooms, and so on. There is a one-to-many relationship between instructors and classes. Can you see that? Instructors often teach several classes, but classes have one instructor (unless there is team teaching). Note that you have to think of exceptions. If the exceptions are very rare, you might choose to ignore them. But if there are more than a rare instance of classes having more than one instructor, it becomes a many-to-many relationship. Then you will need three tables, because you will need a connector table.

Our college database will also need a *room* table. What is the relationship between rooms and courses? Can you see that it is one-to-many? A course is in only one room. (Is it always? What about labs? Or are labs separate courses?) But rooms have more than one course in them at different times, unless we have a terribly inefficient college. So how many tables will we need? One-to-many requires two tables. Which tables do we need? In this case a *course* table and a *room* table. The *course* table will have the room number in it, but the *room* table will have no mention of the courses in it because there are many.

Figure 3. One-to-Many

course		room
Course	--Room-->	Room
Credit		Type
Room		Size
Day		Hall
Time		
Teacher		

To find the size of the room for each course, join the *room* table with the *course* table.

```
$ cat course
Course   Credit   Room    Day    Time    Teacher
------   ------   ----    ----    ----    -------
art-1a        3   RB-8    MWF    10am          3
chem-1        4   HA-18   TTh    2pm           1
cs-101        4   DB-1    MWF    2am           2
econ-1        3   RB-8    TTH    1pm           2
his-10        3   HA-18   MWF    11am          3

$ cat room
Room    Type        Size    Hall
----    ----        ----    ----
DB-1    Lecture      250    Daddy Bucks
HA-18   Lab           17    Hillary Addler
RB-8    Tacky         23    Roberta Bucks
$ sorttable Room < course |
> jointable -j Room - room |
> column Course Room Size > room.size
$ cat room.size
Course   Room    Size
------   ----    ----
cs-101   DB-1     250
chem-1   HA-18     17
his-10   HA-18     17
art-1a   RB-8      23
econ-1   RB-8      23
```

So, it turns out that designing a database is easy. Just practice thinking about these principles with different applications.

6.5 Normalization

The approach we have just discussed is the easiest way to think about designing your database. However, most of the database literature approaches the problem from a different angle. To help you understand that literature, these other approaches are discussed in the following sections. It is more technical and can be skipped on first reading, or if you are just beginning to use databases. In the technical relational database literature, this process of correctly grouping data into tables is called *normalizing*.

6.6 Functional Dependency

Before discussing normalization, several concepts must be understood. *Functional dependency* refers to whether the data in one column determine the data in another. In other words, if you know the data in one column, can you tell what the data in another column will be? If the data in one column are repeated, are the corresponding data in the other column also repeated? If so, there is a functional dependency, otherwise not. For example, look at these two tables. First the *room.size* table we previously created.

```
$ cat room.size
Course   Room       Size
------   ----     -------
cs-101   DB-1         250
chem-1   HA-18         17
his-10   HA-18         17
art-1a   RB-8          23
econ-1   RB-8          23
```

Note that when a value in the *Room* column is repeated, the corresponding *Size* value is also repeated. (See RB-8 is in the *Room* column with the same *Size* of 23. Also the same for HA-18 and 17). Therefore, *Room* functionally determines *Size* or an equivalent way of saying it, *Size* is functionally determined by *Room*. Ordinarily, we do not want to have tables with functional dependencies in them. It is ok here,' because we used a join to put this table together. It is a query of our database and not a proper table of the database.

6.7 Keys

Key columns are the unique identifiers of each row in the table. The key column or columns of a table should always determine each of the other columns of the table. The function of a key is to uniquely identify the data in the other columns. So the rule is that only key columns can functionally determine other columns. Nonkey columns should not functionally determine other columns in a normalized database.

6.8 Universal Relation

The opposite of normalization is the universal relation. Imagine one large table that has all of the tables joined together. It has all of the columns of all of the tables across the top. It is the worst case of a unnormalized database. Why? What is wrong with such a table?

6.9 Problems

We need to avoid unnormalized tables because they create severe problems for us.

6.9.1 Redundancy problems.

One problem is that we have a lot of redundant data. Look at the *room.size* table again and note that the size information for each room is repeated.

```
$ cat room.size
Course   Room    Size
------   ----    ----
cs-101   DB-1     250
chem-1   HA-18    17
his-10   HA-18    17
art-1a   RB-8     23
econ-1   RB-8     23
```

This takes up more space than necessary and slows down the programs that must process it.

6.9.2 Update problems.

Another problem is the extra work and errors that result from trying to update such a table. Suppose we add more chairs to *HA-18*. We have to update the new *Size* twice. In this simple table, that is not much work, but in a large database it is overwhelming. And what happens when we make an error in our updating? It is hard to find and correct. After a while, we will not know which conflicting value is correct. Our database will become hopelessly corrupted.

6.9.3 Insert and delete problems.

There are also insert and delete problems. Suppose we want to add a room and its size to this database. If it does not yet have a course in it, we can't put it into the table unless we give it a blank course. This creates problems when searching and joining. How do you handle blank or null values? Likewise with deleting. What if a course is still assigned to the room after the building has been demolished? You don't want to drop the course, but you need to delete the room from the database.

6.10 First Normal Form

In order for relational functions to work, tables must be simple or, as it is called in the literature, normalized. There are a number of steps to simplifying, or normalizing, a table. Most importantly, you must never have a variable number of columns in a table. For example, in a file of college employees, you might be tempted to have a column for the first name of the children of employees.

```
Emp#       Name      Dept      Child
-------    -------   -------   -------
1          Martin    1204      Sally, Fido
2          Moore     1339
3          Mapes     1045      Jan, Shawn, Peter, Barbara
```

This creates many problems, not the least of which is that the relational functions will not work. The answer is to have two files, one for employees and another for their children. The *child* file would look like this:

```
   Emp#   Child
-------   -------
      1   Sally
      1   Fido
      3   Jan
      3   Shawn
      3   Peter
      3   Barbara
```

If you ever need to put the two files together, you can do so with a join (**jointable** in **/rdb** because there is a UNIX command named **join** which works on files without headers). This is another way of saying that one-to-many relations must be represented in two tables. When all of the one-to-many relations are in separate tables, we say that the database is in first normal form.

6.11 Second Normal Form

Both second and third normal forms require that nonkey functional dependencies be removed by creating additional tables. In the case of second normal form, we look for dependencies on columns within the key. Keys can consist of more than one column. For example, consider a *grade* table.

```
$ cat grade
Course   Student   Grade
------   -------   -------
art-1a   1         3
art-1a   4         4
chem-1   1         3
chem-1   2         2
chem-1   3         2
cs-101   2         1
cs-101   4         4
econ-1   1         3
econ-1   2         3
econ-1   3         2
his-10   1         3
```

Note that it takes two columns to make a unique key for each row. Both the *Course* and the *Student* columns make up the key. *Grade* is a nonkey column. What we must look for is a dependency between one of the columns in the key and the other columns. In this case there are none, so this table is in second normal form. But suppose we added a column for class rooms. Since the *Room* column depends upon the *Course* column, we would not be in second normal form. This is called a *partial* dependency because columns are dependent on a partial key, that is, less than all of the columns of the key.

6.12 Third Normal Form

Third normal form requires that we also eliminate any dependencies between nonkey columns. These are called *transitive* dependencies.

```
$ cat room.size
Course   Room    Size
------   ----    ----
cs-101   DB-1     250
chem-1   HA-18    17
his-10   HA-18    17
art-1a   RB-8     23
econ-1   RB-8     23
```

Here the *Size* column is dependent on the *Room* column. To reach third normal form we must make two tables: one called *course.room* with the *Course* and *Room* columns. The other would be *room* and would have the *Room* and *Size* columns.

6.13 Normalizing Example

Let's start with a simple universal table and normalize it step by step. Suppose we go to the dean of the college to work out the college database for grades. Since the dean does not know about normalization, she lists all of the items she wants to keep track of, but our job is to put them into tables. The universal table she builds might look like this.

```
$ cat universe
Course   Student  Grade  Teacher  Title    Child
------   -------  -----  -------  -----    -----
chem-1      1       3       1     Assist.  Sally, Mike, Joy
chem-1      2       2       1     Assist.  Fred
chem-1      3       2       1     Assist.
cs-101      2       1       2     Prof.    Fred
cs-101      4       4       2     Prof.
econ-1      1       3       2     Prof.    Sally, Mike, Joy
econ-1      2       3       2     Prof.    Fred
econ-1      3       2       2     Prof.
his-10      1       3       3     Assoc.   Sally, Mike, Joy
```

Look at this unnormalized table and see if you can normalize it before we show you how.

First normalization requires that we get rid of the one-to-many relationship between students and their children to remove multiple values in the *Child* column. We create a new table for children of the students.

```
$ cat student.child
Student   Child
-------   -----
      1   Sally
      1   Mike
      1   Joy
      2   Fred
```

We could add more columns about each child to this table as long as we are careful not to include information about the student-parent which should be put into the *student* table. We also remove the *Child* column from the big table.

```
$ column Course Student Grade Teacher Title < universe
Course    Student   Grade   Teacher   Title
------    -------   -----   -------   -----
chem-1          1       3         1   Assist.
chem-1          2       2         1   Assist.
chem-1          3       2         1   Assist.
cs-101          2       1         2   Prof.
cs-101          4       4         2   Prof.
econ-1          1       3         2   Prof.
econ-1          2       3         2   Prof.
econ-1          3       2         2   Prof.
his-10          1       3         3   Assoc.
```

For second normal form we have to realize that we have a multi-column key: *Course* and *Student* which uniquely determines each row. Let's look for dependencies between either of these columns and the other columns. Can you see that *Course* determines *Teacher?* So let's create a new *course.teacher* table.

```
$ column Course Teacher Title < universe > course.teacher
$ cat course.teacher
Course    Teacher   Title
------    -------   -----
chem-1          1   Assist.
chem-1          1   Assist.
chem-1          1   Assist.
cs-101          2   Prof.
cs-101          2   Prof.
econ-1          2   Prof.
econ-1          2   Prof.
econ-1          2   Prof.
his-10          3   Assoc.
$ column Course Student Grade < universe > grade
$ cat grade
Course    Student   Grade
------    -------   -----
chem-1          1       3
chem-1          2       2
chem-1          3       2
cs-101          2       1
cs-101          4       4
econ-1          1       3
econ-1          2       3
econ-1          3       2
his-10          1       3
```

Note that there is a lot of redundancy in the *course.teacher* table. We can reduce the table to unique rows by using the UNIX **uniq** command to remove duplicate rows.

```
$ uniq < course.teacher
Course   Teacher   Title
------   -------   -----
chem-1         1   Assist.
cs-101         2   Prof.
econ-1         2   Prof.
his-10         3   Assoc.
```

The *grade* table is now in second and third normal form, but the new *course.teacher* table is only in second normal form. Note that *Title* depends upon *Teacher*. We need another table.

```
$ column Teacher Title < course.teacher | uniq > teacher
$ cat teacher
Teacher   Title
-------   -----
      1   Assist.
      2   Prof.
      3   Assoc.
$ column Course Teacher < course.teacher
Course   Teacher
------   -------
chem-1         1
cs-101         2
econ-1         2
his-10         3
```

So now the *teacher* and *course.teacher* tables are in third normal form. How many tables do we have? What are their names? What columns are in each table? How would you explain to the dean what you have done to her nice big table? Why have you done it?

6.14 Complex Queries with Joins

When data are distributed to many tables, how can we get the information we want? It is easy to project columns and select rows from a single table and join two tables. But what if the information we want is widely separated?

As an example, let us imagine that you are an instructor in a college and want a phone book of all of your students, just in case you need to call to tell them that the class was canceled or that the final exam date or room had changed. Suppose all you know is your own name and the different tables in the database.

TABLE 10. Table of College Database Tables

```
Table              Columns
-----              -----------
teacher            Teacher First Last Address City State Phone   Title
teacher.course     Teacher Course
course             Course Credit Room Day Time Teacher
course.student     Course Student
student            Student First Last Year Phone
```

Could you produce such a phone book or listing with a single pipeline? The answer is ... drumroll ... Yes! First let's think through the solution. Then we will build the one-line query. You know your name, so you can find your ID number in the *teacher* file. With your teacher ID number, you can get a table of all of your class ID numbers from the *teacher.course* connector file. Then you can pick up the student ID numbers from the *course.student* connector file. Finally you can project the information you want about each of your students. Here is a picture of the join.

Figure 4. Phone Book Pipeline Join

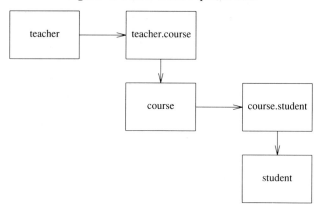

6.15 Pipeline Join

Now let's look at the pipeline. It has been written down the page to make it easier to read and modify. When the (Bourne) shell sees the pipe symbol at the end of a line, it knows to continue to the next line because this line is not finished.

```
$ cat makephonebook
row 'First == "Joy" && Last == "Xi" ' < teacher |
column Teacher |
tee tmp1 |
jointable - teacher.course |
column Course |
sorttable |
tee tmp2 |
jointable - course.student |
column Student Course |
sorttable |
tee tmp3 |
jointable - student |
column Course Last First Phone |
sorttable > phonebook
```

This probably looks overwhelming, but don't worry, we are going to go through each part. First let's look at the output so that we will know where we are going with all of this.

```
$ cat phonebook
Course   Last     First    Year   Phone
------   ----     -----    ----   --------
cs-101   Dunce    Boris      2    765-4321
cs-101   Early    Mary       4    123-4567
econ-1   Early    Mary       4    123-4567
econ-1   Farkel   Freddy     3    123-1234
econ-1   Knott    Why        1    123-7654
```

Note that **tee** *tmp* lines have been inserted in three places in the pipeline. The UNIX **tee** command will write the *standard input* to the *standard output* but also write the stream of characters into the file *tmp*. By looking at the *tmp* files we have a peephole into the pipeline so that we can see how the data look at each point. Therefore, we can see and discuss the data at three points in the pipeline.

6.15.1 tmp1.

Assuming your name is *Joy Xi*, you can select the row in the teacher file in which the first name, *First,* is Joy and the last name, *Last,* is Xi. Then you can project the *Teacher* ID number column only. **column** throws away the other columns. This is to reduce the amount of data flowing through the pipe to speed up the execution. It also avoids conflicts in the names of columns.

```
row 'First == "Joy" && Last == "Xi" ' < teacher |
column Teacher |
tee tmp1 |
```

Now let's see what the data look like by looking at the *tmp1* file:

```
$ cat tmp1
Teacher
-------
2
```

Here we have gotten the *Teacher* ID number in a little table that we can now use to find more data.

6.15.2 tmp2.

The next four lines join the single-line table above with the *teacher.course* table to pickup the courses that *Joy Xi* teaches. Then only the *Course* column is projected. It must be sorted for the next join.

```
jointable - teacher.course |
column Course |
sorttable |
tee tmp2 |
```

By taking a look at our data now, we see that *Joy Xi* teaches two courses.

```
$ cat tmp2
Course
------
cs-101
econ-1
```

6.15.3 tmp3

Now we can join this two-row table to the *course.student* table to pick up the students in her classes. This time we project not only their ID numbers but the courses because we want that information carried on to the phone book. The *Student* column also must be sorted for the next join. We have to tell the **sorttable** command that the *Student* column is numeric, instead of string, to get a correct sort.

```
jointable - course.student |
column Student Course |
sorttable -n |
tee tmp3 |
```

Here is the output of these lines:

```
$ cat tmp3
Student   Course
-------   ------
      1   econ-1
      2   cs-101
      2   econ-1
      3   econ-1
      4   cs-101
```

Note that we have only the *Student* and the *Course* columns and that the *Student* column is correctly sorted.

6.16 Phone Book

The last lines join this table above with the *student* file to get the student information. Then the columns we want for the phone book are projected. Note that we project the *Course* column that was carried along as well as columns from the *student* table. We must e-sort the new phone book by course so that the teacher can see all of the students in one class.

```
jointable - student |
column Course Last First Phone |
sorttable > phonebook
```

Let's see the final output phone book again:

```
$ cat phonebook
Course   Last      First     Year   Phone
------   ----      -----     ----   --------
cs-101   Dunce     Boris       2    765-4321
cs-101   Early     Mary        4    123-4567
econ-1   Early     Mary        4    123-4567
econ-1   Farkel    Freddy      3    123-1234
econ-1   Knott     Why         1    123-7654
```

Note that we have done this in such a way that some students' information is repeated if they are taking more than one class from this teacher. Mary Early, in the table above, is an example. We accept this repetition so that the teacher can call all of the students in a particular class. If we had just a list of all the students, we would not know which student was in what class. But you can change this example many different ways by changing the **column, sorttable,** and **jointable** commands.

7. Shell Programming: Let UNIX do the work

The great advantage of the UNIX system is that most of the work is done for you. Most database systems create a new language that you must learn, but **/rdb** uses UNIX programs and the shell programming language. If you already know these UNIX tools, there is little more to learn. If you don't know the UNIX system, it is much better to learn the general purpose UNIX system than a special language that is only good for a single database package. The UNIX system is better documented, better tested, has more books available in book stores and libraries, and is on more computers than any database system you might consider. UNIX tools as they are delivered on your system can do much of the database application. **/rdb** only extends the UNIX system by adding more than a hundred commands that will make database handling easier and faster.

7.1 Database Programming in UNIX Shell Language

It is the shell programming language that make this approach so easy and powerful. The shell is the user interface to the UNIX system. It prompts you for commands, rewrites your command line to save you typing, and executes the programs you request. It is extremely simple to learn. You start by putting commands that you would type at the terminal, into files called shell programs. These files can be executed simply by typing their names.

But the shell is also a powerful string-oriented programming language with control flow statements like **if, for,** and **while.** You can mix procedural with nonprocedural statements.

Procedural programs are the traditional step-by-step instructions that tell the computer *how* to do something. *Nonprocedural* statements simply tell the computer *what* to do. For example, a traditional procedural program will tell the computer how to sort a file. A nonprocedural statement in the UNIX system would be

```
$ sort file
```

where *file* is the name of the file we want sorted. The UNIX **sort** command knows how to sort a file, so we get what we want with out worrying about details. If we had to write the sort program, it would take 10 to 100 lines of code or more. Nonprocedural is much easier and saves a lot of time. It is also much faster to fix. Options to the **sort** program can reverse the sort. Editing a sort program is much trickier.

Of course, nonprocedural is best, but if a system is all nonprocedural, it has to anticipate everything you will ever want to do! Most fourth generation systems have this problem. They give you a lot of functions, but lack procedural language statements to let you program what they don't have. Third generation languages let you program anything but force you to carefully code too many basic functions over and over. The UNIX system gives you a nice mix of predeveloped programs that cover all of the basic actions, and the shell programming language to allow you to code more complex functions by building up basic functions.

In the UNIX environment you are constantly in a process of automating your work. First you try out a simple program. Then call it, and other programs, from a higher level program. Soon you are able to do many things with simple keystrokes.

There are a number of books on shell programming, in addition to the UNIX documentation. We happen to like the book, *The UNIX^{TM} Shell Programming Language,* [Manis and Meyer, 1986]. Before we discuss shell programming further, we will need some UNIX programs to build applications.

7.2 UNIX Utilities

In addition to the **/rdb** commands, there are several UNIX utilities that you will probably need often. Your UNIX documentation provides detailed descriptions of these commands; we briefly describe some of their database uses.

7.3 awk - Language to Produce Complex Reports

awk is the heart of the **/rdb** system. It provides the important **row, compute** and **validate** commands. It can be used by itself to do powerful things to tables. For advanced applications, please refer to your UNIX manual pages and tutorial.

7.4 cat - Display a Table or List File

cat is used all the time to list out your tables.

7.5 grep - Find All Rows That Contain a Matching String

grep will let you search a table or any text file for a string of characters. If a match is found, the line is printed out. It is a primitive search but easy to use.

7.6 od -c - Octal Dump All Bytes as Characters

od will let you see special characters and can be used to see if your tabs are in place (the **/rdb** or Berkeley **see** command is better for this purpose).

7.7 sed - Stream Editor to Edit File in a Pipe

sed is a very powerful program for editing your tables in a pipe stream. Many of the **/rdb** shell programs use it. You can perform almost any editor command with it.

7.8 sh - UNIX Shell Programming Language

sh is the UNIX shell program that interfaces to the user. It prompts with the dollar ($) or other prompt and reads the commands that the user types in. It is a powerful string oriented (from Snobol) programming language. You can create any complex application with it and the UNIX and **/rdb** commands.

7.9 spell - Check Spelling in a Table or List File

You may find this quite useful for checking spelling in a file. It is also a good example of the power of shell programming.

7.10 tail - Display Bottom Rows of a Table or List File

tail will output the end of a file. You can use it to chop off the head of a table:

```
$ cat mailtable
Number   Name                 Company          Phone
------   ---------------      -------------    --------------
     1   Ronald McDonald      McDonald's       (111) 222-3333
     2   Chiquita Banana      United Brands    1234
$ tail +3 mailtable
     1   Ronald McDonald      McDonald's       (111) 222-3333
     2   Chiquita Banana      United Brands    1234
```

There is also the **/rdb** command **headoff** for the same purpose.

7.11 vi - Text Editor to Enter and Update Files

Any text editor is important to your work, because you will use it to set up tables and lists and to write your shell program applications. **vi** is provided for free with the UNIX system so it is always available.

7.12 Reading and Writing Database Files

When you write programs, you have to open files. In the UNIX environment files usually come to the program from standard-in and output is sent to standard-out. But sometimes you have a shell program that is talking to the user at the terminal through the standard-in and out, but has to open one or more files for reading and writing. This is done with the **exec** command. This code opens *filein* for input (read) and assigns the file descriptor 3. *fileout* is opened for output (write) and assigned file descriptor 4. Then programs can use those file descriptors with the *<&3* and *>&4* conventions.

```
$ exec 3< filein
$ exec 4> fileout
$ cat <&3 >&4
```

The UNIX **sh read** command cannot have its input redirected to a file other than standard-in, except by a trick.

```
$ exec 0< inventory
$ read HEAD
$ echo "$HEAD"
Item    Amount  Cost    Value   Description
```

In a loop you can read a whole file line by line. The **while** statement is a control statement that executes the lines within the **do** and **done** until **read** tries to read the end-of-file and returns a status code indicating false.

```
$ exec 0< inventory
$ while read HEAD
> do
>       echo "$HEAD"
> done
Item    Amount  Cost    Value   Description
----    ------  ----    -----   --------------
  1        3     50      150    rubber gloves
  2      100      5      500    test tubes
  3        5     80      400    clamps
  4       23     19      437    plates
  5       99     24     2376    cleaning cloth
  6       89    147    13083    bunsen burners
  7        5    175      875    scales
```

7.13 Parsing Rows

You can use the **set** command to parse strings in the shell. For example, if you want to get at any field in a row you can read the row into a shell variable and set the words in the row to the shell positional arguments *$1, $2*.

```
$ exec 0< inventory
$ read HEAD
$ set $HEAD
$ echo "The first field is $1 and the fifth field is $5."
The first field is Item and the fifth field is Description.
```

7.14 Tables to Shell Variables

It would be very nice if we could use the column names from a table to refer to the column values in a shell program. Often people assume they have to walk through the row with **for** and, perhaps, **shift** commands. This slow method is not necessary. Here is a neat trick for using column heads as variables in shell programs:

```
$ cat inventory
Item    Amount  Cost    Value   Description
----    ------  ----    -----   --------------
  1        3     50      150    rubber gloves
  2      100      5      500    test tubes
  3        5     80      400    clamps
  4       23     19      437    plates
  5       99     24     2376    cleaning cloth
  6       89    147    13083    bunsen burners
  7        5    175      875    scales
```

```
$ cat onhand
: onhand reports the amount of an item in inventory
USAGE='usage: onhand Item < inventory'
FOUND=0
NOFOUND=1
read HEAD
read DASH
while read $HEAD
do
        if test "$Item" -eq "$1"
        then
                echo We have $Amount $Description on hand.
                exit $FOUND
        fi
done
exit $NOFOUND
$ onhand 2 < inventory
We have 100 test tubes on hand.
```

First we look at the *inventory* file. Then we look at the *onhand* program. Note that we read the first line of the table into a shell variable called *HEAD*. This will assign the whole row of column names to the variable *HEAD*. The dashed line is read into *DASH* and ignored. Within the **while** loop we read each column name. But look carefully at the **read** statement. We use *$HEAD*, which is expanded by the shell into the list of column names, *before* **read** is called. So the **read** command really sees all of the column names as arguments:

```
read Item Amount Cost Value Description
```

The **read** command assigns the first word it reads from standard-in to *Item*, then next to *Amount*, and so on. Therefore, it has automatically assigned the column values to the column names for us and we can use them in the shell program with '*$*' in front. The **test** and **echo** commands both use the variables which will hold the values from the current row. Let's see this with the shell execution trace option turned on:

```
$ sh -x onhand 2 < inventory
+ : onhand reports the amount of an item in inventory
USAGE=usage: onhand Item < inventory
+ read HEAD
+ read DASH
+ read Item Amount Cost Value Description
+ test 1 -eq 2
+ read Item Amount Cost Value Description
+ test 2 -eq 2
+ echo We have 100 test tubes on hand.
We have 100 test tubes on hand.
```

This lets you see how the column names and values are rewritten as each row is read, tested, and processed.

7.15 Lists to Shell Variables

Here is an example of how to get records from a list formatted file and make each column name-value pair a shell *variable=value* pair. It uses the /**rdb** program **list-tosh** to convert the list record to shell format.

```
$ cat mail.list

Number  1
Name    Ronald McDonald
Company McDonald's
Street  123 Mac Attack
City    Menphis
State   TENN
ZIP     30000
Phone   (111) 222-3333

$ listtosh < mail.list

Number='1'
Name='Ronald McDonald'
Company='McDonald´s'
Street='123 Mac Attack'
City='Menphis'
State='TENN'
ZIP='30000'
Phone='(111) 222-3333'
```

See the tabs converted to equal signs (=) and the data protected absolutely by single quotes ('). Also note that a single quote in the data is protected with a back slash (\) in the *Company* line. This is the format for the shell *variable=value* assignments. This program can be executed in a shell program and the *variable=value* pair will become known to the program.

```
$ column Name Phone < mail.list | listtosh
Name='Ronald McDonald' Phone='(111) 222-3333'
```

This one line output from the command substitution is exactly the format the shell uses to assign values to its variables. Yes, Virginia, the shell can read multiple assignments on one line. The single quotes allow anything to be in the data without being expanded by the shell. Only *Name* and *Phone* were projected to keep from having a long line and to show that we can use any command to get the variables we want. Below **eval** is used to rescan and assign the line.

```
eval `column Name Phone < mail.list | listtosh`
echo "$Name's phone number is $Phone."
Ronald McDonald's phone number is (111) 222-3333.
```

Now we can use the values of the variable in a shell program. In this example is an **echo** statement to see that the variable had been correctly assigned to the current shell, and not to some subshell. The next example is more complex. A table is searched for a record and converted to list and then used in the shell program.

```
$ cat sh.list
: sh.list shows how to use lists and tables to set shell variables

echo `row 'Item == 3' < inventory | tabletolist | listtosh`
eval `row 'Item == 3' < inventory | tabletolist | listtosh`
echo "We have $Amount $Description."
$ sh.list
Item='3' Amount='5' Cost='80' Value='400' Description='clamps'
We have 5 clamps.
```

7.16 4GL

UNIX/World magazine printed two articles by Alan Winston about fourth generation programming languages (July 1986 and April 1987). Several competing companies were invited to produce a sample report using their 4GL systems. Most of these languages looked more like COBOL or RPG.

Here are two ways of producing the sample report with the UNIX shell and **/rdb.** The first example is a simple default report (which we think looks better than the report format required in the article). The second report uses the formatting commands necessary to conform exactly to the articles' example.

```
$ pay
number    fname    lname      code   hours   rate   total
------    -------  --------   ----   -----   ----   -----
     1    Evan     Schaffer     2       3     75     225
     1    Evan     Schaffer     2       4     75     300
------    -------  --------   ----   -----   ----   -----
     1                                 7            525

     2    Bill     Robinson     1       4     85     340
     2    Bill     Robinson     2       5     85     425
------    -------  --------   ----   -----   ----   -----
     2                                 9            765

     3    Barbara  Wright       2       5     75     375
     3    Barbara  Wright       1       6     75     450
------    -------  --------   ----   -----   ----   -----
     3                                11            825

                                                    2115
```

Following is the shell script that produces this default report. Note that it only takes only 11 lines of simple, readable code. Actually, it could be written in two lines, but we put each command on a separate line. This example does not require counting columns or characters. There is no ''line-at-a-time'' processing, as with the other so-called 4GLs — rather, whole files are processed at once.

```
$ cat pay
jointable hours employee |
sorttable code |
jointable -j1 code -j2 number - task |
sorttable number |
column number fname lname code hours rate total |
compute 'total = hours * rate' |
justify > tmp
subtotal -1 number hours total < tmp
total total < tmp |
justify |
tail -1
```

The data used in the *UNIX/World* samples were not included in the articles, primarily because their format is virtually unprintable. **/rdb** data are flat ASCII files, as follows:

```
$ cat hours
number  hours   code
------  -----   ----
     1      3      2
     1      4      2
     2      4      1
     2      5      2
     3      5      2
     3      6      1

$ cat employee
number  fname   lname      rate
------  ------- --------   ----
     1  Evan    Schaffer     75
     2  Bill    Robinson     85
     3  Barbara Wright       75

$ cat task
number  name
------  ------------------
     1  unix/world
     2  \rdb
```

Here is the exact report format required in the *UNIX/World* articles of July 1986:

```
$ payexact
  number    Employee Name          code        hours     rate      total
       1    Evan Schaffer            2           3.00    75.00     225.00
       1                             2           4.00    75.00     300.00
                          * Employee Total       7.00              525.00

       2    Bill Robinson            1           4.00    85.00     340.00
       2                             2           5.00    85.00     425.00
                          * Employee Total       9.00              765.00

       3    Barbara Wright           2           5.00    75.00     375.00
       3                             1           6.00    75.00     450.00
                          * Employee Total      11.00              825.00

                            ** Report Total                       2115.00
```

And here is the UNIX shell and **/rdb** program that produces the exact format:

```
$ cat payexact
jointable hours employee |
sorttable code |
jointable -j1 code -j2 number - task |
sorttable number |
column number hours code fname lname rate name total |
compute 'total = hours * rate; name = sprintf("%s %s",fname,lname)' |
column number name code hours rate total > tmp
compute 'if (name == prev) name = ""; prev = name;\
hours = sprintf("%4.2f",hours); rate = sprintf("%6.2f",rate);\
total = sprintf("%7.2f",total)' < tmp |
subtotal -l number hours total |
compute 'if (code ~ / / && code !~ /-/) code = "* Employee Total";\
if (code ~ / / && code !~ /-/) number = ""' > tmp1
rename name "Employee Name" < tmp1 |
justify -r number hours rate total -l "Employee Name" -c code |
sed "/---/d" | sed "s/^/ /" | sed "s/rate/  rate/" |
sed "s/total /  total/"
TOTAL=`column total < tmp |\
total | compute 'total = sprintf("%10.2f",total)'| headoff`
echo "                                      \
** Report Total                     $TOTAL"
```

Note this is still only 22 lines. The powers of the UNIX shell, **awk,** and **sed** programs are used for string and arithmetic processing. The user only needs to know UNIX tools, not yet another language. If you know UNIX tools, you understand this, and if you do not, learning them has much greater value than learning yet another special programming language from a single vendor. As UNIX and DOS/UNIX systems become the standard, you can use your UNIX skills on almost all computers. In fact, with MKS UNIX tools for DOS and **rdb,** you can run these programs on DOS today.

8. Menus: One from column A and ...

When setting up software applications it is usually important to provide menus to the user. These tell the users what options are available and make it easy to choose. As more functions are added to the system, they can also be added to the menus.

There are two levels of menus. In this chapter a simple shell program menu is discussed. For large transaction processing applications, there are excellent packages like **/menu shell**[TM] by Tom Johnson of TelWatch.

8.1 Shell Menu

A simple way to create menus in UNIX is with a shell script. The advantage of using shell programming is that it is so easy and you can do anything with it. A sample menu program is included with **/rdb.** You can copy it into your own directory and edit it to be one or more menus for your system. The menu program is in two parts. For details see the **menu** manual page.

8.2 Screen Menu Example

The first half of the menu simply paints the menu selections on the CRT terminal. It is a simple UNIX **cat** or **echo** command.

```
        cat <<SCREEN
$CLEAR                              UNIX MENU
 Number   Name      For
 -------   -------   --------------------------------------------
      0    exit      leave menu or return to higher menu
      1    Menu      goto another local menu (if any)
      2    sh        get unix shell
      3    vi        edit a file
      4    mail      read mail
      5    send      send mail to someone
      6    cal       see your calendar
      7    who       see who is on the system
      8    ls        list the files in this directory
      9    cat       display a file on the screen
     10    rdb       display rdb commands
Please enter a number or name for the action you wish or DEL to exit:
SCREEN
```

The **cat** command shown uses the *here* file feature of the shell. All of the text from the *<<SCREEN* to the line that consists of only *SCREEN* is sent to the standard input of the **cat** command. The **cat** command sends its output to your terminal. So the

text between the two *SCREEN* lines is displayed on your screen.

This lets you edit any menu you wish. The one shown is only one example. Use your text editor to set up any menu format you desire. Whatever you type will be displayed on the user's terminal screen.

8.3 case Actions

Whatever the user types is assigned to the shell variable *ANSWER*. (After the first word of the reply, any more words are assigned to the shell variable *COMMENT*).

```
read ANSWER COMMENT

case $ANSWER in

0|exit) exit 0 ;;
1|Menu) Menu ;;
2|sh)    sh ;;
3|vi)
         echo 'Which file or files do you wish to edit'
         read ANSWER COMMENT
         vi $ANSWER $COMMENT
         ;;
4|mail) mail ;;
5|send)
         echo 'Please enter login name of person to send mail to'
         read ANSWER COMMENT
         echo 'Type you letter, and end by typing Ctrl-d'
         mail $ANSWER
         ;;
6|cal)  (cd ; calendar) ;;
7|who)  who ;;
8|ls)   ls ;;
9|cat)
         echo 'Please enter the name of the file you wish to see'
         read ANSWER COMMENT
         cat $ANSWER
         ;;
10|rdb) menu.rdb ;;
*)       echo 'Sorry, but that number or name is not recognized.' ;;
esac
```

After the user's answer is read in, the shell **case** statement is used to match the answer to a number of possible cases. If the user types a number 8 or *ls,* then the **ls** command is executed. This sample gives the user the choice of two ways to indicate a menu selection: numbers or short mnemonic string names.

After the **case** pattern, you can type any shell command or call any shell program, or any combination of both. This gives you complete power to do anything, as a result of a user's choice. In the previous examples, you can see how to simply execute a command, invoke another menu, ask for more information and use it in a command, and so on. The *) case is selected if the user does not type any of the patterns previously listed. This gives an error message.

To make this system work, two commands are needed. A **clear** command clears the screen so that the form can be written on it and the **cursor** command moves the cursor to each field of the screen.

8.4 termput and tput Commands

The problem with screen handling is that there are so many CRT terminals with different capabilities and commands. Bill Joy solved this problem when he wrote the **vi** text editor. He created a file of terminal capabilities which is called */etc/termcap*. On the usual UNIX system delivered to you this *termcap* file knows about hundreds of terminals. You only need to find out what it calls your terminal and assign that name to the shell variable **TERM.** (Be sure to also **export** *TERM)*. To pick up the command string for a terminal capability **/rdb** provides the **termput** command. It searches through the **/etc/termcap** file for the terminal name you assigned to *TERM* and then for the capability you indicate.

If you have UNIX System V, you may want to use the new **tput** command which does the same thing but uses the new *terminfo* system. AT&T Bell Labs, for some reason, decided to reinvent this system. So now we have two different systems for doing the same thing.

8.5 clear Command

The **clear** command clears the screen. On the Berkeley UNIX system, there is a **clear** command that you can use. Starting with UNIX System V Release 2.0, there is **tput clear.** Otherwise, you can use the **/rdb termput cl.** Figure out what works on your system.

To speed up clearing the screen, assign the clear command sequence to the shell variable *CLEAR*. Then you can use *$CLEAR* in **echo** and **cat** *<<HERE* statements. This is ten to a hundred times faster because it does not require that you look up the sequence in a file first.

```
$ CLEAR='termput cl'    # all UNIX systems
$ CLEAR='tput clear'    # UNIX System V Release 2.0 and later
$ export CLEAR
$ echo $CLEAR
```

8.6 cursor Command

For the **cursor** command to work correctly you must set up a shell variable called *CURSOR*.

```
$ CURSOR='termput cm'
$ CURSOR='tput cup'
$ export CURSOR
$ cursor 20 40
```

The **cursor** command moves the cursor to line (row) 20, character (column) 40 on the screen. It uses the sequence in the *CURSOR* variable and calls the **tgoto** command from the */usr/lib/libtermcap.a* or */usr/lib/libcurses.a* library.

8.7 Help Facility: How to get help

There are six commands to help the user with programs and syntax. In addition there is a command, **helpme**, to list these commands.

TABLE 11. Help Commands

```
$ helpme
There are many help programs:
Command                 Description
-----------------       ----------------------------------------
"menu"                  a menu with some commands
"rdb"                   a list of the available commands
"commands"              description and syntax of all the commands
"whatis command"        description and syntax of a command
"whatwill feature"      info on commands with that feature
"man command"           the manual page for that command
```

You will find detailed descriptions of each of these commands in the manual. Incidentally, the *rdb/man/*.1* manual commands should be moved, by your system administrator, to */usr/man/man1*. Better still, **nroff** the manual pages into the */usr/man/cat1* directory for much faster response by the **man** command. Usually, the manual pages are **nroff**'ed each time **man** is executed. This is not too bad on a very powerful computer, but often it is too slow. The cat directories have pages already **nroff**'ed. They are simply **cat**'ed out, which is fast. But this cat directory feature is a Berkeley enhancement. If you don't have these enhancements, you can modify your UNIX **man** command, because it is a shell program.

9. Screen Forms: Forms and more forms

In addition to menus, it is usually important to give the users simple forms on their CRT screen to fill out for data entry and to use such screen forms to display data on their screens. The two can be mixed with a form in which some fields are filled in and the data from the database is written into the remaining form fields. /**rdb** comes with several forms systems: **ve,** described earlier, and a shell level forms system, described here. **ve** was designed to make creating and entering data into /**rdb** databases easy, using a **vi** style interface. **screen** and **update,** on the other hand, are more general purpose application development tools that can be customized for any specific application.

To make the shell level system work, you need the **clear** and **cursor** commands, described in the previous menu chapter.

9.1 Building a Screen Form

You can write a shell script that paints a screen and accepts input. You can clear the screen and use the **cursor** command to move to any location. There you can use the **echo** or **cat** command to display whatever you wish. You can use the **read** command to read in anything the user types and assign it to a shell variable. You can take the users information and look up data in the database, using the database query commands, and display it anywhere on the screen. See **update.inv.**

9.2 screen Command

To automate the process of screen building and to make it a lot easier, there is an /**rdb screen** program. You create a screen form in any text editor (just like the /**rdb report** program form).

```
$ cat inv.f
Makeapile, Inc.            Inventory Update            <!date!>

Item Number: <Item>

Item        Cost      Value      Description
----        ----      -----      -----------
<Item>      <Cost>    <Value>    <Description>

Amount Onhand: <Amount>
```

Then you input that form into the **screen** program.

```
$ screen < inv.f > inv.s
$ cat inv.s
: paint crt screen
exec 3>&1 1>&2
cat <<SCREEN
${CLEAR}Makeapile, Inc.               Inventory Update

Item Number:

Item        Cost      Value      Description
----        ----      -----      -----------


Amount Onhand:
SCREEN

: read user input
cursor  0 56 ; date;
cursor  2 13 ; read Item;
cursor  6  0 ; read Item;
cursor  6 12 ; read Cost;
cursor  6 23 ; read Value;
cursor  6 34 ; read Description;
cursor  8 15 ; read Amount;

: output table head
exec 1>&3
echo "Item     Item    Cost    Value    Description    Amount"
echo "----     ----    ----    -----    -----------    ------"
: append row
echo "$Item    $Item   $Cost   $Value   $Description   $Amount"
```

The output is a shell program that will paint the screen, read the user's input, and output a table of the user's responses. This shell program is simple, but you can edit it to do any advanced operation you like.

9.3 update.inv: Advanced Screen Program

The **/rdb update.inv** program is an example of an advanced application that uses the features mentioned in this chapter, plus the fast access methods, record locking, and so on.

```
$ cat update.inv
: %W% SCCS ID Information

: update.inv - updates the inv table with form entry and record locking

USAGE='usage: update.inv'

  MSEEKING="${MS}Seeking record.$ME   "
  MLOCKING="${MS}Locking record.$ME   "
  MREADING="${MS}Reading record.$ME   "
MREPLACING="${MS}Replacing record.$ME"
MUNLOCKING="${MS}Unlocking record.$ME"
    MBLANK='
```

```
while :
do
: paint crt screen
exec 3>&1 1>&2
cat <<SCREEN
${CLEAR}Makeapile, Inc.              Inventory Update

Item Number: $SO        $SE       (or hit Return key to exit.)

Item        Cost      Value     Description
----        ----      -----     -----------


Amount Onhand: $SO          $SE


$MB$MESSAGE$ME
SCREEN
cursor 0 60 ; set `date` ; echo $1 $2 $3, $6

MESSAGE=

: read user input
cursor  2 13 ; echo "$SO\c" ; read Item; echo "$SE\c"

if test -z "$Item"
then
        echo "$CLEAR"
        exit 0
fi

: seek Item in inv
cursor 12 0 ; echo "$MSEEKING"

LOCATION=`echo "$Item" | seek -mb -o tmp inv Item`

if test -z "$LOCATION"
then
        MESSAGE="Item $Item not found."
        continue
fi

: lock record
: lock command adds line to lock file /tmp/Lfilename
cursor 12 0 ; echo "$MLOCKING"

if lock inv $$ $LOCATION
then
        cursor 12 0 ; echo "$MREADING"
else
        MESSAGE="That record is already locked."
        continue
fi

: we could also write a blank record into the file
: blank < tmp | replace inv $LOCATION

: replace the record if this program abnormally exits
: trap "replace inv $LOCATION < tmp" 1 2 3 15

: read record
exec 4<&0 0< tmp
read    HEAD
read    DASH
read    $HEAD
cursor 12 0 ; echo "$MBLANK"
```

```
: display record
cursor  6  0 ; echo $Item;
cursor  6 12 ; echo $Cost;
cursor  6 23 ; echo $Value;
cursor  6 34 ; echo $Description;
cursor  8 15 ; echo "$SO$Amount$SE";

: read new Amount
exec 0<&4
cursor  8 15 ; echo "$SO\c" ; read A ; echo "$SE\c"
Amount=${A:-$Amount}

: output table
cursor 12 0 ; echo "$MREPLACING"
exec 1>&3
cat <<TABLE  | replace inv $LOCATION
$HEAD
$DASH
$Item    $Amount $Cost    $Value  $Description
TABLE

trap 0

: unlock record

cursor 12 0 ; echo "$MUNLOCKING"
unlock inv $$ $LOCATION
cursor 12 0 ; echo "$MBLANK"
done
```

This is a large shell script that shows how to do many different operations. You can study it or skip it for now and come back to it as an example when you need it. Another example is the **update.sh** script in the manual at the end of this book.

10. Fast Access Methods: How to get data fast

Fast access methods allow you to get rows from a table or list file faster than sequentially reading the file. This is very important for large databases. Where sequentially reading a huge file would take minutes, the right fast access method might take only a few seconds to find the records you want. Traditionally, these methods were very important to database management systems. For very large databases, they will continue to be important. But one or a few users on a microprocessor with small to medium sized tables will seldom need these speedups.

10.1 When Appropriate

It is important to point out that these methods are not always faster and usually require significant time to set up. They are almost never justified unless the file is large (over 1000 rows), and the extra time to index or sort the table is worthwhile.

row will find rows that match complex logical conditions and regular expression (string patterns). But these fast access methods require that the key value be expressed more specifically. No *greater than*, *less than*, or string pattern matches: only *equals*, and *partial initial matches* (for example, the first few letters of a key).

We've implemented five fast access methods: sequential, record, inverted, binary, and hash. **/rdb** has two commands which use these methods: **index** and **search**. **index** creates secondary indexes or sorts a table for the **search** command.

10.2 index

We will use a two row table to show the **index** and **search** commands. Here is a *mailtable:*

```
$ cat mailtable
Number  Name             Company        Phone
------  ---------------  -------------  --------------
     1  Ronald McDonald  McDonald's     (111) 222-3333
     2  Chiquita Banana  United Brands  1234
```

The hash method is often the fastest, so let's use it as an example.

```
$ index -mh mailtable Name
```

The *-m* means *method* and the *h* specifies hash. The **index** command builds a hash secondary index table. You can see it, if you are curious, by listing out the table name followed by the *.h* secondary index extension *table.h*. For example, *mailtable.h*

```
$ cat mailtable.h
 Offset
 --------
       0
     156
       0
     104
       0
```

Each of the names in the *Names* column of the *mailtable* was *hashed* into row 4 (104) or 2 (156). The offset in the hash table (the nonzero numbers) is the location (in bytes) in the main file, of the row with that key value.

10.3 search

The **search** command allows you to search for one or more rows in the table in four different ways. You can input a key two ways, and you can input a table of keys two ways.

10.3.1 Interactive

Now you can search the mailtable by name in an interactive way:

```
$ search -mh mailtable Name
Number   Name            Company        Phone
------   --------------  -------------  --------------
Ronald McDonald
     1    Ronald McDonald  McDonald's     (111) 222-3333
```

The **search** command first prints out the table head line and then waits for you to type in a key value. In this case enter the name you are searching for. After you type the name and hit the return key, the row will print almost immediately, even if the file is huge. You may continue to type keys. When you are finished you can type *control-d* (that is a control (CTRL) key held down and *d* key pressed at the same time).

10.3.2 Pipe Key

The **search** command can also be used in a pipe. You can input a table or list of keys through a pipe and the **search** command will output a table or list of rows which match your input keys. This becomes a fast join, with keys coming in and a table of rows coming out.

```
$ echo "Ronald McDonald"| search -mh mailtable Name
Number   Name            Company        Phone
------   --------------  -------------  --------------
     1    Ronald McDonald  McDonald's     (111) 222-3333
```

10.3.3 File Input

In addition to sending a single key to **search** you can also send a whole table of keys. **search** will look up each key and output a whole table of matching rows. It is like a high speed join; keys in, records out.

Here we have our name keys in a table called *name*. We direct it to the standard input of the **search** command and get the matching records out.

```
$ cat name
Name
---------------
Ronald McDonald
Chiquita Banana
$ search -mh mailtable < name
Number   Name             Company        Phone
------   ---------------  -------------  --------------
     1   Ronald McDonald  McDonald's     (111) 222-3333
     2   Chiquita Banana  United Brands  1234
```

Note that you do not have to tell the **search** command the name of the column to search on, if you send it a table with the column name, because **search** can pick up the column name from that input table.

10.3.4 File Input by Pipe

You can also put the **search** program in a pipeline and it will send to its right a table of rows that match the table of keys coming from its left. In other words, keys in, matching records out.

```
$ cat name
Name
---------------
Ronald McDonald
Chiquita Banana
$ cat name | search -mh mailtable
Number   Name             Company        Phone
------   ---------------  -------------  --------------
     1   Ronald McDonald  McDonald's     (111) 222-3333
     2   Chiquita Banana  United Brands  1234
```

The **cat** command simulates any program or pipeline that produces a table of keys, including other **search** commands.

10.4 Multi-Rows, Multi-Columns, and Multi-Keys

The **search** command will produce multi-rows, if more than one row matches the key. You can have multi-column keys consisting of more than one column. You can also send more than one key, multi-keys, to **search** and it will output all matching rows.

10.5 Methods

The five different fast access methods each have their own advantages and disadvantages. It is an art and a science to figure out which to use in a given situation, or whether to use them at all.

10.5.1 Sequential

Sequential is the simplest and slowest method. It is hardly a fast access method at all, but is included for completeness. This method simply looks at every record in the table for a match. With a big file, this will take a long time.

When might you use it? It is better than **grep** because it will look at only a single column for a match, instead of the whole row. Thus it avoids matching strings in the wrong columns of the row.

Also, use the sequential method to time how fast it takes. You will often be surprised that this method is fast enough for your system. If it is fast enough, use it since it requires no indexing or overhead to use. The table can be in any order and can be updated randomly.

10.5.2 Record

One problem with variable length records is that there is no simple computation of where a row such as number 7 is. Without this method, we would have to sequentially search the table, counting records, until we came to the one we wanted. On the average we would have to search half the file. When we index with this method, the **index** program runs through the whole file and builds a secondary file which contains the offsets to each row. The secondary index table is named by adding a *.r* to the end of the table name. It contains fixed length rows so that the record number can be computed. At that address is the offset of the corresponding record in the database table.

```
$ index -mr mailtable
$ cat mailtable
Number   Name              Company         Phone
------   ---------------   -------------   --------------
     1   Ronald McDonald   McDonald's      (111) 222-3333
     2   Chiquita Banana   United Brands   1234
$ cat mailtable.r
   Offset
---------
      104
      156
```

Note that each of the offsets in the secondary index table *mailtable.r* is the byte address of that row in the main *mailtable* table.

10.5.3 Binary

The binary method requires that the table be sorted on the key columns. The **index** command simply sorts the table. The **search** command can find the desired row by first looking at a row in the middle of the table. It can use the UNIX **seek** system call for fast access to any byte in the file. **search** compares the key value of that center row with the key it is looking for. If the row's key is too high, it jumps to the one-quarter point in the file, if too low, to the three-quarter point in the file. Each probe cuts the file in half so that the record can be found quickly.

If there are a thousand records in the table, only 10 probes are needed to find the record you wish. One million records require only 20 probes. A billion records need only 30. This is called *log n* search time, where *n* is the number of records in the file and the log to the base of 2 is the number of probes needed to find a record. The sorting takes *n log n* time with the fastest sort routines.

```
$ index -mb mailtable Name
$ cat mailtable
Number   Name              Company        Phone
------   ---------------   ------------   --------------
     2   Chiquita Banana   United Brands  1234
     1   Ronald McDonald   McDonald's     (111) 222-3333
```

Note that the *Name* column is now sorted so that the binary search will work. This is a good method when you have to keep the file in sorted order anyway. Then your sorting pays off twice. It is a painful method, if you are adding and deleting records often and have to resort often.

10.5.4 Hash

The hash method takes the key and performs a mathematical operation on it that converts it into a single number. Each ASCII character in the key is added together and modulo-ed with the size of the hash table to produce a number that is its location in the hash table. That number is an index into a secondary hash table. At that location should be the offset to the record in the main table. The row at that offset in the main table is checked to see if its key column(s) match the key we are looking for. If it is, we have found our record.

It might not match because more than one key may *hash* to the same number by accident. If it does not match, the next offset in the hash table is selected and tested. Each offset is tested until a match is found, or until a value of zero is found. This indicates that there is no matching record in the database table. So the search fails. No error message is produced, just no record is output.

```
$ index -mh mailtable Name
$ cat mailtable
Number   Name              Company        Phone
------   ---------------   ------------   --------------
     1   Ronald McDonald   McDonald's     (111) 222-3333
     2   Chiquita Banana   United Brands  1234
$ cat mailtable.h
   Offset
---------
        0
      156
        0
      104
        0
```

The 104 in the fourth row of the hash table *mailtable.h* is the byte offset of the first record in the database *mailtable* table. 4 (4th row) is the result of adding the ASCII values of *Ronald McDonald* together and modulo with 5, the number of rows in the hash table. The size of the hash table is two times the number of rows in the table to be indexed, plus one. Having twice as many hash rows makes it likely that there will be lots of zeros to stop the search for keys. If the hash table is twice as big as the number of keys to hash, then only two probes are needed on average.

Hash is usually the fastest method. But it is best for a static file that you are not updating and do not need to keep sorted.

10.5.5 Inverted or Indexed Sequential

The inverted method projects the key columns and the offset of each row and sorts on the key columns to create a secondary index file. Then the **search** command can use a binary search on the key columns to find the right offset into the database table.

```
$ index -mi mailtable Name
$ cat mailtable
Number   Name              Company        Phone
------   ---------------   -------------  --------------
     1   Ronald McDonald   McDonald's     (111) 222-3333
     2   Chiquita Banana   United Brands  1234
$ cat mailtable.i
   Offset   Name
---------   -------
      156   Chiquita Banana
      104   Ronald McDonald
```

Note that the *Name* column has been projected and sorted and that the offset column contains the corresponding offset in the main table.

10.5.6 Partial Inital Match

The *-x* option specifies that partial initial match is to be used. This means you can use only the first few letters of a key, and a match will be made on all those records whose key is matched up to that point.

```
$ search -mi -x mailtable Name
Number   Name              Company        Phone
------   ---------------   -------------  --------------
Ron
     1   Ronald McDonald   McDonald's     (111) 222-3333
```

10.5.7 B-tree

B-tree subroutines are now a standard on UNIX System V releases for those who want to return to software prisons, but of course the easiest to use and most general tree routines are to be found, as usual, in the power of UNIX itself. What is the hierarchical directory structure but a collection of shell level programs to manipulate a tree? You can use the directory structure itself to implement the first few levels of (tree structured) indices. For example, in a company database, you can have a directory for each city; within each city directory, a directory for each department; within each department directory, a file for each employee, each such file having header records and one employee record. Then, to retrieve all the New York sales employees whose names begin with J, one could say:

```
% union nyork/sales/J*
```

and, to retrieve all sales employees,

```
% union */sales/*
```

UNIX itself has many programs to manipulate trees. So there was no point in duplicating the power of UNIX.

The tree method is occasionally appropriate but usually the most expensive in space requirements. Its advantages are in rapid updates, deletes, and inserts of new records in very large databases. If you have a very large database that requires lots of updates, it's really quite fast to build the first few levels of indexing into the UNIX directory structure, but it does involve extra file system overhead.

10.6 Analysis

It takes analysis and testing to determine which is the best method for a given situation. Each has its advantages and disadvantages. Theory only takes one so far. You can time the different methods on your computer to determine the fastest.

In order to determine the best method to use in a situation, you must both analyze and test your different options. The advantages and disadvantages of each method is discussed earlier. You should also test any strategy you adopt. You might find that a simpler method is fast enough, or the overhead of a fast method outweighs the benefits of speed.

10.7 Management

Fast access methods need to be managed. If the files are being updated, they may have to be reindexed. Reindexing takes time. You may want to schedule it when users are not accessing the data and perhaps when the computer is not being used much. A nightly reindexing may be appropriate. UNIX has an **at** command that lets you schedule big jobs like this, at say 3 A.M., when the system is more likely to be quiet. When you choose an access method, you must plan for any management that is needed.

11. Swiss Army Knife: A program for all reasons

/rdb has over 100 programs to help develop software applications. Here is a brief discussion of some of them, grouped together by subject. For details on all of the programs see the **/rdb** *Users Manual* at the end of this book.

11.1 Record Locking: It´s Mine.

When your application requires that several people must update the same file at the same time you will need to lock records. When one operator gets a record to change, it is important that no other operator pulls out the same record and edits it also. If you allow this, the second record written back will clobber the first record. So the results of the first operator's changes will be lost.

Many complain that the UNIX system does not have a record locking system. Future UNIX releases will have it built in. But it is trivial to create record locking with UNIX tools. **/rdb** provides **lock** and **unlock** commands that you can use or modify for this purpose.

11.1.1 seek

To find out the location of a record use the **seek** command. It uses the fast access method of your choice to find the record and returns the starting and ending byte location which can be assigned to a shell variable.

```
$ LOCATION=`echo 5 | seek -mb -o tmp inventory Item`
$ echo $LOCATION
207 245 0 9
```

A lot is going on here so let's take it step by step. The **echo** command sent the number *5* to the **seek** command. **seek** looks for an *Item* numbered 5 in the *inventory* file using the binary fast access method (-mb) and writes out the record into the *tmp* file (-o tmp). **seek** sends a string of four numbers to standard out which is assigned to the shell variable *LOCATION*. The four numbers are the beginning byte, ending byte of the record and the beginning byte and ending byte of the offset in the secondary index file, in case that might be needed some time. In this case it is meaningless because the binary method does not use a secondary file.

11.1.2 lock and unlock

The **lock** command writes the string from the *LOCATION* shell variable into a file in the */tmp* directory. It checks to see if that area of the file has been previously locked.

The **unlock** command removes the location line from the lock file.

11.1.3 Blanking a Record

For added protection, or as an alternative, you can also blank out the record in the file. Use **seek** to get the location, use **blank** to blank the record and use **replace** to write the blank record into the file.

```
$ LOCATION='echo 5 | seek -mb -o tmp inventory Item'
$ blank < tmp | replace -mb inventory $LOCATION
$ cat inventory
Item  Amount  Cost  Value  Description
----  ------  ----  -----  --------------
   1       3    50    150   rubber gloves
   2     100     5    500   test tubes
   3       5    80    400   clamps
   4      23    19    437   plates

   6      89   147  13083   bunsen burners
   7       5   175    875   scales
```

11.2 Dates: Conversion and Math

A few programs help you handle dates.

11.2.1 Julian and Gregorian

Gregorian is the kind of dates we are all familiar with: January 1, 1989, 1/1/89, 890101, and so on. Unfortunately there are two problems with this kind of date: Gregorian dates can not be added or subtracted and they have several different formats. Fortunately, there is another form of date, called Julian, that solves these problems. A Julian date is a number of days from over a thousand years ago. Therefore, one can add days to and subtract days from a Julian date and get the correct new date.

/rdb has two commands that are used for this purpose. **julian** will convert a date from the standard Gregorian to Julian. It converts a whole column of dates so that they can be operated upon. After some addition or subtraction, the column can be converted back to Gregorian dates with the **gregorian** command.

Suppose you are planning a project. You can put the plan into a table called *project*.

```
$ cat project
 Date   Description
------  -----------
890601  Start project
890701  Project crises
890801  Abandon project
890901  Coverup blame
891001  Write off losses
```

Now you find that you need to put off the start date of the project by 45 days. First, you need to convert the Gregorian *Date* to Julian.

```
$ julian Date < project > tmp
$ cat tmp
   Date    Description
-------   -----------
1752623   Start project
1752653   Project crises
1752684   Abandon project
1752715   Coverup blame
1752745   Write off losses
```

Those huge numbers under *Date* are Julian days. We can now add 45 days to the column with the **compute** command.

```
$ compute 'Date += 45' < tmp > tmp1
$ cat tmp1
   Date    Description
-------   -----------
1752668   Start project
1752698   Project crises
1752729   Abandon project
1752760   Coverup blame
1752790   Write off losses
```

Note that all of the Julian dates are 45 days later. Now we can convert back to Gregorian.

```
$ gregorian Date < tmp1 > project
$ cat project
  Date    Description
------   -----------
890716   Start project
890815   Project crises
890915   Abandon project
891016   Coverup blame
891115   Write off losses
```

This can also be done in one pipeline.

```
$ julian Date < project |
> compute 'Date = Date + 45' |
> gregorian Date > tmp
$ mv tmp project
$ cat project
  Date    Description
------   -----------
890716   Start project
890815   Project crises
890915   Abandon project
891016   Coverup blame
891115   Write off losses
```

11.2.2 *Difference*

You can also find the difference between two dates. For example we may build houses and have start and stop dates for each phase. To compute the number of days for each step we can use the **julian** and **gregorian** programs on the *house* building table.

```
$ cat house
  Start     Stop   Days    Step
  -----    ------   ----    ----
 890101   890118            Lay concrete
 890121   890212            Setup frame
 890215   890302            Build walls
 890305   890401            Install fixtures
 890408   890425            Sell at a loss
$ julian Start Stop < house | compute 'Days = Stop - Start'
  Start      Stop   Days    Step
  -----     ------   ----    ----
 1752837   1752854    17   Lay concrete
 1752857   1752899    22   Setup frame
 1752882   1752897    15   Build walls
 1752900   1752927    27   Install fixtures
 1752934   1752951    17   Sell at a loss
$ julian Start Stop < house |
> compute 'Days = Stop - Start' |
> gregorian Start Stop
  Start     Stop   Days    Step
  -----    ------   ----    ----
 890101   890118    17   Lay concrete
 890121   890212    22   Setup frame
 890215   890302    15   Build walls
 890305   890401    27   Install fixtures
 890408   890425    17   Sell at a loss
```

11.2.3 Formats

There are a number of different formats that people use to express dates. The **julian** and **gregorian** programs also allow you to convert between three different formats.

11.2.4 Computer

Computer date format is: *890101* for the 1st of January, 1989. It is best because it can be sorted and is the most compact. You can also test to see if one date is greater than another. Most users can quickly get used to it.

11.2.5 US

In the United States of America, dates are written in the strange sequence: month day, year. For example: *January 31, 1989* and *01/31/89*.

11.2.6 European

The Europeans have the more sensible sequence: day month year. For example: *31 January 1989* or *31/01/89*.

11.2.7 Conversions

The **/rdb julian** and **gregorian** commands allow you to convert between these different formats. Simply specify the current format to the **julian** command and another format that you want to the **gregorian** command and the format will change.

The default format is *computer* format. Let's change the computer format in the proj-ect table to US format.

```
$ julian Date < project | gregorian -u Date
Date       Description
--------   -----------
 6/01/89   Start project
 7/01/89   Project crises
 8/01/89   Abandon project
 9/01/89   Coverup blame
10/01/89   Write off losses
```

You can see one of the problems of the standard date is that it is eight characters. Since the tabs are also eight characters, the next column has to move over. You can use the **justify** command to pretty things up.

```
$ julian Date < project | gregorian -u Date | justify Date
Date       Description
--------   ----------------
 6/01/89   Start project
 7/01/89   Project Crises
 8/01/89   Abandon project
 9/01/89   Coverup blame
10/01/89   Write off losses
```

11.3 Set Theory Commands

In addition to the basic relational commands, there are several that come from relational set theory.

11.3.1 union

The **union** command will append one table to another making a larger table consisting of all of the rows of each. Below we consolidate several subsidiary journals to create the general journal.

```
$ cat journalcash
Date      Account  Debit  Credit  Description
------    -------  -----  ------  ----------------------------------
891222        101  25000          cash from loan
891223        101          5000   cash payment
891224        101         15000   cash payment to CCPSC for parts

$ cat journalloan
Date      Account  Debit  Credit  Description
------    -------  -----  ------  ----------------------------------
891222    211.1           25000   loan number #378-14 Bank Amerigold
891223    211.2            5000   note payable to Zarkoff Equipment

$ cat journaladjust
Date      Account  Debit  Credit  Description
------    -------  -----  ------  ----------------------------------
891224        130  30000          inventory - parts from CCPSC
```

```
$ union journalcash journalloan journaladjust > journal
$ cat journal
Date     Account   Debit   Credit   Description
------   -------   -----   ------   --------------------------------
891222   101       25000            cash from loan
891223   101                5000    cash payment
891224   101               15000    cash payment to CCPSC for parts
891222   211.1             25000    loan number #378-14 Bank Amerigold
891223   211.2              5000    note payable to Zarkoff Equipment
891224   130       30000            inventory - parts from CCPSC
```

11.3.2 *difference*

difference lets us subtract one table from another to give the rows that are in the first table but not in the second table.

```
$ difference journal journalloan
Date     Account   Debit   Credit   Description
------   -------   -----   ------   --------------------------------
891222      101    25000            cash from loan
891223      101             5000    cash payment
891224      101            15000    cash payment to CCPSC for parts
891224      130    30000            inventory - parts from CCPSC
```

11.3.3 *intersect*

intersect lets us find the rows that are in both tables, the intersection of the set.

```
$ intersect journal journaladjust
Date     Account   Debit   Credit   Description
------   -------   -----   ------   --------------------------------
891224      130    30000            inventory - parts from CCPSC
```

12. How to Solve Traditional Database Problems

Much of your database work can be done with UNIX commands. Many of the traditional problems of databases disappear when you have a UNIX system. If you have only one or a few users, problems like security, distributed data, concurrent access to files, backup, checkpoint and recovery, validation, audit trails and logging, and others, are minimized. Here are some suggestions for using both /**rdb** and UNIX tools to develop solutions to these problems. This is not to say that there are no longer any problems. There is still a role for programmers and system/analysts. But it is important for these professional people, who got their experience on older systems, to rethink what they know in light of the new tools and the new economics of our changing technology.

12.1 Multi-User Concurrent Access to Files

On small systems, you can assign each file to only one person. Then only one person need access it at a time. Any number can append new records to a file at one time with the **enter** command. Also, any number of users can read a table into their /**rdb** and UNIX commands, since reading does not change the table.

The only problem that arises is when two or more people must edit a table or list file at the same time. Files can be locked in several ways. There is a **lock** and an **unlock** command for this purpose. With the **blank** and **replace** commands, you can blank out a record while you have it out for edit. The **update** commands does this.

Each user can move (**mv**) the file to a new name before editing it. Perhaps they might move it into their own directories, make their changes and move it back. That way other users will not find the file when they try to edit it. This is how the **vilock** command works. Application programs can change the permission of a file so that it is *read only* to others on the system, when our user is updating it.

There are also the **lock** and **unlock** commands, which are shell scripts to show how easy it is to solve this problem with UNIX tools.

12.2 Screen Form Entry

If you want to put forms on the terminal screen for the users to input data into, you can use **ve** or the **screen** program. **screen** takes a form you create in a text editor, as with the **report** command, and creates a shell script that will display the form, read the user's input and output a table. Since it is a shell script, it can be edited to do a lot more including validation, table lookup, and others. See the /**rdb** program **update.inv** for an example. **ve** also takes a form, like the report command's form, and creates a table.

12.3 Security

You can handle security by physically protecting the computer and the terminal, by using the UNIX security permissions on files and directories, and by encrypting files. **ve** contains special security features like unwriteable and invisible fields. There are read, write, and execute permissions for the owner of the file, the group, and anyone on the computer. See the UNIX commands **chmod** and **encrypt**.

12.4 Distributed Data

The new network technology and high-speed communications are doing a lot for this problem. They tremendously increase the speed at which we can update data. This eliminates the necessity of having data in different locations that diverge. Now, or soon, data anywhere will be effectively local. The **diff** command can be used to find differences in two files. Much work on UNIX is aimed at communication and networking, both at AT&T Bell Laboratories and at U.C., Berkeley. The new UNIX System V Release 3 makes a network of computers appear as one file system. Software developed on one computer can now work with the whole network.

12.5 Backup

One should backup the **/rdb** tables and list files just like regular UNIX files. You can simply copy a file or a whole directory to a backup media like mag tape, cassette tape, floppy disk, or Bernoulli Box, or transmit to another computer for backup. The UNIX **tar** and **cpio** commands can be used for putting an entire directory structure into a single file.

12.6 Checkpoint and Recovery

You can always create a copy of a file that you are working on. **/rdb** commands do not alter their input files. They simply create new files or pass their output (pipe) to another program. In a crash, the original file is not harmed. Only the editors modify the existing file and at least one, **vi**, has a crash recovery system.

12.7 Validation

ve provides programmable validity checks for data as it is entered. **Awk** scripts and other programs can be developed to check the validity of operator input. The **vi** editor has the ability to assign to a single key a complex program. It can be used to validate each line typed. The **/rdb validate** command is available to do any data validation from simple to complex. See the sections on validation in the **/rdb** manual and the **ve** chapter.

12.8 Audit Trails and Logging

This is very easy because of the **diff** and SCCS commands. At the end of each day's work the **diff** program can be run like this:

```
$ diff todaysfile yesterdaysfile > todayslog
```

The file *todayslog* will contain all lines that have changed since yesterday. Save it and you have a log or audit trail. It can also be used for recovery to any date in the past.

If you want more power than that, use the SCCS commands in UNIX System III or above. These commands are for archiving the work of software developers, but can be used for any purpose including as an audit trail. They minimize storage space, keep records of who made a change and why, allow only certain people to make changes, keep anyone from editing a file when someone else has it out for edit, and allow you to recreate your data at any point in time from the first entry to the most current. You can use it to create an accounting audit system. At the end of each day, all of the journals could then be **delta**'ed back into the archive files under SCCS control. You would have a record of every change. You could recreate the journals, and therefore all of the books and financials, as of any day in the past!

13. Comparing Systems: Who's on first?

There are many database management systems available for UNIX and DOS systems. They are all good in their own ways. Each has its strengths and weaknesses. However, they usually take a traditional approach. Such systems were developed on operating systems that provide only a fraction of the services that the UNIX system provides. Therefore, the database developers had to write as much functionality into their database packages as they could. When these database management systems are moved to the UNIX environment, they require that you leave UNIX tools and all of their power behind, and go into a software box where you are limited to the functions that the database developers have supplied. There are many other database packages running on UNIX systems, but they all take this traditional *big box* approach. One usually finds that functions UNIX tools could provide are not available inside those database system boxes. There is usually no good way to get the data out to UNIX and back. It was the frustration of knowing that we could do what we needed to do with UNIX tools, but that our data was locked up in the database package, that prompted the development of /**rdb.** With /**rdb** you always have access to the full power of the UNIX system, because /**rdb** commands are UNIX commands that can be piped together with other UNIX commands. They extend the power of UNIX tools rather than waste it. /**rdb** works at the shell level and allows you to use all of the UNIX utilities and powers. With shell programming you can build applications easily with both UNIX and /**rdb** commands mixed and piped together.

With other database systems, you must learn a whole new language/syntax that is unique to that database package. Learning /**rdb** is learning the UNIX system, which is useful in many applications. Or you can use the UNIX knowledge you have already acquired. In fact, it is an excellent way to learn UNIX tools, just as many people learned computers starting with a spreadsheet program.

13.1 Resource Use

When developers duplicate UNIX functions, their programs become huge. These programs take up tremendous amounts of computer memory and other resources. Most database packages will bring large expensive computers to their knees with only a few users. By doing things the UNIX way, only the small programs that are needed are brought in from the disk, putting only a light load on the system. This can save hundreds of thousands of dollars in computer hardware.

13.2 C Programming Unnecessary

The UNIX system has many programming languages, including the C language. Although many programmers naturally think they must use such programs in their work, it is usually unnecessary. Putting together UNIX programs will usually accomplish whatever is needed.

Although with work almost everything can be done with the basic UNIX system as delivered, some database facilities and tools are missing or are hard to create. Therefore, a number of relational database management systems have been developed for the UNIX system. Unfortunately, most come from other operating systems and ignore the power of UNIX. On other operating systems, virtually nothing exists to help the developer and user. Everything must be programmed from scratch. If the developer or the user is to have a feature, it must be programmed into the database program.

On UNIX the reverse is true. Almost everything you need is available in the UNIX environment. The traditional database management systems, when moved to UNIX, prevent the developer and user from getting access to these powerful and familiar UNIX tools. It is as if these systems create an unfamiliar box that you must go into, leaving the power of UNIX behind.

/rdb, however, was built for the UNIX environment. It consists of over 100 UNIX-like commands that fit together nicely with other UNIX commands. It has the tools that were found to be needed from real experience of developing software applications. Using UNIX shell programming, developers can quickly put together applications from both UNIX and **/rdb** commands. Users face a unified environment. They may not know or care whether the commands they use come from the UNIX system or **/rdb.** This is the correct way to extend the UNIX system: keeping the power and genius of the UNIX system and adding functions to it.

13.3 Speed

Most of the research on databases and their problems assumes that you have huge files, need to find a record (row) very quickly, and have many users. Not many years ago, few could afford to have the power that a microcomputer offers today. Then computers cost millions of dollars and had to be shared by many users. Only large volume applications were cost effective enough to computerize. Thus the tremendous concern for speed and size. The early 8 bit microcomputer systems reinforced this thinking. With weak computers, small memories, and floppy disks, size and speed were still overriding issues.

Today, and more so in the future, we have powerful 16- and 32-bit microcomputers with large memories and big disks, but so inexpensive that they are ubiquitous. Applications will run faster and handle larger databases. Now we want ease of use and powerful systems. For most of us, the bulk of database applications will be for relatively small data files. Perhaps a few hundred records, to several tens of thousands. As much as a person or a small company, department, or group could type in. We want to see our data manipulated in many ways as soon as we think of them. Traditional database systems are optimized for only one or a few searches. If you think of something new to do that was not planned for in the development of the application, you will usually find it very difficult or impossible to do. These traditional databases often require complicated setups, lots of training to use and are difficult to modify.

Worse still, they are huge programs that take up much of the memory and CPU cycles of the computer. Only a few users can slow a big expensive computer down to an unacceptable response. These traditional database systems have features built into a large program. The UNIX system has lots of features, but they are in the hundreds of programs stored on the hard disk. UNIX only brings in the code it needs for a particular function. The average UNIX utility is about 40 K bytes. Traditional database programs are often a quarter of a megabyte and larger.

/**rdb** takes a much different approach. It is much closer to the ideas of a text editor, spreadsheet and, of course, the UNIX system. It handles small databases as well as large. /**rdb** is aimed at ease of use and maximum power. Even so, it is usually very fast. But when more speed is needed, /**rdb** also has not one but five fast access methods to give a variety of ways to access large files. We have seen studies that indicate that /**rdb** is as fast or faster than any other database management system. Furthermore, even **grep** with its sequential search is not so bad. **grep** is a UNIX program which looks for a string pattern and prints out each line in which it finds a match. Remember that there is computing overhead for the traditional fast access methods. Binary searches require sorting, hash tables must be computed, B-trees must split their pages when they fill, linked lists must maintain their pointers, and so on. As the size of our tables diminishes, so do the advantages of the fast access methods. See the chapter on fast access methods.

13.4 Size

Many database comparisons put great emphasis on the size of the database that can be handled. This is really a problem for database systems that are one large program. /**rdb,** however, is a group of small programs which can be piped together. Its only limits are those of your hardware and UNIX itself.

So a table can be as big as the available free space on your disk, or as big a file as your UNIX system can handle. The **justify** command builds a temporary file as big as its input file. So, if you are going to justify a file, there must be as much free space on your disk (and in your file system) as the file you are justifying.

However, UNIX occasionally has problems with lines longer than 256 bytes. Also, some UNIX implementations have problems with **printf** handling more than 128 bytes. **printf** is a UNIX utility for doing formatted printing. You will run into UNIX limits long before you run into /**rdb** limits.

14. Database Theory: Ways of thinking about data

14.1 Can You Say that in English?

If you are not a mathematician, you may find the literature on relational databases incomprehensible. One problem is the terms used in the literature. Different terms are used by the mathematicians, computer people, and other humans. We try to use human terms throughout the /**rdb** documentation. We lapse into computer terms either by mistake, or when we think we are talking to programmers and analysts about the more technical details. We ignore the mathematicians, since they seem to ignore us. But we love them. Without them we would not have relational theory. Here is a table that will help each group translate terms used by another group.

TABLE 12. Relational Database Term Translations

most humans	computer people	mathematicians
table	file	relation
column	field	attribute (domain)
row	record	tuple
number of columns	number of fields	degree
number of rows	number of records	cardinality
list of tables	schema	data model
user's tables	user view	data submodel
simplified	simplified	normalized
no repeated columns	no multi fields	normalized
one concept per table		3rd normalized
get rows	get records	select
get columns	get fields	project
combine tables	concatenate	join, union
new command	shell script	view

14.2 Database Models

A database model is a way of structuring and thinking about data. We use the relational model, but there are several others. There are three major types of database models that have been implemented in several commercially successful database management systems: relational, network, and hierarchical. In addition there are at least four more important models discussed in the literature, but for which few implementations exist as yet: entity-relationship, binary, semantic network, and infological [Tsichritzis 1982]. We will probably see more of them in the future.

The major difference between these models is their structure. As you read through these descriptions, you will probably have a sense of *deja vu.* Each is quite similar to the other with some differences. Remember that information in each model can be converted or transformed into the other models.

14.3 Hierarchical

The hierarchical database has a tree structure. (In computer science, trees have their roots at the top and grow their branches and leaves downward. Computer scientists are not botanists.)

Figure 5. Hierarchical Structure

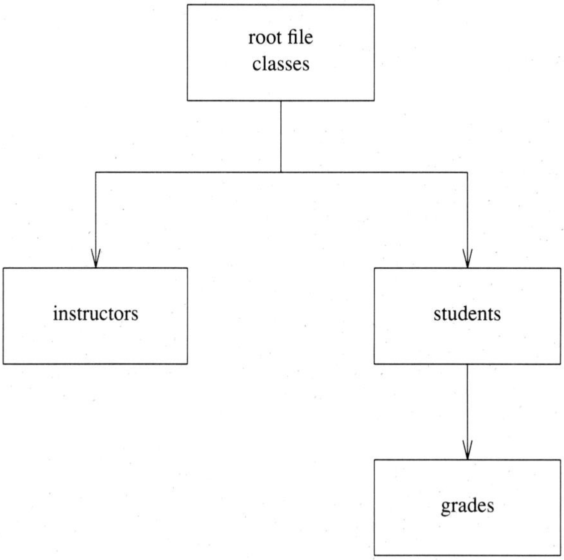

This type of database was popularized by IBM. Remember them? Their IMS database management system has been widely used in the past. When the users build a database, this structure must be imposed upon their data. Push, squeeze, force. Some searches are speeded up (such as from classes to grades). Others become difficult or impossible: *What grades did an instructor give?* The emphasis is on speedy responses from older, slower, and usually heavily burdened computers. The speed is achieved by anticipating standard searches and optimizing them. But *ad hoc* queries (ones you just think up as you are working) are not only slow, but are often difficult, even impossible, to do.

14.4 Network

The network type of database has a two level structure:

Figure 6. Network Structure

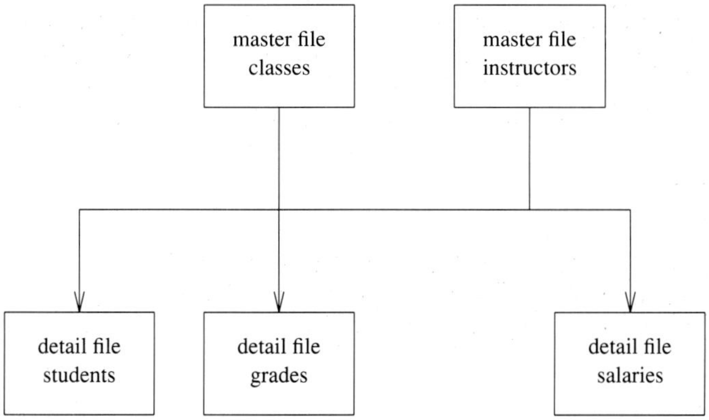

```
  ┌──────────────┐        ┌──────────────┐
  │ master file  │        │ master file  │
  │   classes    │        │  instructors │
  └──────────────┘        └──────────────┘



  ┌──────────┐  ┌──────────┐        ┌──────────┐
  │detail file│  │detail file│        │detail file│
  │ students │  │  grades  │        │ salaries │
  └──────────┘  └──────────┘        └──────────┘
```

Both Total and Image/Query are examples of this approach. This model comes from a CODASYL committee standard. This system is a little easier to build and use than hierarchical, but still requires that the user know the structure and *navigate* through the links. It is difficult, if not impossible to get from one detail file to another.

14.5 Relational

Relational databases have what are called a *flat* file structure. All files are at the same level.

Figure 7. Relational Structure

With such a structure and a set of commands like **project, select,** and **join,** one can get all of the information out of the database that has been put into it.

E.F. Codd of the IBM San Jose Research Laboratory proposed this relational model in the early 1970s [Codd 1970]. Since then the relational approach has captured the attention and approval of most of the academic, and now business, researchers in the field. IBM is converting to relational with its new System R database management system. It uses SQL for a user interface. Almost all of the database systems that have been built for UNIX are relational.

A relational database management system is considered by most researchers in the field as the best for several reasons. Relational databases have a solid mathematical base in relational set theory, relational algebra and relational calculus. There are theorems in this relational math that prove that any data put into a relational database can be extracted. The mathematical base also assures us that the manipulations we perform will have correct results, just as arithmetic assures us that the math functions we perform on the computer have correct results.

The relational structure is the simplest. All information is kept in simple tables. The user does not have to navigate through complex networks (network model) or tree structures (hierarchical model). Relational theory has tables (relations) with rows (tuples) and columns (attributes of domains), which anyone can understand.

It also has functions on tables: **project (column)**, **select (row)**, **join (jointable)**, and so on. These functions both input and output tables, just as the functions in algebra which we are familiar with input and output numbers (scalars), lists of numbers (vectors), or arrays of numbers (matrixes). These commands we've discussed earlier. They are the most frequently used. There are also several commands from set theory that are not as often used but are important for completeness. There has been a lot written on relational database systems and theory. See the Bibliography.

14.6 Entity-Relationship

The entity-relationship model was put forth by Chen [Chen 1976]. This model sees the universe, or more practically the company or institution, as composed of entities and relations between them. Things, people, departments, and so on, are entities. Entities have relationships between them. A department is part of an enterprise. People work in departments as staff members. Equipment is assigned to departments. Some people are heads of departments. One can draw a diagram of these entities and relationships.

Figure 8. Entity-Relationship Diagram

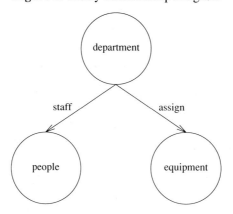

Entities are boxes and relationships are connecting lines. There is a one-to-many relationship. A department can have many staff people and many pieces of equipment. But each employee and piece of equipment is assigned to only one department. If the rules of the organization change, so will this graph.

This model has similarities to the three classic models. The relational model holds entities in tables (also called relations). It provides the **jointable** command to combine tables on keys in which there is a relationship between the entites of one table and another. It can also be seen as hierarchical and network because of the structures. This model tries to capture the overall structure of the enterprise regardless of how it is implemented. It is the *big picture*.

14.7 Binary

The binary model sees data as a graph in which each node is a simple column or field of data and the arcs that join the nodes represent simple relationships between them. It is based on graph theory. As we move to computer systems with powerful graphic screens, this model might become more common.

14.8 Semantic Network

The semantic network model comes from the field of artificial intelligence (AI). (See Quillian [1968] and Sowa [1983]). AI is the part of computer science that trys to get computers to be *intelligent.* Its subfields are games, expert systems, vision, robotics, natural language recognition, and others. Researchers came up with this model in trying to structure data for these efforts, trying to understand the human associative memory, and trying to understand natural language.

There are many variations of the semantic network model because many researchers have written about different versions in the technical literature. In the broadest sense any graph model is a semantic network model, including the entity-relationship and the binary model.

The new graphic terminals will make this graph model easier to display and input. Since all information can be represented in this way, it will be a very powerful way to interact with computers.

14.9 Infological

An infological model is the user's view of the application. There is a dream that some day a user can simply communicate the structure of the application to the computer and the database system will be set up automatically. — somewhere between a general database management system and a specific application. Some elements exist today. The new graphic terminal systems provide powerful tools to communicate with the user and give the user the ability to specify needed applications pictorially. Work in this field will be fun and productive for future users.

14.10 Prolog: Programming in Logic

Finally, the Prolog language adds logic programming on top of a database model. Prolog is discussed more in the next chapter.

14.11 The Grand Unified Field Theory of Information

The *Grand Unified Field Theory of Information* is that all of the different structures of information are simply transformations of each other. Natural language sentences and their parses, predicate calculus, tables and relational algebra, graphs, and semantic networks are simply different representations and transformations of information. Each has its advantages and uses. People speak language and understand graphs. Computers can parse language, store tables, and manipulate them through relational algebra and predicate logic. Sentences can be converted to predicate calculus formulas and solved by comparing with the table database.

Figure 9. Grand Unified Field Theory of Information

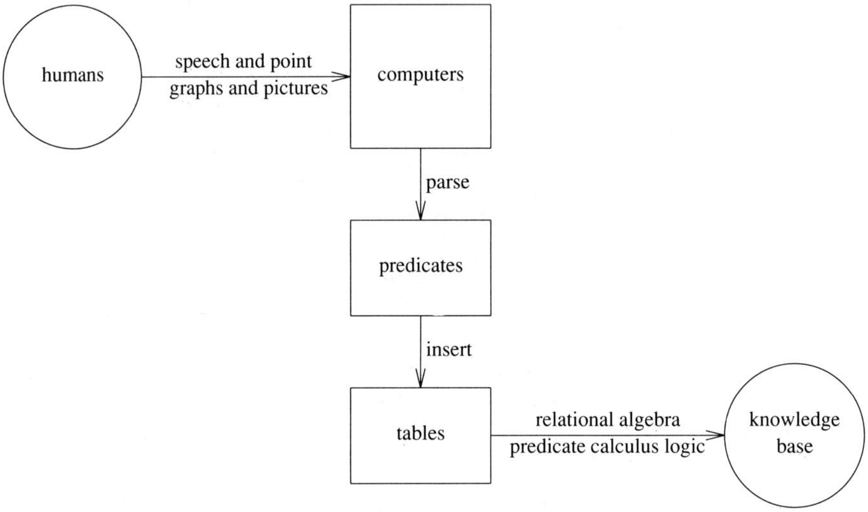

This offers enormous power and possibilities. In the years ahead the written literature of many fields can be scanned by computer, parsed, and inserted into tables.
Then written or spoken queries can be parsed and converted into predicate calculus
formulas which can be evaluated against the relational table database. The computer
can then speak, write, or draw a graph or a picture of the answer. Watch out
universe, here comes the humans!

15. AI and Prolog: Programming in Logic

Artificial intelligence programs, like most programs, rely heavily on databases. **/rdb** has several facilities to assist AI, and especially expert system programs.

15.1 Prolog Language and Environment

Prolog is a programming language that allows you to program in logic. It was developed in Europe and has been adopted as the language for the Japanese Fifth Generation Computer project. It is used in artificial intelligence work. It provides a powerful new method to make logical inferences from databases. Instead of being able to find data only, it can reason from that data to answer questions that are not in the database, but are logically derivable from the data. This is an enormous leap in getting the computer to be smart.

Prolog is an entire programming language and environment, mainly because it was developed on non-UNIX operating systems where almost nothing was provided. But we are only interested in the logical searching features which are its major contribution. The logic programming of Prolog would be best placed in a UNIX environment with its many tools, rather than in the primitive Prolog environment. There are now several Prologs available for UNIX.

15.1.1 Predicate Calculus

The branch of logic that Prolog uses is predicate calculus. This is not the calculus you learned in math classes, but refers to the manipulation of formulas, of which the calculus you are familiar with is only one form.

Almost all sentences in a natural language can be converted into predicate calculus statements and manipulated logically. The sentence: **Bill loves Kathy** is written: **loves(Bill, Kathy).** This says that there is a relationship, **love,** and that the first argument, *Bill,* has that relationship with the second argument, *Kathy.* This predicate calculus formula can also be expressed as a table:

```
$ cat loves
Subject   Object
-------   ------
Bill      Kathy
```

15.1.2 Facts

Prolog stores facts in the predicate calculus notation. Since almost any sentence can be expressed, almost any information can be stored in the database.

```
Prolog                          Means
----------------------          ---------------------------
female(michele)                 michele is a female
female(jane)                    jane is a female
male(john)                      john is a male
male(shawn)                     shawn is a male
parent(shawn, jane)             shawn is a parent of jane
parent(michele, jane)           michele is a parent of jane
```

These facts are entered into Prolog by simply typing them in or having Prolog get them from a file with the Prolog **consult** command.

15.1.3 Questions

Once entered into the Prolog database, you can ask questions.

```
?- parent(shawn,jane)
yes
?- female(shawn)
no
?- mother(michele,jane)
no
```

The first query is found in the database and *yes* is returned. The second and third queries are not found in the database, so *no* is returned. None of this is very exciting because any database management system can do this. However, we humans know that the third query is true because we know that if *michele* is the parent of *jane* and that *michele* is *female*, than *michele* must be the mother of *jane*. But no database can know this rule and logically deduce this conclusion except Prolog.

15.1.4 Rules

This great innovation of Prolog comes when we add rules and logical inference to the database of facts. A rule is stated in this form:

```
mother(X,Y) :- parent(X,Y), female(X).
```

In English this rule says that the relationship **mother** exists between two entities X and Y if (:-) X is the **parent** of Y and (,) X is a **female.** This rule is stored by Prolog. Now we can ask again:

```
?- mother(michele,jane)
yes
```

This time Prolog gives the right answer. Not because it found the fact in the database, but because it inferred the fact from facts and rules in the database. Prolog failed to find the fact in the database, so it searched its list of rules for one that started with **mother.** It then assigned *michele* to X and *jane* to Y. It went to the facts after the if (:-) symbol. Prolog first looked for the fact *parent(michele,jane)*. It found that successfully, so it then searched for the fact *female(michele)*. This was also successful so it responded with *yes*.

With a simple mechanism, we now have the ability to logically infer facts from other facts and rules!

15.2 /rdb Interface to Prolog

/rdb provides an interface to Prolog with two commands **tabletofact** and **tabletorule.** These convert **/rdb** tables into the predicate calculus formulae that Prolog needs to see. Therefore, we can logically query our database.

15.2.1 tabletofact

The **tabletofact** command converts a table to predicate calculus. First let's look at our **/rdb** fact tables.

```
$ cat female
Female
------
michele
beth
sandy
jan
$ cat male
Male
----
kirk
rod
shawn
durk
$ cat parent
Parent    Child
------    -------
michele   rod
kirk      rod
$ cat isa
Name      Isa
----      ---
rod       human
human     mammal
mammal    animal
animal    lifeform
```

Now let's convert them to Prolog format. We see several tables representing relations converted to Prolog facts.

```
$ tabletofact female male parent isa > fact
$ cat fact
```

```
female(michele).
female(beth).
female(sandy).
female(jan).
male(kirk).
male(rod).
male(shawn).
male(durk).
parent(michele,rod).
parent(kirk,rod).
isa(rod,human).
isa(human,mammal).
isa(mammal,animal).
isa(animal,lifeform).
```

15.2.2 tabletorule

Rules can also be stored in **/rdb** tables and converted to Prolog format with the **tabletorule** command.

```
$ cat ruletable
True             If
-------------    ----------------------
mother(X,Y)      female(X) , parent(X,Y)
father(X,Y)      male(X) , parent(X,Y)
son(X,Y)         male(X) , parent(Y,X)
isa(X,Y)         isa(X,Z) , isa(Z,Y)
$ tabletorule ruletable > rule
$ cat rule
mother(X,Y) :- female(X) , parent(X,Y).
father(X,Y) :- male(X) , parent(X,Y).
son(X,Y) :- male(X) , parent(Y,X).
isa(X,Y) :- isa(X,Z) , isa(Z,Y).
```

Then you can consult these files within Prolog with the **consult** command.

```
$ prolog
consult ("fact").
yes
consult ("rule").
yes
```

Now you are ready to ask questions. With this database you can now ask questions about motherhood and fatherhood, and questions like *is rod a lifeform?* Prolog will answer yes, showing the limits of this approach. Garbage in, garbage out.

15.3 Problems of Prolog

Richard Forsyth [Forsyth 1984, page 16] lists many complaints about Prolog including: *Prolog provides a relational database for free - a big bonus, but the trouble is that it resides in main memory, and is consequently very greedy on storage.* He also quotes Feigenbaum and McCorduck [1983]: *The last thing a knowledge engineer wants is to abdicate control to an 'automatic' theorem-proving process that conducts massive searches without step-by-step control exerted by knowledge in the knowledge base.*

The reason for all of the problems in Prolog is that it is a great idea AND a programming environment. On non-UNIX systems, when you want to do something, you wind up having to do everything else also. You have to write editors, floating point handlers (some Prologs don't), trace, input/output, and on, and on. In addition, both Prolog and LISP do everything in memory. This is fine for small prototype and demo programs in a university AI research lab but unworkable for large databases.

The same is true for LISP. Peter Jackson [Jackson 1986] writes about a classic expert system: *The difference between MYCIN's score and those of Stanford experts was not significant, but its score is as good as the experts and better than the non-expert physicians. However, MYCIN is not currently used in wards for a number of reasons...it is written in INTERLISP, is slow and heavy on memory...*

This problem is not new to the computer world. It was solved decades ago in commercial computing. There needs to be a shift from memory to secondary storage as AI moves from the research labs to real users. See *Expert Database Systems: Proceedings From the First International Workshop* [Kerschberg 1986].

We also need to shift from Prolog and LISP to UNIX and a powerful database management system like **/rdb.** As radical as this sounds, one of the leading expert system companies converted its system from LISP to UNIX and C. They got a **50** fold increase in speed! The other expert system companies are in various stages of converting to UNIX.

On UNIX you can simply add a new capability to an excellent environment. Prolog's environment is quite primitive and its inference system narrow and limited. The Prolog rule inference and search mechanism should be added to UNIX as simply more programs. We expect to see all of the AI ideas added to UNIX in the years ahead. We should see different logics, that is, fuzzy logic, Bayesian logic, multi-valued logic and certainty factors. We should also see many new search strategies. Heuristic searches guided by data in the database are needed. Then we will see many new expert systems developed with these vastly enhanced tools. By concentrating on only what is new, developers can do a much better job. They won't have to waste most of their time reinventing environment wheels.

15.4 searchtree: Database Tree Searching

Most AI programs search databases that can be visualized as trees or networks. Speeding those searches and controlling them is a very important area of research. Usually, these trees are kept in memory and searched with pointers. This limits the size of the database that a LISP or Prolog language program can handle. It is not as fast as one might imagine. Memory searches are fast, but the overhead of bringing the data in off the disk, and hogging so much memory that programs must swap frequently, quickly wipes out any theoretical speed advantage.

searchtree is a **/rdb** shell program that shows another way to search a tree. It can use the fast access methods to do a breadth first search of any sized data table. It is a shell program example which can be edited to handle many search situations. Heuristics can be built into the code to speed, or otherwise improve, the performance of the search. Examples of its use are in the **/rdb** manual.

16. C Interface: Speak C to the database

You can call UNIX and the **/rdb** database commands from C programs. This chapter gives you several example programs starting from the most simple to the most complex.

16.1 Don't

Before we start, it is strongly recommended that you think twice before writing C or other language programs. The shell, UNIX tools, and **/rdb** commands are so powerful, fast, and easy to develop, you seldom need to bother with the old *third generation programming languages*. If you think of writing a program in C by habit, try to break the habit. Always try to do things in the UNIX shell and **/rdb** first. Only resort to C when there is a compelling reason, as opposed to a compulsion. We consider resorting to C as a failure of imagination, or lack of knowledge or insight, in most cases. If you think you need a C program, you may really need to know more shell programming tricks. Think of your problems as a more general problem, and check to see if there is a UNIX or **/rdb** program that will do the job.

Speed is the most common excuse for descending to C coding. Remember that computers are getting faster and cheaper. The new UNIX V Release 2 shell is so fast that it significantly narrows the speed penalty with respect to C programming. RAM disk also greatly speeds up UNIX programs. Finally, try using the shell for a fast prototype. You can see if it is too slow before coding. Often our intuitions are wrong in these matters. Also, the users might change their minds and decide on a different way to approach the problem. Your fast prototype will then save you a lot of unnecessary C coding.

If you do descend to C, try to write small programs that can be used in future shell programming. Only write what is necessary. Read from standard-in and write to standard-out. Make your programs table driven and use **/rdb** database table and list formats so that the full power of UNIX and the database can manipulate the tables that drive your programs. Of course, if you are a devotee of pain and suffering, forget this advice.

16.2 System

The easiest way for C programs to access both UNIX and the **/rdb** database is with the UNIX **system(2)** call. It only needs a character string, or pointer to a character string containing a shell command. **system** will execute the command, just as though you typed the command at the terminal or entered it into a shell program. In the example below are three different ways of setting up the command string.

```
$ cat system.c
#define COMMAND   "ls | wc"

main (argc, argv)

int     argc;
char    *argv [];
{
        system ("echo hello world");
        system (COMMAND);
        system (argv [1]);
}
```

The first **system** function call hard codes the command in the code of the function call. The second call uses a previously defined name **COMMAND.** Note the *#define COMMAND* line at the beginning of the code. Finally, the first argument on the command line is used as a command string for **system** (*argv[1]*). This allows the user to type a command as the first argument and it will be executed. The UNIX **make** command is used to compile the program. It uses the *Makefile*.

```
$ cat Makefile
system: system.o
        cc system.o -o system
$ make system
        cc -O -c system.c
        cc system.o -o system
```

Now that the **system** program has been compiled, it can be run with a command as an argument.

```
$ system date
hello world
      7       7      65
Thu Apr  3 02:10:04 PST 1986
$
```

Note that the first system call produced the *hello world* line. The second call executed the defined command. Finally, the date and time were displayed when the **date** argument to the **system** program was executed by the **system** call.

16.3 Execl

The next step from simple to complex is the **execl** system call. This function will replace the current process with another program. It is usually called *chaining*. Once called, the calling process dies and is never reentered. The executed program takes over the process table entry of the calling program and all of the open input and output files. Here is an example.

```
$ cat execl.c
#include        <stdio.h>
#define FIRST   "First"

char    *p1 = "argument";
char    *p2;

main (argc, argv)

int     argc;
char    *argv [];
{
        p2 = "is:";
        fflush (stdout);
        execl ("/bin/echo", "echo", FIRST, p1, p2, argv[1], NULL);
}
$ make
        cc -O -c execl.c
        cc execl.o -o execl
$ execl ARG1 ARG2
First argument is: ARG1
```

All of the arguments to **execl** are character pointers and you can have as many as
you want. The last one must be the *NULL,* as a sentinel or end marker. In the first
argument the full path to the program to be executed must be given because the
PATH variable is not searched by **execl.** It is not good to hard code paths. The
second argument is the zero'th argument, which is the name of the called program.
The rest of the arguments are the normal arguments as you would type on the command line at the shell level. Several possible ways of setting up the arguments are
shown. The first regular argument is a defined constant. The *p1* and *p2* are each
pointers to characters. The first is initialized to a string when it is declared and the
second is assigned later in the code. Finally, the first argument passed to the calling
program is passed on through the second pointer in the *argv* array of pointers.

16.4 Execl Shell Programs

If you try to use the **execl** system call to execute a shell script file, it will fail. You
have to execute a **sh** shell program to read the text of the shell file. Here a shell file
called *listargs* is executed. It simply echoes out its arguments separated by newlines.

```
$ cat listargs
for I in $*
do
        echo $I
done
```

```
$ cat execl.sh.c
#include         <stdio.h>
#define FIRST   "First"

char    *p1 = "argument";
char    *p2;

main (argc, argv)

int     argc;
char    *argv [];
{
        p2 = "is:";
        fflush (stdout);
        execl ("/bin/sh", "sh", "listargs", FIRST, p1, p2, argv[1], NULL);
}
$ make
        cc execl.sh.o -o execl.sh
$ execl.sh arg1
First
argument
is:
arg1
```

Note that **sh** is the program executed, and that its first argument is *listargs*. This is like typing:

```
$ sh listargs
```

16.5 Fork

Sometimes we want to run another program without killing ourselves. The **fork** system call will create a child process that is identical to the calling program. The return value of the **fork** command can be tested to see which process the code is in, parent or child. Therefore, the same program, with the same code, can branch to different statements, depending upon whether it is the parent or child process. The child code can do its thing, including executing another program. The parent process can wait for the child to finish before going on. But it does not have to, because the UNIX system is a multi-processing environment.

```
$ cat fork.c
#include         <stdio.h>

#define FAIL     -1
#define CHILD    0
#define PARENT   1

main (argc, argv)

int     argc;
char    *argv [];
{
```

```
        switch (fork())
        {
        case -1:        /* error */
                fprintf (stderr, "fork system call failed.\n");
                exit (FAIL);
        case 0:         /* child process */
                execl ("/bin/echo", "echo", "I am the child.", NULL);
                exit (CHILD);
        default:        /* parent process */
                if (wait(NULL) != -1)
                {
                        fflush (stdout);
                        printf ("I am the parent.\n");
                }
                else
                {
                        fflush (stdout);
                        fprintf (stderr, "wait system call failed.\n");
                }
        }
        exit (PARENT);
}
$ make
        cc -O -c fork.c
        cc fork.o -o fork
$ fork
I am the child.
I am the parent.
```

In this example the C **switch** command is used to execute the **fork** system call because it has three different return values. A -1 return indicates a failure to fork a new process. Perhaps the number of processes has reached a limit. We want to handle this error condition. A zero return means that the code is now in a child process, so the code should do the child's thing. In this case, the child process executes an **echo** command with the **execl** system call. Thus it changes into another program. Finally the parent process will get the child's process ID number, which is some number greater than zero. Here the parent waits for the child to die before printing its message. It flushes the standard-out buffers before printing its own message. You can see when we execute this program that both processes send output to the standard-out.

16.6 One-Way Pipe

A very important use of this mechanism is to open a pipe between the two processes so that they can pass data. This can go either way, from parent to child, or from child to parent. The first example here is of a one-way pipe. The next section will demonstrate a two-way pipe.

```
#include        <stdio.h>

#define FAIL    -1
#define CHILD   0
#define PARENT  1
#define MESSAGE "Hi, kid"

main (argc, argv)

int     argc;
char    *argv [];
{
        int     pd [2];
        char    childbuf [BUFSIZ];

        if (pipe(pd) == FAIL)
        {
                fprintf (stderr, "pipe system call failed.\n");
                exit (FAIL);
        }

        switch (fork())
        {
        case -1:        /* error */
                fprintf (stderr, "fork system call failed.\n");
                exit (FAIL);
        case 0:         /* child process */
                if (close (pd [1]) == FAIL)
                {
                        fprintf (stderr, "close pipe failed.\n");
                        exit (FAIL);
                }
                read (pd [0], childbuf, BUFSIZ);
                execl ("/bin/echo", "echo",
                        "child read:", childbuf, NULL);
                exit (CHILD);
        default:        /* parent process */
                if (close (pd [0]) == FAIL)
                {
                        fprintf (stderr, "close pipe failed.\n");
                        exit (FAIL);
                }
                printf ("parent wrote: %s\n", MESSAGE, sizeof(MESSAGE));
                if (write (pd[1], MESSAGE, sizeof(MESSAGE)) == FAIL)
                {
                        fprintf (stderr, "pipe write filed\n");
                        exit (FAIL);
                }
        }
        exit (PARENT);
}
$ make
        cc -O -c pipe1.c
        cc pipe1.o -o pipe1
$ pipe1
parent wrote: Hi, kid
child read: Hi, kid
```

pd is the pipe descriptor buffer which holds two integers, one for each pipe direction. The parent writes into *pd[1]* and the child reads from *pd[0]*. Each closes its other pipe with the **close** system call. The **fork** call creates the child process. The parent process writes its message to the pipe with the **write** system call. It uses the C **sizeof** facility to count the characters of the *MESSAGE*. This allows us to edit the message and not have to look through the code to find, count and change its size. The child process reads the pipe with the **read** system call and executes the **echo** program to display the message it got from the parent process.

Of course this is not very useful, but it is simple enough to follow. It can be used in any situation in which we want to crank up a background process and periodically send it data to act upon. This mechanism is especially useful in UNIX because there are so many programs that are available to save us the effort of writing them.

16.7 Pipe to Standard-in

In the previous example, the **write** system call was used to read the pipe and the message was passed on to the executed **echo** program as an argument. But we also want to write to the standard-in of a UNIX program. In the following example, the child executes a process that reads from its standard-in. The child connected the pipe to its standard-in using the **dup** system call.

```c
#include        <stdio.h>

#define FAIL    -1
#define CHILD   0
#define PARENT  1
#define PM      "Hi, kid"
#define CM      "Hi, parent"

main (argc, argv)
int     argc;
char    *argv [];
{
        int     pd [2];
        char    buffer [BUFSIZ];

        if (pipe(pd) == FAIL)
        {
                fprintf (stderr, "pipe system call failed.\n");
                exit (FAIL);
        }

        switch (fork())
        {
        case -1:        /* error */
                fprintf (stderr, "fork system call failed.\n");
                exit (FAIL);
        case 0:         /* child process */
                if (close () == FAIL)
                {
                        fprintf (stderr, "close pipe failed.\n");
                        exit (FAIL);
                }
                if (dup (pd [0]) != 0)
                {
                        fprintf (stderr, "dup pipe failed.\n");
                        exit (FAIL);
                }
```

```
                    if (close (pd [0]) == FAIL || close (pd [1]) == FAIL)
                    {
                            fprintf (stderr, "dup pipe failed.\n");
                            exit (FAIL);
                    }
                    execl ("/bin/cat", "cat", NULL);
                    fprintf (stderr, "execl cat failed.\n");
                    exit (FAIL);
        default:        /* parent process */
                    if (close (pd [0]) == FAIL)
                    {
                            fprintf (stderr, "close pipe failed.\n");
                            exit (FAIL);
                    }
                    printf ("parent wrote: %s\n", PM, sizeof(PM));
                    if (write (pd[1], PM, sizeof(PM)) == FAIL)
                    {
                            fprintf (stderr, "pipe write filed\n");
                            exit (FAIL);
                    }
                    if (close (pd [1]) == FAIL)
                    {
                            fprintf (stderr, "close pipe failed.\n");
                            exit (FAIL);
                    }
/*
                    read (pd [0], buffer, BUFSIZ);
                    printf ("parent read: %s\n", buffer);
*/
        }
        exit (PARENT);
}
$ make
        cc -O -c pipe2.c
        cc pipe2.o -o pipe2
$ pipe2
parent wrote: Hi, kid
Hi, kid
```

This is similar to the example before, except that the **cat** command reads from its standard-in. The pipe is closed by the parent after writing with a **close** system call. This sends an end-of-file to the pipe and the standard-in of the **cat** program so that the program will terminate.

16.8 Two-Way Pipe

In addition to sending data one way, we sometimes want to get replies. Two-way pipes make possible coroutines that send data back and forth.

```
$ cat pipe2.c
/*
pipe2 - sends first argument thru pipe to child program,
        and reads the childs replay and sends it to standard-out.
*/
```

```
#include        <stdio.h>

/* program return status */
#define OK      0
#define FAIL    -1


/* fork return codes distinguished child from parent process */
#define CHILD   0
#define PARENT  1


/* pipe descriptor array elements */
#define READ    0
#define WRITE   1


/* standard-io file descriptors */
#define STDIN   0
#define STDOUT  1
#define STDERR  2


/* program for child to execl */
#define PATH    "/usr/bin/bc"
#define PROGRAM "bc"


/* standard-error handling macro */
#define error(message) {fprintf (stderr,"%s: %s\n", argv [0], message);\
                     exit (FAIL); }
char    buffer [BUFSIZ];        /* buffer to read into */

main (argc, argv)

int     argc;
char    *argv [];
{
        register char  *p;      /* pointer for scanning strings */
        int     pcpipe [2];     /* pipe from parent to child */
        int     cppipe [2];     /* pipe from child to parent */

        if (pipe (pcpipe) == FAIL || pipe (cppipe) == FAIL)
                error("pipe system call failed.");

        switch (fork())
        {
        case FAIL:      /* error */
                error("fork system call failed");

        case CHILD:     /* child process */

                /* close stdin to free for pipe connection */
                if (close (STDIN) == FAIL)
                        error("close stdin failed");

                /* connect pipe to stdin of child */
                if (dup (pcpipe [READ]) != STDIN)
                        error("dup stdin pipe failed");

                /* close stdout to free for pipe connection */
                if (close (STDOUT) == FAIL)
                        error("close stdout failed");

                /* connect pipe to stdout of child */
                if (dup (cppipe [WRITE]) != STDOUT)
                        error("dup stdout pipe failed");
```

```
                    /* close all pipes so child reads from stdin/out */
                    if (    close (pcpipe [READ])  == FAIL ||
                            close (pcpipe [WRITE]) == FAIL ||
                            close (cppipe [READ])  == FAIL ||
                            close (cppipe [WRITE]) == FAIL )
                            error("close child pipes failed");

                    /* execute basic calculator */
                    execl (PATH, PROGRAM, NULL);

                    /* if we get here, execl failed */
                    error("execl failed");

        default:        /* parent process */

                    /* close unused ends of the pipes */
                    if (    close (pcpipe [READ])  == FAIL ||
                            close (cppipe [WRITE]) == FAIL )
                            error("parent close pipe failed");

                    /* write command line argument into pipe to child */
                    if (write (pcpipe [WRITE], argv [1], strlen(argv [1]))
                            == FAIL)
                            error("parent pipe write argv failed");

                    /* bc needs a newline to execute a line */
                    if (write (pcpipe [WRITE],"\n", 1) == FAIL)
                            error("parent pipe write nl failed");

                    /* close pipe sends end-of-file to kill child */
                    if (close (pcpipe [WRITE]) == FAIL)
                            error("parent close pipe failed");

                    /* read childs reply */
                    if (read (cppipe [READ], buffer, sizeof(buffer))
                            == FAIL)
                            error("parent pipe read failed");

                    /* be sure string is terminated by NULL */
                    for (p = buffer; *p != '\n'; p++);
                    *p = NULL;

                    /* output the answer */
                    puts (buffer);

                    exit (OK);
        }
}
$ make
        cc -O -c pipe2.c
        cc pipe2.o -o pipe2
$ pipe2 '2+2'
4
$ pipe2 'scale=2 ; (100/3) * 5'
166.65
```

The **bc** command is the UNIX basic calculator. It takes equations from standard-in and sends solutions to standard-out. This program takes an equation from its first command line argument and sends it through one pipe to a child process. The child process has executed the **bc** program after connecting pipes to its standard-in and standard-out. **bc** reads the equation and sends the answer to the parent through the second pipe. The parent reads the second pipe and sends the solution to its standard-out.

This program is not very useful, but is a template. You can use this mechanism to give your C programs access to all of the UNIX, /rdb and other programs as if they were subroutines. This will save you a lot of programming. If a program exists to do what you want, use it.

16.9 Programming Style

The previous program also introduces a more advanced programming style. Most *magic* numbers have been defined to mnemonic constants to make the code easier to read and to simplify changes. A zero appearing in the code usually means nothing to the reader, but a name helps us understand what it is. In addition, if you have to change a magic number, it is much easier to edit it once at the top of the code than to search through all of the code to find it. It is especially difficult when the magic number is a common number like 0 or 1. You can not globally change such numbers because they are used in many different ways. You must carefully search the code for the correct numbers to change.

Notice that the error condition is now handled by a simple macro called **error.** It saves a lot of typing, makes the code easier to read, and standardizes the way errors are handled and reported. Finally, every major section of code is commented. It takes a little more time, but saves a lot of time when we are debugging, changing, and maintaining the program.

16.10 Fast Access

This final example shows a more practical program. This fast access program creates the **search** program and sends it a key through the first pipe. This child process finds a row in the *inventory* table and sends it back through the second pipe to the parent. The parent writes it to standard-out, but the parent can be modified to do other operations to the row.

```
$ cat fastaccess.c
/*
fastaccess - sends first argument thru pipe to child seek program,
        and reads the childs offset replay, seeks the record,
        reads it and sends the record to standard-out.
*/

#include        <stdio.h>


/* program return status */
#define OK      0
#define FAIL    -1


/* fork return codes distinguished child from parent process */
#define CHILD   0
#define PARENT  1
```

```
/* pipe descriptor array elements */
#define READ    0
#define WRITE   1


/* standard-io file descriptors */
#define STDIN   0
#define STDOUT  1
#define STDERR  2


/* program for child to execl */
#define PATH    "/usr/rdb/bin/search"
#define PROGRAM "search"
#define METHOD  "-mb"
#define TABLE   "inventory"
#define KEY     "Item"

/* standard-error handling macro */
#define error(message) {fprintf (stderr,"%s: %s\n", argv [0], message);\
                  exit (FAIL); }

char    buffer [BUFSIZ];        /* buffer to read into */

main (argc, argv)

int     argc;
char    *argv [];
{
        register char   *p;     /* pointer for scanning strings */
        int     pcpipe [2];     /* pipe from parent to child */
        int     cppipe [2];     /* pipe from child to parent */
        int     file;           /* file descriptor for table file */
        int     from, to;       /* offsets of record in table */
        int     xfrom, xto;     /* offsets in secondary index file */

        if (pipe (pcpipe) == FAIL || pipe (cppipe) == FAIL)
                error("pipe system call failed.");


        switch (fork())
        {
        case FAIL:      /* error */
                error("fork system call failed");


        case CHILD:     /* child process */
                /* close stdin to free for pipe connection */
                if (close (STDIN) == FAIL)
                        error("close stdin failed");


                /* connect pipe to stdin of child */
                if (dup (pcpipe [READ]) != STDIN)
                        error("dup stdin pipe failed");


                /* close stdout to free for pipe connection */
                if (close (STDOUT) == FAIL)
                        error("close stdout failed");
```

```
                        /* connect pipe to stdout of child */
                        if (dup (cppipe [WRITE]) != STDOUT)
                                error("dup stdout pipe failed");


                        /* close all pipes so child reads from stdin/out */
                        if (    close (pcpipe [READ])  == FAIL ||
                                close (pcpipe [WRITE]) == FAIL ||
                                close (cppipe [READ])  == FAIL ||
                                close (cppipe [WRITE]) == FAIL )
                                error("close child pipes failed");


                        /* execute program */
                        execl (PATH, PROGRAM, METHOD, TABLE, KEY, NULL);


                        /* if we get here, execl failed */
                        error("execl failed");


             default:        /* parent process */
                        /* close unused ends of the pipes */
                        if (    close (pcpipe [READ])  == FAIL ||
                                close (cppipe [WRITE]) == FAIL )
                                error("parent close pipe failed");

                        /* write command line argument into pipe to child */
                        if (write (pcpipe [WRITE], argv [1], strlen(argv [1]))
                                == FAIL)
                                error("parent pipe write argv failed");

                        /* needs a newline to execute a line */
                        if (write (pcpipe [WRITE],"\n", 1) == FAIL)
                                error("parent pipe write nl failed");

                        /* close pipe sends end-of-file to kill child */
                        if (close (pcpipe [WRITE]) == FAIL)
                                error("parent close pipe failed");

                        /* read childs reply */
                        if (read (cppipe [READ], buffer, sizeof(buffer))
                                == FAIL)
                                error("parent pipe read failed");

                        /* output the answer */
                        puts (buffer);

                        exit (OK);
             }
}
$ make
        cc -O -c fastaccess.c
        cc fastaccess.o -o fastaccess
$ fastaccess 2
Item    Amount  Cost    Value   Description
----    ------  ----    -----   --------------
   2      100     5       500   test tubes
$
```

This is similar to the last example. But here several arguments are given to the **search** program. These are defined with the *#define* preprocessor statements, but they could be passed from the command line arguments of the parent program or created within the program, or read from another file, a technique which is called *table driven* programming.

The best way to program is to write simple code that gets its parameters and data from database tables. Then the programs can be easily modified by simply editing the driving data tables, without having to reedit and recompile the source code. Users can modify these programs without calling back the programmer.

16.11 tabletostruct

A useful **/rdb** command is **tabletostruct.** It converts an **/rdb** table to a C language **struct** (record) type and initializes it to the values in the table. You can compile this **struct** into your C program and access any field. This makes possible table driven code. You can use the database to enter and update your tables, and recompile the program when you wish. This is the fastest access to tables, but requires compiling, and the inflexibility of not being able to change the programs internally compiled tables while the program is running.

Here we start with a simple table, convert to **struct,** make it an include file (.h is a header file), and compile it into a simple program that prints out each field.

```
$ cat table
A       B       C
-       -       -
1       2       3
$ tabletostruct Table table < table > table.h

$ cat table.h
struct Table
{
char    *A;
char    *B;
char    *C;
}       table [] =
{ "1","2","3" }
;
$ cat Makefile
printtable:     printtable.o
        cc -o printtable printtable.o

$ cat printtable.c
#include        "table.h"

main ()

{
        printf ("A=%s\n", table[0].A);
        printf ("B=%s\n", table[0].B);
        printf ("C=%s\n", table[0].C);
}
```

```
$ make
        cc -O -c printtable.c
        cc -o printtable printtable.o
$ printtable
A=1
B=2
C=3
```

Note that the **struct** is an array and that we have to give a subscript for each row we want. We can also put the **tabletostruct** into the *Makefile* to further automate the recompilation.

```
$ cat Makefile
printtable:     table.h printtable.o
        cc -o printtable printtable.o

table.h:        table
        tabletostruct Table table < table > table.h
```

This says that the printable program depends upon *table.h* being up to date, and *table.h* depends upon *table* being up to date. If you modify *table* since the last compile, the **tabletostruct** command will be reexecuted.

Here is a bigger table:

```
$ tabletostruct Inventory inventory < inventory
struct Inventory
{
char    *Item;
char    *Amount;
char    *Cost;
char    *Value;
char    *Description;
}       inventory [] =
{ "1","    4"," 50","  150","rubber gloves" }
,{ "2","  100","   5","  500","test tubes" }
,{ "3","    5","  80","  400","clamps" }
,{ "4","   23","  19","  437","plates" }
,{ "5","   99","  24"," 2376","cleaning cloth" }
,{ "6","   89"," 147","13083","bunsen burners" }
,{ "7","    5"," 175","  875","scales" }
;
```

You can refer to the *Description* of the third item with this code:

```
printf ("Item Name = %s\n", inventory [2].Description);
```

Remember that tables in C start with element 0. You can convert the strings to integers with the **atoi** (ASCII to int) function.

```
int     item;           /* current inventory item number */
int     row;            /* current row number starting from 0 */
item = atoi (inventory [row].Item);
```

16.12 Read Table into Memory: getfile and fsize

To get tables from the database at run time, you can read the table into memory and set up an array of pointers to reference any field by row and column number. Use the UNIX **open** system call, and the **stat** system call to get the size of the table, and the **malloc** system call to get that much memory. Then use the **read** call to copy the whole table into memory and run through it with a loop that sets a two-dimensional array of pointers to point to every field in the array. Then you can reach any field with:

```
char    *field, *p_table [][];
int     row, column;

field = p_table [row][column];
```

To keep from having to hard code the size of your pointer table, first find out how many columns and rows you have by running through the memory counting newline '\n' characters. You might turn tabs '\t' and newlines into NULL while you go. Then **malloc** enough memory to hold this array of pointers and run through the memory again to set the pointer array to pointing to fields. Here are some routines that show examples of how to do this.

```
$ cat getfile.c
static char    Sccs [] = "%W%";        /* SCCS Information */
/*
Copyright (c) 1983 Rod Manis

getfile - reads a file into memory and returns pointer and size
*/
#include        "rdb.h"
#include        <sys/types.h>
#include        <sys/stat.h>

char    *filebuffer, *malloc();
int     file, open(), read();
long    fsize ();

char    *getfile (filename, p_size)

char            *filename;
unsigned        *p_size;
{
        *p_size = 0;

        /* open the file */

        if ((file = open (filename, 0)) < 0)
        {
                fprintf (stderr, "Can't open file %s.\n", filename);
                fflush (stderr);
                perror ("getfile");
                return (NULL);
        }
```

```
        /* get the memory to hold the table */

        /* get size adding a byte for a trailing NULL */

        *p_size = (unsigned) (fsize (file) + 1); /* byte for NULL end */

        /* get a buffer in memory for the system */

        if ((filebuffer = malloc ((unsigned) *p_size)) == NULL)
        {
                fprintf (stderr,
                        "Can't malloc the size of file %s.\n", filename);
                fflush (stderr);
                perror ("getfile");
                return (NULL);
        }

        /* read in the file and reset p_size to number of bytes read */

        if ((*p_size = (unsigned) read (file, filebuffer, *p_size)) < 1)
        {
                fprintf (stderr, "Can't read file %s.\n", filename);
                fflush (stderr);
                perror ("getfile");
                return (NULL);
        }
        /* write NULL at the end of the buffer */

        *(filebuffer + *p_size) = NULL;

        return (filebuffer);
}
```

getfile calls **fsize** which gets the file size from the operating system by calling the **fstat** system call.

```
$ cat fsize.c
static char     Sccs [] = "%W%";           /* SCCS Information */
/*
Copyright (c) 1983 Rod Manis

fsize   get the size of a file by calling the fstat routine
*/
#include         "rdb.h"
#include         <sys/types.h>
#include         <sys/stat.h>

extern  int     Debug;          /* global for debugging */

long    fsize (file)

int     file;
{
        int     fstat ();               /* system call */
        struct  stat    statusbuffer;  /* info on file */

        /* get status information including size */

        if ((fstat (file, &statusbuffer)) < 0)
        {
                fprintf (stderr,
                        "fsize: Can't get the size of file %d\n", file);
                perror ("fsize");
                return (FAIL);
        }
```

```
      if (Debug)
            fprintf (stderr, "fsize: file size=%d\n",
                  statusbuffer.st_size);

      /* return size */

      return ((long) statusbuffer.st_size);
```

16.13 /rdb Functions: librdb.a

In the /rdb/lib directory is an archive file, librdb.a, which contains all of the functions called by the /rdb programs. You can call them like any function if you add
the file to your compile line:

```
cc -o prog prog.c librdb.a
```

If you or your system administrator moves the file to the /usr/lib directory, you only
need to add -lrdb to your compile line:

```
cc -o prog prog.c -lrdb
```

16.14 Colroutines

Another file in /rdb/lib is named Colroutines. Col stands for column because the
functions largely handle the columns of a table. Colroutines contains documentation
on each of the C functions in librdb.a. It is the header of the source code for each
routine. It shows the description, function name, arguments and argument types. It
should be enough information to use the function, without being able to see the code.

16.15 Display Example

The display.c program is a sample program that calls the /rdb functions.

```
$ cat display.c
static char    Sccs [] = "%W%";          /* SCCS Information */
static char    Copyright []="Copyright (c) 1982 Rod Manis";
/*
display will read a table or list file and send to standard-out
*/
#define USAGE    "usage: display < tableorlist\n"
#include "rdb.h"

int     Debug; /* global for debugging */

struct rowstruct row;                     /* row  information */
int     colgeth (), colgetr ();           /* input   functions */
int     colputh (), colputr ();           /* output  functions */
int     colinit (), coldump ();           /* utility functions */
```

```c
main (argc, argv, envp)

int argc;
char *argv [];
char *envp [];
{
        register        columns;        /* columns returned */
        register        i;              /* index for loops  */

        /* handle command line arguments */
        for (i = 1; i < argc; i++)
        {
                if (argv [1][0] == '-')
                {
                        switch (argv [1][1])
                        {
                        case 'D':
                                if (argv [1][2] != EOS)
                                {
                                        Debug = atoi (&(argv [1][2]));
                                }
                                else
                                {
                                        Debug = TRUE;
                                }
                                break;
                        /* add other options here */
                        default:
                                break;
                        }
                }
                else
                {
                        /* get non-option arguments, like files, here */
                }
        }

        /* get table or list headlines */
        if ((columns = colgeth (&row)) == EOF)
                exit (EOF);

        /* output headlines */
        colputh (&row);


        /* read in each row till end-of-file */
        while ((columns = colgetr (&row)) != EOF)
        {
                /* output each row, or do other row processing */
                colputr (&row);
        }
        /* return status code becomes shell $? variable for testing */
        exit (OK);
}
```

```
$ make
        cc -O -c display.c
        cc display.o -o display librdb.a
$ display < inventory
Item    Amount  Cost    Value   Description
----    ------  ----    -----   --------------
   1         3    50      150    rubber gloves
   2       100     5      500    test tubes
   3         5    80      400    clamps
   4        23    19      437    plates
   5        99    24     2376    cleaning cloth
   6        89   147    13083    bunsen burners
   7         5   175      875    scales

$ display < maillist

Number  1
Name    Ronald McDonald
Company McDonald's
Street  123 Mac Attack
City    Menphis
State   TENN
ZIP     30000
Phone   (111) 222-3333

Number  2
Name    Chiquita Banana
Company United Brands
Street  Uno Avenito De La Revolution
City    San Jose
State   Costa Rica
ZIP     123456789
Phone   1234
```

The first line is for the SCCS (Source Code Control System) routines, which maintain large software packages. The *%W%* is replaced by information about the module. The next line is the copyright notice. Both of these strings are declared *static char* so that they will appear in the object module and the binary code. The next comment is a description of the purpose of the program. The *USAGE* definition gives the syntax of the program. It can be displayed when a syntax error is detected. The debugging system is described in the next section.

The *row* structure is defined in the *rdb.h* header file that can be included (*#include*) in your programs. *row* contains lots of information about the head line and rows of the input table or list file. It is passed to the various *col* functions, which are declared below *row*. After the **main** function call, command line arguments are handled. Only the *Debug* variable is set, but this code can be edited to get all expected options and other arguments. The *col* functions read in the head line and display it, followed by each row in the table or list. The **return** command returns an exit status so that the program can be tested with the shell **if, while,** and **for** statements.

You can copy this program to start your own program. You can process each row of the table as it is read in by inserting your code within the **while** loop. Have fun, but remember, shell programming is much easier.

16.16 Debugging

The *Debug* variable is an external global that can be seen by all of the functions. There are several methods of handling debugging. The advantage of this approach is that it is in the final product so that diagnostics can be run when errors are found by users and service people. On the command line one can put *-D* to turn on debugging traces. These messages are printed out as the program runs to show the value of certain key variables. To control the quantity of output, one can follow the option with a number. The higher the number, the more output. *-D9* turns on all output, which is a lot to wade through, but shows everything. In the following example, all diagnostics are dumped. Each function gives its name and the value of various variables. *colgeth* is the column-get-header function which calls *colinit* to initialize the row buffers. The **malloc** UNIX system call is invoked to get memory for head and row data. This is part of the dynamic buffering that allows the programs to get as much memory as they can to handle large heads and rows. In this way the /**rdb** programs are not limited by software, but only by available hardware memory.

Since pointers are often a problem in C, several pointers are printed out. Their values don't mean much, but can be checked to see that they have been set to reasonable numbers. **coldump** lists all of the variables and their values in the row structure. You can also call **coldump** from your program if you wish. Of course you can use a C on-line debugger, if you prefer.

colgetr also displays the columns as they are read, so that you can see what it is seeing. All of this is coming to you through the standard-error (*stderr*) file output so that you can redirect it. It is not buffered, so it comes out before the table which is coming through the buffered standard-out and is not sent until the buffer is full or the file is closed on program termination.

```
$ display -D9 < inventory
colgeth: row=14976 filein=0
colinit: row=14976
colinit: bufsize=2048
colinit: colsize=2
colinit: p_buffer allocated
colinit: maxcolumns=1024
colinit: p_heads allocated
colinit: p_columns allocated
colinit: p_collengths allocated
coldump:-------------------------------------
        row pointer
row=14976
        file pointer for input file
row->p_filein=14754
        fileout pointer for input fileout
row->p_fileout=0
        points to buffer to write into
row->buffer=16224
        points to (offset) buffer to write into
row->p_buffer=16224
        buffer size
```

```
row->bufsize=2048
      points to end of buffer
row->p_endbuffer=18272
      points to each head found in lists
row->p_heads=18274
      to number of head columns found
row->heads=0
      points to each column found
row->p_columns=20324
      number of columns
row->columns=0
      number of colsize
row->colsize=2
      number of maxcolumns
row->maxcolumns=1024
      each column's length
row->collengths=22374
      entire row length
row->rowlength=0
      boolean fixed or variable
row->fixed=0
      boolean list or table
row->list=0
coldump:---------------------------------------
Item
Amount
Cost
Value
Description
colgetr: end-of-row.  row->rowlength = 37
colgeth: row->heads=5
----
------
----
-----
-------------
colgetr: end-of-row.  row->rowlength = 37
colgeth: row->columns=5 length=38 fixed=0 list=0
colputh: row->p_fileout=0
   1
     3
  50
  150
rubber gloves
colgetr: end-of-row.  row->rowlength = 36
   2
  100
   5
  500
test tubes
colgetr: end-of-row.  row->rowlength = 33
   3
     5
  80
  400
clamps
colgetr: end-of-row.  row->rowlength = 29
   4
    23
  19
  437
```

```
plates
colgetr: end-of-row.  row->rowlength = 29
    5
     99
  24
 2376
cleaning cloth
colgetr: end-of-row.  row->rowlength = 37
    6
     89
 147
13083
bunsen burners
colgetr: end-of-row.  row->rowlength = 37
    7
      5
 175
  875
scales
colgetr: end-of-row.  row->rowlength = 29
colgetr: eof
Item    Amount  Cost    Value   Description
----    ------  ----    -----   --------------
   1        3     50      150   rubber gloves
   2      100      5      500   test tubes
   3        5     80      400   clamps
   4       23     19      437   plates
   5       99     24     2376   cleaning cloth
   6       89    147    13083   bunsen burners
   7        5    175      875   scales
```

17. Converting from Other Databases to /rdb

17.1 SQL: How to talk SQL to /rdb

SQL is a language for querying a database. It was developed by IBM for their System R relational database management system. Originally called SQUARE and SEQUAL. We find it harder to use and less flexible than the **/rdb** and UNIX system. When they developed SQL, they did not have the advantage of UNIX. So they had to develop an entire system to express queries. Therefore SQL is *another whole system* to learn, with no use outside of itself.

Scientific studies show that SQL commands are very difficult for users to write correctly. If you do not know SQL, do not bother to learn it. It is more difficult to use and not as powerful as **/rdb** and UNIX. For example, the SQL commands only work on database files, while UNIX commands work on any file on the system. Getting away from these walls that stand between our data is very important. In fact, it was the principal reason databases were developed. This idea goes under the name *integrated* and *modeless* software.

But if you have already learned SQL, here is a conversion table from SQL queries to **/rdb** queries:

```
SQL                              UNIX and /rdb
------------------------------   ---------------------------
select col1 col2 from filename   column col1 col2 < filename
where column = expression        row 'column == expression'
compute column = expression      compute 'column = expression'
group by                         subtotal
having                           row
order by column                  sorttable column
unique                           uniq
count                            wc
nesting                          pipes "|"
insert, update and delete        editors, forms software, etc.
```

17.2 dBASE: How to talk dBASE to /rdb

dBASE II™ and dBASE III™ is a another database system. It was developed and is marketed by Ashton Tate. You can use a program like **dBx** from Desktop Ai, to convert from dBase II and III to the C programming language, which you can compile on a UNIX or DOS computer. Or you can convert the dBase commands to UNIX and **/rdb** queries. This table shows corresponding commands in the two systems.

```
dBASE Commands
        UNIX and /rdb commands

ACCEPT Comment TO Variable
        echo Comment ; read Variable
APPEND BLANK
        echo >> Fileout
APPEND FROM Filename FOR Condition
        row 'Condition' < Filename >> Fileout
BROWSE
        pg, more, cat, vi, ve, update, any editor, etc.
CANCEL
        DEL (any character set with stty)
CHANGE Range FIELD Fieldname FOR Condition
        compute 'Range && Condition {Fieldname = Value}' < Filein
CLEAR
CLEAR GETS
        clear, or tput clear on System 5.2
CONTINUE
        continue  (shell statement)
COPY TO Filename FIELD Fieldnames FOR Condition
        row 'Condition' < Filein | column Fieldnames > Filename
COUNT FOR Condition TO Variable FOR Condition
        row 'Condition' < Filein | tail +3 | wc -l
CREATE Filename
        > Filename ; vi Filename ; ve Filename ; cmd > Filename
DELETE RECORD Number
        (sed $NUM+1}q Filename ; tail +$NUM+3}) > tmp; mv tmp Fieldname
DELETE NEXT Number
DELETE ALL
        sed 2q Filename > tmp ; mv tmp Filename
DELETE NEXT Number FOR Condition
DELETE FILE Fieldname
        > Filename
DISPLAY Range FOR Bedingung Field OFF
        row 'Range && Dedingung' < Filename | column Fieldnames
DISPLAY STRUCTURE
        for I in * do sed 2q; done
DISPLAY MEMORY
        df ; du
DISPLAY FILES ON Disk LIKE Datatype
        ls *Datatype ; ls Disk/*Datatype
) Program
        Program
CASE Condition
        Condition) (shell case statement)
OTHERWISE
        *) (shell case statement)
DO WHILE Condition CR ENDDO
        while Condition CR do done
EDIT
        vi, ve, update, ex, ed, other editors and commands
ECT
ENDDO
        do (in shell while, until, for statements)
```

```
ERASE
        clear
FIND Text
        /Text (in vi, ve, update)
INDEX ON Fieldname TO Filename
        index Filename Fieldname ...
USE Filename INDEX Keyfield
        search Filename Keyfield
INPUT Text To Variable
        Variable=Text
INSERT
        sed ${NUM}q Filename; echo $RECORD; tail +$NUM Filename
JOIN TO Filename FOR Condition FIELDS Fieldnames
        jointable Filename1 Filename2
        row 'Condition' < Filename2 | jointable Filename1 -
        column Fieldnames < Filename2 | jointable Filename1 -
Column,Row SAY Comment GET Variable PICTURE
        tput Column ; tput Row ; echo Comment ; READ Variable
GO
GOTO
GO RECORD n
        ve nG
GO Fieldname
        ve /
GO TOP
        ve H
GO BOTTOM
        ve L
IF Condition Statement2 ELSE Statement2 ENDIF
        if Condition then Statement1 else Statement2 fi
LOCATE FOR Condition
        row 'Condition' < Filename
LOOP
        while, until, for (shell statements)
MODIFY STRUCTURE
        column New Fieldnames < Filename
NOTE
REMARK
        : Old Comment
        # New Comment
MOVE Old-Filename TO New-Filename
        mv Old-Filename New-Filename
REPLACE Range Fieldname WITH Expression FOR Condition
        compute 'Fieldname = Expression' < Filename
        compute 'Range && Condition {Fieldname = Expression}' < Filename
REPORT Form FOR Condition TO PRINT
        report Form < Filename
        row 'Condition' < Filename | report Form | print
PACK
        pack, unpack (UNIX)
QUIT
        Ctrl-d
READ
        read Variable
RECALL Condition
        row 'Condition' < Filename
RELEASE Variable
        Variable=
RESET
RESTORE FROM Filename
```

```
RETURN
        return (shell)
SAVE TO Filename
SELECT
        row, column, etc.
SET
        set (shell)
SKIP
SORT ON Fieldname TO Filename
        sorttable Fieldname > Filename
STORE Expression TO Variable
        Variable=`Expression`
SUM Fieldname TO Variable FOR Condition
        Variable=`row 'Condition' < Filename | column Fieldname`
TOTAL ON Keyfield TO Filename FIELDS Fieldnames FOR Condition
        row 'Condition' | subtotal Keyfield Fieldnames > Filename
UPDATE FROM Filename ON Keyfield
        update, vi, ve, replace, append, delete, etc.
USE Filename
        cmd < Filename
WAIT
        wait (shell)
@ Row,Column SAY expression
        cursor Row Column; echo EXPRESSION
        ve screen and validation file
```

The UNIX programs **awk**, **sh**, **expr**, **bc**, **test**, etc., handle many of the functions of dBASE.

17.3 R:base: How to talk R:base to UNIX and /rdb

R:base 4000 and 5000 are database management systems developed by Microrim, Inc. The R:base series is *another whole system* to learn. But if you have already learned R:base, here is a conversion table to UNIX and **/rdb** queries:

```
R:base Commands
        UNIX and /rdb equivalents
*(
        # comment
APPEND table1 TO table2 WHERE conditions
        row 'conditions' < table1 > table2
ASSIGN column TO value IN table WHERE conditions
        compute 'conditions { column = "value" }' < table
BREAK
        break
BUILD KEY FOR column IN table
        index [-m[bhirs]] table column
CHANGE column TO value IN table WHERE conditions
        compute 'conditions { column = "value" }' < table
CHANGE COLUMN columnold TO columnnew datatype length
        rename columnold columnnew < table > tmp ; mv tmp table
CHDIR or CD drive path
        cd path
CHDRV
        not appropriate
```

```
CHECK/NOCHECK
        not appropriate
CHKDSK drive
        df drive
CHOOSE variable FROM menu IN file
        menu
CLEAR variable / CLEAR ALL VARIABLES
        VARIABLE=
CLOSE
        not appropriate
COLOR
        see prelude plot graphics
COMPUTE variable AS option column FROM table WHERE conditions
        row 'conditions' < table | math -option column
COMPUTE ALL column FROM table WHERE conditions
        row 'conditions' < table | math -alloptions column
COMPUTE variable AS ROWS FROM table
        VARIABLE='tail +3 table | wc -l'
COMPUTE COUNT column FROM table WHERE conditions
        select 'conditions' < table | total column
COMPUTE SUM column FROM table WHERE conditions
        row 'conditions' < table | column column | total column | tail -1
COPY file1 file2
        cp file1 file2
DELETE DUPLICATES FROM table
        uniq table > tmp ; mv tmp table
DELETE KEY FOR column IN table
        rm table.[bhirs]
DELETE ROWS FROM table WHERE conditions
        row '!(conditions)' < table > tmp ; mv tmp table
DELETE ROWS FROM table WHERE variable FAILS
        row 'variable != "" ' < table > tmp ; mv tmp table
DIR
        ls
DISPLAY
        cat
DRAW
        cat draw escape sequences
EDIT column FROM table SORTED BY column WHERE conditions
        ve
EDIT USING form SORTED BY column WHERE conditions
        ve
EDIT VARIABLE variable USING form RETURN key
        ve
END
        exit
ENTER form FROM file FOR n ROWS
        ve
ENTER VARIABLE variable USING form RETURN key
        ve
ERASE file
        rm file
EXIT
        exit
EXPAND table WITH column datatype length
        column 'sed 1q table' column < table > tmp ; mv tmp table
FILL/NOFILL
        no loading and no null character
FILLIN variable USING "message" AT row column
        cursor row column ; echo "message"FORMS file
        vi file
```

```
GOTO
        use control structures instead of goto and label
HELP command
        info command
        whatis command
IF condition THEN command1 ELSE command2 ENDIF
        if test condition then command1 else command2 if
INPUT file
         file
INTERSECT table1 WITH table2 FORMING table3 USING column
        jointable -j column table1 table2 > table3
JOIN table1 USING column1 WITH table2 USING column1 FORMING table3
        jointable -j1 column1 -j2 column2 table1 table2 > table3
LABEL label
        use control structures instead of goto and label
LINES

LIST table
        cat table
LOAD table WITH PROMPTS FROM file USING column
        enter table
MKDIR drive path directory
        mkdir path/directory
MOVE n FROM variable1 AT position1 TO variable2 AT position2
        use compute substr and split
NEWPAGE
        tput clear      # clear screen of TERM terminal
        echo ^L         # printer
NEXT #n variable

OPEN database
        unnecessary,  perhaps cd to different directory
OUTPUT device1 TO device2
        1> /dev/device2
OWNER password
        user chmod, chown, chgrp, passwd, etc.
PACK database
        compress < database > tmp ; mv database
PASSWORDS
        user chmod, chown, chgrp, passwd, etc.
PAUSE
        read PAUSE  # ignore PAUSE
PRINT reportform SORTED BY column WHERE conditions
        row 'conditions' < table | sort column | report reportform
PROJECT tablenew FROM tableold USING column... SORTED BY sortcolumn...
        WHERE conditions
        row 'conditions' < tableold | sorttable sortcolumn... |
column column...
PROMPT command
        prompt command
QUIT TO file
        exec file
REEDIT file
        ve
RELOAD database
        compress, rmblanks
REMOVE table
        rm table
REMOVE COLUMN column FROM table
        column `sed 1q table | sed "s/column//"` < table
```

```
RENAME file newfile
        mv file newfile
RENAME COLUMN column to newcolumn IN table
        rename column newcolumn < table > tmp ; mv tmp table
RENAME OWNER password TO newpassword
        passwd, chown, chgrp
RENAME TABLE table TO newtable
        mv table newtable
REPORTS report
        report report
RETURN
        exit
RMDIR drive path directory
        rmdir path/directory
RUN command IN procedurefile USING parameter...
        command parameter...
OUTPUT PRINTER WITH SCREEN
        | tee PRINTER # where PRINTER is /dev/lp
OUTPUT SCREEN
        > /dev/tty
SELECT column ... FROM table
        column column ... < table
SELECT column ... FROM table WHERE conditions
        row 'conditions' < table | column column ...
SELECT ALL FROM table WHERE LIMIT = number
        sed <number>q table
SELECT ALL FROM table WHERE column GE date
        row 'variable >= date' < table > tmp
SELECT ALL FROM table WHERE variable EXISTS
        row 'variable != "" ' < table > tmp
SET DATE MMM/DD/YYYY
        set `date` ; echo $2/$3/$6
SET ECHO
        set -xv
SET NULL
        NULL=ON NULL=OFF
SET ERROR VARIABLE variable
        variable=errorcode
SET POINTER variable FOR table SORTED BY column WHERE condition
        index, sort, row
SET VARIABLE variable type
        variable=        # no typing
SET VARIABLE variable TO value
        VARIABLE=value          # make variables uppercase
SHOW variable
        echo $VARIABLE
SHOW ERROR variable AT row column
        cursor row column ; echo $VARIABLE
SHOW VARIABLES
        set
SORTED BY column =A | =D
        sorttable -r column
SUBTRACT table1 FROM table2 FORMING table3 USING columns
        difference table1 table2 | column columns > table3
TABLES: table WITH column
        cat column... > table
TALLY column FROM table WHERE conditions
        row 'conditions' < table | column column | sorttable | uniq -c
TYPE file
        cat file
```

```
UNION table1 WITH table2 FORMING table3 USING column
        union table1 table2 > table3, jointable -j column
UNLOAD DATA FOR table
        cat data
UNLOAD DATA FOR table USING column AS format SORTED BY sortcolumn
        WHERE conditions
        row 'conditions' < table | sorttable sortcolumn
USER password
        passwd password
WHILE conditions THEN command... ENDWHILE
        while conditions do command ... done
WRITE "message" AT row column
        cursor row column ; echo "message"
WRITE VARIABLE AT row column
        cursor row column ; echo $VARIABLE
```

18. Installation: How to set up /rdb

18.1 Step 1: tar from Tape, Floppy or Cassette

Your first decision is where do you want the **/rdb** directory to go. The old system is to put it under *usr*. The new approach at AT&T Bell Labs is to have directories under the root (/). Let's assume you are putting it under *usr* (you can put it anywhere). First, go to the directory of your choice:

```
$ cd /usr
```

You may need to be the super user (root). Change to super user like this:

```
$ su
Passwd:
```

Type the super user password here (it will not echo). Now make the *rdb* directory, and get into it:

```
$ mkdir rdb
$ cd rdb
```

Insert the **/rdb** floppy disk, or mount tape or cassette onto your system. Then **tar** the software package from your floppy, tape or cassette. The UNIX command **tar** may already know the name of your tape drive. If so, you need only type:

```
$ tar xv
```

tar is the UNIX tape archive program. *xv* are options. Note it is not '-*xv*'. *x* means extract from the tape and *v* means verbose. *v* will print out each file as it copies it. If the **tar** command runs successfully, the *rdb* directory will consist of several files and directories:

.profile	- profile to set shell variables
DATE	- date this copy way copied to media
Menu	- installation menu
Makefile	- installation make file
bin	- the /rdb programs in binary or shell scripts
demo	- the /rdb sample tables and lists for you to play with
man	- the /rdb manual pages in Unix "man" format before "nroff"
lib	- the /rdb library of C interface programs and other goodies
ve	- the ve help files

If you get source code:

```
src       - the /rdb c programs and col routines source code
shell     - shell programs
ve/src    -the ve source code
```

If the **tar** previous command gives you an error indicating that there is no tape drive, you may have to find out the name of your device driver for your floppy, tape or cassette. You can list all of the device names by typing:

```
$ ls /dev
```

For example, on the VAX-780 with BSD 4.1, the single-sided, single-density floppy (inside the cabinet at the bottom) is named */dev/floppy*. To **tar** from it you type:

```
$ tar xvf /dev/floppy
```

The *f* after *xv* means the device driver name follows. The */dev/floppy* is that name.

The Compaq 286 with Venix System 5.2 from Venturcom calls its floppy: */dev/f0*. It also has */dev/f0.40.d.9,* etc, for 40 track, double density, 9 sectors. But it defaults to the floppy, so you only need to type:

```
$ tar xv
```

Another example, on the PC/IX, Codata and the Cyb computers, the double sided, double density floppy device driver is named */dev/rfd0*. To tar from these floppies type:

```
$ tar xvf /dev/rfd0
```

If you get your **/rdb** files from another computer with a **cu** or **uucp** command, then you will have one or more *tarfiles*. You can **tar** them by typing:

```
$ tar xvf tarfile
```

18.2 Step 2: Change Path Name

Before you can execute any of your new **/rdb** commands, you must set up your *PATH* shell variable, (or *path* on the cshell), so that UNIX can find these new commands.

When you type the **/rdb** commands, you want the UNIX shell to know where the commands are. This is done by adding the path to your directory *rdb/bin* to your current *PATH* variable in your environment.

For example, if the path to your **/rdb** is */usr/rdb,* and you have the regular Bourne or Bell shell (**sh** with a prompt of $), you could type:

```
$ PATH=:/bin:/usr/bin:/usr/rdb/bin
$ export PATH
```

or if you have other *bin*'s in your *PATH*, you might try:

```
$ PATH=$PATH:/usr/rdb/bin
$ export PATH
```

or if you have put **/rdb** somewhere other than under */usr,* try:

```
$ cd bin
$ PATH=$PATH:`pwd`
$ export PATH
```

The **pwd** is your *present working directory.* Since you **cd**'ed down into bin, it will be the complete path name of the *rdb/bin*. The output of **pwd** will be written on the command line in place of '**pwd**'. You might want to try this and test some of the commands. You can go to the *rdb/demo* directory. It has tables that you can try out the commands on.

However, when you logout, your *PATH* will revert to its old ways. So, you need to do something more permanent. You can add the *PATH* and **export** commands above to your *.profile* in your home directory. Then it will be set each time you login. A sample *.profile* is included. You can edit it for your situation and copy (**cp**) it to your home directory.

If you use the cshell, **csh,** you will want to put the following line in the *.login* file in your home directory.

```
% set path=(. /bin /usr/bin /usr/rdb/bin)
```

However, this only works for you. If you want others to have automatic access to **/rdb,** you will have to add these lines to their *.profile* or *.login* files. Or, better still, you can make the **/rdb** commands available to everyone on your computer by adding the preceding lines to the file */etc/profile*. This file is looked at first by the shell when logging everyone in.

```
Shell Prompt File    Line to add
----- ------ -------- ------------------------------------
sh    $      .profile PATH=:/bin:/usr/bin:/usr/rdb/bin
                      export PATH
csh   %      .login   set path=(. /bin /usr/bin /usr/rdb/bin)
```

If you have other directories you want searched, you can add them.

18.3 Step 3: Set RDB Environment Variable

Add the following lines to your *.profile:*

```
RDB=/usr/rdb
export RDB
```

or the following to your *.cshrc* file:

```
setenv RDB /usr/rdb
```

Of course, if **/rdb** resides somewhere other than */usr/rdb,* change the preceding lines to reflect its actual location.

18.4 Step 4: Source Installation (If you have source code)

If you need to compile the source code on your computer and you have **tar**'ed in the source directory along with the other **/rdb** directories, then you can make, install and test by simply typing:

```
$ Menu
                     /rdb Installation Menu
Number  Name    For
-------  ------  ---------------------------------------------------------
0        exit    leave menu or return to higher menu
1        all     make all programs
2        5.2-286 8088, 8086, 286: IBM AT, Compaq,etc: split i-d
3        a5-286  AT&T: 286: AT compatible; split i-d
4        x5-286  Xenix V-286: IBM, Compaq, etc: split i-d: sick make
5        x3-286  Xenix III-286: IBM, Compaq, etc: split i-d: sick make
6        68000   68000 computer
7        3B2     AT&T: 3B2 computer: floating point software: -f
8        x6300   AT&T: 6300 Olivetti: xenix and venix: split i and d: -i
9        pdp11   DEC: pdp-11: split i and d space: -i
10       v3-pc   Venix System III on IBM PC/XT
11       pcix-xt INTERACTIVE PC/IX on IBM PC/XT and SCI-1000
12       4.1bsd  Berkeley BSD 4.1
13       4.2bsd  Berkeley BSD 4.2

20       clean   remove all object, temporary, etc files
Please enter a number or name for the action you wish or DEL to exit:
```

Then select your system from the menu. Hopefully, it will compile and install correctly. If not, you have lots of examples and can edit in an entry for your system. While testing your own version, you can type:

```
$ make
```

You can examine the *Makefile* to see what **make** will do. **make** will first compile the col routines in the col directory, and will then link the object files (*.o) to the *rdb/src/c* directory. **make** will then compile the files in the rdb/src/c directory. **make** will install by moving the binary programs to the *rdb/bin* directory. Then **make** will copy all of the shell directory's shell files to *rdb/bin* and change their mode (chmod) to executable. Finally, **make** will run the **testall** and the **testsearch** programs in the *demo* directory and report any **diff**'erences with the old test results.

18.5 Summary

Following is a list of all of the new directories and special files that **/rdb** will create (assuming you **tar**'ed while in */usr/rdb).*

```
/usr/rdb
/usr/rdb/bin
/usr/rdb/demo
/usr/rdb/man
/usr/rdb/lib
/usr/rdb/ve
```

Add new line to */etc/profile*, or *.profile* or *.login* file. For **sh** shell:

```
$ PATH=:/bin:/usr/bin:/usr/rdb/bin
$ RDB=/usr/rdb
$ export PATH RDB
```

For **csh** shell:

```
% set path=(. /bin /usr/bin /usr/rdb/bin)
% setenv RDB /usr/rdb
```

19. /rdb Commands

19.1 Features

Feature	Description
UNIX compatible	UNIX commands, standard I/O, pipes, shell scripts, etc.
flat ASCII files	readable by UNIX commands and people, not binary
powerful	full power of UNIX and /rdb commands working together
simple	easy to enter data and easy to get data out
inexpensive	one of the lowest priced database systems for UNIX
portable	written in portable C, is running on over 40 computers
micro to super	runs on computers from the IBM XT to CRAY2 supercomputer
zero load time	no need for time consuming 'loading' of the database
easy data entry	can use any text editor, forms package, or program
query language	UNIX command queries with full access to your data
report writer	produce any kind of report easily
menu	powerful and easy to use shell menu
form entry	create screen forms for data entry
lock and unlock	lock from whole file, to record, to single byte
views	easily create queries, use by simply typing their names
mail label	easily produce mailing labels selected and sorted
form letters	easily produce form letters to selected destination
cashflow	compute cash flow table to manage your cash flow
many utilities	useful utility commands to help you manage your data
fully relational	all the power of relational algebra and calculus
file compression	minimum file size to save space, execution time
data validation	easy to use and extremely powerful validation
fast access	get record in a file of over 20,000 in less than 3 sec.
many methods	hash, binary, record, indexed and sequential methods
help facility	six programs to help the user
secure	full UNIX file permissions, password access and encrypt
distributed data	files can be anywhere, can be networked together
backup facility	UNIX file backup facility
audit trail	UNIX diff and SCCS programs for complete file history
programmable	commands accessible by both UNIX shell, C, others
C interface	C access to 'system' call and same routines /rdb calls
partial string	can find string patterns (regular expressions)
variable length	both records and fields are variable length
decentral access	no centralized access bottleneck
dynamic buffers	to handle large tables, records and fields
system limits	UNIX, awk and hardware limit rows and columns, not /rdb
huge files	the only limit is the size of your available disk space

19.2 Most Important Commands

Command	Description
column	project columns of a table in any order
row	select rows by logical conditions including regular expressions
jointable	joins two tables together on a common key column
compute	calculates columns as a function of almost any equation
sorttable	like UNIX™ sort, but knows about /rdb™ tables
total	sums columns
subtotal	subtotals columns
ve	vi like form input screen editor with scores of functions
report	report writer: reports, invoices, labels, form letters, etc.
menu	display menu screen and perform any action selected
screen	easily create form input screen shell programs
validate	check data in table and print helpful messages
search	fast access methods: record, binary, inverted, sequential, hash
lock	lock and unlock byte to multi-records for multi-user access
cashflow	keep track of your cash flow
tax	find tax in a tax table
translate	convert from one language to another

19.3 Commands Grouped by Function

AI	Artificial Intelligence, Logic, Prolog Interface
not	logical not reverses return status of command
searchtree	find path from root to goal in tree table
tabletofact	converts table format to prolog fact file format
tabletorule	converts table format to prolog rule file format

Business	Business and Accounting Programs
cashflow	compute balance column of cash table
explode	find all children of parent
tax	compute tax from income and tax table

Conversion	Convert Table and List Formats
tabletolist	converts a file from table to list format
listtotable	for converting from list to table format
tabletotbl	converts /rdb table to nroff/tbl table format

Database	Basic Data Base Commands: Project, Select, Join
column	display columns of a table in any order (project)
compute	calculates columns of a table
jointable	joins two tables into one where keys match
row	outputs selected rows (select)

Date	Date Conversions and Calculations
computedate	adds the date plus given number of days
gregorian	convert column of dates for math and format change
julian	convert column of dates for math and format change
todaysdate	output the current date in the format: 890415

Fast Access	Get and Put Records Fast In Large Tables
append	add row to table and update index tables
blank	replaces all data in a record with spaces
delete	blank record and update index file
hashkey	returns the hash offset for key strings
index	set up table for search by access methods
pad	adds extra spaces at end of last column
replace	put a record into a file at specified location
search	search indexed table by access methods
seek	returns the offset and size of a record

Help	User Help Commands
commands	describes /rdb commands
helpme	lists the help commands available
howmany	displays the number of commands in a directory
rdb	lists all /rdb programs in rdb/bin directory
whatis	displays the command description and syntax
whatwill	displays the commands with function in description
yourprog	one line description of yourprog goes here

Input	Programs for Inputing Data into the Database
ask	prompts questions, validates and writes answerlist
clear	clears the crt terminal screen
cursor	moves the cursor to the row and column requested
enter	adds rows to a table or list file without an editor
menu	root menu with some UNIX commands
screen	converts form into screen input shell program
termput	get terminal capability from /etc/termcap file
update	displays and edits records in any sized file
update.inv	multiuser update with screen form and record locking
update.sh	update table with blank record locking

Locking	From File to Record to Byte Locking for Multi-user Access
lock	locks a record of field of a file
unlock	unlocks a record or field of a file
vilock	locks a table before vi and unlocks afterwards

Mailing Lists	Print Labels and From Letters from Mailing Lists
label	for printing mailing labels from a mailing list
letter	prints form letters from a mailing list
report	writes reports using a form and a table

Math Stat	Perform Math on Tables
maximum	displays the maximum value in each column selected
mean	displays the mean (average) of each column selected
minimum	displays the minimum of each column selected
precision	displays the precision of each column selected
subtotal	outputs the subtotal of columns in a table
total	sums up each column selected and displays
width	displays the width of each column selected

Output	Report Writing Programs
report	writes reports using a form and a table
reportwriter	sample program to produce standard reports

Relational Theory	Advanced Theory Programs
difference	outputs table of rows that are in only one table
fd	tests for functional dependency of columns

| intersect | outputs table of rows that are in both input tables |
| union | appends tables together |

Translation	Language Translation
translate	word for word substitution using translation files
tabletom4	converts table format to m4 define file format
tabletosed	converts table format to sed file format
uniondict	combines three tables into translate dictionary
word	converts text file to list of unique words

Utilities	Useful Programs for Any Files
ascii	returns the ascii value of any character
cap	converts first letter of each word to uppercase
chr	outputs the character corresponding to number
cpdir	copies one directory tree to another directory
filesize	returns the number of characters in a file
length	returns the length of its argument or input file
lowercase	returns the lowercase of its argument or input file
padstring	add bytes to string
paste	outputs two or more tables sides by side
path	finds the full path of a command: /usr/rdb/bin/path
prompt	echo string without newline
rmcore	remove all core files to free up space on the disk
see	displays non-printing as well as printing characters
substitute	replace old string with new string in files
trimblank	remove leading and trailing blanks
tset	return the termcap entry for TERM terminal
uppercase	returns the uppercase of its argument or input file

Utilities Database	Useful Programs for Table and List Files
compress	squeezes out all leading and trailing blanks
display	writes table or list file to standard out
headoff	removes the head from both table and list files
insertdash	insert dash line as second line in table
justify	left and right justifies the columns of a table
listtosh	list format to shell variable
number	insert a column row number in a table or list
record	return record of given number
rename	change column name in headline
rmblank	removes blank rows from the input table
schema	list database dictionary from tables
sorttable	sorts a table by one or more columns
splittable	divide table in smaller tables
structtotable	struct to table
tabletostruct	table to C struct
testall	tests all /rdb programs in demo directory
testsearch	test the fast access methods in demo directory
timesearch	times the fast access methods in demo directory
trim	squeezes a table for printing
widest	return width of each column

Validation	Data Validation
check	reports any rows in which columns do not match head
domain	displays invalid values in a column
validate	finds invalid data and prints messages

20. Case Study: /act^{TM} Accounting

This is a case study of **/act,** a business operations and accounting system for a small business. It is a model, that can be copied and edited to computerize a company. It has menus, forms, database tables, and shell programs all set up for you. The source code is listed after each **/act** shell program manual page included in the following **/rdb** manual. It shows how easy it is to computerize your business with the UNIX tools approach and helps you get started by showing you a lot of examples.

/act covers both operations and accounting of a simple business.

1. Operations are the activities of a business such as manufacturing, figuring out what to purchase, keeping track of inventory, taking sales orders, and so forth. It is what the business does.

2. Accounting includes the general ledger, financial statements, tax forms, accounts receivable and payable, inventory, and payroll. It keeps track of how the business is doing.

This system integrates both functions so that the operations automatically update the journals of the accounting system. The whole company is computerized with the same system so that all of the data for the company are in the same database and accessible by UNIX shell scripts and **/rdb** database commands.

The I Hate Accounting Book

Whatever your business is, the part you probably hate the most is the accounting side. You want to do the exciting purpose of the business, not get caught up in the boring paper work and annoying government forms. We felt the same way, so we computerized all that stuff in order to get on to the fun part of our businesses.

For Beginner and Expert in Business and Computers

This tutorial will show you how to run a business with a computer. Whether you are new to both business and computing, or have great experience in both, the tutorial and the software system it describes should be easy for you to understand.

If you are just starting, this tutorial is simple to understand and use. If you have computer experience, you will find UNIX and these software tools an enormous improvement over what has come before. We are going through a revolution in computing in both hardware and software. Hardware is getting so cheap that every business, corporate department, research lab, university and college department, government office, yes, even every individual can have great computing power. UNIX allows one to accomplish a great deal without the difficult, tedious and error prone programming that other systems require. One can accomplish in minutes and hours on UNIX, what takes days and weeks on other systems to accomplish.

20.1 Model Business

The best way to setup a system is to start with an example. The next few chapters take you though the operations and accounting of a small business, called Makeapile, Inc. It is a model business that is easy to understand and also easy to extend to any real business. This example system has been deliberately kept simple so that it can be understood. But the system can be copied to a new directory in your computer and modified to handle your own business.

All businesses are different. Some are large and some are small. Some do manufacturing, some just buy and sell, some sell services instead of goods. As such, some businesses may not need all of the modules in our model system while others will want to expand and modify them to fit their business.

With a simple text editor, you can change the name of our model company to your company's name, change the dates of the accounting period, add your company's data to the tables, and modify and add new menus, tables and shell programs to suit your needs. Soon your business will be computerized with a custom system.

20.2 Tools to Grow with Rather than an Inflexible System

The editing never stops because you will always want more. Your business will grow and change, people will come and go. It is the constant change of business that makes a hard coded computer system so unacceptable.

Most systems that we can buy, or develop, are hard to change. They try to force all businesses into a tight mold. These systems look good at first. They seem to have done everything for us. But as you study them closely and work with them, you soon find that modifying them is painful or impossible. You try to get help and find that even for experts, it is very difficult, time consuming, and expensive to make the changes you need.

Dr. Brad J. Cox, in his book *Object Oriented Programming*, [Cox 1986], writes: *In fact, software systems are usually the least responsive element in many organizations today. The organization as a whole is able to adapt more fluidly than the software upon which it has grown dependent.*

We have been down that road in the past, which is why we insist on the flexible approach. Change is the constant of any business. The business changes, the people change, the people want different things from their computer system. Furthermore, computerizing anything is a learning experience. No one knows it all at the beginning. We learn from the early systems we set up that we must be able to modify the software easily. The system described here is aimed at being easy to change. Changes that might take weeks or months or even be impossible to make in other systems can be made within hours or minutes in this one using any text editor.

20.3 Speaking from Experience

The authors have each been in the computer business for 20 years or more. We have both consulted for large organizations, and run small successful businesses. I have seen this problem of change so many times. In the early years it was the big corporations that spent mega-bucks on computing. They went through this cycle of buying fixed packages, or developing them in-house, and then trying to use and modify them. We spent many years working in that environment. Even though it created lots of work for us, it seemed so terribly wasteful.

When we started our own businesses, we looked at leading accounting packages for microcomputers. We found that half of the functions we needed were missing, and were difficult to add. And that half the data the packages forced us to enter were useless to our business. The whole approach was an ancient, 1950-60's way of handling the processing. Transactions files updated a master file in batch mode, instead of the interactive, time-shared, multi-user, immediate-access system that we needed.

We had already fallen in love with UNIX because it offered an easy solution. We added tools to UNIX for my own consulting work. They were so easy to use that we decided to make them available to everyone trying to computerize a company.

20.4 Access to Data

When data are put into the computer, two purposes are served. They are originally entered to produce some standard report such as income statement, tax form, invoice, bill-of-material, paychecks, and so on. However, with all of that data in a database, the management can ask a multitude of different questions and get understandable tables, forms, and graphs back. Suddenly, the company is understandable. The data are not lost in piles of paper and long lines of file cabinets. They are alive. Having all of this information stored in a database for easy access by management can dramatically improve the operations of a business.

The presidents of small companies with a terminal on their desks, and this system, have more access to the company data than the presidents of giant companies that spend millions of dollars a year on computers and staff. People on the computer staff of the largest bank in the world, which spent billions of dollars on computing, once told us that they could not figure out whether the worldwide operations were making a profit or a loss, or what the assets and liabilities were!

Querying the database becomes a fascinating activity. Our experience is that everyone in the company has a different idea of what is going on, but that the numbers tell another story. We have had employees tell us that most of the inventory was of a certain type, and then the numbers showed that it was mostly of the opposite type. Employees have said that most of our customers were in one part of the country, when the numbers proved that they were somewhere else. Employees have been upset about problems that the data showed to be trivial, and yet they missed serious problems that the data revealed. Managing with information is a whole new experience. Fascinating, fun, and profitable. It also significantly reduces the anxieties of running a business. Now you can know, rather than guess and worry.

20.5 Shell Programming

All of this ease of setup and ease of change comes from using UNIX tools and shell programming. This is called a fourth generation programming language. It frees the developer and maintainer from a multitude of details that must be struggled with when using third generation languages like COBOL, PL/I, Fortran, Basic, C or

Pascal. A single line of UNIX shell code can often do what takes 100 lines of COBOL to do. Even more important, it is much easier to change one line than 100.

20.6 System Overview

To begin, let's look at an overview of a typical business.

```
$ Menu
                        Makeapile, Inc.
                Operations and Accounting System Overview
```

Owners	Managers	Employees
1 gl	6 opr	5 pay
General Ledger/Tax	Operations	Payroll
Update Journals	Manufacturing	Enter Hours
Make Financials	Bill of Materials	Compute Tax and Net
Print Financials	Print Bill-of-Mat	Print Pay Check Info
Calculate Tax Forms	Update Parts List	Print W2 Forms
2 sales	3 inv	4 pur
Accounts Receivable	Inventory	Accounts Payable
Enter Sale Order	Ship	Enter Purchase Ord.
Print Invoice	Print Invoice	Print Purchase Ord.
Enter Deposits	Backorder	Enter Checks
Create AR Ledger	Receive	Create AP Ledger
Print Statements	Print PO	Print Vendor State.
Update Customer	Fill Backorder	Update Vendor Table
Customers	Carriers	Vendors

Each box represents a different part of a typical business. In each box are some the basic functions performed in that system. Note that different people see the business from different points of view. The owners and the tax people see the general ledger and tax system. The customers see sales and accounts receivable, and so on.

You can copy this system and modify it to serve your own business. You can pick up only the modules that you want. For example, if you are a sole professional person, you will only need the general ledger and tax module (1 gl). If you buy and sell, you will need to add only the three modules: sales and accounts receivable (2 sales), inventory (3 inv), and purchasing and accounts payable (4 pur). If you decide to do your own payroll (5 pay) and manufacturing (6 opr), you will need the last two modules. A hospital or medical clinic does not do manufacturing, but its operations consist of patient records, admissions, scheduling, and medical programs to help doctors, nurses, and technicians do their jobs. These programs will replace the manufacturing programs in the *opr* operations module.

So we have gone around counterclockwise, picking up what we need. You can implement the computerization of your company this way also. Just do one module at a time. Let the organization settle down before starting the next module. It is like a snake eating a buffalo: eat and rest, eat and rest. Don't underestimate the human problems of changing an operation. If you are starting a new business, you can train everyone on the new system from the start.

20.7 Menus

This model system is delivered with menus, which list all of the functions, and allow you to execute the functions with as little as a single keystroke. You can execute the different programs by simply typing the name or number of the functions listed in the menu. However, to understand the workings of the system, you will be shown each of the programs at the UNIX command level. Once you understand them, you can use and modify menus. You can also train your operators to use menus. But you can always go back to the lower level to make changes, fix problems, and so on.

20.8 Simple Example

We are going to be showing you this system as if we are sitting together at a computer terminal. If you have the system, you can go to the general ledger directory (gl) and run all of the following examples.

When UNIX wants us to enter another command, it types a dollar sign prompt:

```
$ _
```

The underline is the cursor, the place where the next character you type goes on the screen. The prompt can be changed from a dollar sign to practically anything else, so it may be different on your computer. After the prompt you can type a command. One command we will use is **cat** to display a file:

```
$ cat filename
```

where filename is the name of the file we want to see. We will also type in other commands like **make.**

```
$ make
```

20.9 Manual

The following sections cover each module in turn. After this tutorial is a manual for all of the **/rdb** commands and many of the **/act** commands. It contains one or more pages of documentation for each program, in alphabetical order. Each manual page shows examples of each program and lists the source codes for all shell programs. It is aimed at the computer knowledgeable person who will maintain the system. This tutorial is aimed at the managers and operators of the business who will think about how to run the system.

20.10 gl - General Ledger and Tax System

The general ledger is the customary name for the system that keeps the general journals and ledgers of the company, and produces financial statements such as income statements and balance sheets, and fills in the appropriate tax form. This is the major concern of accountants and book keepers, but the information is vital to seeing how the business is doing. Every business, from a single consultant to a giant corporation, needs this module.

First, a quick sample of how this system works. Then a more detailed look at the steps that the computer takes to do all of this. I will show you how to set up your own books, how to modify the system, and how to troubleshoot. In other words, we are going top down, from big picture to details. First a very general overview of the system, then we will zoom in on the details later.

20.10.1 Quick Overview.

The general ledger system is very simple to use. You only need to enter your income and expenses into a couple of journals and the system will produce your financial statements, fill in your tax forms and calculate your taxes.

20.10.2 ji - journal income.

Let us begin by looking at a journal of income.

```
$ cat ji
Date      Amount   Account   Ref     Description
------    -------  -------   ------  -----------
860118   3286.66   income    c101    consulting
860125    250.00   royalty   c1459   book fees
```

ji is the short name for the journal of income. It is a file you edit with a text editor such as **vi,** or a form editor like **ve.** Note that we have five columns in this table. For each item of income (check, deposit, cash, and so on) we record five pieces of information. We need to know the date, amount, and a description of each item. The *Account* is a name for the account in which we want this item assigned. We will see the *chart* of accounts later which will show us the names of all of our accounts. You can change the accounts and their names as you wish with your text editor.

Ref is a reference to your paper documentation. It helps you find that scrap of paper you need to prove that this is a real income (or expense) item. In the case above it is the check number of the customer's check, which, along with the *Date* and *Amount,* should help you locate the item in your bank statements or box of receipts.

So you simply type in all of your income items into this file. If you have a large number of small items, they can be recorded in other journals, on or off the computer, and simply totaled and entered here as one item. We will see this when we discuss the accounts receivable and sales system. For example, if you do a thousand sales a day, just enter the total of the cash register receipts at the end of each day.

20.10.3 je - journal expense.

```
$ cat je
Date      Amount   Account   Ref     Description
------    -------  -------   ----    --------------------
860101      2.25   parking   r       parking at clients
860103     15.00   travel    c115    shuttle bus to airport
860104     12.93   travel    v       meal
860105     12.86   travel    c116    meal
860106    114.23   travel    r       hotel
```

Here we record all of our expenses, checks, credit cards, cash receipts, and so on.

This is our outgo. There is an old economics joke: *If your income does not keep up with your outgo, then your upkeep will be your downfall.*

These items should be the legitimate business expenses of your company. They are important as deductions which reduce your tax burden. Keeping good records can save you taxes — much more than computer hardware and software costs.

Of course, you will still have to keep all of your receipts to prove each of these items. Here, *Ref* is a reference to your own records, such as check books, credit cards receipts, bank statements, little paper receipts stuck away in envelopes named for months, or accounts, or whatever. They should be kept in such a way that by looking at the line of information in the journal, you can use the *Date,* or *Account,* or *Ref* information to find the physical receipt.

20.10.4 make

Now that you have these two journals created, just type:

$ make

make is a UNIX program that uses information in a file called *Makefile* to run all of the programs which create all of the ledgers, financial statements, and filled and calculated tax forms in the system. **make** will take from a few minutes to over an hour, depending upon how fast your computer is and and how big your journals are.

After **make** finishes, you can look at your statements and tax forms, and so on. In fact you can always see every file. In the next section we look at each of the programs that were called an the files they read and the files they produced.

20.10.5 Overview

Here is an overview of the general ledger and tax system:

```
                 getjournal
journalincome  | <---------- ji, je, ja, etc.
journalexpense |
journaldeposit |
journalcheck   | consolidate          post         foot
journalpay       --------------> journal ----> ledger ----> footed
journaladjust  ---|                             |
                 adjust                trial     |
adjustedtrial <-------- trialbalance <-----------
|  |  |  |
|  |  |  | income
|  |  |  ---------> incomestatement
|  |  |   balance
|  | -----------> balancesheet
|  |       close
| ---------------> journalnext
|      fillform              1120S.calc
-----------------> 1120S.filled -----------> 1120S
          edit               1040.calc
1040.blank -------> 1040.filled  -----------> 1040
```

Here is a list of files that you must create and maintain:

```
Table     Description
-------   -----------------------------------------------------------
ji        journal of income (deposits from accounts receivable)
je        journal of expense (checks from accounts payable)
ja        journal of adjustments for adjusted trial (inventory, etc.)
chart     chart of accounts (edit from time to time for your accounts)
1040      1040 tax form (input data including from business tax form)
```

Finally, a look at the programs we'll use and the input and output of each:

```
Programs      Input Tables                    Output Tables
-----------   -----------------------------   ---------------------
make          all                             all
consolidate   ji (income), je (expense)       journal
post          journal                         ledger
foot          ledger                          footed (ledger)
trial         ledger                          trialbalance
adjust        trialbalance, ja (adjustments)  adjustedtrial (balance)
income        adjustedtrial                   incomestatement
balance       adjustedtrial                   balancesheet
close         adjustedtrial                   jn - journal next period
fill(bus)     adjustedtrial, bustaxform       bustaxform.filled
calc(bus)     bustaxform.filled               bustaxform (1120,S,C)
calc(1040)    1040.filled                     1040
```

20.10.6 Menu.

```
Number    Name      For
-------   -------   ------------------------------------------------
0         exit      Return to Higher Menu
1         ov        Overview of General Ledger and Tax

2         ji        Enter and Edit Journal Income   (deposits)
3         je        Enter and Edit Journal Expenses (checks, pay)
4         ja        Enter and Edit Journal of Adjustments (inventory)
5         1040      Edit 1040 Tax Form
6         chart     Edit Chart of Accounts

7         make      Make All Financial Statements
8         show      Display Output of Make Command, All Programs
9         step      Menu of Individual Programs to Run Step by Step
10        print     Menu of Financial Statements to Print
```

20.10.7 Step 1: getjournal -> journalincome journalexpense journaladjust, ...

getjournal is a program that will create each of the journals. It will simply copy *ji* to *journalincome, je* to *journalexpense,* and *ja* to *journaladjust.* This keeps you from editing the official journal. If you mess it up, you can always get a copy of the official journal and start again.

getjournal also gets three more journals from the other modules of the business. It gets the *journaldeposit* from the *deposit* file in the accounts receivable system, the *journalcheck* from the *check* file in the accounts payable system (pur), and gets the value of current inventory from the inventory module (inv) and adds it to the *journaladjust.*

If you do not use these modules, you can turn off the feature by editing the *Makefile*.
But it is very nice to see all of the information being collected automatically for you.
You can run this system every hour of the day, if you want to know exactly where
you stand at all times. You will know more about your business than the heads of
the giant corporations that spend billions on computing. You can run this program
by simply typing:

```
$ getjournal
```

and it will get all of the journals, or you can name a specific journal you want:

```
$ getjournal journaldeposit
```

20.10.8 *Step 2:* `consolidate < journals > journal`

The next program is **consolidate.** It consolidates all of those journals (except *journaladjust* which comes in later) into the general journal named *journal*. Here is an
example of a journal.

```
$ cat journal
Date     Account     Debit    Credit   Ref       Description
------   ------     -------   -------   ------    --------------------
860101   4370          2                r         parking at clients
860103   4380         15                c115      shuttle bus to airport
860104   4380         13                v         meal
860105   4380         13                c116      meal
860106   4384        114                r         hotel
860118   3100                   3286    c101      consulting
860125   3080                    250    c1459     book fees
861231   1010                   5858              double entry
861231   1010      17036                          double entry
861231   3010                  13500    deposit   from sales/deposit
861231   4020       3601                check     from pur/check
861231   4030       2100                payroll   from pay/journalpay
```

A journal keeps every item sorted by date, whereas a ledger is sorted by account.
Otherwise they are the same. All of the items from all of the journals are here.

Note that we now have *Debits* and *Credits* columns. That means we now have a
double entry bookkeeping system. But we did not have to enter every item twice to
get it. We simply assume that every income item was put into the cash account and
every expenditure came out of cash. This is why we keep two journals, income and
expense, to make this trick work.

Note the two items with *Account* number *1010*. They are counterbalancing entries.
They debit all of the expenses to the cash account (1010) and credit all of the income
at once, so you do not have to do it yourself. When you need to do debit and credit
entries, you can use the *ja journaladjust* journal. Note also that we have the deposit
and check summary items from the sales and purchasing departments.

If you want to check to see if it is in balance, type:

```
$ total Debit Credit < journal
Date      Account    Debit    Credit   Ref     Description
------    ------     -------   -------  ------  -----------
                     20794     20794
```

Looks good, so let's go on.

20.10.9 Step 3: `post < journal > ledger`

The next step is to post the general journal to the general ledger with the **post** program.

```
$ post
ledger
Account   Date       Debit    Credit   PostRef  Name
-------   -------    -------   -------  -------  -------------------
                     20794     20794
```

Note the table named *ledger* after the **post** command. It is the totals of the ledger's *Debit* and *Credit* columns. Use this to check that your ledger is in balance before going to the next step. If it is not, go back and check the journals with standard accounting techniques. We will discuss these under troubleshooting later on.

To look at the whole ledger, **cat** it out, or use **more** or **pg** UNIX commands. Note that *ledger* is the same as *journal,* except that the *Account* and *Date* columns have been reversed and the whole file has been sorted on *Account*.

```
$ cat ledger
Account   Date      Debit    Credit   Ref       Short     Description
-------   ------    -----    ------   -------    -------   ------------
1010      861231             5858               cash      double entry
1010      861231    17036                       cash      double entry
3010      861231             13500    deposit   sales     from sales/deposit
3080      860125             250      c1459     royalty   book fees
3100      860118             3286     c101      income    consulting
4020      861231    3601              check     merch     from pur/check
4030      861231    2100              payroll   wages     from pay/journalpay
4370      860101    2                 r         parking   parking at clients
4380      860103    15                c115      travel    shuttle bus airport
4380      860104    13                v         travel    meal
4380      860105    13                c116      travel    meal
4384      860106    114               r         hotel     hotel
```

20.10.10 Step 4: `foot < ledger > footed`

You can foot this ledger with the **foot** program to produce the *footed* file. **foot** subtotals all of the entries per account. The accountants call this *footing.* Technically footing then subtracts the larger of *Debit* or *Credit* from the smaller. You don't have to do the footing. The trial program does its own footing from the ledger. The foot program is provided so you can get this listing for your own information.

```
$ foot
$ cat footed
Account   Date     Debit   Credit   Ref       Short     Description
-------   ------   -----   ------   -------   -------   -----------
1010      861231            1758               cash
1010      861231   5137                        cash
-------   ------   -----   ------   -------   -------   -----------
1010               5137    1758

3010                       1601     deposit   sales
-------   ------   -----   ------   -------   -------   -----------
3010                  0    1601

3080      860125             250     c1459     royalty   book fees
-------   ------   -----   ------   -------   -------   -----------
3080                  0     250

3100      860118            3286     c101      income    sales
-------   ------   -----   ------   -------   -------   -----------
3100                  0    3286

4020               1601              check     merch
-------   ------   -----   ------   -------   -------   ------------
4020               1601       0

4370      860101      2              r         parking   parking at clients
-------   ------   -----   ------   -------   -------   ------------------
4370                  2       0

4380      860103     15              c115      travel    shuttle bus
4380      860104     13              v         travel    meal
4380      860105     13              c116      travel    meal
4380      860106    114              r         travel    hotel
-------   ------   -----   ------   -------   -------   ------------------
4380                155       0
```

foot gives you an excellent view of your business. It shows you all of your items with their descriptions grouped together by account. You can see both the totals and the individual items. You get the big picture and the details in one listing. You can see where your money is coming from (yea) and where it is going to (boo). This is an important management tool for you. This is also the document you take to your IRS audits along with your paper receipts, so that you can find anything that is asked for.

20.10.11 *Step 5:* `trial < ledger > trialbalance`

The next step is to get your trial balance. It is like the footed ledger we just saw, but without the detail. To get your *trialbalance*, run **trial**.

```
$ trial
trialbalance
Account   Debit   Credit   Format   Taxline   Short     Name
-------   -----   ------   ------   -------   -------   -------------
          17036   17036
```

Looks like we are still in balance. Here is what *trialbalance* looks like.

```
$ cat trialbalance
Account   Debit    Credit   Format   Taxline   Short     Name
-------   -----    ------   ------   -------   -------   ----------------
1010      11178             B-A      4L01      cash      Cash
3010               13500    I-I      101a      sales     Sales
3080                 250    I-I      106       royalty   Gross royalties
3100                3286    I-I      108       income    Other Income
4020       3601             I-COGS   102-A2    merch     Misc Merchandise
4030       2100             I-COGS   102-A3    wages     Salary and Wages
4370          2             I-E      122       parking   Business parking
4380         41             I-E      122       travel    Business travel
4384        114             I-E      122       hotel     Business hotel
```

Note we just have the subtotals for each account. Also we have three new columns: *Format, Taxline,* and *Name.* These have been picked up from the chart of accounts (*chart*) which we will see later. The information in these columns will be needed for the financial statements and the tax forms, which in this case, is *1120S* for an s-corporation. A *Format* of *B-A* tells the *balance* program that the account goes to the balance sheet under assets. *Taxline* of *4L01* tells us to put this account on page four, schedule L, line 1 of our 1120S tax form.

20.10.12 Step 6: `adjust < trialbalance > adjustedtrial`

Now let's get an adjusted trial balance. But first we must look at *ja.* We talked about it earlier but now is the time to look at it closely.

```
$ cat ja
Account   Debit    Credit   Format   Taxline   Name
-------   -------  -------  -------   -------   --------------------
1110               20000    B-A      4L06      Beginning Inventory
1110         0              B-A      4L06      Ending Inventory
1310                  0     B-A      4L09a        Accum Depreciation
1330                  0     B-A      4L10a        Accum Depletion
1420                  0     B-A      4L12a        Accum Amortization
4010      20000            I-COGS   102-A3    Beginning Inventory
4080                  0    I-COGS   102-A4    Ending Inventory
4170         0             I-E      121       Depreciation
4180         0             I-E      118       Depletion
4215         0             I-E      122       Amortization
```

This is the journal in which you make what the accountants call adjustments. They are double entry, so you will have to put in each number twice, one under *Debit* and one under *Credit. ja* has been set up with zero entries. If you do not have values, just leave it zero, or remove it.

getjournal *journaladjust* will copy this *ja* file to the *journaladjust.* **getjournal** *inventory* will also copy *ja* to *journaladjust,* but will fill in the value of the inventory from the inventory department of the company.

```
$ getjournal inventory

$ cat journaladjust
Account     Debit     Credit    Format    Taxline    Name
-------     -------   -------   -------   -------    ---------------------
1110                   20000    B-A       4L06       Beginning Inventory
1110        22130               B-A       4L06       Ending Inventory
1310                       0    B-A       4L09a        Accum Depreciation
1330                       0    B-A       4L10a        Accum Depletion
1420                       0    B-A       4L12a        Accum Amortization
4010        20000               I-COGS    102-A3     Beginning Inventory
4080                   22130    I-COGS    102-A4     Ending Inventory
4170            0               I-E       121        Depreciation
4180            0               I-E       118        Depletion
4215            0               I-E       122        Amortization
```

Note that the total value of our inventory has been added in. You can do this by hand if you prefer. Then run the **adjust** program to get the *adjustedtrial.*

```
$ adjust
adjustedtrial
Account   Debit   Credit   Format   Taxline   Short    Name
-------   -----   ------   ------   -------   -------   -----------------
          39166   39166
```

Ok, our adjustments table hasn't thrown us out of balance. The *adjustedtrial* is the same as the *trialbalance,* except the adjustments have been pulled in. Let's look.

```
$ cat adjustedtrial
Account   Debit   Credit   Format   Taxline   Short    Name
-------   -----   ------   ------   -------   -------   -----------------
1010      11178            B-A      4L01      cash     Cash
1110       2130            B-A      4L03      inv      Inventory
1310          0            B-A      4L09a     adeprec    Accum Deprec
1330          0            B-A      4L10a     adeplet    Accum Deplet
1420          0            B-A      4L12a     aamort       Accum Amortiz
3010              13500    I-I      101a      sales    Sales
3080                250    I-I      106       royalty  Gross royalties
3100               3286    I-I      108       income   Other Income
4010      20000            I-COGS   102-A1    beginv   Begin Inventory
4020       3601            I-COGS   102-A2    merch    Misc Merchandise
4030       2100            I-COGS   102-A3    wages    Salary and Wages
4080              22130    I-COGS   102-A6    endinv   Ending Inventory
4170          0            I-E      117a      deprec   Depreciation
4180          0            I-E      118       deplet   Depletion
4215          0            I-E      122       amort    Amortization
4370          2            I-E      122       parking  Business parking
4380         41            I-E      122       travel   Business travel
4384        114            I-E      122       hotel    Business hotel
```

Getting pretty sick of this little company by now, heh? Well, hold on — we are about to see the bottom line.

20.10.13 Step 7: `income < adjustedtrial > incomstatement`

Now for the profits and losses: the **income** program shows your *incomestatement*.

```
$ income
Account   Debit    Credit   Format   Taxline   Short    Name
-------   -----    ------   ------   -------   -------   ------------------
4997               13308    B-LE                         Earnings (Profit)
```

Oh, goody. We made some money. Unfortunately, it looks like we were only making $1.82 an hour for all the time we put in. Now let's see the income statement.

```
$ cat incomestatement
       Makeapile, Inc.
     Income Statement
          1986

          13500    Sales
            250    Gross royalties
           3286    Other Income
-----    ------   -----------------------
          17036    Income


20000             Beginning Inventory
 3601             Misc Merchandise
 2100             Salaries and Wages
          22130    Ending Inventory
-----    ------   -----------------------
          -3571    Cost of Goods Sold


    0             Depreciation
    0             Depletion
    0             Amortization
    2             Business parking
   41             Business travel
  114             Business travel hotel
-----    ------   -----------------------
           -157    Expenses
-----    ------   -----------------------
          13308    Net Profit or Loss
```

You may notice that a new file has appeared in your directory named *profit* that holds the computed net profit or loss. It will be used by the **balance** program to produce the balance sheet.

```
$ cat profit
Account   Debit    Credit   Format   Taxline   Short    Name
-------   -----    ------   ------   -------   -------   ------------------
4997               13308    B-LE                         Earnings (Profit)
```

20.10.14 Step 8: `balance < adjustedtrial > balancesheet`

Now type **balance** to get a *balancesheet:*

```
$ balance
-----   ---------------------------
13308   Total Assets
-----   ---------------------------
13308   Total Liabilities and Equity
```

balance prints out the Assets and Liabilities and Equity so you can verify that all is in balance. **balance** also puts *profit* into the *adjustedtrial* ledger. If you want to rerun the **balance** program, be sure to go back and rerun *adjust* and *income* first. Otherwise you will get multiple entries of profit in the *adjustrial*. Let's look at the balance sheet.

```
$ cat balancesheet
        Makeapile, Inc.
        31 December 1986
          Balancesheet
 11178     Cash
  2130     Inventory
     0        Accumulated Depreciation
     0        Accumulated Depletion
     0        Accumulated Amortization
------     ---------------------------
 13308     Total Assets

 13308     Retained Earnings (Profit)
------     ---------------------------
 13308     Total Liabilities and Equity
```

20.10.15 Step 9: `close < adjustedtrial > journalnext`

Finally close the books with the **close** command:

```
$ close
Usage: close next-period-start-date (Example: close 820101)
```

Oops! This is one of the few general ledger programs that wants an argument passed to it. It wants to know the date for the new accounting period. **close** will put the date you give it into the *Date* column of the *journalnext* ledger. **close** needs the date in the format: YYMMDD (YY=year MM=Month DD=day). So let's give it 870101 (1 Jan 1987).

```
$ close 870101
Account   Date      Debit   Credit   Ref       Description
-------   -------   -----   ------   -------   ---------------
                    13308   13308
```

```
$ cat journalnext
Account   Date      Debit   Credit   Ref      Description
-------   -------   -----   ------   -------   ---------------
1010      860101    11178            jl        brought forward
1110      860101    2130             jl        brought forward
1310      860101    0                jl        brought forward
1330      860101    0                jl        brought forward
1420      860101    0                jl        brought forward
4997      860101            13308    jl        brought forward
```

This starts you off for the new accounting period. When you are all finished with doing the old period, save the old *journallast* by moving it to something like *journal860101*. Then move (UNIX **mv**) the *journalnext* table to *journallast*. From now on, the **post** command will pick it up each time it posts to the *ledger*. In other words, the new ledgers will be the *journallast* from last period and the journal entries from this accounting period.

20.10.16 Step 10: `fillform < adjustedtrial > 1120S.filled`

The *fillform* program fills in your business tax form from your *adjustetrial* balance. In this sample business we are an S corporation so we use form *1120S*.

```
$ fillform 1120S
```

Note we must tell the **fillform** command the name of the form we want to fill in.

20.10.17 Step 11: `1120S.calc < 1120S.filled > 1120S`

The 1120S.calc program calculates the 1120S tax form for us.

```
$ 1120S.calc
Taxline   Amount   Description
-------   ------   -------------------------------------
    124   13308    Net Profit or -Loss
```

It also gives us a summary of what our profit is. Now let's look at the filled and computed form.

```
$ cat 1120S
Taxline  Amount  Description
-------  ------  ------------------------------------
101a      13500  Sales
101b          0  Returns and Allowances
101c      13500  Net Sales
102           0  Cost of Goods Sold
102-A1    20000  Beginning Inventory
102-A2     3601  Misc Merchandise
102-A3     2100  Salaries and Wages
102-A4        0  Other Costs
102-A6    22130  Ending Inventory
103        9929  Gross Profit
104           0  Nonqualifying Interest and Dividends
105           0  Gross rents
106         250  Gross royalties
107           0  Net Gain Form 4797
108        3286  Other Income
109       13465  Income
110           0  Compensation of Officers
111a          0  Salary and Wages
111b          0  Salary and Wages Job Credits
111c          0  Salary and Wages Balance
112           0  Repairs
113           0  Bad Debt
114           0  Rent
115           0  Taxes
116a          0  Total deductible interest
116b          0  Interest on Sch. K and K-1
116c          0  Interest
117a          0  Depreciation from Form 4562
117b          0  Depreciation from Sch. A
117c          0  Depreciation
118           0  Depletion
119           0  Advertising
120           0  Retirement Plans
121           0  Cemployee Benefit Programs
122         157  Other Expenses
123         157  TOTAL deductions
124       13308  Net Profit or -Loss
125a          0  Excess net passive income tax
125b          0  Tax from Schedule D Part IV
125c          0  Add line 25a and 25b
126a          0  Tax deposited with Form 7004
126b          0  Federal tax fuels and oils (Form 4136)
126c          0  Add line 26a and 26b
127           0  TAX DUE
128           0  OVERPAYMENT
4L01      11178  Cash
4L02          0  Accounts Receivable
4L02a         0  Allow for Bad Debt
4L03       2130  Inventory
4L04a         0  Gov Obligations - Fed and State
4L05          0  Other Current Assets
4L06          0  Loans to Stockholders
4L07          0  Mortgage Loans
4L08          0  Other Investments
4L09          0  Buildings, Depreciable Assets
4L09a         0  Accumulated Depreciation
4L10          0  Depletable Assets
4L10a         0  Accumulated Depletion
```

```
4L10a        0   Land (net of amortization)
4L12         0   Intangible Assets (amortizable)
4L12a        0   Accumulated Amortization
4L13         0   Other Assets
4L14     13308   Assets
4L15         0   Accounts Payable
4L16         0   Notes Payable Short Term
4L17         0   Other Current Liabilities
4L18         0   Loans from Stockholders
4L19         0   Notes Payable Long Term
4L20         0   Other Liabilities
4L21         0   Capital stock
4L22         0   Paid-in or Capital Surplus
4L23         0   Retained Earnings - Approp
4L24         0   Retained Earnings - UnAppr
4L25         0   Shareholders undistrib income taxed
4L26         0   Accumulated adjustments account
4L27         0   Other adjustments account
4L28         0   Cost of treasury stock
4L29         0   Liabilities and Equity
```

This can now be hand copied onto the official tax form. (If you want to, you can use the **/rdb report** command to print your own form.)

20.10.18 Step 12: `1040.calc < 1040.filled > 1040`

Finally, the **make** command executes your **1040.calc** program to give you a *1040* tax form.

```
$ 1040.calc X
Line   Amount   Description
----   ------   -----------
56       1973   Total tax
```

The X is the name of the tax schedule you use. X is the single, Y the married filing jointly, YS the married filing separately, and so forth.

```
$ cat 1040
Line   Amount   Description
----   ------   -----------
6           1   Exemptions
7        2000   Wages, salaries, tips, etc.
8           0   Interest income
9a          0   Dividends (Schedule B if over $400)
9b          0   Exclusion
9c          0   Total Dividends
10          0   Refunds of State and local income taxes from worksheet
11          0   Alimony received
12          0   Business income or (loss) (attach Schedule C)
13          0   Capital gain or (loss) (attach Schedule D)
14          0   Capital gain distributions not reported on line 13
15          0   Supplemental gains or (losses) (attach Form 4797)
16          0   Fully taxable pensions, IRA distributions, etc.
```

```
17a        0    Other pensions and annuities, including rollovers
17b        0    Taxable amount, if any, from worksheet on page 10
18     15408    Rents, royalties, partnerships, estates, trusts (Sch E)
19         0    Farm income or (loss) (attach Schedule F)
20a        0    Unemployment compensation (insurance).  Total received.
20b        0    Taxable amount, if any, from worksheet on page 11.
21a        0    Social security benefits.
21b        0    Taxable amount, if any, from the worksheet page 10
22         0    Other income
23     17408    Total income. Add 7-12.
24         0    Moving expense (sttach Form 3903 or 3903F)
25         0    Employee business expense (attach Form 2106)
26a     2000    IRA deduction, from the worksheet on page 12
26b        0    Enter here IRA payments you made in 1984 included
27         0    Payments to a Keogh (H.R. 10) retirement plan
28         0    Penalty on early withdrawal of savings
29         0    Alimony paid
30         0    Deduction for a married couple when both work (Sch W)
31      2000    Total adjustments. Add 23-30
32     15408    Adjusted gross income. Subtract 31 from 22.
33     15408    line 32.
34a        0    If you itemize, enter Schedule A, line 28
34b        0    If do not itemize, charitable contributions
35     15408    Subtract line 34a or 34b from line 33
36      1000    Multiply $1,000 by the number of exemptions line 6
37     14408    Taxable Income.  Subtract line 36 from line 35.
38      1973    Tax.
39         0    Additional Taxes.
40      1973    Total. Add lines 38 and 39.
41         0    Credit for child and dependent care expenses (Form 2441)
42         0    Credit for elderly (attach Schedule R)
43         0    Residential energy credit (attach From 5695)
44         0    Partial credit for political contributions
45         0    Total personal credits. Add lines 41 through 44.
46      1973    Subtract line 45 from 40. Enter the result (not less 0)
47         0    Foreign tax credit (attach Form 1116)
48         0    General business credit. Check if form ...
49         0    Total credits
50      1973    Balance
51       223    Self-employment tax (attach Schedule SE).
52         0    Alternative minimum tax (attach Form 4625).
53         0    Tax from recapture of investment credit (Form 4255)
54         0    Social security tax on tip income no reported employer
55         0    Tax on an IRA (attach Form 5329)
56      2196    Total tax
57         0    Federal income tax withheld
58      2000    Estimated 1984 tax payments and applied from 1983 return
59         0    Earned income credit
60         0    Amount paid with Form 4868
61         0    Excess social security tax and RRTA tax withheld
62         0    Credit for Federal tax on special fuels and oils (4136)
63         0    Regulated investment Company credit (attach Form 2439)
64      2000    Total payments
65         0    If line 67 is larger than line 59, enter OVERPAID
66         0    REFUNDED TO YOU
67         0    Applied to your 1984 estimated tax
68       196    AMOUNT YOU OWE
69         0    Penalty for not paying estimated. (Form 2210).
```

Note that only one exemption is claimed on line 6. The profit from the S-corporation was copied into line 18 from Schedule E. An IRA deduction was taken on line 26a. Self-employment tax of $223 on the $2000 wages was entered into line 51. The values in this form can now be copied to your 1040.

Gee, wasn't that fun?

20.10.19 Setting Up the System for Your Business.

Can't wait to set up your own books? Ok, here is how.

First copy the /act directory in you /rdb system to the directory you want for your business. (You can use the /rdb cpdir command). Now you can edit your files while keeping your original /act copy for reference and backup. Look at this table which lists all of the files that you might need to edit. Once you are set up, you may only need to edit the *ji* and *je* journals.

```
File             Edit
---------------  -------------------------------------------------------
Makefile         top lines for company name dates and tax form
income.head      company name, year
balance.head     company name, year
journallast      edit from last periods books, or cp journalnext
ji               enter all income items (deposits)
je               enter all expense items (checks)
ja               enter all adjustments (inventory, depreciation, etc.)
1120S.blank      edit for new year tax forms s-corporation
1120S.calc       edit for new year tax forms
1040.blank       edit for new year tax forms individual
1040.calc        edit for new year tax forms
chart            edit if you wish to change from the sample
```

20.10.20 Makefile.

You need to edit the *Makefile* to give the name of your company, the business tax form you use, the end of the tax period, and so forth.

```
COMPANY=Makeapile, Inc.   # Your company name
FORM=1120S                # The tax form your company must fill out
DATE=861231               # The last day of the accounting period
NEXTDATE=870101           # First day of next accounting period
YEAR=1986                 # The calendar or physical
SCHEDULE=X                # The 1040 tax schedule
```

20.10.21 Incomestatement and Balancesheet Headers.

To get nice headers in the income statement and balance sheet, edit the headers files income.h and balance.h.

```
cat income.h

        Makeapile, Inc.
        Income Statement
For the Year Ended 31 December 1986
```

```
cat balance.h

        Makeapile, Inc.
        31 December 1986
        Balancesheet
```

20.10.22 jl - journallast.

For the first accounting period you will need to build a *journallast* ledger table. It should contain all the accounts that were carried forward from the last accounting period. At the end of the first accounting period, the **close** program will generate the *journalnext* for the next period. From then on you will simply rename (**mv**) *journalnext* to *journallast.* You will not have to create it by hand again.

```
$ cat journallast
Account   Date      Debit   Credit   Ref      Description
-------   -------   -----   ------   -------   ---------------
1010      870101    11178            jl        brought forward
1110      870101    2130             jl        brought forward
1310      870101    0                jl        brought forward
1330      870101    0                jl        brought forward
1420      870101    0                jl        brought forward
4997      870101            13308    jl        brought forward
```

20.10.23 ji - journalincome and je journalexpense.

You should bring the *ji* and *je* tables up in an editor and delete from the third line on. Then you can start editing in your own income and expense items.

20.10.24 ja - journaladjust.

ja is a template of adjustments. You can leave zero values in the accounts that you don't want. Just fill in the accounts that you do want. Remember, this file is double entry. For each *Debit,* you must also enter a *Credit.* Understanding debit and credit is as close as you need to get to real accounting. Don't get scared, you can do it.

20.10.25 chart of accounts.

Here is an example of a chart of accounts of a software company. Note that it has four columns. Under *Account* is the account number column and under *Name* is the description of the accounts. The *Format* column tells the programs that generate the income statement and the balance sheet where the accounts go. The *Taxline* is used by the programs that fill in your tax form. It shows where the sums of the accounts go on a tax form. In this case the numbers refer to line numbers on the Federal S-Corporate Tax Form (*1120S*) for 1986. *4L01* means page 4, schedule L, line 1.

Account	Format	Taxline	Name
1010	B-A	4L01	Cash
1020	B-A	4L02	Accounts Receivable
1030	B-A	4L02a	Allow for Bad Debt
1110	B-A	4L03	Inventory
1130	B-A	4L04a	Gov Obligations - Fed
1140	B-A	4L04b	Gov Obligations - State
1150	B-A	4L05	Other Current Assets
1160	B-A	4L06	Loans to Stockholders
1170	B-A	4L07	Mortgage Loans
1180	B-A	4L08	Other Investments
1210	B-A	4L09	Equipment
1310	B-A	4L09a	Accum Depreciation
1320	B-A	4L10	Depletable Assets
1330	B-A	4L11	Accum Depletion
1410	B-A	4L12	Intangible Assets
1420	B-A	4L12a	Accum Amortization
1430	B-A	4L13	Other Assets
1999	B-A	4L14	Assets
2010	B-LE	4L15	Accounts Payable
2020	B-LE	4L16	Notes Payable Short Term
2030	B-LE	4L17	Other Current Liabilities
2110	B-LE	4L18	Loans from Stockholders
2120	B-LE	4L19	Notes Payable Long Term
2130	B-LE	4L20	Other Liabilities
2199	B-LE		Liabilities
2209	B-LE	4L21a	Preferred stock
2210	B-LE	4L21b	Common Stocks
2220	B-LE	4L22	Paid-in or Capital Surplus
2310	B-LE	4L23	Retained Earnings - Approp
2320	B-LE	4L24	Retained Earnings - UnAppr
2400	B-LE	4L25	Cost of Treasury Stock
2899	B-LE		Equity
2999	B-LE	4L26	Liabilities and Equity
3010	I-I	101a	Sales
3015	I-I	101b	Returns and Allowances
3019	I-I	101c	Net Sales
3030	I-I	103	Gross Profit
3040	I-I	104	Dividends
3050	I-I	105	Interest on US Notes
3060	I-I	106	Other Interest
3070	I-I	107	Gross rents
3080	I-I	108	Gross royalties
3090	I-I	109a	Capital Gain
3092	I-I	109b	Net Gain Form 4797
3100	I-I	110	Other Income
3999	I-I	111	Income
4010	I-COGS	2A2	rdb Software
4020	I-COGS	2A2	act Software
4057	I-COGS	2A3	Beginning Inventory
4058	I-COGS	2A4	Ending Inventory
4059	I-COGS	102	Cost of Goods Sold
4060	I-E	123	Advertising
4070	I-E	126	Bank Charges
4080	I-E	117	Taxes
4090	I-E	126	Hair Analysis
4100	I-E	126	Insurance
4105	I-E	112	Compensation of Officers
4110	I-E	113	Salary and Wages
4120	I-E	126	Legal Fees

```
4130      I-E       126        Supplies
4140      I-E       126        Office Supplies
4150      I-E       126        Telephone
4160      I-E       126        Postage
4170      I-E       126        Printing
4180      I-E       126        Professional Services
4190      I-E       116        Rent
4200      I-E       126        Research and Development
4210      I-E       126        Subscription
4220      I-E       126        Misc. Expenses
4310      I-E       114        Repairs
4320      I-E       115        Bad Debts
4330      I-E       118        Interest
4340      I-E       119        Contributions (<5% 130)
4350      I-E       120        Amortization
4360      I-E       121        Depreciation
4370      I-E       122        Depletion
4380      I-E       124        Pension, Profit-Sharing
4390      I-E       125        Employee Benefit Programs
4399      I-E       127     Expenses
4999      I-E       130        Net Profit or Loss
```

20.10.26 Business Tax Forms.

These are the tax forms for the major types of taxpayers.

```
Form    Business
----    --------
1040    Individual
C       Sole Proprietorship (Schedule C of 1040)
4697    Partnership
1120S   S-corporation (Small business)
1120    Corporation
```

Every individual will have to enter their own 1040 individual tax form, but all of the business forms can be filled in by the computer from the data in the financial statements. For each tax form there are several tables.

```
Table             Description
--------------    -------------------------------------------------
1120S.chart       chart of accounts for this form
1120S.blank       blank form
1120S.filled      filled by program
1120S.calc        program that calculates the tax form from filled
1120S             calculated form
```

You have to tell the system which business tax form you use by editing the *Makefile*. Then you will have to copy the appropriate chart of accounts to *chart*.

```
$ cp 1120S.chart chart
```

Then you can edit the chart of accounts to fit your company. When you type **make,** the appropriate tax form will be filled in and calculated.

20.10.27 Personal 1040 Tax Form.

Finally, you can copy the *1040.blank* to the *1040.filled* table and you can use a text editor to edit the *1040.filled* table. Put in your wages and income from all of your businesses, and so on. Then you can type:

```
$ make
```

or

```
$ 1040.calc
$ cat 1040
Line  Amount  Description
----  ------  -------------------------------------------
6          1  Exemptions
 ...
```

You can cat or print your tax forms now that they are filled. Then just write the numbers into you official government tax form. You should do some checking to see if you made any mistakes. Don't believe the results just because the computer printed them. You have good tools to help you look at your numbers. Use the footed ledger as a good overview and detail document. See if everything is reasonable. Do spot checks. You will learn a lot about your business as you go over the numbers.

20.10.28 Interface with the Other Modules.

We have also integrated the general ledger and tax system with the rest of the business. A program that **make** calls, **getjournal,** gets subsidiary journals from other systems.

20.10.29 journaldeposit from sales.

In the sales and accounts receivable section, all money that comes into the business from customers is recorded in the *deposit* journal. **getjournal** totals that table and creates a *journaldeposit*. It sets the account to be *sales*.

20.10.30 journalcheck from pur.

The checks are all entered into the *check* table in the accounts payable department. That table is totaled and placed in the *journalcheck*. The account is set to *merch* for merchandise bought for sale.

20.10.31 inventory.

From the inventory department we get the total value of the inventory which we insert into the *journaladjust*. Then when you type **make,** the financial statements will reflect the current state of the business as of that moment.

20.10.32 Modifying the System.

Of course you will probably want to modify the system and do some things differently. Some departments you will not have. Other departments will need a lot more functions. We have deliberately kept this simple to make it easy to learn. You have powerful tools with UNIX and **/rdb** to modify the software as your business changes and grows.

20.10.33 Troubleshooting.

The biggest problem in the general ledger and tax system is misspelling an account name or entering one that does not exist. The **post** program checks for that and displays a list of accounts that you entered into the journals, that are not in the chart of accounts. Edit the journals, or the chart of accounts, to make the account names match.

Fortunately, you can see everything that you want. You can list or print out each table. You can see the debit and credit totals after each program. When you find a problem, you can trace it back to where it happened. Then you can edit the data to correct it. Since the **/act** programs are all shell programs, you have the source. So you can even modify the programs and add new ones easily. Be sure to keep a copy of the originals, in case of momentary failure of omniscience.

20.11 sales - Accounts Payable and Sales

The sales system is the interface with the customer. It takes the sales orders and adds new customers to the customer file. It generates invoices for each order and customer statements periodically, usually monthly. It credits the customer payments to the deposits file. It also maintains an accounts receivable ledger. If the company extends credit to customers, this ledger keeps track of all orders and deposits so that it knows the balance for each customer.

20.11.1 menu - Menu of Sales and Accounts Receivable.

Here is the menu for the sales system:

```
Number    Name       For
-------   -------     -------------------------------------------------
0         exit       Exit This Menu
1         ov         Overview of Sales and Accounts Receivable System
2         sale       Enter Sales Order
3         invoice    Print Invoice
4         deposit    Enter Deposit
5         postar     Post AR Ledger, Update Customer Balance
6         cstate     Print Customer Statement
7         cust       Update Customer File
8         cmail      Print Customer Mailing Labels
```

20.11.2 ov - Overview of Sales and Accounts Receivable.

The overview menu shows the general outline of the sales system and the programs and files used.

```
            Sales and Accounts Receivable System Overview
sale
---------> customer  ----------|             invoice
     |--> saleorder -----------------------------> INVOICE
     |--> saleitem  ----------|
deposit                   postar |           cstate
---------> deposit -------------> ledgerar ---------> STATEMENT


Programs   Description
--------   -----------------------------------------------
cstate     print customer statement
invoice    print invoice for customer
onhand     report the quantity in inventory of an item
postar     post deposits and orders to accounts receivable ledger
sale       take sales order, update customer, saleorder and item

Files in Sales and Accounts Receivable System


Files          Description of Major Files
--------       -----------------------------------------
customer       customer information, address, etc.
deposit        journal of money into the business
ledgerar       ledger of accounts receivable, by customer
saleitem       table of items sold
saleorder      table of sales orders


Files          Description of Minor Files
--------       -----------------------------------------
catalog        list of items to sell and in inventory
cstate.f       form for customer statement
customer.f     form for customer file
customer.s     screen program to get customer info
invoice.f      form for printing invoice
mail.f         form to print customer mailing list
nextorder      next sales order number for sale program
shipaddress    table of separate shipping addresses
```

20.11.3 sale - Enter Sales Order.

sale enters a sales order into the *saleorder* table and items into the *saleitem* table and can update the customer information file *customer*. The customer comes in or calls and the order taker can add a new customer or check old information. Then the order information and item information are added.

The program is interactive allowing you to confirm each action. First it asks for customer number. If you give it a number, it looks the number up in the *customer* file. If the customer is found, information is displayed for you to confirm. If you do not have the customer number, you can search with the slash string option (/string) or enter the question mark (?) to get into the customer file. There you can search for the customer or add a new customer.

In the following examples, bold face type means that the user types in these characters. *$CLEAR* is a shell variable that clears the screen if it has been set with some command like:

```
$ CLEAR='termput cl`
$ export CLEAR
```

or nothing if it has not been set.

```
$CLEAR
MakeaPile, Inc.                    saleorder
Enter Customer Number (? for new, /string search, Return to exit)
Vendor Number 1
Mr. Luke  Skywalker   CEO

Rebel Enterprises
123 Lea Street
Space Port City, Far Side  123456789  Tatooy

Code      Qty
-------   -------
rdb       1
Order     Number    Code      Backord   Qty       Price     Total     Name
-------   -------   -------   -------   -------   -------   -------   ----
1         1         rdb           10    1              1500  1500.00   /rdb
Number    Cust      Date      Shipped   Gross     Tax       Total
-------   ----      -------   -------   -------   -------   -------
1         2         850723    0         1500.00   75.00     1575.00
```

```
Is this correct? (y, n) y
$ cat saleorder
Number    Cust      Date      Shipped    Gross       Tax         Total
-------   ----      -------   -------    -------     -------     -------
     1      2       850723    860525     1500.00      75.00      1575.00
     2      2       850724    860525     3000.00     150.00      3150.00
     3      3       850902    860525    22500.00    1125.00     23625.00
     4      3       850902         0    36000.00    1800.00     37800.00
     5      3       850902         0    21000.00    1050.00     22050.00
$ cat saleitem
  Order    Number    Code      Backord       Qty      Price      Total     Name
  -------  -------   -------   -------     -------    -------    -------    ----
     1       1       rdb           10          1       1500     1500.00    /rdb
     2       1       rdb           10          2       1500     3000.00    /rdb
     3       1       rdb           10          5       1500     7500.00    /rdb
     3       2       act           10         10       1500    15000.00    /act
     4       1       rdb           10          5       1500     7500.00    /rdb
     4       2       rdb           10         19       1500    28500.00    /rdb
     5       1       rdb           10          5       1500     7500.00    /rdb
     5       2       act           10          9       1500    13500.00    /act
```

Once you enter the correct customer number, you are given a table of items to enter. You type in the product *Code* **rdb** and *Qty* **1**, and the program looks up the other information in the inventory. You can verify that the information is correct and make sure that you have enough in inventory to satisfy the order. You continue entering items until through. A carriage return, or enter key, will indicate you are finished, and the program will calculate the totals for the order, including tax. It then prompts you for the next customer so that you can have one or more terminals taking orders all day.

This program uses the **cursor** and **termput** programs to move about the screen.

20.11.4 invoice - Print Invoice.

invoice will prompt you for an order number. It then prints an invoice by looking up information in the *customer, saleorder,* and *saleitem* files.

```
$ invoice
Please enter order number (or Return to exit): 1
                        Invoice
                        -------
Makeapile, Inc., 123 Bigbucks Blvd., Dallas, TX 12345, 1-800-SOF-WARE

Order Number   1
Date Ordered   850723
Date Shipped   0

Mailing Address for Customer Number  2
Vendor Number 2
Mr. Thomas  Boomer   President

Ye Olde Thermonuclear Bombe Shoppe
54321 Blooy Road
Livermore, California    USA

Order     Number    Code     Backord     Qty   Price     Total     Name
-------   -------   -------   -------   -------  -------   -------   ----
1         1         rdb           10         1    1500   1500.00   /rdb

                                             Gross   1500.00
                                             Tax        75.00
                                             Total   1575.00

Please enter order number (or Return to exit):
```

The *saleorder* file has a column for customer number. With that number the program finds the customer row and displays it with a special form *customer.f.* It also displays the sales items as a table and the order total information. This all can be directed to a printer, by setting up the *PRINTER* shell variable in your *.profile.* (See */act/.profile.*)

20.11.5 deposit - Enter Deposit.

When the customer pays money, information should be entered into the *deposit* journal. This journal will be read by the general ledger system and used to post to the accounts receivable ledger.

```
Date      Amount     Cust      Ref
-------   -------   -------   -------
860101    3000.00        1     1490
860103    1500.00        2      312
860105    9000.00        3     3347
```

Cust is the customer number and *Ref* is the reference, such as customer check number, and so on.

20.11.6 postar - Post Acc Receivable, Update Customer Balance.

postar will put together both the *deposit* and the *saleorder* files to make a ledger of accounts receivable *ledgerar*.

```
$ postar
$ cat ledgerar
Cust    Date        Amount    Ref
----    ------    ---------    ----
1       860101     3000.00    1490
2       850723    -1575.00       1
2       850724    -3150.00       2
2       860103     1500.00     312
3       850902   -22050.00       5
3       850902   -23625.00       3
3       850902   -37800.00       4
3       860105     9000.00    3347
```

This file is sorted by customer so that it is a running record of each customer's orders and deposits. It will be pulled out by the customer statement printing program **cstate.**

20.11.7 cstate - Print Customer Statement.

cstate simply prints some customer information from the *customer* file and the activity from the accounts receivable ledger *ledgerar*.

```
$ cstate
Please enter customer number (or all, Return to exit): 2
                Customer Statement
                ------------------
Makeapile, Inc., 123 Bigbucks Blvd., Dallas, TX 12345, 1-800-SOF-WARE

Mailing Address for Customer Number  2

Mr. Thomas  Boomer  President

Ye Olde Thermonuclear Bombe Shoppe
54321 Blooy Road
Livermore, California    USA

Now Due and Payable is your balance of: 7950.00


Details of Your Orders (-) and Payments
Cust    Date        Amount    Ref
----    ------    ---------    ---
   2    850723    -1575.00       1
   2    850724    -3150.00       2
   2    850902    -4725.00      19
   2    860103     1500.00     312
----    ------    ---------    ---
                  -7950.00


Please enter customer number (All for all customers, Return to exit):
```

cstate will prompt you for the customer. *all* will get you all of the customer statements.

20.11.8 cust - Update Customer File.

The *customer* file can be updated by several programs. Here is what the *customer* file looks like in list format.

```
$ tabletolist < customer
Number    1
Pretitl   Mr.
Fname     Luke
Mname
Lname     Skywalker
Postitl
Title     CEO
MS
Dept
Company   Rebel Enterprises
Street    123 Lea Street
City      Space Port City
State     Far Side
Zipcode   123456789
Country   Tatooy
Wphone    Unlisted
Hphone
Bought    0
Paid      0
Balance     3000.00
Comment   Don't tell the Empire
Date      850717


Number    2
Pretitl   Mr.
Fname     Thomas
Mname
Lname     Boomer
Postitl
Title     President
MS
Dept
Company   Ye Olde Thermonuclear Bombe Shoppe
Street    54321 Blooy Road
City      Livermore
State     California
Zipcode
Country   USA
Wphone    (415) 123-4567
Hphone
Bought    0
Paid      0
Balance   -7950.00
Comment
Date      850717
```

```
Number    3
Pretitl   Ms
Fname     Ute
Mname
Lname     Unix
Postitl   Ph.D.
Title     President
MS
Dept
Company   UniUniUniUni Software Sellers
Street    12345 Nixuni Street
City      Union
State     New Jersey
Zipcode   11111
Country   USA
Wphone    (201) 123-4567
Hphone
Bought
Paid
Balance   -107550.00
Comment   Distributor
Date      850723
```

20.11.9 cmail - Print Customer Mailing Labels.

cmail prints the mailing labels for your customers. You can use this to send out promotional mailings and/or customer statements.

```
$ cmail
Customer Number 1
Mr. Luke  Skywalker   CEO

Rebel Enterprises
123 Lea Street
Space Port City, Far Side  123456789  Tatooy

Customer Number 2
Mr. Thomas  Boomer  President

Ye Olde Thermonuclear Bombe Shoppe
54321 Blooy Road
Livermore, California    USA

Customer Number 3
Ms Ute  Unix Ph.D. President

UniUniUniUni Software Sellers
12345 Nixuni Street
Union, New Jersey  11111  USA
```

The *mail.f* file can be edited to put as many spaces between labels as your perforated labels need. The customer number is included so that if the mailer is returned or the customer calls, it is faster to enter the sales order.

20.12 inv - Inventory

The inventory department has two parts, shipping and receiving.

20.12.1 Shipping.

Shipping involves sending items from inventory out to customers, to the manufacturing department or to other users within the company.

20.12.1.1 invoice - print invoice.

In order to send goodies to customers or company departments, you need to print invoices. Then you can walk through the stock room and pick out the items to send. Or you could print a separate picklist. You can send the invoice, or a copy, along with the goods. You can also mark the invoice for any backordered items.

```
$ invoice
Please enter order number (or Return to exit): 1
                        Invoice
                        -------
Makeapile, Inc., 123 Bigbucks Blvd., Dallas, TX 12345, 1-800-SOF-WARE

Order Number            1
Date Ordered            860523
Date Shipped            860525

Mailing Address for Customer Number  2
Customer Number 2
Mr. Thomas  Boomer  President

Ye Olde Thermonuclear Bombe Shoppe
54321 Blooy Road
Livermore, California    USA

   Order   Number   Code    Backord     Qty    Price    Total    Name
   -----   ------   ----    -------     ---    -----    -----    ----
       1        1   rdb          10       1     1500  1500.00    /rdb
                                               Gross  1500.00
                                                 Tax    75.00
                                               Total  1575.00

Please enter order number (or Return to exit):
```

20.12.1.2 back - Note backorder.

It is possible that you may not have in inventory an item that has been ordered. Shame on you. You need to keep track of it in a backorder table. To update the backorder column in the *sales/saleitem* table you can select *back* in the menu or use one of the update programs like **vi** or **ve.**

```
$ vi saleitem
   Order   Number   Code    Backord     Qty    Price    Total    Name
   -----   ------   ----    -------     ---    -----    -----    ----
       1        1   rdb           0       1     1500  1500.00    /rdb
       2        1   rdb           0       2     1500  3000.00    /rdb
       3        1   rdb           0       5     1500  7500.00    /rdb
       3        2   act           0       1     1500  1500.00    /act
       4        1   rdb           3       5     1500  7500.00    /rdb
       5        1   rdb           5       5     1500  7500.00    /rdb
```

Note the *Backord* and *Qty* columns. If we only have ten *rdbs* to start with, eight are sent out on orders 1, 2, and 3. (See the *Qty* column). That leaves only two. Order 4 wants five *rdbs,* but we can only send two and backorder three. Order 5 wants five *rdbs,* but there are none, so we backorder all five. To get the total backorders we need to subtotal the *Backord* column, after sorting and breaking on the *Code* column. When items come in, we can look for backorders in this table and find the orders.

20.12.1.3 ship - *Send out an order.*

When you finish shipping out the goods, you need to record the date shipped in the *saleorder* table. You do this by running the **ship** program.

```
$ ship
Please enter order number (Return to exit): 1
Number   Cust     Date   Shipped    Gross     Tax      Total
------   ----   -------  -------   -------   -------  -------
     1      2   860523   860525   1500.00     75.00  1575.00
Please enter order number (Return to exit):
```

Note that the ship dates have been updated.

20.12.2 *Receiving.*

Receiving involves getting items into inventory from outside vendors, from the manufacturing department, or from other departments within the company.

20.12.2.1 po - *Print purchase order.*

When an item arrives from an outside vendor, the purchase order should be checked against the items received to see what we actually got. To get a purchase order to check we run the *po* program.

```
$ po
Please enter order number (or Return to exit): 1
                    Purchase Order
                    --------------
Makeapile, Inc., 123 Bigbucks Blvd., Dallas, TX 12345, 1-800-SOF-WARE

Order Number          1
Date Ordered          860524
Date Received         0
Mailing Address
Vendor Number 2
Mr. Sally  Johnson  Grand Poo Bah
 Vendor Relations
Beyond the Valley of the Silicon, Inc.
123 St. Tomas Road
Silly Valley, California  94000  USA
```

```
    Order   Number   Code    Backord     Qty     Price    Total    Name
    -------  -------  ------- -------   -------  -------  -------   ----
       1        1     binder     100        50       20  1000.00   bind
                                                     Gross  1000.00
                                                       Tax    50.00
                                                     Total  1050.00
Please enter order number (or Return to exit):
```

20.12.2.2 receive - Receive goods.

When we are satisfied with the shipment, we need to record the date in the *purchaseorder* table. We run the **receive** program to update that table with today's date.

20.12.2.3 back - Check backorder.

Now that we have new items in inventory, we need to check to see if anyone has them backordered. Find all of the backorders for the item in the *salesitem* table, fill as many as you can, and correct the number in the *Backord* column.

```
$ vi saleitem
    Order   Number   Code    Backord     Qty     Price    Total    Name
    -------  -------  ------- -------   -------  -------  -------   ----
       1        1     rdb        0         1      1500  1500.00   /rdb
       2        1     rdb        0         2      1500  3000.00   /rdb
       3        1     rdb        0         5      1500  7500.00   /rdb
       3        2     act        0         1      1500  1500.00   /act
       4        1     rdb        3         5      1500  7500.00   /rdb
       5        1     rdb        5         5      1500  7500.00   /rdb
```

If you just got *rdbs* in, you can try to fill orders 4 and 5. You can reprint the invoices for those orders with the invoice program, and mark the items as backorder shipments.

20.12.3 Other.

20.12.3.1 inv - Update inventory file.

When we add or subtract items from inventory, we must·update our inventory table.

```
$ vi inventory
Code    Price   Cost   Onhand  Value   Rate   Lead   Name
-----   ------- ------ ------- ------- ------- ------- ----
rdb      1500    900     10     9000      1     10    /rdb
act      1500    900     10     9000      1     10    /act
rdbdoc     50     12    100     1200      1     30    rman
actdoc     50     12    120     1440      1     30    rman
binder     20     10    100     1000      1     30    bind
f1          5      5     30      150    0.5      2    f2s2d
f2          8      8     20      160    0.4      3    f2s4d
tape       15     15     12      180    0.1      8    1600
```

Edit the *Onhand* column.

20.12.3.2 catalog - Print a catalog (order form).

You can print an *orderform* from the *inventory* table with the **makecatalog** program.

```
$ makecatalog
$ cat catalog
Code      Qty          Price   Total     Name
-----     -------      ------- -------   -------------
rdb            _____x   1500   =$_____   /rdb
act            _____x   1500   =$_____   /act
rdbdoc         _____x     50   =$_____   /rdb manual
actdoc         _____x     50   =$_____   /act manual
binder         _____x     20   =$_____   binders
f1             _____x      5   =$_____   floppy 2s2d
f2             _____x      8   =$_____   floppy 2s4d
tape           _____x     15   =$_____   tape 1600bpi
-----     -------      ------- -------   -------------
                               _____   Total
                               _____   - Discount
                               _____   Net
                               _____   - Sales Tax
                               _____   Amount Due
```

20.13 pur - Accounts Payable and Purchasing

20.13.1 Symmetry with Sales.

Purchasing is the mirror image of the sales department. Here are the corresponding programs in the two departments. They are really each the same program (linked), with the name tested to decide which department they are in. This saves a lot of coding.

```
Sales     Pur          Description
-----     ---          -----------
sale      purchase     enter order
invoice   po           print purchase order
check     check        update journals for checks and checks
postar    postap       post ledger for accounts receivable and payable
cstate    vstate       print customer and vendor statements
```

The purchasing system is the interface with the vendor. It creates the purchase orders and adds new vendors to the vendor file. It generates purchase orders for each order, and vendor statements periodically, usually monthly. It credits the vendor payments to the *check* file. It also maintains an accounts payable ledger. If the vendors extend credit to the company, this ledger keeps track of all orders and checks so that it knows the balance for each vendor.

20.13.2 menu - Menu of Purchasing and Accounts Payable.

Here is the menu for the purchasing system:

```
Number   Name     For
-------  -------  ---------------------------------------------------------
0        exit     Exit Menu
1        ov       Overview of the Purchasing and Accounts Payable System
2        onhand   Find Out How Much Inventory is Onhand and Onorder
3        pur      Enter Purchase Order
4        po       Print Purchase Order
5        check    Enter Check Journal
6        postap   Create Accounts Payable Ledger, Update Vendor Balance
7        vstate   Print Vendor Statement
8        vendor   Update Vendor Table
9        vmail    Print Vender Mailing Labels
10       vitem    Update Vendor/Item Table
```

20.13.3 ov - Overview of Purchasing and Accounts Payable.

The overview menu shows the general outline of the purchasing system and the programs and files used.

```
           Purchasing and Accounts Payable System Overview
purchase
---------> vendor  ----------|            po
     |--> purchaseorder -------------------------> PO
     |--> purchaseitem  ----|
check                 postap |           vstate
---------> check ------------> ledgerar -----------> STATEMENT


Programs      Description
----------------------------------------------------------------------
vstate  print vendor statement
po      print po for vendor
onhand  report the quantity in inventory of an item
postap  post checks and orders to accounts receivable ledger
purchase       take purchase order, update vendor, order and item


         Files in Purchasing and Accounts Payable System
Files   Description of Major Files
----------------------------------------------------------------------
vendor  vendor information, address, etc.
check   journal of money into the business
ledgerar       ledger of accounts receivable, by vendor
purchaseitem   table of items sold
purchaseorder  table of purchases orders


Files   Description of Minor Files
----------------------------------------------------------------------
catalog list of items to sell and in inventory
vstate.f       form for vendor statement
vendor.f       form for vendor file
vendor.s       screen program to get vendor info
po.f    form for printing po
mail.f  form to print vendor mailing list
nextorder      next purchases order number for purchase program
shipaddress    table of separate shipping addresses
```

20.13.4 *purchase - Enter Purchase Order.*

purchase enters a purchase order *purchaseorder* and items *purchaseitem* and can update the vendor information file *vendor*. The purchasing agent for the company decides what to buy, perhaps with the help of the *onhand* program and the *vendor.item* file. When a vendor comes in or calls, the agent can check the information. When a new vendor is found, the agent can add its information to the *vendor* file. Then the order information and item information are added.

The program is interactive, allowing you to confirm each action. First it asks for vendor number. If you give it a number, it looks the number up in the *vendor* file. If the vendor is found, information is displayed for you to confirm. If you do not have the vendor number, you can search with the slash string option (*/name*) or enter the question mark (?) to get into the vendor file. There you can search for the vendor or add a new vendor.

```
$ purchase
                purchaseorder
Enter Vendor Number (? for new, /string search, Return to exit) 2
Vendor Number 2
Mr. Sally  Johnson  Grand Poo Bah
 Vendor Relations
Beyond the Valley of the Silicon, Inc.
123 St. Tomas Road
Silly Valley, California  94000  USA
Code       Qty
-------    -------
binder     5
Order      Number    Code      Backord  Qty      Price    Total     Name
-------    -------   -------    -------  -------  -------  -------   ----
4          1         binder        100  5             20  100.00    bind
Number     Vendor    Date      Receive  Gross    Tax      Total
-------    -------   -------    -------  -------  -------  -------
4          2         860524    0        100.00   5.00     105.00
Is this correct? (y, n) y
```

Once you enter the correct vendor number, you are given a table of items to enter. You type in *Code* and *Qty* and the program looks up the other information in the *inventory* table. You can verify that the information is correct and make sure that you have enough in inventory to satisfy the order. You continue entering all of the items of the order. A carriage return will indicate that you are finished, and the program will calculate the totals for the order, including sales tax and discounts. It then prompts you for the next vendor so that you can have one or more terminals making purchase orders all day. This program uses the **cursor** and **termput** programs to move about the screen.

20.13.5 *po - Print Purchase Order.*

po will prompt you for an order number. It then prints a purchase order by looking up information in the *vendor, purchaseorder,* and *purchaseitem* files.

```
$ po
Please enter order number (or Return to exit): 1
                         Purchase Order
                         --------------
Makeapile, Inc., 123 Bigbucks Blvd., Dallas, TX 12345, 1-800-SOF-WARE

Order Number    1
Date Ordered    860524
Date Received   0

Mailing Address
Vendor Number 2
Mr. Sally  Johnson  Grand Poo Bah
 Vendor Relations
Beyond the Valley of the Silicon, Inc.
123 St. Tomas Road
Silly Valley, California  94000  USA

Order    Number    Code     Backord     Qty   Price      Total   Name
-------  -------   -------   -------   -------  -------   -------  ----
1        1         binder       100        50       20   1000.00  bind

                                                Gross     1000.00
                                                Tax         50.00
                                                Total     1050.00

Please enter order number (or Return to exit):
```

The *purchaseorder* file has a column for vendor number. With that number the program finds the vendor row in and displays it with a special form *vendor.f.* It also displays the purchasing items as a table and the order total information.

This all can be directed to a printer, by setting up the *PRINTER* shell variable in */act/.profile.*

20.13.6 check - Enter Check.

When you pay the vendor money, information should be entered into the *check* journal. This journal will be read by the general ledger system and used to post to the accounts payable ledger *ledgerap.*

```
$ cat check
Date       Amount    Vendor      Ref
-------    -------   -------    -------
860101     1253.50         1      101
860102     1113.00         2      102
860119     1234.34         3      103
```

Vendor is the vendor number and *Ref* is the reference, such as company's check number.

20.13.7 postap - Create Accounts Payable and Update Vendor Balance.

postap will put together both the *check* and the *purchaseorder* files to make a ledger of accounts payable *ledgerap.*

```
$ postap
$ cat ledgerap
Vendor   Date       Amount   Ref
------   ------    --------   ---
     1   860101    1253.50   101
     2   860102    1113.00   102
     2   860524   -1050.00     1
     2   860524   -5250.00     2
     3   860119    1234.34   103
     3   860524   -5250.00     3
```

This file is sorted by vendor so that it is a running record of each vendor's orders, and check. It will be pulled out by the vendor statement printing program *vstate*.

20.13.8 vstate - Print Vendor Statement.

vstate simply prints vendor information from the *vendor* file and the activity from the accounts payable ledger *ledgerap*.

```
$ vstate
Please enter vendor number (of all, Return to exit): 1
                     Vendor Statement
                     ----------------
Makeapile, Inc., 123 Bigbucks Blvd., Dallas, TX 12345, 1-800-SOF-WARE

Mailing Address for Customer Number  1

Mr. Simon  Sayes   Order Taker

All Hype, Inc.
P.O. Box 234
New York, NY  10001  USA

Our records show you have a balance of: 1253.50

Details of Our Orders and Payments

Vendor  Date      Amount   Ref
------  ------   -------   ---
     1  860101   1253.50   101
------  ------   -------   ---
                 1253.50

Please enter vendor number (or all, Return to exit):
```

vstate will prompt you for the vendor. *all* will get you all of the vendor statements.

20.13.9 cust - Update Vendor File.

The *vendor* file can be updated by several programs. In this simple example the **ve** program is used. Here is what the *vendor* table looks like in list format.

```
$ tabletolist < vendor

Number    1
Pretitl   Mr.
Fname     Simon
Mname
Lname     Sayes
Postitl
Title     Order Taker
MS
Dept
Company   All Hype, Inc.
Street    P.O. Box 234
City      New York
State     NY
Zipcode   10001
Country   USA
Wphone
Hphone
Bought    0
Paid      0
Balance   0
Comment   Watch out
Date      850717
Amount    0


Number    2
Pretitl   Mr.
Fname     Sally
Mname
Lname     Johnson
Postitl
Title     Grand Poo Bah
MS
Dept      Vendor Relations
Company   Beyond the Valley of the Silicon, Inc.
Street    123 St. Tomas Road
City      Silly Valley
State     California
Zipcode   94000
Country   USA
Wphone    (408) 123-4567
Hphone
Bought    0
Paid      0
Balance   0
Comment
Date
Amount    0
```

```
Number    3
Pretitl   Herr
Fname     Wolfgang
Mname
Lname     Gutenburg
Postitl   V
Title     Master Printer
MS
Dept      Old Docs
Company   Der Alt Verlag GmbH.
Street    123 Old Street
City      Mainz
State     Reinland-Palz
Zipcode   12345
Country   West Germany
Wphone    (001) 49-35-070-96
Hphone
Bought
Paid
Balance   0
Comment   Guten Tag, Gutenburg
Date      850723
Amount    0
```

20.13.10 vmail - Print Vendor Mailing Labels.

vmail prints the mailing labels for your vendors. You can use this to send out vendor statements and/or promotional mailings.

```
$ report mail.f < vendor
Vendor Number 1
Mr. Simon  Sayes   Order Taker

All Hype, Inc.
P.O. Box 234
New York, NY  10001  USA

Vendor Number 2
Mr. Sally  Johnson  Grand Poo Bah
 Vendor Relations
Beyond the Valley of the Silicon, Inc.
123 St. Tomas Road
Silly Valley, California  94000  USA

Vendor Number 3
Herr Wolfgang  Gutenburg V Master Printer
 Old Docs
Der Alt Verlag GmbH.
123 Old Street
Mainz, Reinland-Palz  12345  West Germany
```

The *mail.f* file can be edited to put as many spaces between labels as your perforated labels need. The *vendor number* is included so that if the mailer is returned, or the vendor calls, it is faster to enter the purchase order.

20.14 pay - Payroll

Payroll is the department that everyone understands. It collects our time cards and produces paychecks and annual W2 forms. It is independent of the rest of the business and is often handled by a bank or outside service company. There are so many details, and it changes so much, it may not be something your company wants to bother with. This sample is not at all complete. It must be customized for your state, for your retirement programs and other deductions. You will have to update the tax tables every year for FICA, federal, state, and any local tax bites. On the other hand, the tools are here to customize your own system if you desire.

20.14.1 Menu.

Here is the menu of the payroll department:

```
Number    Name     For
-------   -------   -------------------------------------
0         exit      Return to Higher Menu
1         hour      Enter Employee Hours
2         calcpay   Compute journalpay
3         checks    Print Pay Checks
4         emp       Edit Employee Table
5         w2        Print Annual W2 Forms
6         taxcol    Recalculate the Cumulative Tax Column
```

20.14.2 ov - Overview of Payroll System.

```
              Payroll System Overview
taxcol
------> federal, state...
                 |
        hour        calcpay          paycheck
TIMECARDS ----> hours -------> nextpay --------> PAYCHECKS
                  |     emp            |
                  |   -------> employee |
                  |     postpay        | ` w2
                journalpay -------> ledgerpay ------> W2
```

```
Programs                    Description
--------------              -------------------------------------
hour Enter Employee Hours
calcpay                     Compute journalpay
paycheck                    Print Pay Checks
emp                         Edit Employee Table
w2                          Print Annual W2 Forms
taxcol                      Recalculate the Cumulative Tax Column
```

```
           Files in Payroll System
Files              Description           ·
---------------    --------------------------------------
employee           employee information table
employee.l         employee information list
federal            federal tax table for withholding
hour               hours worked by employees this period
journalpay         journal of pay
lastpay            table of just the last, or current pay
ledgerpay          ledger of pay sorted by employee
paycheck.f         form used to print pay checks
state              state withholding tax table
w2.f               form for printing w2 forms
```

20.14.3 hour - Enter Employee Hours.

Employee hours are entered in the *hour* table with **vi** or **ve**.

```
$ cat hour
Number    Hours
-------   -------
1            80
2            80
3            30
```

20.14.4 calcpay - Compute Payroll.

calcpay will take the *hour* table, look up rates in the *employee* table, calculate taxes from the *federal, state*, and local tax tables and compute the *journalpay* and *nextpay* tables.

```
$ cat journalpay
tabletotbl: datatype: not found
Date       Number    Hours   Salary   Rate    Gross    Federal   Net
----       -------   -------  ------   ----    -------   -------   ---
860518        1         80     1000       0     1000         70   920
860518        2         80        0      10      800         42   752
860518        3         30        0      10      300          0   300
```

20.14.5 paycheck - Print Paychecks.

From *nextpay* the paychecks are printed.

```
$ paycheck
Makeapile, Inc., 123 Bigbucks Blvd., Dallas, TX 12345, 1-800-SOF-WARE
                                             860518
Pay to the order of Ms. Sally  Slinky
                                    $ 920

Memo: Paycheck          _____

Makeapile, Inc., 123 Bigbucks Blvd., Dallas, TX 12345, 1-800-SOF-WARE
                                             860518
Pay to the order of Mr. Nick  Nerd
                                    $ 752

Memo: Paycheck          _____

Makeapile, Inc., 123 Bigbucks Blvd., Dallas, TX 12345, 1-800-SOF-WARE
                                             860518
Pay to the order of Mr. Hi  Hype
                                    $ 300

Memo: Paycheck          _____
```

20.14.6 emp - Edit Employee Table.

Occasionally, the *employee* file will have to be edited.

```
$ cat employee.1

Number    1
Pretitl   Ms.
Fname     Sally
Mname
Lname     Slinky
Postitl
Title     Vice President
Dept.     Shipping and Customer Relations
M/S:
Street    123 Armadillo Road
City      Houston
State     TX
Zipcode   77244
Country   USA
Wphone    (714) 123-4567
Hphone
Salary    1000
Rate      0
Deduct    1
Status    Single
SocSec    987-65-4321
Comment
Date      830402

Number    2
Pretitl   Mr.
Fname     Nick
Mname
Lname     Nerd
Postitl
Title     Vice President
```

```
Dept.    Software Development
M/S:
Street   Sliderule
City     Houston
State    TX
Zipcode  77244
Country  USA
Wphone   (714) 765-4321
Hphone
Salary   0
Rate     10
Deduct   2
Status   Married
SocSec   123-45-6789
Comment
Date     810402

Number   3
Pretitl  Mr.
Fname    Hi
Mname
Lname    Hype
Postitl
Title    Vice President
Dept.    Marketing, Sales, and Bambozzeling
M/S:
Street   123 Sleezy
City     New York
State    NY
Zipcode  10000
Country  USA
Wphone   (212) 765-4321
Hphone
Salary   0
Rate     10
Deduct   3
Status   Married
SocSec   456-12-6789
Comment
Date     800402
```

20.14.7 w2 - Print W2 Form Information.

At the end of the year the W2 forms must be printed. They take information from the *employee* and *ledgerpay* tables.

```
$ w2
W2 Form Information

Company Tax ID: 12-1234567
Makeapile, Inc.
123 Bigbucks Blvd.
Dallas, TX 12345
1-800-SOF-WARE
```

```
Employee Tax ID: 987-65-4321
Employee Number: 1
Ms. Sally  Slinky          Vice President
123 Armadillo Road
Houston, TX  77244  USA

  Gross   Federal    State      Net
 -------  -------   -------   -------
   1000        70         0       920

------------------------- cut here -------------------------
W2 Form Information

Company Tax ID: 12-1234567
Makeapile, Inc.
123 Bigbucks Blvd.
Dallas, TX 12345
1-800-SOF-WARE


Employee Tax ID: 123-45-6789
Employee Number: 2
Mr. Nick  Nerd          Vice President
Sliderule
Houston, TX  77244  USA

  Gross   Federal    State      Net
 -------  -------   -------   -------
    800        42         0       752
------------------------- cut here -------------------------
W2 Form Information

Company Tax ID: 12-1234567
Makeapile, Inc.
123 Bigbucks Blvd.
Dallas, TX 12345
1-800-SOF-WARE


Employee Tax ID: 456-12-6789
Employee Number: 3
Mr. Hi  Hype          Vice President
123 Sleezy
New York, NY  10000  USA

  Gross   Federal    State      Net
 -------  -------   -------   -------
    300         0         0       300
------------------------- cut here -------------------------
```

20.14.8 taxcol - Recalculate the Cumulative Tax Column.

taxcol is a utility program that helps you edit tax tables. Since these must be typed in each year, this saves you from having to calclulate and update the cumulative tax column. Here is a tax table:

```
$ cat federal
 Income      Tax   Percent
 -------    -------  -------
    500        0       14
   1000       70       16
   1500      150       18
   2000      240       20
   3000      440       25
   4000      690       30
   5000      990       40
   7500     1990       50
```

The column named *Tax* is the cumulative tax column. It is computed from the other two columns.

20.15 opr - Operations (Manufacturing)

This section deals with the operations of the company which can vary widely from business to business. A mailorder business may have no manufacturing. Its sole operation may be buying and selling. A large manufacturer may need extensive programming in this area. A consultant may keep her or his expert system here. A hospital or clinic may keep medical record programs and patient care programs here.

We have gone from the general ledger/tax system which is very standard from company to company, to this operations system which is quite different from firm to firm. The point of this whole software system is to be a starter. In operations we see the biggest need to be able to modify and change to meet the needs of the business. This is the reason for taking an integrated tools approach. One system for all companies, or one system for the same company through time, is not practical. This operations section only has a few simple demo programs.

20.15.1 ov - System Overview.

```
                 Payroll System Overview
part -----------|     bom
                |---------------> bom
salesitem ------|


Programs          Description
--------------    ------------------------------------------
bom               Create Bill of Materials
print             Print Bill of Materials
part              Update Part List


        Files in Payroll System
Files             Description
--------------    ------------------------------------------
bom               Bill of Materials
part              Part/Subpart Table
```

20.15.2 Menu - System Menu.

```
Number   Name     For
-------  -------  --------------------------------------------
     0   exit     Return to Higher Level Menu or to Unix
     1   ov       Overview of Manufacturing Operations
     2   bom      Create Bill of Materials
     3   print    Print Bill of Materials
     4   part     Update Part List
```

20.15.3 bom - Create Bill of Materials.

A manufacturing company may need a **bom** program to compute the bill of materials necessary to make all of the items that have been ordered by customers.

20.15.4 print - Print Bill of Materials.

To see the *bom* table select the **print** command in the menu.

```
$ cat bom
Code        Qty
-------   -------
actdoc        38
binder       112
f1           560
rdbdoc        74
```

This shows us how many items we will have to make or buy to meet current orders.

20.15.5 part - Update Part List.

The parts list is a table of which parts are needed to make the products to be sold.

```
$ cat part
Code      Subpart    Count
-------   -------   -------
act       binder        2
act       actdoc        2
act       f1           10
rdb       binder        2
rdb       rdbdoc        2
rdb       f1           10
```

Appendix: /rdb^{TM} Manual

The UNIX-formatted manual pages in this chapter are arranged in alphabetical order and include the following sections:

TABLE 13. Manual Sections

NAME	one line description of the program
SYNOPSIS	the syntax of the program
DESCRIPTION	description of the function of the program
OPTION	lists of any options and their descriptions
EXAMPLE	one or more examples of the use of the program
SOURCE	the shell program listing for you to study and copy

/e -l -r	-c -t'c'] [column ...] <	justify
	calculates columns of a	compute
	capability	termput
/get terminal	capability from	termput
/compute balance column of	cash table	cashflow
/print	catalog from inventory	makecatalog
dates for math and format	change	gregorian
dates for math and format	change	julian
	change column name in	rename
the ascii value of any	character	ascii
/displays the	character corresponding to	chr
as well as printing	characters	see
/returns the number of	characters in a file	filesize
names and accounts in	chart	chartdup
	check for duplicate names	chartdup
	clears the crt terminal	clear
	close accounting period	close
/converts names into soundex	codes	soundex
row	col [CURSOR]	cursor
invalid values in a	column	domain
extra spaces at end of last	column	pad
[1] [	column ...] < table	datatype
[1] [	column ...] < table	maximum
[1] [	column ...] < table	mean
[1] [	column ...] < table	minimum
[1] [	column ...] < table	precision
[1] [	column ...] < table	total
[1] [	column ...] < table	width
/e -l -r -c -t'c'] [	column ...] < table	justify
[1] [break-column	column ...] < table	subtotal
table [ke	column [: decode-column]	vindex
the length of widest	column in a table	widest
/change	column name in headline	rename
/compute balance	column of cash table	cashflow
/convert	column of dates for math	gregorian
/convert	column of dates for math	julian
the cursor to the row and	column requested	cursor
/insert a	column row number in a	number
the datatype of each	column selected	datatype
the maximum value in each	column selected	maximum
the mean (average) of each	column selected	mean
the minimum of each	column selected	minimum
the precision of each	column selected	precision
/displays the width of each	column selected	width
/sums up each	column selected and	total
functional dependency of	columns	fd
a table by one or more	columns	sorttable
/reports any rows in which	columns do not match head	check
/outputs the subtotal of	columns in a table	subtotal
/calculates	columns of a table	compute
and right justifies the	columns of a table	justify

/display	columns of a table in any	column
/adds	columns to a table	addcol
	combine all subsidiary	consolidate
	combines three tables into	uniondict
reverses return status of	command	not
/finds the full path of a	command	path
	command	whatis
	command ...	not
[	command ...]	path
/displays the	command description and	whatis
/display list of all /act	commands	act
/describes /rdb	commands	commands
/root menu with some UNIX	commands	menu
/lists the help	commands available	helpme
/displays the number of	commands in a directory	howmany
/displays the	commands with function in	whatwill
	compute balance column of	cashflow
	compute each taxform listed	calculate·
	compute tax from income and	tax
where rows match logical	condition	row
'column	condition colum or-value	row
'column	condition colum or-value' <	select
	convert column of dates for	gregorian
	convert column of dates for	julian
	convert table to C language	tabletostruct
/for	converting from list to	listtotable
	converts a file from table	tabletolist
	converts first letter of	cap
	converts fixed length	fixtotable
	converts form into screen	screen
	converts list format to	listtosh
	converts names into soundex	soundex
	converts /rdb table format	tabletotbl
	converts /rdb table format	tabletofix
	converts table format to m4	tabletom4
	converts table format to m4	tabletosed
	converts table format to	tabletofact
	converts table format to	tabletorule
	converts text file into	word
	copies journals for sales,	getjournal
	copies one directory tree	cpdir
/remove all	core files to free up space	rmcore
/displays the character	corresponding to number	chr
table of subparts and their	count for a part	explode
	create and display ve	vindex
	create incomestatement from	income
	creates adjusted trial	adjust
	creates balancesheet from	balance
/close accounting period	creating journal for next	close
/clears the	crt terminal screen	clear
/output the	current date in the format:	todaysdate

/moves the	cursor to the row and	cursor
saleorder and item, update	customer	sale
/produce	customer statement	cstate
/insert	dash line as second line in	insertdash
with adjusted trial balance	data	fillform
/finds invalid	data and prints messages	validate
/replaces all	data in a record with	blank
/lists the	database dictionary from	schema
/prints a	database dictionary: the	dbdict
/visually edit a	database table	ve
/displays the	datatype of each column	datatype
given number of days to a	date	computedate
	date days	computedate
/output the current	date in the format: 840415	todaysdate
/convert column of	dates for math and format	gregorian
/convert column of	dates for math and format	julian
date	days	computedate
/adds given number of	days to a date	computedate
/converts table format to m4	define file format	tabletom4
< table >	definefile	tabletom4
langtolang >	definefile	uniondict
/tests all /rdb programs in	demo directory	testall
the fast access methods in	demo directory	testsearch
the fast access methods in	demo directory	timesearch
determinecolumn	dependcolumn < table	fd
/tests for functional	dependency of columns	fd
	describes /rdb commands	commands
commands with function in	description	whatwill
/displays the command	description and syntax	whatis
/one line	description of yourprog	yourprog
	determinecolumn	fd
three tables into translate	dictionary	uniondict
/lists the database	dictionary from table	schema
directory tree to another	directory	cpdir
the number of commands in a	directory	howmany
/rdb programs in rdb/bin	directory	rdb
all /rdb programs in demo	directory	testall
fast access methods in demo	directory	testsearch
fast access methods in demo	directory	timesearch
/copies one	directory tree to another	cpdir
to free up space on the	disk	rmcore
	display columns of a table	column
	display list of all /act	act
/create and	display ve look-up tables	vindex
up each column selected and	displays	total
	displays and edits records	update
	displays invalid values in	domain
	displays non-printing as	see
	displays the character	chr
	displays the command	whatis
	displays the commands with	whatwill

/create incomestatement	from adjustedtrial	income
/removes the head	from both table and list	headoff
/get terminal capability	from /etc/termcap file	termput
/compute tax	from income and tax table	tax
/print catalog	from inventory table	makecatalog
/for converting	from list to table format	listtotable
/produces bill-of-materials	from parts list	bom
/finds and outputs record	from table	record
the database dictionary	from table	schema
/converts a file	from table to list format	tabletolist
/removes blank rows	from the input table	rmblank
/filename processid	from to indexfrom indexto	lock
tableorlist processid	from to indexfrom indexto	unlock
/a] [-m[bhirs] tableorlist	from to [xfrom xto] </	replace
/fill a tax	from with adjusted trial	fillform
	fromdirectory todirectory	cpdir
/finds the	full path of a command	path
	function	whatwill
/displays the commands with	function in description	whatwill
/tests for	functional dependency of	fd
all subsidiary journals to	general journal	consolidate
	get terminal capability	termput
/adds	given number of days to a	computedate
/m[bhirs]] table root	goal column1 column2	searchtree
/looks for	goal string node in tree	searchtree
description of yourprog	goes here	yourprog
syntax	goes here	yourprog
/n[n] -fc -mc -i -s [file]	-h [file] -a [file] -v/	ve
/reports whether the file	has a table or list format	tableorlist
/returns the	hash offset for key strings	hashkey
which columns do not match	head	check
/removes the	head from both table and	headoff
/adds a /rdb	head to a table	headon
/change column name in	headline	rename
/lists the	help commands available	helpme
[table n[n] -fc -mc	-i -s [file] -h [file] -a/	ve
	income < taxtable	tax
/compute tax from	income and tax table	tax
/create	incomestatement from	income
/blank record and update	index file	delete
< file > file.x ;	index mb file.x Soundex	soundex
/add row to table and update	index tables	append
/filename processid from to	indexfrom indexto	lock
/processid from to	indexfrom indexto	unlock
processid from to indexfrom	indexto	lock
processid from to indexfrom	indexto	unlock
length of its argument or	input file	length
of its argument or	input file	lowercase
of its argument or	input file	uppercase
/converts form into screen	input shell program	screen
/removes blank rows from the	input table	rmblank

	print catalog from	makecatalog
	print invoice for sale	invoice
/squeezes a table for	printing	trim
/non-printing as well as	printing characters	see
/for	printing mailing labels	label
	prints a database	dbdict
	prints form letters from a	letter
/finds invalid data and	prints messages	validate
/filename	processid from to indexfrom	lock
tableorlist	processid from to indexfrom	unlock
	produce customer statement	cstate
/sample program to	produce standard reports	reportwriter
	produces bill-of-materials	bom
	produces table of subparts	explode
into screen input shell	program	screen
/sample	program to produce standard	reportwriter
/tests all /rdb	programs in demo directory	testall
/lists all /rdb	programs in rdb/bin	rdb
[	project ...] < tableorlist	project
/outputs selected	projects (same as project)	project
/converts table format to	prolog fact file format	tabletofact
/converts table format to	prolog rule file format	tabletorule
table ... >	prologfactfile	tabletofact
table ... >	prologrulefile	tabletorule
	prompts questions,	ask
	put a record into a file at	replace
	questiontable answerlist	ask
/e -1	-r -c -t'c'] [column ...]	justify
/blank	record and update index	delete
/finds and outputs	record from table	record
/put a	record into a file at	replace
update with screen form and	record locking	update.inv
/updates table with blank	record locking	update.sh
/locks a	record or field of a file	lock
/unlocks a	record or field of a file	unlock
/replaces all data in a	record with spaces	blank
/displays and edits	records in any sized file	update
	remove all core files to	rmcore
	removes blank rows from the	rmblank
	removes leading and	trimblank
	removes the head from both	headoff
	replace old string with new	substitute
	replaces all data in a	blank
program to produce standard	reports	reportwriter
	reports any rows in which	check
/writes	reports using a form and a	report
	reports whether the file	tableorlist
to the row and column	requested	cursor
/logical not reverses	return status of command	not
	returns string with blanks	padstring
	returns the ascii value of	ascii

[-m[bhirs] tableorlist from	to [xfrom xto] </	replace
fromdirectory	todirectory	cpdir
/appends tables	together	union
out all leading and	trailing blanks	compress
/removes leading and	trailing blanks for a	trimblank
/combines three tables into	translate dictionary	uniondict
language < text >	translatedtext	translate
for word substitution using	translation files	translate
for goal string node in	tree table	searchtree
/copies one directory	tree to another directory	cpdir
balancesheet from adjusted	trial balance	balance
a tax from with adjusted	trial balance data	fillform
/creates adjusted	trial balance table	adjust
/outputs	two or more tables sides by	paste
/joins	two tables into one where	jointable
[c -e	-u] [Column ...] <	gregorian
[c -e	-u] [Column ...] <	julian
text file into list of	unique words	word
	unlocks a record or field	unlock
/locks a table before vi and	unlocks afterwards	vilock
/enter saleorder and item,	update customer	sale
/blank record and	update index file	delete
/add row to table and	update index tables	append
/multiuser	update with screen form and	update.inv
letter of each word to	uppercase	cap
/returns the	uppercase of its argument	uppercase
/writes reports	using a form and a table	report
/word for word substitution	using translation files	translate
[file] -h [file] -a [file]	-v [file]]][-b]	ve
/prompts questions,	validates and writes/	ask
/displays the maximum	value in each column/	maximum
/returns the ascii	value of any character	ascii
/displays invalid	values in a column	domain
list format to shell	variable	listtosh
/create and display	ve look-up tables	vindex
/locks a table before	vi and unlocks afterwards	vilock
	visually edit a database	ve
/displays non-printing as	well as printing characters	see
/joins two tables into one	where keys match	jointable
/makes new table	where rows match logical	row
outputs the length of	widest column in a table	widest
/displays the	width of each column	width
to a table or list file	without an editor	enter
	word for word substitution	translate
/word for	word substitution using	translate
first letter of each	word to uppercase	cap
file into list of unique	words	word
questions, validates and	writes answerlist	ask
	writes reports using a form	report
	writes table or list file	display
/m[bhirs]] [-h -s -n	-x +x] [-l [2> location]]/	search

/**rdb**User´s Manual

/one line description of   yourprog goes here   yourprog

NAME

intro   command descriptions and syntax

COMMAND NAMES AND SYNOPSES

```
act             - display list of all /act commands
act

addcol          - adds columns to a table
addcol          newcolumn... < table

adjust          - creates adjusted trial balance table
adjust

append          - add row to table and update index tables
append          [-h -m[bhirs]] table [keycolumn ...] < tableorrow

ascii           - returns the ascii value of any character
ascii           character...

ask             - prompts questions, validates and writes answerlist
ask             questiontable answerlist

balance         - creates balancesheet from adjusted trial balance
balance

blank           - replaces all data in a record with spaces
blank           < tableorlist

bom             - produces bill-of-materials from parts list
bom

calcpay         - post payroll to ledgerpay
calcpay

calculate       - compute each taxform listed
calculate       taxform ...

cap             - converts first letter of each word to uppercase
cap             < textfile

cashflow        - compute balance column of cash table

chartdup        - check for duplicate names and accounts in chart
chartdup

check           - reports any rows in which columns do not match head
check           < tableorlist

chr             - displays the character corresponding to number
chr             number ...

clear           - clears the crt terminal screen
clear

close           - close accounting period creating journal for next
close

column          - display columns of a table in any order
column          [ Column ... ] < tableorlist

commands        - describes /rdb commands
commands

compress        - squeezes out all leading and trailing blanks
compress        [-b] < tableorlist

compute         - calculates columns of a table
compute         'column = expression [ ; ... ]' < tableorlist

computedate     - adds given number of days to a date
computedate     date  days

consolidate     - combine all subsidiary journals to general journal
consolidate     nextdate

cpdir           - copies one directory tree to another directory
cpdir           fromdirectory todirectory

cstate          - produce customer statement
```

```
      cstate

      cursor           - moves the cursor to the row and column requested
      cursor           row col [ CURSOR ]

      datatype         - displays the datatype of each column selected
      datatype         [ -l ] [ column ... ]  < table

      dbdict           - prints a database dictionary: the field names
      dbdict            < table

      delete           - blank record and update index file
      delete           [-m[bhirs]] table keycolumn ... < keytable

      difference       - outputs table of rows that are in only one table
      difference       table1 table2

      display          - writes table or list file to standard out
      display           < tableorlist

      domain           - displays invalid values in a column
      domain           domaintable [string ...] [< one-column-table]

      enter            - adds rows to a table or list file without an editor
      enter            [-limit] tableorlist

      explode          - produces table of subparts and their count for a part
      explode

      fd               - tests for functional dependency of columns
      fd               determinecolumn dependcolumn < table

      filesize         - returns the number of characters in a file
      filesize         filename ...

      fillform         - fill a tax from with adjusted trial balance data
      fillform         form

      fixtotable       - converts fixed length format to /rdb table format
      fixtotable       column [= n1,n2] ... < fixtdb

      foot             - foot or subtotal Debits and Credit of ledger
      foot

      getjournal       - copies journals for sales, pur, pay systems
      getjournal       journalname

      gregorian        - convert column of dates for math and format change
      gregorian        [ -c -e -u ] [ Column ... ] < tableorlist

      hashkey          - returns the hash offset for key strings
      hashkey          rows keystring ...

      headoff          - removes the head from both table and list files
      headoff          < tableorlist

      headon           - adds a /rdb head to a table
      headon           < table

      helpme           - lists the help commands available
      helpme

      howmany          - displays the number of commands in a directory
      howmany

      income           - create incomestatement from adjustedtrial
      income

      index            - set up table for search
      index            [-m[bhirs]] [-h -s -l [2> location]] tableorlist
                       [keycolumn ...] [ < keytable ]

      insertdash       - insert dash line as second line in table
      insertdash       < table-without-dashline

      intersect        - outputs table of rows that are in both input tables
      intersect        table1 table2

      invoice          - print invoice for sale order
      invoice

      jointable        - joins two tables into one where keys match
```

jointable	[-a[1|2]] [-j[1|2] column]... -n -] table1 [table2]
julian	- convert column of dates for math and format change
julian	[-c -e -u] [Column ...] < tableorlist
justify	- left and right justifies the columns of a table
justify	[-e -l -r -c -t'c'] [column ...] < table
label	- for printing mailing labels from a mailing list
label	< list
length	- returns the length of its argument or input file
length	[string] [< file]
letter	- prints form letters from a mailling list
letter	letter.1 ... < maillist
like	- finds names that sound like similar name
like	similar-name file [name-column]
listtosh	- converts list format to shell variable
listtosh	< list
listtotable	- for converting from list to table format
listtotable	[-e -l] < listfile
lock	- locks a record or field of a file
lock	filename processid from to indexfrom indexto
lowercase	- returns the lowercase of its argument or input file
lowercase	[string ...] [< file]
makecatalog	- print catalog from inventory table
makecatalog	
maximum	- displays the maximum value in each column selected
maximum	[-l] [column ...] < table
mean	- displays the mean (average) of each column selected
mean	[-l] [column ...] < table
menu	- root menu with some UNIX commands
menu	
minimum	- displays the minimum of each column selected
minimum	[-l] [column ...] < table
not	- logical not reverses return status of command
not	command ...
number	- insert a column row number in a table or list
number	< tableorlist
pad	- adds extra spaces at end of last column
pad	[-number] < tableorlist
padstring	- returns string with banks to fill a field
padstring	size string
paste	- outputs two or more tables sides by side
paste	table1 table2 [...]
path	- finds the full path of a command
path	[command ...]
precision	- displays the precision of each column selected
precision	[-l] [column ...] < table
project	- outputs selected projects (same as project)
project	[project ...] < tableorlist
prompt	- like echo but no return
prompt	string ...
rdb	- lists all /rdb programs in rdb/bin directory
rdb	
record	- finds and outputs record from table
record	[-h] number < table'
rename	- change column name in headline
rename	[oldcolumn newcolumn ...] < tableorlist

replace	- put a record into a file at specified location	
replace	[-a] [-m[bhirs] tableorlist from to [xfrom xto] < intableorlist	
report	- writes reports using a form and a table	
report	form < tableorlist	
reportwriter	- sample program to produce standard reports	
reportwriter		
rmblank	- removes blank rows from the input table	
rmblank	< table	
rmcore	- remove all core files to free up space on the disk	
rmcore		
row	- makes new table where rows match logical condition	
row	'column condition column-or-value ...' < table	
sale	- enter saleorder and item, update customer	
sale		
schema	- lists the database dictionary from table	
schema	tableorlist ...	
screen	- converts form into screen input shell program	
screen	< form > shellprogram	
search	- set up table for search	
search	[-m[bhirs]] [-h -s -n -x +x] [-l [2> location]]	
	tableorlist [keycolumn ...] [< keytable]	
searchtree	- looks for goal string node in tree table	
searchtree	[-m[bhirs]] table root goal column1 column2	
see	- displays non-printing as well as printing characters	
see	< tableorlist	
seek	- returns the beginning and ending offset of a row	
seek	[-m[bihrs]] [-o outfile] tableorlist [keycol...] < file	
select	- outputs selected rows	
select	'column condition column-or-value' < table	
sorttable	- sorts a table by one or more columns	
sorttable	[sort options] [columnname ...] < tableorlist	
soundex	- converts names into soundex codes	
soundex	< file > file.x ; index -mb file.x Soundex	
splittable	- divide table into smaller tables	
splittable	[-n] table	
substitute	- replace old string with new string in files	
substitute	oldstring newstring file ...	
subtotal	- outputs the subtotal of columns in a table	
subtotal	[-l] [break-column column ...] < table	
tableorlist	- reports whether the file has a table or list format	
tableorlist	[tableorlist...] [< tableorlist]	
tabletofact	- converts table format to prolog fact file format	
tabletofact	table ... > prologfactfile	
tabletofixt	- converts /rdb table format to fixed length format	
tabletofixt	column=n [r] ... < tableorlist	
tabletolist	- converts a file from table to list format	
tabletolist	[-l] < table	
tabletom4	- converts table format to m4 define file format	
tabletom4	< table > definefile	
tabletorule	- converts table format to prolog rule file format	
tabletorule	table ... > prologrulefile	
tabletosed	- converts table format to m4 sed file format	
tabletosed	< table > sedfile	
tabletostruct	- convert table to C language struct (record)	
tabletostruct	tag name	

```
tabletotbl      - converts /rdb table format to UNIX tbl/nroff format
tabletotbl      < tablefile > tblfile

tax             - compute tax from income and tax table
tax             income < taxtable

termput         - get terminal capability from /etc/termcap file
termput         capability

testall         - tests all /rdb programs in demo directory
testall         [ > testall.new ]

testsearch      - test the fast access methods in demo directory
testsearch

timesearch      - times the fast access methods in demo directory
timesearch      [ > timesearch.new ]

todaysdate      - output the current date in the format: 840415
todaysdate

total           - sums up each column selected and displays
total           [ -l ] [ column ... ]  < table

translate       - word for word substitution using translation files
translate       language < text > translatedtext

trim            - squeezes a table for printing
trim            [-[l|n|ln] col...][-r[n] col...][-t'c']...< table

trimblank       - removes leading and trailing blanks for a string
trimblank       [string] [ < file ]'

tset            - returns the termcap entry for the TERM terminal
tset            [ TERM ]

union           - appends tables together
union           tableorlist ... [-] [< tableorlist ]

uniondict       - combines three tables into translate dictionary
uniondict       langtolang > definefile

unlock          - unlocks a record or field of a file
unlock          tableorlist processid from to indexfrom indexto

update          - displays and edits records in any sized file
update          [-l -m[bhirs] -v] tableorlist [keycolumn...]

update.inv      - multiuser update with screen form and record locking
update.inv

update.sh       - update table with blank record locking
update.sh       -m[bhirs] tableorlist keycolumn

uppercase       - returns the uppercase of its argument or input file
uppercase       [string ...] [< file]

validate        - finds invalid data and prints messages
validate        'pattern { action } ...' < tableorlist

ve              - visually edit a database
ve              [data [-n[n] -fc -mc -i -s [file] -h [file] -a [file] -v [file]]] [-b]

vilock          - locks a table before vi and unlocks afterwards
vilock          tableorlist

vindex          - create and display ve look-up tables
vindex          data [ key field   [: decode field ] ... ]]

whatis          - displays the command description and syntax
whatis          command

whatwill        - displays the commands with function in description
whatwill        function

widest          outputs the length of widest column in a table
widest          < table'

width           - displays the width of each column selected
width           [ -l ] [ column ... ]  < table
```

```
word              - converts text file into list of unique words
word              < text > table

yourprog          - one line description of yourprog goes here
yourprog          syntax goes here
```

DESCRIPTION
/rdb

is a group of relational database commands for the UNIX and DOS systems. They operate on table or list files created in a text editor, or in the many input programs, or by other programs. They output new tables from old tables by extracting columns or rows or by joining, sorting, computing, totaling, subtotaling, and so on. They are flat ASCII files and the programs can be piped together. So /**rdb** is the only database system that works with and enhances the UNIX system. You can write programs in C and the UNIX shell programming language, which gives you complete access to the power of the UNIX system.

An example of a table is:

```
Date       Amount   Account   Description
-------    -------   -------   -----------
890601      20.00   car       car repair
890602       5.00   meal      dinner with client
```

There are only three rules for making a table:

1. Put a single tab between each column.
2. Put a column name at the top of each column, separated by tabs.
3. Put a dash line as the second line (minus sign, not underscore).

/**rdb** also has a list format. It is useful when data does not easily fit into a table. **listtotable** and **tabletolist** commands convert the files from one format to another.

List format looks like this:

```
Name      John Q. Public
Company   Makeapile
Street    1 Main
City      Anytown
State     CA
Zip       90000

Name      Sally Q. Public
 ...
```

The three rules for lists are:

1. Put a single tab between column (or field) name and data.
2. Put a return (newline) as first character (line) of the file.
3. Put a return between each row (or record, group of fields).

NAME
act   - display list of all **/act** commands

SYNOPSIS
act

DESCRIPTION
act will list the **/act** commands.

EXAMPLE
```
$ act
act          close       income       postap    shorttoaccount
adjust       consolidate invoice      postar    start
balance      cstate      makecatalog  postpay   tax.calc
bom          fillform    onhand       purchase  trial
calculate    foot        po           sale      vstate
chartdup     getjournal  post         ship      w2
```

SOURCE
```
: act menu shows programs available in accounting system

echo '
act          chartdup    getjournal   po        receive    trial
adjust       close       income       post      sale       vstate
balance      consolidate invoice      postap    ship       w2
bom          cstate      makecatalog  postar    ship.back
calcpay      fillform    onhand       postpay   shorttoacc
calculate    foot        paycheck     purchase  tax.calc
'
```

NAME
addcol   - adds columns to a table

SYNOPSIS
addcol   newcolumn... < table

DESCRIPTION
addcol appends new blank column(s) with the column names specified on the command line.

EXAMPLE
```
$ addcol New < inventory
Item      Amount   Cost    Value    Description      New
----      ------   ----    -----    --------------   -------
1         3        50      150      rubber gloves
2         100      5       500      test tubes
3         5        80      400      clamps
4         23       19      437      plates
5         99       24      2376     cleaning cloth
6         89       147     13083    bunsen burners
7         5        175     875      scales
```

SOURCE
```
read HEAD
read DASH
(echo "$HEAD" ; echo "$DASH" ; cat) |  column $HEAD "$@"
```

NAME

adjust   - creates adjusted trial balance table

SYNOPSIS

adjust

DESCRIPTION

adjust produces an adjusted trial balance sheet *adjusttrial* from the trial balance *trialbalance* sheet by adding in the journal of adjustments *journaladjust*. Adjustments are made at the end of the accounting period by the accountant to reflect changes in inventory, depreciation, depletion, amortization, and so on. These are computed costs of doing business that are assigned to each accounting period.

EXAMPLE

```
$ cat trialbalance
Account  Debit   Credit   Format   Taxline   Short     Name
-------  -----   ------   ------   -------   -------   ------------------

1010     11178            B-A      4L01      cash      Cash
3010             13500    I-I      101a      sales     Sales
3080               250    I-I      106       royalty   Gross royalties
3100              3286    I-I      108       income    Other Income
4020     3601            I-COGS   102-A2    merch     Misc Merchandise
4030     2100            I-COGS   102-A3    wages     Salary and Wages
4370        2            I-E      122       parking   Business parking
4380       41            I-E      122       travel    Business travel
4384      114            I-E      122       hotel     Business hotel
$ cat journaladjust
Account   Debit    Credit   Format   Taxline   Name
-------   -------  -------  -------  -------   --------------------

1110               20000    B-A      4L06      Beginning Inventory
1110      22130             B-A      4L06      Ending Inventory
1310                   0    B-A      4L09a     Accum Depreciation
1330                   0    B-A      4L10a     Accum Depletion
1420                   0    B-A      4L12a     Accum Amortization
4010      20000            I-COGS   102-A3    Beginning Inventory
4080               22130    I-COGS   102-A4    Ending Inventory
4170         0            I-E      121       Depreciation
4180         0            I-E      118       Depletion
4215         0            I-E      122       Amortization
$ adjust
$ cat adjustedtrial
Account  Debit   Credit   Format   Taxline   Short     Name
-------  -----   ------   ------   -------   -------   ------------------

1010     11178            B-A      4L01      cash      Cash
1110      2130            B-A      4L03      inv       Inventory
1310         0            B-A      4L09a     adeprec   Accum Deprec
1330         0            B-A      4L10a     adeplet   Accum Depletion
1420         0            B-A      4L12a     aamort    Accum Amort
3010             13500    I-I      101a      sales     Sales
3080               250    I-I      106       royalty   Gross royalties
3100              3286    I-I      108       income    Other Income
4010     20000            I-COGS   102-A1    beginv    Begin Inventory
4020     3601            I-COGS   102-A2    merch     Misc Merchandise
4030     2100            I-COGS   102-A3    wages     Salary and Wages
4080             22130    I-COGS   102-A6    endinv    Ending Inventory
4170         0            I-E      117a      deprec    Depreciation
4180         0            I-E      118       deplet    Depletion
4215         0            I-E      122       amor      Amortization
4370        2            I-E      122       parking   Business parking
4380       41            I-E      122       travel    Business travel
4384      114            I-E      122       hotel     Business hotel
```

Note that the *journaladjust* items have been added to the *trialbalance* to produce the *adjustedtrial*.

SEE ALSO
trial income balance

SOURCE
```
: adjust puts the journaladjust into the trialbalance to give
:      ajustedtrial

TMP=adjust$$
trap 'rm -f $TMP; trap 0; exit 0' 0 1 2 3 15

union  trialbalance journaladjust |
sorttable Account > adjustedtrial

: trial subtotals each account debits and credits
: and subtracts smallest

column Account Debit Credit < adjustedtrial |
subtotal |
compute 'Debit -= Credit;
      if (Debit < 0) Credit = 0 - Debit;
      if (Debit < 0) Debit = ""; else Credit = "";' > $TMP

: join with chart to get account names
: and justify Debit and Credit

jointable $TMP chart |
justify Debit Credit > adjustedtrial

echo adjustedtrial
total Debit Credit < adjustedtrial
```

NAME

append   - add row to table and update index tables

SYNOPSIS

append   [-h -m[bhirs]] table [keycolumn ...] < tableorrow

DESCRIPTION

append writes the row of the input *tableorrow* to the end of the *table*. It also updates the appropriate index table so that the next search will find it.

For the *record* method, it adds a new record offset to the end of the index table. For the *inverted* method, it adds a record and then sorts it.

OPTIONS

-h The input *tableorrow* has no **/rdb** head line and dash line. Useful when you only have a row to append to a table, but it does not have a head line.

-m[bhirs] See **index** for fast access methods.

EXAMPLE

We start with the *inventory* and *newrecord* tables.

```
$ cat inventory
Item   Amount   Cost   Value   Description
----   ------   ----   -----   -----------
   1        3     50     150   rubber gloves
   2      100      5     500   test tubes
   3        5     80     400   clamps
   4       23     19     437   plates
   5       99     24    2376   cleaning cloth
   6       89    147   13083   bunsen burners
   7        5    175     875   scales
$ cat newrecord
Item   Amount   Cost   Value   Description
----   ------   ----   -----   -----------
   8       35    105       0   pipettes
```

The *record* index table is also updated. First, let's see it before it is updated.

```
$ index -mr inventory
$ cat inventory.r
 Offset
--------
     76
    113
    147
    177
    207
    245
    283
```

Now we can append the *newrecord*.

```
$ append -mr inventory < newrecord
$ cat inventory
Item   Amount   Cost   Value   Description
----   ------   ----   -----   --------------
   1        3     50     150   rubber gloves
   2      100      5     500   test tubes
   3        5     80     400   clamps
   4       23     19     437   plates
```

```
     5      99     24    2376    cleaning cloth
     6      89    147   13083    bunsen burners
     7       5    175     875    scales
     8      35    105       0    pipettes

$ cat inventory.r
 Offset
--------
      76
     113
     147
     177
     207
     245
     283
     313
```

Note the new 313 entry in the secondary index table *inventory.r*. It is the offset to record 8.

SEE ALSO
delete replace

SOURCE
```
: %W% SCCS ID Information

: append - adds a record to the end of a file
:   it also updates the index file

USAGE='usage: append [-h -m[bhirs]] table [keycolumn ...] < tableorrow'
EUSAGE=1

HASHFULL='Hash index table is full.  Please reindex.'
EHASHFULL=2

TMP=/tmp/$$append

OFFSETWIDTH=9
METHOD=-ms

: handle arguments
while test -n "$1"
do
    case "$1" in
    -m*)    METHOD=$1 ;;
    -h)     NOHEAD=true ;;
    *)      TABLE=$1
            shift && KEYCOLUMNS="$*"
            break
            ;;
    esac
    shift
done

if test -z "$TABLE"
then
    echo $USAGE 1>&2
    exit $EUSAGE
fi

case "$METHOD" in
-ms)
    if test -n "$NOHEAD"
    then
            cat >> $TABLE
    else
            tail +3 >> $TABLE
```

```
        fi
        ;;
-mb)
    if test -n "$NOHEAD"
    then
            cat >> $TABLE
    else
            tail +3 >> $TABLE
    fi
    sorttable $KEYCOLUMNS < $TABLE > $TMP
    mv $TMP $TABLE
    ;;
-mr)
    END=`filesize $TABLE`
    if test -n "$NOHEAD"
    then
            cat >> $TABLE
    else
            tail +3 >> $TABLE
    fi
    awk     "END { printf (\"%${OFFSETWIDTH}d\\n\",\
                        $END);}" >> ${TABLE}.r < /dev/null
    ;;
-mi)
    END=`filesize $TABLE`
    cat > $TMP
    if test -n "$NOHEAD"
    then
            cat < $TMP >> $TABLE
    else
            tail +3 < $TMP >> $TABLE
    fi
    KEYROW="`column $KEYCOLUMNS < $TMP | tail -1`"
    awk     "END { printf (\"%${OFFSETWIDTH}d\\t%s\\n\", $END, \"$KEYROW\");}"\
    >> ${TABLE}.i < /dev/null
    sorttable +1 < ${TABLE}.i > $TMP; mv $TMP ${TABLE}.i
    ;;
-mh)
    END=`filesize $TABLE`
    cat > $TMP
    if test -n "$NOHEAD"
    then
            cat < $TMP >> $TABLE
            HEAD="`sed 1q $TABLE`"
            for KEY in $KEYCOLUMNS
            do
                    I=1
                    for COL in $HEAD
                    do
                            if test "$COL" = "$KEY"
                            then
                                        COLUMNS="$COLUMNS $I"
                            fi
                            I=`expr $I + 1`
                    done
            done
            KEYROW="`headon < $TMP | column $COLUMNS | tail -1`"
    else
            tail +3 < $TMP >> $TABLE
            KEYROW="`column $KEYCOLUMNS < $TMP | tail -1`"
    fi
    XROWS=`wc -l < ${TABLE}.h`
    ROWS=`expr $XROWS - 2`
    HASH=`hashkey $ROWS $KEYROW`
    awk     " NR != ($HASH + 3) { print; }
            NR == ($HASH + 3) {
                    while (\$1 > 0) {
                            print;
                            getline ;
                            }
                    printf (\"%${OFFSETWIDTH}d\\n\", $END);
```

```
                              }
                      " < ${TABLE}.h > $TMP
              if test "$XROWS" != "`wc -l < $TMP`"
              then
                      awk     "NR != 3 { print; }
                              NR == 3 {while (\$1 > 0) {
                                      print;
                                      if (getline == 0) {
                                                          }
                                          }
                              printf (\"%${OFFSETWIDTH}d\\n\", $END);
                              }
                              " < ${TABLE}.h > $TMP
                      if test "$XROWS" != "`wc -l < $TMP`"
                      then
                              echo $HASHFULL 1>&2
                              exit $EHASHFULL
                      fi
              fi
              mv $TMP ${TABLE}.h
              ;;
      esac
```

NAME

ascii   - returns the ASCII value of any character

SYNOPSIS

ascii   character...

DESCRIPTION

ascii converts each of the characters in the first argument string of its command line to a space delimited series of numbers. It is used to find out the internal computer representation of a character. This is a code called ASCII (pronounced ask-key), which stands for the American Standard Code for Information Interchange. Any strings following the first are ignored. If you have spaces in your string, be sure to put quotes around them.

EXAMPLE

Here we convert several characters.

```
$ ascii aA1
97 65 49
$ ascii ' '
32
```

Note that the single blank space, enclosed in single quotes, is converted to its ASCII code in decimal (32).

SEE ALSO

chr

NAME

ask   - prompts questions, validates and writes answerlist

SYNOPSIS

ask   questiontable answerlist

DESCRIPTION

ask will prompt the user with questions from the question table, validate the answers from information in the question table, and write the answers out to a list formatted answer file.

To use the **ask** program, simply edit the question table for your application. The *Var* column contains the name of the field you wish to enter.

The *Valid* column contains the validation criterion. A *number-number* value will cause **ask** to test to see if the user's answer is within that range of numbers. A file name here will cause **ask** to grep through the file for a match of the answer string that the user types. Anything else in the *Valid* column will cause **ask** to accept anything the user types.

The *Question* column contains the literal question to be asked.

EXAMPLE

First let's look at the question file:

```
$ cat questions
Var       Valid    Question
---       -----    --------
name      LETTERS  What is your name?
sex       sex      What is your sex?
weight    0-1000   What is your weight in pounds?
eye       eye      What is the color of your eyes?
```

Now let's run the **ask** program.

```
$ ask questions answers
What is your name? (LETTERS)
Rod  Manis
What is your sex? (choose from list below)
female
male

male
What is your weight in pounds? (0-1000)
160
What is the color of your eyes? (choose from list below)
black
blue
brown
green
hazel

hazel
$
```

Finally, let us see the answers as they have been put into list format.

```
$ cat answers
name      Rod Manis
sex       male
weight    160
eye       hazel
```

TECHNICAL

ask is a shell program that you can modify for your own use. Note that it uses the UNIX shell **read** command to read from the question file, as well as the standard-in. This is done by saving the standard input in a spare slot in the file table under file descriptor 4. Then standard input can be switched back and forth between the question table (file descriptor 3) and the user input (file descriptor 4).

SOURCE

```
: %W% SCCS Information
: ask - asks questions from a table and writes out the answers

USAGE='usage: ask questions answers'
EUSAGE=1
MACCEPT='Error: Can not find a file named $ACCEPT'
EACCEPT=2

if test "$#" -ne 2
then
      echo $USAGE
      exit $EUSAGE
fi


: get file names
QUESTIONS=$1
ANSWERS=$2

: start answer list if it does not exit
if test ! -w $ANSWERS
then
      echo > $ANSWERS
fi

: read questions form file descriptor 3 so we can get replys from 1

exec  3< $QUESTIONS

: save standard in file table entry

exec  4<&0

: save standard IFS, so that we can add tabs

OLDIFS=$IFS

: first skip question table headlines

exec 0<&3
read HEAD
read DASH

: read each line from question table, and switch back to stdin

read LINE
exec 0<&4

: big loop ask question, get reply, validate, write out

while test -n "$LINE"
do
      : parse question table row

      OLDIFS=$IFS
      IFS='        '
      set $LINE
      IFS=$OLDIFS
      VAR=$1 ; ACCEPT=$2 ; QUESTION=$3
```

```
        : test if domain or range

        if test "$ACCEPT" = "$VAR"
        then
                echo "$QUESTION (choose from list below)"
                cat $ACCEPT || ( echo $MACCEPT ; exit $EACCEPT )
                echo
        elif test "$ACCEPT" = "ANY"
        then
                echo $QUESTION
        else
                echo "$QUESTION ($ACCEPT)"
        fi

        : get answer from user

        ANSWER=
        while test -z "$ANSWER"
        do
                read ANSWER

                : validate answer

                case "$ACCEPT" in
                ANY): accept anyting
                break
                ;;
                [0-9]*-[0-9]*): this a a numeric range
                IFS=-
                set $ACCEPT
                IFS=$OLDIFS
                LOW=$1
                HIGH=$2
                if test "$ANSWER" -lt "$LOW" -o "$ANSWER" -gt "$HIGH"
                then
                echo Sorry, but your answer must be between $LOW and $HIGH.
                echo Please enter another answer.
                ANSWER=
                fi
                ;;
                *): this is a domain, check against table

                grep "^$ANSWER\$" $ACCEPT 2> /dev/null 1> /dev/null
                if test "$?" -ne 0
                then
                echo Sorry, but the acceptable answers are:
                cat $ACCEPT
                echo Please enter another answer.
                ANSWER=
                fi
                ;;
                esac
        done

        : write out answer and get next question

        echo "$VAR $ANSWER">> $ANSWERS

        : switch to question file and than back to stdin

        exec 0<&3
        read LINE
        exec 0<&4
done

: add one blank line as record separator

echo >> $ANSWERS
```

NAME
balance - creates balance sheet from adjusted trial balance

SYNOPSIS
balance

DESCRIPTION
balance produces the balance sheet.

EXAMPLE
```
$ cat adjustedtrial
Account   Debit   Credit    Format   Taxline   Short     Name
-------   -----   ------    ------   -------   -------   ------------------
1010      11178             B-A      4L01      cash      Cash
1110       2130             B-A      4L03      inv       Inventory
1310          0             B-A      4L09a     adeprec   Accum Depreciation
1330          0             B-A      4L10a     adeplet   Accum Depletion
1420          0             B-A      4L12a     aamort    Accum Amortization
3010              13500     I-I      101a      sales     Sales
3080                250     I-I      106       royalty   Gross royalties
3100               3286     I-I      108       income    Other Income
4010      20000             I-COGS   102-A1    beginv    Begin Inventory
4020       3601             I-COGS   102-A2    merch     Misc Merchandise
4030       2100             I-COGS   102-A3    wages     Salary and Wages
4080              22130     I-COGS   102-A6    endinv    Ending Inventory
4170          0             I-E      117a      deprec    Depreciation
4180          0             I-E      118       deplet    Depletion
4215          0             I-E      122       amor      Amortization
4370          2             I-E      122       parking   Business parking
4380         41             I-E      122       travel    Business travel
4384        114             I-E      122       hotel     Business hotel
$ balance
$ cat balancesheet
        Makeapile, Inc.
      31 December 1985
        Balancesheet

    11178   Cash
     2130   Inventory
        0       Accumulated Depreciation
        0       Accumulated Depletion
        0       Accumulated Amortization
    -----   -----------------------
    13308   Total Assets

    13308   Retained Earnings (Profit)
    ------  --------------------------
    13308   Total Liabilities and Equity
```

SOURCE
```
: balance will produce balancesheet

TMP=balance$$
TMP1=balance1$$
TMP2=balance2$$
trap 'rm -f $TMP $TMP1 $TMP2; trap 0; exit 0' 0 1 2 3 15

: get the right accounts from the adjusted trial balance

row 'Format ~ /^B-/' < adjustedtrial > $TMP

: add in the profit

tail -1 < profit>> $TMP
```

```
: add up the Assets first

row 'Format ~ /B-A/' < $TMP |
compute 'Debit -= Credit' |
justify Debit Credit > $TMP1

total Account Debit < $TMP1 |
compute 'Name = "Total Assets"' |
tail -2 >> $TMP1

: then add up the Liabilities and Equity

row 'Format ~ /B-LE/' < $TMP |
compute 'Credit -= Debit' |
justify Debit Credit > $TMP2

total Account Credit < $TMP2 |
compute 'Name = "Total Liabilities and Equity"' |
tail -2 >> $TMP2

: start with headline

cp balance.head balancesheet

: put each table, without head, into balancesheet

column Debit  Name < $TMP1 | tail +3 >> balancesheet
tail -2 balancesheet

echo >> balancesheet
column Credit Name < $TMP2 | tail +3 >> balancesheet
tail -2 balancesheet

# rm $TMP $TMP1 $TMP2
```

NAME

blank   - replaces all data in a record with spaces

SYNOPSIS

blank   < tableorlist

DESCRIPTION

blank allows you to replace with spaces all of the values in each record of a table or list file. It is used by the **update** program to lock (blank out) records that are being updated.

blank is used by the **update** command to put a blank record back into a file while the original record is being edited. This is a record lock against other users reading or updating the record while it is being worked on. However, the whole file is still available for use. Instruct your operators that when they pull up a blank record, it means that it is being updated by someone else. They should come back to it later, or find out who has it and when they will return it.

EXAMPLE

If you had a table, and you wanted to blank out the data fields and **see** the result, you could type:

```
blank < maillist | see
$
Number^I $
Name^I              $
Company^I        $
Street^I              $
City^I        $
State^I    $
ZIP^I     $
Phone^I              $
$
Number^I $
Name^I              $
Company^I          $
Street^I                      $
City^I        $
State^I        $
ZIP^I        $
Phone^I     $
$
```

Note the spaces between the tab (^I) and the dollar sign ($) which indicates the end of the line. The spaces replaced the characters, including spaces, that were in the original records.

Note also that the column names are left alone, so that this is a perfectly correct file as far as the **/rdb** commands are concerned, just no data.

NAME

bom   - produces bill-of-materials from parts list

SYNOPSIS

bom

DESCRIPTION

bom creates a bill-of-materials table from a table of parts (a list of all of the items that are required to make a product) and the sales items from the sales department. This tells how many items must be manufactured or purchased to meet current sales orders.

EXAMPLE

```
$ cat ../sales/saleitem
Order      Number   Code     Backord    Qty    Price    Total    Name
-------    -------  -------   -------   ------- -------  -------  ----
1                1  rdb          10        1     1500    1500.00  /rdb
2                1  rdb          10        2     1500    3000.00  /rdb
3                1  rdb          10        5     1500    7500.00  /rdb
3                2  act          10       10     1500   15000.00  /act
4                1  rdb          10        5     1500    7500.00  /rdb
4                2  rdb          10       19     1500   28500.00  /rdb
5                1  rdb          10        5     1500    7500.00  /rdb
5                2  act          10        9     1500   13500.00  /act
$ cat part
Code      Subpart     Count
-------   -------     -------
act       binder          2
act       actdoc          2
act       f1             10
rdb       binder          2
rdb       rdbdoc          2
rdb       f1             10
$ bom
$ cat bom
Code        Qty
-------   -------
actdoc        38
binder       112
f1           560
rdbdoc        74
```

You can see that we have orders for 19 copies of **act**s in the *salesitem* table. Each package has two (2) documents for a total of 38 *actdoc*. Note that the *bom* table lists 560 floppies (19 act x 10 + 37 rdb x 10). We can order these, regardless of which software packages are being put onto them.

SOURCE

```
: bom produces a bill of materials from the sales orders

TMP=/tmp/`basename $0`$$
TMP1=/tmp/`basename $0`1$$
trap 'rm -f $TMP $TMP1; trap 0; exit 0;' 0 1 2 3 15

row 'MakeBuy ~ /make/' < ../inv/inventory |
column Code |
search -ms ../sales/saleitem Code |
column Code Qty |
sorttable |
subtotal > $TMP

if test `tail +3 $TMP | wc -l` -le 0
```

```
then
       exit 1
fi

echo 'Code         Qty
-------         -------' > bom

while test 'jointable part $TMP | tee $TMP1 | tail +3 | wc -l' -gt 0
do
       compute 'Qty *= Count' < $TMP1 |
       column Subpart Qty |
       rename Subpart Code > $TMP
       tail +3 $TMP >> bom
done

sorttable < bom |
subtotal Code Qty > $TMP
mv $TMP bom

rm -f $TMP1
```

NAME
calcpay - post payroll to ledgerpay

SYNOPSIS
calcpay

DESCRIPTION
calcpay will post the payroll journal *journalpay* to the payroll ledger *ledgerpay*.
This ledger groups the pay checks by employee and is used to create the W2 form.

EXAMPLE
```
$ cat journalpay
Date      Number   Hours   Salary   Rate    Gross    Federal  State   Net
----      -------  ------- ------   ----    -------  -------  -----   -------
860518      1       80     1000      0      1000        70     10     920
860518      2       80        0     10       800        42      6     752
860518      3       30        0     10       300         0      0     300
$ calcpay
```

SOURCE
```
: 'calcpay computes journalpay: gross pay, deductions and net pay'
USAGE='usage: calcpay [ date ]'

: 'you will have to update these variables'
FICA=.07

: 'initialize variables'

EUSAGE=1
EFILES=2
MCORRECT='Is this correct? (y or n) '
TMP=/tmp/calcpay$$
TMP1=/tmp/calcpay1$$
trap 'rm -f /tmp/calcpay*; trap 0; exit 0' 0 1 2 3 15

DATE=${1:-`todaysdate`}

: 'check for needed files'

for I in employee hour journalpay féderal state
do
        if test ! -r $I
        then
                echo 'Must have file $I in this directory.'
                exit $FILES
        fi
done

: 'get needed data'
listtotable < employee |
jointable hour - |
column `sed 1q journalpay` |
compute "Gross = Salary + ( Rate * Hours) ;
        Date = \"$DATE\" ;
        FICA = $FICA * Gross ;" > $TMP

# compute taxes from tax tables
# redirect tmp file to stdin so that read can read it
exec 0< $TMP

# get headline
read HEAD
echo "$HEAD" > $TMP1
```

```
# tricky shell programming to get values
# make output line by putting $ in front of head column names
ROWOUT="`echo \"$HEAD\" | sed 's/[A-Za-z]*/\$&/g'`"

read DASH
echo "$DASH" >> $TMP1
while read $HEAD
do
        Federal=`tax $Gross < federal`
        State=`tax $Gross < state`
        eval echo \""$ROWOUT"\" '>> $TMP1'
done

# compute net
compress < $TMP1 |
compute 'Net = Gross - Federal - State - FICA;' |
justify |
tee lastpay |
tail +3 >> journalpay
```

NAME

calculate- compute each tax form listed

SYNOPSIS

calculate taxform ...

DESCRIPTION

calculate is a simple shell script that will calculate each tax form listed on its command line.

EXAMPLE

```
$ calculate 1040
```

SOURCE

```
: calculate will calculate each tax form
USAGE='usage: calculate taxform ...

for i
do
        $i.calc
done
```

NAME

cap　　　- converts first letter of each word to uppercase

SYNOPSIS

cap　　　< textfile

DESCRIPTION

cap capitalizes the first letter of each word in the input text file.

EXAMPLE

Note that the *Description* column has lower case names in it.

```
$ cat inventory
Item     Amount   Cost    Value   Description
----     ------   ----    -----   -------------
   1          3     50      150   rubber gloves
   2        100      5      500   test tubes
   3          5     80      400   clamps
   4         23     19      437   plates
   5         99     24     2376   cleaning cloth
   6         89    147    13083   bunsen burners
   7          5    175      875   scales
```

If we want to capitalize the first letter of each word in the inventory file we can type:

```
$ cap < inventory
Item     Amount   Cost    Value   Description
----     ------   ----    -----   -------------
   1          3     50      150   Rubber Gloves
   2        100      5      500   Test Tubes
   3          5     80      400   Clamps
   4         23     19      437   Plates
   5         99     24     2376   Cleaning Cloth
   6         89    147    13083   Bunsen Burners
   7          5    175      875   Scales
```


SEE ALSO

uppercase lowercase

NAME
cashflow- compute balance column of cash table

SYNOPSIS
cashflow< cashtable

DESCRIPTION
cashflow helps you manage your cash flow. It will compute a running balance in a *Balance* column (which must be column 3) from the *Amount* column (which must be column 2) of a special cash flow table.

Both individuals and businesses run the risk of spending more than they receive. This is not the problem of not having enough coming in to meet expenses. It is the problem in which your income is sufficient to cover your expenses, but it comes and goes in lumps that do not match. Cash flow analysis lets you see if your income will cover your out go on a day to day basis. It makes cash management possible by telling you whether to put off an expense until a check arrives, ask for an advance, get to work and make more money, or control your spending.

EXAMPLE
With an editor, create a table, which we will call **cashtable,** that looks like this:

```
$ cat cash

Date      Amount   Balance   Description
----      ------   -------   -----------
890101              512      current balance
890101    -450               rent check
890101    1000               pay check
890115    -300               estimated tax payment
890115    1000               pay check
890115    -1000              living expenses
890120    -900               big purchase

890201    1000               pay check
890201    -450               rent check
890215    1000               pay check
890115    -1000              living expenses
```

cashflow needs two columns, named *Amount* and *Balance*. (If you use different these column names, you must edit the **cashflow** shell script). Any other columns are optional. Each row in your table represents a projected income item (positive) or a projected expense (negative). This is your flow of cash. To find out if your cash flow is negative:

```
$ cashflow < cash

Date      Amount   Balance   Description
------    ------   -------   -----------
860101    512      512       current balance
860101    -450     62        rent check
860101    1000     1062      pay check
860115    -300     762       estimated tax payment
860115    1000     1762      pay check
860115    -1000    762       living expenses
860120    -900     -138      big purchase

860201    1000     862       pay check
860201    -450     412       rent check
860215    1000     1412      pay check
860115    -1000    412       living expenses
```

Oops! That *big purchase* is going to give us a negative balance in 890120. Now that you know, you can do something about it. One move is to put the big purchase off until the first of February.

```
$ cat cash

Date     Amount  Balance  Description
------   ------  -------  -----------
890101            512
890101    -450            rent check
890101    1000            pay check
890115    -300            estimated tax payment
890115    1000            pay check
890115   -1000            living expenses
890201    1000            pay check
890201    -900            big purchase
890201    -450            rent check
890215    1000            pay check
890115   -1000            living expenses
```

Now let's see if that works:

```
$ cashflow < cash

Date     Amount  Balance  Description
----     ------  -------  -----------
890101     512      512   current balance
890101    -450       62   rent check
890101    1000     1062   pay check
890115    -300      762   estimated tax payment
890115    1000     1762   pay check
890115   -1000      762   living expenses
890201    1000     1762   pay check
890201    -900      862   big purchase
890201    -450      412   rent check
890215    1000     1412   pay check
890115   -1000      412   living expenses
```

Ok. This will work. You can also try other options. Of course, if the purchase is **/rdb** software, then buy it immediately, and put off the rent and food.

You can do all of the inputting and editing in the text editor. You can execute commands in **vi** using the **vi** exclamation point (!) shell feature. You also might want to write out to a *tmp* file and **mv** it back to *cash* so that your *cash* file is up to date. For example in **vi** you can type:

```
:!cashflow < cashtable > tmp ; mv tmp cashtable
:e!
```

The first line computes the *Balance* column, puts the result in a *tmp* file, and moves the *tmp* file to be the new *cashtable*. All of this is necessary because in UNIX you cannot have one file as both input and output without wiping out the file. The second line, *:e!* pulls the new file into the **vi** editor and displays it on your screen.

SOURCE
```
: %W% SCCS ID Information
: cashflow - computes the balance column of a cashflow table

USAGE='usage: cashflow < table
Amount must be column 2 and Balance must be column 3'

awk    'BEGIN  { FS="    " ; OFS="            "; }
       NR < 3  { print }
       NR > 2  { $3 = sprintf ("%7d", ($2 + prev ));
               prev = $3; print }'
```

NAME
chartdup - check for duplicate names and accounts in chart

SYNOPSIS
chartdup

DESCRIPTION
chartdup checks to see if there are any duplicates in the account numbers or the short names of the chart of accounts. This is the most common error people make updating the chart of accounts.

EXAMPLE
```
$ chartdup
Duplicate Account numbers in chart.  See chart.Account
4150   I-E   115   taxes    Taxes
4150   I-E   115   taxes    Taxes
Duplicate Short names in chart.  See chart.Short
4150   I-E   115   taxes    Taxes
4150   I-E   115   taxes    Taxes
```

SOURCE
```
: chartdup checks to see if there are any duplicates in the
:    account numbers or the short names of the accounts

column Account < chart | tail +3 | sort | uniq -d > chart.Account

column Short   < chart | tail +3 | sort | uniq -d > chart.Short

if test -s chart.Account
then
    echo Duplicate Account numbers in chart.  See chart.Account
    cat chart.Account
    exit 1
fi

if test -s chart.Account
then
    echo Duplicate Short names in chart.  See chart.Short
    cat chart.Short
    exit 1
fi
```

NAME

check   - reports any rows in which columns do not match head

SYNOPSIS

check   < tableorlist

DESCRIPTION

check counts the columns (tabs + 1) in the head line of a **/rdb** table or list formatted file. Use it to see if your editing has messed up the tabs. Then it displays
information on each row that does not match the number of columns in the first
head line row. If your head line row is incorrect, then all of your rows will likely
be reported as errors.

check returns a zero status when all is ok and nonzero when it has found errors.
This returned status value ($?) can be used in shell programming to take different
actions depending upon the validity of the table or list file.

EXAMPLES

Here is a bad table:

```
$ cat badtable

Date      Account  Debit  Credit  Description
----      -------  -----  ------  -----------
820102    101      25000          cash from loan
820102    211.1            25000  loan #378-14 Bank Amerigold
820103    150.1            10000  test equipment from Zarkoff
820103    101      5000           cash payment
820103    211.2    5000           note payable to Zarkoff
820104    130      30000          inventory - parts from CCPSC
820104    201.1            15000  accounts payable to CCPSC
820104    101      15000          cash payment to CCPSC for parts
```

It is hard to see anything wrong with it.

```
$ check < badtable

check: Columns (4) do not equal headline columns (5) in row 3 (line 5).
820103 150.1   10000 test equipment from Zarkoff
```

Now if we see the table with the **see** command:

```
$ see < badtable

Date^IAccount^IDebit^ICredit^IDescription$
----^I ------^I-----^I------^I-----------$
820102^I101^I25000^I^Icash from loan$
820102^I211.1^I^I25000^Iloan number #378-14 Bank Amerigold$
820103^I150.1   10000^I^Itest equipment from Zarkoff$
820103^I101^I^I5000^Icash payment$
820103^I211.2^I^I5000^Inote payable to Zarkoff Equipment$
820104^I130^I30000^I^Iinventory - parts from CCPSC$
820104^I201.1^I^I15000^Iaccounts payable to CCPSC^I$
820104^I101^I15000^I^Icash payment to CCPSC for parts$
```

Note that in row 3 (line 5) of the table, there is a tab missing between 150.1 and
10000. The spaces hide the fact that it is missing.

When working with a large file, run **check** first. It will find the tab problems and
give you the information you need to find them. Use the text editor. On **vi**, turn
on the number option so you can see line numbers (it won't show row numbers).

```
$ vi table
```

```
:set number
```

You can move down to the first bad line with a vi *colon* command: (Get the colon in vi by simply typing a colon).

```
:5
```

This will take you to line 5. Then list it to see it:

```
:l
```

(This is the letter *ell,* not the number one (1)). Or to do it in one step (move and list), type:

```
:5l
```

Or you can set all of the lines in the file to display tabs with this colon command:

```
:set list
```

Turn it back to normal display with:

```
:set nolist
```

Edit in whatever changes you need, and go to the next bad line. You can change a space to a tab with:

```
:s/ /^I/
```

where the *^I* is the key on your keyboard that produces a tab. If you want to list several lines above and below the bad line, type:

```
:-3,+3l
```

If you use **ve** to enter your data, you will have fewer problems like this. Data from foreign sources should be checked carefully before use with **rdb**.

NAME

chr   - displays the character corresponding to number

SYNOPSIS

chr   number ...

DESCRIPTION

chr converts each of the integer numbers on its command line to the corresponding ASCII character. It is used to send special characters to the screen. This gives you a nice way to produce special characters that are hard to type or are interpreted by the shell.

EXAMPLE

Here we convert several characters.

```
$ chr 97 65 49
aA1
$ chr 7
(beep)
$ echo `chr 7`Wake up
(beep)Wake up
```

The *(beep)* is the sound. It does not print on your terminal.

SEE ALSO

ascii

NAME
    clear   - clears the crt terminal screen

SYNOPSIS
    clear

DESCRIPTION
    clear cleans your terminal screen of all characters and leaves the cursor in the upper left corner. It is useful for menus and forms which look better on a clear screen.

    clear uses the */etc/termcap* file of terminal capabilities to find the string of special characters that are needed to clear your screen. To work correctly, your *TERM* shell variable must be set correctly to the name of your terminal as listed in the */etc/termcap* file.

    The UNIX System 5 Release 2 has a new command which does the same thing.
```
$ tput clear
```

    /**rdb** also has a command called **termput** which does the same thing.
```
$ termput cl
```

    The difference is that **termput** uses the */etc/termcap* file, while **tput** use the *terminfo* directory.

SPEED
    This **clear** is quite fast, but there is a much faster way. About ten to twenty times faster on our computer. Set a shell variable *CLEAR* to the output of **clear** like this:
```
$ CLEAR='clear'
$ export CLEAR
```

    Then you can use:
```
$ echo "$CLEAR"
```

    in your shell programs for a fast clear. Put it in your *.profile* so that it will always be available. Use double quotes around the shell variables in case they might have special characters in them.

EXAMPLE
```
$ clear
```

    How do we show nothing? A blank screen?

SOURCE
```
: %W% SCCS ID Information
: 'clear screen using termput'

USAGE='usage: clear'

if test -n "$CLEAR"
then
        echo ${CLEAR}\\c
else
        termput cl
fi
```

NAME

　　close　　- close accounting period creating journal for next

SYNOPSIS

　　close

DESCRIPTION

close will close an accounting period, like a month, quarter, or year and will create the next period's journal, *journalnext*. When you start the next period, carry the *journalnext* forward by renaming it *journallast,* (**mv** *journallast journalnext*).

```
$ close
$ cat journalnext
Account   Date     Debit    Credit   Ref      Description
-------   -------  -----    ------   -------  ---------------
1010      850101   11178             jl       brought forward
1110      850101   2130              jl       brought forward
1310      850101   0                 jl       brought forward
1330      850101   0                 jl       brought forward
1420      850101   0                 jl       brought forward
4997      850101            13308    jl       brought forward
```

SOURCE

```
: copy all the balance sheet accounts into new journalnext

if test  $# = 0
then
        echo What is the next period starting date? \(example: 860101\)
        read NEXTDATE
else
        NEXTDATE=$1
fi

: get the balance sheet accounts from adjustedtrial balance

union adjustedtrial profit |
row 'Format ~ /B-/' |
column Account "Date    " Debit Credit Ref Description |
compute "Date = \"$NEXTDATE\"; Ref = \"jl\";
        Description = \"brought forward\";" > journalnext

total Debit Credit < journalnext
```

NAME

column - display columns of a table in any order

SYNOPSIS

column [Column ...] < tableorlist

DESCRIPTION

column will take in a table (or list) and produce a new table (or list) consisting of only the columns selected and in the order that they are listed on the command line.

If you give a column name that is not one of the columns for the file, **column** will create a new column by that name, in that location, and leave it empty. This allows you to create new columns. If you want to compute a column that does not exist, use this **column** facility to create it, then use the **compute** command to compute it. However, if you misspell a column name, you will get an empty column.

If no columns are specified on the command line (seems silly), the whole file is passed to the standard output without change. An inefficient **cat** program.

EXAMPLE

To make a new table from an inventory table like this:

```
$ cat inventory
Item#    Amount   Cost    Value   Description
-----    ------   ----    -----   -----------
    1        3    5.00        0   rubber gloves
    2      100    0.50        0   test tubes
    3        5    8.00        0   clamps
    4       23    1.98        0   plates
    5       99    2.45        0   cleaning cloth
    6       89   14.75        0   bunsen burners
    7        5     175        0   scales
```

type a column command like this:

```
$ column Cost Amount Description < inventory
Cost    Amount   Description
----    ------   -----------
 5.00        3   rubber gloves
 0.50      100   test tubes
 8.00        5   clamps
 1.98       23   plates
 2.45       99   cleaning cloth
14.75       89   bunsen burners
  175        5   scales
```

Note that the *Cost* and *Amount* columns have been reversed. We only have the columns we asked for and in the order we requested.

You can also project list formatted files columns. For example, the mailing list called *maillist* looks like this:

```
$ cat maillist

Number    1
Name      Ronald McDonald
Company   McDonald's
Street    123 Mac Attack
City      Memphis
State     TENN
```

```
ZIP        30000
Phone      (111) 222-3333

Number     2
Name       Chiquita  Banana
Company    United Brands
Street     Uno Avenido de la Reforma
City       San Jose
State      Costa Rica
ZIP        123456789
Phone      1234
```

If you only wanted the names and numbers, you could type:

```
$ column Name Phone < maillist
```

```
Name    Ronald McDonald
Phone   (111) 222-3333

Name    Chiquita  Banana
Phone   1234
```

SEE ALSO
project row

SOURCE

```
: column.sh - input table and output only selected columns of the table

read HEAD

if test -z "$HEAD"
then
     (echo; cat) | listtotable | $0 $* | tabletolist
     exit 0
fi

read DASH

for ARG
do
     C=1
     for I in $HEAD
     do
                     if test "$I" = "$ARG"
                     then
                     COL="$COL,\$$C"
                     shift
                     fi
     C=`expr "$C" + 1`
     done
done

COL=`expr "$COL" : ',\(.*\)'`

(echo "$HEAD"; echo "$DASH"; cat) |
awk "BEGIN {FS=OFS=\"  \";} {print $COL;}"
```

NAME
commands   - describes /rdb commands

SYNOPSIS
commands

DESCRIPTION
commands displays a table of **/rdb** commands, with both the one line description and the syntax of each command.

SOURCE
```
: %W% SCCS ID Information

: commands will list all of the commands
: in commands/bin from file lib/Commands

USAGE='usage: commands'

DIR=`path commands`

if test -r ${DIR}/../lib/Commands
then
        cat ${DIR}/../lib/Commands
else
        echo "Command list not in ${DIR}/../lib/Commands"
fi
```

NAME
compress   - squeezes out all leading and trailing blanks

SYNOPSIS
compress   [-b] < tableorlist

DESCRIPTION
compress removes all leading and trailing blanks from each column or field. It is used to save disk space. It is almost the opposite of justify. Your files are not as pretty when compressed as justified, but they are smaller. Usually one third the size or less. Therefore, they take less disk space and are much faster to process because most of the time used to execute database programs consists of moving data from the disk to the memory and, sometimes, back to the disk.

Multiple blanks separating words are left alone.

OPTIONS
-b   Leave out blank lines also. Don't use this option with list files!

EXAMPLE
For example, we might have a file called *oldjournal* like this:

```
$ cat oldjournal

Date      Account   Debit   Credit   Description
----      -------   ----    -----    -----------
890102    101       25000            cash from loan
890102    211.1             25000    loan number #378-14 Bank Amerigold
890103    150.1     10000            test equipment from Zarkoff
890103    101       5000             cash payment
890103    211.2             5000     note payable to Zarkoff Equipment
890104    130       30000            inventory - parts from CCPSC
890104    201.1             15000    accounts payable to CCPSC
890104    101       15000            cash payment to CCPSC for parts
```

It has no extra spaces. We can see this by using the **see** command:

```
$ see < oldjournal

Date^IAccount^IDebit^ICredit^IDescription$
----^I-------^I-----^I------^I-----------$
890102^I101^I25000^I^Icash from loan$
890102^I211.1^I^I25000^Iloan number #378-14 Bank Amerigold$
890103^I150.1^I10000^I^Itest equipment from Zarkoff$
890103^I101^I^I5000^Icash payment$
890103^I211.2^I^I5000^Inote payable to Zarkoff Equipment$
890104^I130^I30000^I^Iinventory - parts from CCPSC$
890104^I201.1^I^I15000^Iaccounts payable to CCPSC$
890104^I101^I^I15000^Icash payment to CCPSC for parts$
```

Note that **see** turns all of the tabs into (^I) and puts a dollar sign ($) at the end of each row to show us that there are no spaces at the end.

justify will insert spaces in order to justify the file.

```
$ justify < oldjournal

Date      Account   Debit   Credit   Description
----      -------   -----   ------   -----------
890102    101.0     25000            cash from loan
890102    211.1             25000    loan number #378-14 Bank Amerigold
```

```
890103    150.1   10000              test equipment from Zarkoff
890103    101.0            5000      cash payment
890103    211.2            5000      note payable to Zarkoff Equipment
890104    130.0   30000              inventory - parts from CCPSC
890104    201.1           15000      accounts payable to CCPSC
890104    101.0           15000      cash payment to CCPSC for parts
```

To see what has happened let's use **see** again:

```
$ justify < oldjournal > journal ; see < journal
Date    ^IAccount  ^IDebit    ^ICredit   ^IDescription                                     $
------  ^I-------  ^I-------  ^I-------  ^I----------------------------------             $
890102  ^I 101.0   ^I 25000   ^I          ^Icash from loan                                $
890102  ^I 211.1   ^I         ^I 25000    ^Iloan number #378-14 Bank Amerigold            $
890103  ^I 150.1   ^I 10000   ^I          ^Itest equipment from Zarkoff                   $
890103  ^I 101.0   ^I         ^I 5000     ^Icash payment                                  $
890103  ^I 211.2   ^I         ^I 5000     ^Inote payable to Zarkoff Equipment             $
890104  ^I 130.0   ^I 30000   ^I          ^Iinventory - parts from CCPSC                  $
890104  ^I 201.1   ^I         ^I 15000    ^Iaccounts payable to CCPSC                     $
890104  ^I 101.0   ^I         ^I 15000    ^Icash payment to CCPSC for parts               $
```

Note all the spaces that have been inserted by justify. They can be removed by **compress.**

```
$ compress < journal > newjournal
```

To see what **compress** has done, type:

```
$ see < newjournal

Date^IAccount^IDebit^ICredit^IDescription$
-------^I-------^I-------^I-------^I---------------------$
890102^I101.0^I25000^I^Icash from loan$
890102^I211.1^I^I25000^Iloan number #378-14 Bank Amerigold$
890103^I150.1^I10000^I^Itest equipment from Zarkoff$
890103^I101.0^I^I5000^Icash payment$
890103^I211.2^I^I5000^Inote payable to Zarkoff Equipment$
890104^I130.0^I30000^I^Iinventory - parts from CCPSC$
890104^I201.1^I^I15000^Iaccounts payable to CCPSC$
890104^I101.0^I^I15000^Icash payment to CCPSC for parts$
```

SEE ALSO
rmblank

NAME
compute - calculates columns of a table

SYNOPSIS
compute 'column = expression [; ...]' < tableorlist

DESCRIPTION
compute allows you to do math on columns. A column can be computed as a function of other columns, itself and constants.

compute uses the UNIX **awk** program (a powerful interpreted programming language) just as **row** does. The advantage of **compute,** over **awk,** is that **compute** knows about the names of the columns. Therefore, you can use column names instead of column positional numbers. (In **awk** the second column is named *$2.)* To really understand the full power of **compute** and **row,** read the UNIX **awk** tutorial. If you need to do very complex manipulations of tables, use **awk.** It is a cross between a spreadsheet, the C programming language and a Basic interpreter. **awk** knows about tables, columns and rows (or lines). It has the capabilities of many different programs such as **grep, sed, dc,** or **lex.**

If you need to create a new empty column for **compute** to put values into, use **column. column** will create an empty column for any column name it cannot find in the header line.

EXAMPLE
To compute a column from other columns:

```
compute 'Value = Cost * Amount' < inventory

Item#    Amount    Cost    Value    Description
-------  -------  -------  -------  ----------------
      1        3     5.00    15.00  rubber gloves
      2      100     0.50    50.00  test tubes
      3        5     8.00    40.00  clamps
      4       23     1.98    45.54  plates
      5       99     2.45   242.55  cleaning cloth
      6       89    14.75  1312.75  bunsen burners
      7        5   175.00   875.00  scales
```

Here are a lot more examples of what you can do with compute:

```
compute 'column = number' < tableorlist
compute 'column = "string"' < tableorlist
compute 'column1 = column2 + column3' < tableorlist
compute 'column1 = expression; column2 = expression;' < tableorlist
compute '/startstring/,/endstring/ {column = expression}' < tableorlist
```

Change the format of *column* with C language *sprintf:*

```
compute 'column = sprintf ("%8.2f", column)' < tableorlist
```

Set *column* equal to the length of the string in *column2*:

```
compute 'column = length (column2)' < tableorlist
```

Set *column* equal to the natural logarithm of *column2*:

```
compute 'column = log (column2)' < tableorlist
```

Increment *column2* whenever *column* is greater than *number*:

```
compute 'if (column > number) column2 += 1' < tableorlist
```

EXPRESSIONS

As you can see, you can write rather complex expressions. By *expression,* we mean many kinds of equations. For example, a variable or a column is an expression. So is variable + variable. So are rather complex equations. The following SYMBOLS indicate some of the more complex expressions.

SYMBOLS

column	name of a column exactly as it appears at the top of the column
=	make the column on the left equal the expression on the right
+	add
-	subtract
*	multiply
/	divide
%	modulo (zero if left value is equally divisible by right)
;	statement separator needed if more than one equation
log ()	natural logarithm of value or column in ()
length ()	string length of string in column

You can also use C language like statements:

if then else:

```
        if (expression) equation [ else equation ];

        if (Value > 10000) Status = "Special"; else Status = "Normal";
```

while loop:

```
        while (expression) equation;

        while (column => 0) column -= 1 ;
```

for loop:

```
        for (expression; condition; expression) equation;

        for (i = 0; i < column1; i++) array [i] = column2 + i ;
```

You can also use the **awk** format: *pattern { action }* . For example:

```
$ compute 'length > 80 { print NR, "Line too long." }' < table
```

awk recognizes *length* as a function that returns the length of the row and *NR* as the line number. Note that the line numbers of a file starts with the head line, while row numbers of a table starts after the dash line (line 3).

WHAT IS A COLUMN NAME

Each word that **compute** finds in the command line program, it looks up in the column header of the input file. If there is a match, **compute** converts the column name to $1 or $2, etc., depending upon the relative location of the column. These $1, etc. column numbers are needed by **awk.**

compute defines a column name to be a string of the following characters:

1. upper and lower letters, numbers, and the underscore (_) or

2. any string that is enclosed by single (') or double (") quotes.

Therefore, if you want special characters in your column names, put quotes around them when you use them.

```
$ compute ' "Item#" = NR ' < inventory
```

Note the double quotes around the column head *Item#* because of the number character (#). Also, note that we used double quotes, because the whole program was enclosed in single quotes. If you use one kind of quote around the whole program, use the other kind of quote around the column names that have special characters in them.

RESERVED WORDS TO AVOID IN COLUMN

Some words are understood by **awk.** Therefore, they should not be used in column names. A simple way to avoid a conflict is to start your column names with a capital letter. **awk** will not confuse *Print* with *print*. Here is a list of **awk's** built-in functions.

Reserved Words	Description
BEGIN	pattern that matches before first input record
END	pattern that matches after last input record
break	get out of for or while loop
continue	goto next iteration of for or while loop
else	used in "if then else" expression
exit	leave program entirely as if end of input
exp	raise number to a power
for	for (expression ; condition ; expression) statement
getline	get next input line
if	if (condition) statement [else statement]
in	for (variable in array) statement
index	index (string1, string2)
int	truncate argument to integer
length	returns current line length, or length of argument
log	returns log (to base 2) of argument
next	skip to next record and reexecute all commands
print	outputs variables
printf	printf ("format", variable, ...)
split	split (string, arrayname, separator)
sprintf	sprintf ("format", variable, ...)
sqrt	returns square root of argument
substr	substr (string, start, number)
while	while (condition) statement

USING SHELL VARIABLES IN PROGRAMS

Often you want to use a shell variable in a **compute** command. It is easy, if you understand what is going on.

```
$ DATE=860101
$ compute "Date = $DATE" < journal
Date    Account Debit    Credit  Description
------  ------- -----    ------  --------------------------------
860101  101     25000            cash from loan
860101  211.1            25000   loan number #378-14 Bank Amerigold
860101  150.1   10000            test equipment from Zarkoff
860101  101              5000    cash payment
860101  211.2            5000    note payable to Zarkoff Equipment
860101  130     30000            inventory - parts from CCPSC
860101  201.1            15000   accounts payable to CCPSC
860101  101              15000   cash payment to CCPSC for parts
```

We set a shell variable named *DATE* to a date. Then we used the variable in the

compute command line program. But note that we had to use double quotes (") instead of our usual single quote ('). To the shell, single quotes protect absolutely. With single quotes, the shell would not see the dollar sign ($) in front of *DATE* and would not convert it to its value. The double quote protects the enclosed from the shell, also, except for shell variables and command substitution ('cmd'). With double quotes, the shell will still replace variables (which start with a dollar sign character).

There is one further complication. The previous worked fine because the value of date was a number. But if we want to use strings in **awk** they must have double quotes (not single) around them.

```
$ COMPANY='Makeapile, Inc.'
$ compute "Company = \"$COMPANY\"" < maillist

Number   1
Name     Ronald McDonald
Company  Makeapile, Inc.
Street   123 Mac Attack
City     Menphis
State    TENN
ZIP      30000
Phone    (111) 222-3333

Number   2
Name     Chachita Banana
Company  Makeapile, Inc.
Street   Uno Avenito De La Revolution
City     San Jose
State    El Salvadore
ZIP      123456789
Phone    1234
```

Here we set a shell variable COMPANY to a company name. We want to update the maillist because these characters have been hired by a new company. Note what we had to do. We needed double quotes around the whole program to let the shell substitute the value of the shell variable. But we also needed double quotes around the string "Makeapile, Inc." for **awk.** So we have to protect the innermost double quotes with back slashes.

There is another way which opens up a little window in the program for the shell to insert strings. But it fails when there are spaces in the window string. So use the method previously discussed.

PROBLEM WITH AWK FLOATING POINT FORMAT

On some computers the value column is computed to much greater precision than you are likely to want. This is a bug in the UNIX port of **awk.** For example one computer will produce this table:

```
Item#   Amount   Cost    Value   Description
-------  -------  -------  -------  ---------------
    1        3     5.00   15         rubber gloves
    2      100     0.50   50         test tubes
    3        5     8.00   40         clamps
    4       23     1.98   45.539997100830078125   plates
    5       99     2.45   242.5499725341796875    cleaning cloth
    6       89    14.75   1312.75  bunsen burners
    7        5   175.00   875        scales
```

To control the precision of the floating point values in a column you can use the *sprintf* function from the C programming language that has been implemented in **awk:**

```
compute 'Value = sprintf ("%7.2f", ( Cost * Amount ))' < inventory
or
compute 'Value = Cost * Amount; \
        Value = sprintf("%7.2f", Value)'< inventory
```

These commands will produce the first table under EXAMPLES above.

On some Berkeley UNIX systems *$0,* which is supposed to mean the entire line, was replaced with the command line instead. This is all very embarrassing to our UNIX porting people, but they are getting better. Hopefully these problems will disappear with time and experience. If so, we will not have to work around them for long.

SOURCE

```
: compute.sh - input table or list and compute selected columns

read HEAD

if test -z "$HEAD"
then
        (echo; cat) | listtotable | $0 $* | tabletolist
        exit 0
fi

read DASH
echo $HEAD
echo $DASH

C=1
for I in $HEAD
do
        COLIN="$COLIN $I=\$$C;"
        COLOUT="$COLOUT \$$C=$I;"
        C=`expr "$C" + 1`
done

if test -n "$COLIN"
then
        awk "BEGIN {FS=OFS=\"    \";} {$COLIN $1; $COLOUT print;}"
fi
```

NAME
computedate   - adds given number of days to a date

SYNOPSIS
computedate   date days

DESCRIPTION
computedate adds days to a date and displays the new date. **computedate** takes a date in the format 890301 for 1 Mar 89, and a number of days (including negative -days), and computes the new date. **computedate** displays the new date in the same format 890301.

This is the best format for entering dates in a column because they will sort correctly and they only take six characters.

Internally **computedate** converts the date to **julian,** adds days and converts back to **gregorian.** Suppose we want to know the date 45 days from March 31, 1989. We can type:

```
$ computedate 890331 45
890515
```

That is May 15, 1989. Another trick is to combine the **todaysdate** and the **computedate** programs. **todaysdate** gives the date of today in the preferred format:

```
$ todaysdate
890302
```

This command shows us the date, 45 days from today.

```
$ computedate 'todaysdate' 45
890416
```

DATA VALIDATION
Another trick is to validate a date with **computedate.** If you add zero days to a date, and get a different date, then the original date was not valid. Lets test the 32nd day of January, 1989.

```
$ computedate 890132 0
890201
```

As we would expect, we get a different date. We can test this with this kind of shell programming:

```
if test $DATE = 'computedate $DATE 0'
then
        echo OK
else
        echo Invalid DATE
fi
```

SEE ALSO
julian gregorian

NAME

consolidate   - combine all subsidiary journals to general journal

SYNOPSIS

consolidate   nextdate

DESCRIPTION

consolidate will put together all of the subsidiary journals, such as *journalincome, journalexpense,* or *journaldeposit* into the general journal named *journal*. It also converts from single entry to double-entry bookkeeping by totaling *Debits* and *Credits* and inserting counterbalancing adjustments to the cash account. It needs the *nextdate* for these accounts.

EXAMPLE

```
$ consolidate $NEXTDATE
$ cat journal
Date     Account    Debit    Credit    Ref       Description
------   ------    -------   -------   ------    --------------------
890101   4370          2               r         parking at clients
890103   4380         15               c115      shuttle bus to airport
890104   4380         13               v         meal
890105   4380         13               c116      meal
890106   4384        114               r         hotel
890118   3100                   3286   c101      consulting
890125   3080                    250   c1459     book fees
891231   1010                   5858             double-entry
891231   1010      17036                         double-entry
891231   3010                  13500   deposit   from sales/deposit
891231   4020       3601               check     from pur/check
891231   4030       2100               payroll   from pay/journalpay
```

Note the double-entry adjustments, and the totals of journals from sales, purchasing and pay departments. The *Date* came from the *NEXTDATE* shell variable, which is set in the *.profile*.

SEE ALSO

getjournal

SOURCE

```
: consolidate will consolidate journals into a general journal
USAGE='usage: consolidate date'

TMP=/usr/tmp/$$consol
TMP1=/usr/tmp/$$1consol
trap 'rm -f /usr/tmp/$$*; trap 0; exit 0;' 0 1 2 3 15

: get date if first argument
DATE=$1
export DATE

: get cash account
CASH='row 'Name ~ /Cash/' < chart |
column Account |
tail -1'

: sort chart by Short name for convension to Account number
if test ! -r chart.short
then
      sorttable Short < chart > chart.short
fi
```

```
: income

union journalincome journaldeposit |
rename Amount Credit Account Short |
compute 'Credit = sprintf ("%7.0f", Credit)' |
sorttable Short |
jointable -a1 -j Short - chart.short |
column Date Short Account Debit Credit Ref Description > journal

: add balancing Debit to cash account for income

total Credit < journal |
compute "Date = \"$DATE\"; Debit = sprintf (\"%7.0f\", Credit) ; Credit = \"\" ;\
     Account = \"$CASH\"; Description=\"double entry\";" > $TMP1
tail +3 $TMP1 >> journal

: display income total

echo 'Total of journalincome is debited to the cash account:'
column Account Debit < $TMP1


: expense

union journalexpense journalcheck journalpay |
rename Amount Debit Account Short |
compute 'Debit = sprintf ("%7.0f", Debit)' |
sorttable Short |
jointable -a1 -j Short - chart.short |
column Date Short Account Debit Credit Ref Description > $TMP

tail +3 $TMP >> journal

: add Credit to Cash for expenses

total Debit < $TMP |
compute "Date = \"$DATE\"; Credit = sprintf (\"%7.0f\", Debit) ; Debit = \"\" ;\
     Account = \"$CASH\"; Description =\"double entry\";" > $TMP1
tail -1 $TMP1 >> journal

: display expense total

echo 'Total of journalexpense is credited to the cash account:'
column Account Credit < $TMP1

: check for unknown accounts

row 'Account == ""' < journal | trim -l30 Description > $TMP

if test "`wc -l $TMP`" -gt 2
then
     echo 'The short names for these entries are not in the chart.'
     cat $TMP
     exit 1
fi

column Date Account Debit Credit Ref Description < journal > $TMP
mv $TMP journal

: sort journal on Date column

sorttable Date < journal > $TMP
mv $TMP journal

: display results

echo total journal
total Debit Credit < journal
```

NAME
cpdir   - copies one directory tree to another directory

SYNOPSIS
cpdir   fromdirectory todirectory

DESCRIPTION
cpdir copies the directory tree, that is, all the directories and all of their files under the *fromdirectory* to the *todirectory*.

cpdir uses the tar command in a special way. It is a shell program so you can cat it out and see how it does it.

cpdir conforms to the **cp** and **ln** command's format. In other words it copies from olddirectory to newdirectory; left to right. The first directory is the source and the second is the destination.

The UNIX System III and higher **cpio** command can accomplish the same thing, but with a lot more options to get right.

EXAMPLE
You might use this for backing up a large directory:

```
$ cpdir /usr/rdb /usr/rdb.backup
```

Or to move a directory to a preferred place:

```
$ cpdir /usr/he.left/goodstuff /usr/project/goodstuff
```

SEE ALSO
tar

SOURCE
```
: %W% SCCS ID Information

: 'cpdir - copies a directory tree to another directory tree'

USAGE='usage: cpdir fromdirectory todirectory'
EUSAGE=1

if test $# != 2
then
        echo $USAGE 1>&2
          exit $EUSAGE
else
        cd $1; tar cf - . | ( cd $2 ; tar xf - )
fi
```

NAME
cstate   - produce customer statement

SYNOPSIS
cstate

DESCRIPTION
cstate generates the customer statement from the *salesorder* and *deposit* tables. It shows what the customer has ordered and paid and the net. It is printed as a form to be sent to the customer as a bill.

EXAMPLE
```
$ cstate
Please enter customer number (or all or Return to exit): 3
                Customer Statement
                ------------------
Makeapile, Inc., 123 Bigbucks Blvd., Dallas, TX 12345, 1-800-SOF-WARE

Mailing Address for Customer Number  3

Ms Ute  Unix Ph.D. President

UniUniUniUni Software Sellers
12345 Nixuni Street
Union, New Jersey  11111  USA

Now Due and Payable is your balance of: 107550.00

Details of Your Orders and Payments

Cust  Date      Amount    Ref
----  ------   ---------  ----
   3  850902    -6300.00    17
   3  850902   -14175.00    16
   3  850902   -22050.00    15
   3  850902   -23625.00    12
   3  850902   -37800.00    13
   3  850903   -12600.00    23
   3  860105     9000.00  3347
----  ------   ---------  ----
                -107550.00
Please enter customer number (or all or Return to exit):
```

SEE ALSO
vstate

SOURCE
```
: statement print bill for one or all customers

PROGRAM=`basename $0`

MGETCUST='Please enter customer number (or all, Return to exit):'
MGETVENDOR='Please enter vendor number (or all, Return to exit):'

case $PROGRAM in
cstate)
    MGETNUMBER=$MGETCUST
    FILE=customer
    ;;
vstate)
    MGETNUMBER=$MGETVENDOR
    FILE=vendor
    ;;
```

```
*) echo "$PROGRAM: This program must be named cstate or vstate"
   ;;
esac


echo $MGETNUMBER

while read NUMBER
do
    case $NUMBER in
    "")     exit 0 ;;
    A*|a*)
            report $PROGRAM.f < $FILE
            ;;
    [0-9]*)
            echo $NUMBER |
            search -ms $FILE Number |
            report $PROGRAM.f
            ;;
    esac

    echo
    echo $MGETNUMBER
done
```

NAME
cursor   - moves the cursor to the row and column requested

SYNOPSIS
cursor   row col [CURSOR]

DESCRIPTION
cursor will move your cursor to any location on your computer screen. You can do some very nice screen handling from a shell script with this and the **clear** commands. You can paint your screen with cursor moves and **echo** commands. Then use the **read** command to get the user's input. Then you can test the input with the full power of UNIX and **/rdb.** You can also clear fields of the screen by moving the cursor and writing blanks.

You must give the row and column you want. It also needs the cursor movement (cm) entry from the */etc/termcap* file. This can be given as an argument, but the easiest way is to set up the shell variable called *CURSOR*. Then **cursor** will find it in its environment automatically.

To set up the *CURSOR* variable:

```
$ CURSOR=`termput cm`
```

On UNIX System 5 Release 2, use **tput:**

```
$ CURSOR=`tput cup`
```

Another way is to use your text editor to find the entry in */etc/termcap* and copy its *cm* entry for your terminal to your *.profile* file.

```
CURSOR=^[[%p1%d;%p2%dH
```

This is the entry for the *pc* terminal. The uparrow bracket (^[) is the ESC key or CNTL-[. It gets the terminals attention and indicates that a command string to the terminal is following. It is converted into the proper escape string by the *tgoto* function from the **termcap(3)** library.

EXAMPLE
```
$ cursor 11 38
```

Now imagine that your cursor is sitting in the middle of your screen and blinking at you.

SPEED
This **cursor** command is quite fast, but there is a much faster way. Set a shell variable like *L22* to move to the 22nd line like this:

```
$ L22=`cursor 23 0`
```

Then you can use:

```
$ echo "$L22$MESSAGE\c"
```

in your shell programs for a fast cursor movement and to print a message. Note the double quotes around the messages in case there are special characters. Also note the \c which tells **echo** not to put out a carriage return. In older versions of UNIX it is *-n* instead of \c.

An even better trick is to use the shell feature that tests to see if a variable has been set and only gives it a value when it needs one.

```
$ echo "${L22:='cursor 22 0'}$MESSAGE\c"
```

All of this magic causes the shell to check if *L22* has a value. If not it executes the **cursor** command and assigns the value to *L22*. Then, if this line is called in a loop, the next time the value will have been set and will be about 20 times faster.

SOURCE

```
: %W% SCCS Information

: 'cursor - move the cursor to the row and column on the screen'
: '      like tput in system V release 2, but portable'

USAGE='usage: cursor row column'
EUSAGE=1

if test "$#" -ne 2
then
        echo $USAGE 1>&2
        exit $EUSAGE
fi

echo 'echo "$CURSOR"|
sed     "s/%./$1/
        s/%./$2/"'\\c
```

NAME
datatype - displays the data type of each column selected

SYNOPSIS
datatype [-l] [column ...] < table

DESCRIPTION
datatype displays the type of data in each column selected. If no columns are listed, all of the columns will be calculated and displayed.

OPTIONS
-l   option will cause the entire file to be listed also.

CODE
-1   character strings with nonnumeric data
0   integer number
1,2...   floating point (number of digits to the right of the decimal)

EXAMPLE
```
$ datatype -l < typetable
Int     Char    Float2  Float4
---     ----    ------  ------
1       a       1.2     1.1234
745     zzzz    8.54    12.3
---     ----    ------  ------
  0      -1        2       4
```

Note that the *Int* column has only integers in it (code 0), the *Char* column has characters in it (code -1), and the two *Float* columns have different precisions (positive numbers codes). Note that the float precision is the maximum.

SEE ALSO
dbdict

NAME
dbdict   - prints a database dictionary: the field names

SYNOPSIS
dbdict   < table

DESCRIPTION
dbdict prints a table of two columns consisting of the field names and field numbers of the input table.

EXAMPLE
For example, we might have a table named *journal* which looks like this:

```
$ cat journal
Date     Account  Debit  Credit  Description
------   -------  -----  ------  ----------------------------------------
861222   101      25000          cash from loan
861222   211.1           25000   loan number #378-14 Bank Amerigold
861223   150.1    10000          test equipment from Zarkoff
861223   101             5000    cash payment
861223   211.2           5000    note payable to Zarkoff Equipment.
861224   130      30000          inventory - parts from CCPSC
861224   201.1           15000   accounts payable to CCPSC
861224   101             15000   cash payment to CCPSC for parts
```

dbdict produces the following:

```
$ dbdict < journal
field   name
-----   ----
    1   Date
    2   Account
    3   Debit
    4   Credit
    5   Description
```

SOURCE
```
sed 1q |
awk 'BEGIN {OFS="                    ";
print "field","name";
print "-----","----"}
{n=split($0,field,"                    ");
for (i=1; i<=n; i++)
       print i,field[i]}'
```

NAME

delete   - blank record and update index file

SYNOPSIS

delete   [-m[bhirs]] table keycolumn ... < keytable

DESCRIPTION

delete writes a blank record on the row whose key matches the row in the *keytable*. It also deletes the offset row in the appropriate fast access offset table, or, in the case of the *hash* method, replaces the deleted offset with -1.

EXAMPLE

We start with the *inventory* table.

```
$ cat inventory
Item      Amount   Cost    Value    Description
----      ------   ----    -----    --------------
   1           3     50      150    rubber gloves
   2         100      5      500    test tubes
   3           5     80      400    clamps
   4          23     19      437    plates
   5          99     24     2376    cleaning cloth
   6          89    147    13083    bunsen burners
   7           5    175      875    scales
```

The *record* index looks like this.

```
$ index -mr inventory
$ cat inventory.r
 Offset
--------
      76
     113
     147
     177
     207
     245
     283
```

Now we can delete the first record, *Item* 1.

```
$ echo 1 | delete -mr inventory Item
$ cat inventory
Item      Amount   Cost    Value    Description
----      ------   ----    -----    --------------

   2         100      5      500    test tubes
   3           5     80      400    clamps
   4          23     19      437    plates
   5          99     24     2376    cleaning cloth
   6          89    147    13083    bunsen burners
   7           5    175      875    scales
$ cat inventory.r
 Offset
--------
     113
     147
     177
     207
     245
     283
```

Note that we have blanked out the record and removed the offset from the *inventory.r* file.

SEE ALSO
  append replace

SOURCE
```
 : %W% SCCS ID Information

 : 'delete - writes a blank record into the location of the file
 :        it also updates the index file'

 USAGE='usage: delete [-m[bhirs] table keycolumn ... < keytable'
 EUSAGE=1

 NOSEEK='Can not find a row with that key.'
 ENOSEEK=2

 TMP=/tmp/$$delete

 OFFSETWIDTH=9
 METHOD=-ms

 : handle arguments
 while test -n "$1"
 do
         case "$1" in
         -m*)    METHOD=$1 ;;
         *)      TABLE=$1
                 shift && KEYCOLUMNS="$*"
                 break
                 ;;
         esac
         shift
 done

 if test -z "$TABLE"
 then
         echo $USAGE
         exit $EUSAGE
 fi

 LOCATION="`seek $METHOD -o $TMP $TABLE $KEYCOLUMNS`"

 if test -z "$LOCATION"
 then
         echo $NOSEEK
         exit $ENOSEEK
 fi

 blank < $TMP | replace $METHOD $TABLE $LOCATION

 : delete the offset
 set $LOCATION

 case "$METHOD" in
 -mr)    XTABLE=${TABLE}.r
         sed "/^ *$1\$/d" < $XTABLE > $TMP
         mv $TMP $XTABLE
         ;;
 -mh)    XTABLE=${TABLE}.h
         sed "s/^ *$1\$/      -1/" < $XTABLE > $TMP
         mv $TMP $XTABLE
         ;;
 -mi)    XTABLE=${TABLE}.i
         sed "/^ *$1      /d" < $XTABLE > $TMP
         mv $TMP $XTABLE
         ;;
 esac
```

NAME
difference   - outputs table of rows that are in only one table

SYNOPSIS
difference   table1 table2

DESCRIPTION
difference uses the UNIX **sort** and **uniq** commands to logically subtract the second table from the first. It produces a new table consisting of only the rows that are in one of the tables, but not in the other table. The two input tables must have the same columns (*union compatible* in the technical database literature) and the rows have to be exactly identical including every space, tab, and nonprinting character. If two rows look the same to you, but not to **difference,** try the **see** command to see any blank spaces and nonprinting characters.

EXAMPLE
```
$ cat journal

Date     Amount   Account  Ref     Description
-------  -------  -------  -------  ------------------------------
820107    14.00   meal     v       meal with jones
820113   101.62   car      v       car repairs
820114    81.80   insur    c       car insurance allstate
820114    93.00   car      c       car registration dmv
820119    81.72   vitamin  c       sundown vitamins
820121    20.83   meal     v       meal with scott
820121  2500.00   keogh    c       keogh payment
820125    99.00   dues     v       dues to uni-ops unix conference

$ cat carexpense

Date     Amount   Account  Ref     Description
-------  -------  -------  -------  ------------------------------
820113   101.62   car      v       car repairs
820114    81.80   insur    c       car insurance allstate
820114    93.00   car      c       car registration dmv

$ difference journal carexpense

Date     Amount   Account  Ref     Description
-------  -------  -------  -------  ------------------------------
820107    14.00   meal     v       meal with jones
820119    81.72   vitamin  c       sundown vitamins
820121    20.83   meal     v       meal with scott
820121  2500.00   keogh    c       keogh payment
820125    99.00   dues     v       dues to uni-ops unix conference
```

SOURCE
```
: %W% SCCS ID Information
: 'difference produces table with rows in table1 that are not in table2'

USAGE='usage: difference table1 table2'
EUSAGE=1
if  test $# -ne 2
then
        echo $USAGE 1>&2
        exit $EUSAGE
fi

: first output the head of the first file
sed 2q $1
(tail +3 $1 ; tail +3 $2 ) | sort | uniq -u
```

NAME
display - writes table or list file to standard out

SYNOPSIS
display < tableorlist

DESCRIPTION
display copies the table or list file that comes in, to the *standard out*. This is not a very useful program, but is a template for the C interface programs. If you have its source code, you have an example of how to process tables and lists and can modify it for your own programs.

display is slower than the **cat** command because it does more processing. **display** knows about table and list formats and reads in and puts out one row at a time.

SEE ALSO
See the C interface chapter for the source of **display**.

NAME
domain - displays invalid values in a column

SYNOPSIS
domain domaintable [string ...] [< one-column-table]

DESCRIPTION
domain displays all strings or all rows in the input table that do not match any column in the *domaintable*. This program is useful for validating that each item in a column is legitimate. First you build a file consisting of a list of all acceptable values. In relational theory these values are called the **domain** of the column. (The **validate** command can also be used to validate numbers and short lists of valid strings). To check the domain of a column in a multicolumn table, simply project the column you wish with the **column** command.

The *domaintable* must be sorted because it will be searched by the **search** command using the binary fast access method (-mb). **domain** is a shell script, so if you wish to change its search method, you can edit it.

EXAMPLE
You might have an order file for cars like this:

```
$ cat orders
Qty     Model    Colors   Options
-------  -------  -------  -------
1        sedan    black    3
1        sedan    green    1
1        sedan    farble   4
3        sedan    red      5
2        convert  white    1
1        sedan    purple   2
1        sedan    yellow   4
3        convert  blue     2
```

You would also need a file of possible car colors that had been sorted:

```
$ cat colors
Colors
------
black
blue
carmel
green
purple
red
silver
white
```

Now we can validate the *Color* column and see all unacceptable colors:

```
$ column Colors < orders | domain colors
Colors
------
farble
yellow
```

So, **domain** complains about *farble* and *yellow*. Neither color is in our list. So you can call the *orders* file up in the text editor and edit it. Or add those colors to the approved list, if they are ok. In the **vi** editor, use the */pattern* command to find all of the *patterns* in the orders file. Or type something like:

```
:g/farble/s//purple/g
```

This **vi** editor command will find all instances of *farble* and change them to *purple*.
You can also validate strings written on the command line.

```
$ domain colors red blue purple farble yellow green
farble
yellow
```

These command line stings should be quoted if they have any special characters in
them. They are searched for by **grep.** If they contain a dollar sign ($), it should be
protected with three backslashes. It will be scanned both by the shell and the **grep**
command. It takes three backslashes to get one backslash through to **grep.**

SOURCE

```
: %W% SCCS ID Information

: 'domain - searches the domain file for each field of input column
:        or string on the command line'

USAGE='usage: domain domaintable [string ...] [< one-column-table]'
EUSAGE=1

EDOMAIN=2

TMP=/tmp/$$domain
trap 'rm -f /tmp/$$*' 0 1 2 3 15

case "$#" in
0)
        echo $USAGE >&2
        exit $EUSAGE
        ;;
1)
        cat > $TMP
        search -mb $1 < $TMP >> $TMP
        sort $TMP | uniq -u
        ;;
2)
        if grep "ˆ$2\$" $1 > /dev/null
        then
                exit 0
        else
                echo "$2"
                exit EDOMAIN
        fi
        ;;
*)
        FILE=$1
        shift
        for I
        do
                if grep "ˆ$I\$" $FILE > /dev/null
                then
                        :
                else
                        echo "$I"
                        ERROR=true
                fi
        done
        if test -n "$ERROR"
        then
                exit EDOMAIN
        fi
        ;;
esac
```

NAME

enter   - adds rows to a table or list file without an editor

SYNOPSIS

enter   [-limit] tableorlist

DESCRIPTION

enter is a simple way to type in one or more rows at the end of a table or list. It displays each column name and waits for you to type in each item.

Note that this is one of the few **/rdb** commands that does not use the left-arrow (< or less than symbol) to input a table, but rather needs the name of a table to be appended to. It is a stand alone program. **enter** is a substitute for using the editor. It is easier to use but very limited.

If you make an error in entering a record, you can go back to the last line with the caret or hat (ˆ) key. After you type the caret key, **enter** will prompt you with the previous line. If you need to go up two lines, keep typing carets until you get a prompt for the line you wish to reenter.

OPTIONS

-limit   allows the software developer to limit the number of rows to be entered. For example, the user needs to only enter one row. -1 will prompt for one row and then exit. Thus it can be used in a shell script.

RULES

To set up and enter a file in list format instead of table format there are several rules and suggestions.

First, let's discuss terminology. A list is like a table that is turned sideways. For example, a wide table looks like this:

```
Number    Name              Company      Street            City   State  ZIP
Phone
------    ----              -------      ------            ----   -----  ---
-----
1         Ronald McDonald   McDonald's   123 Mac Attack
Memphis   TENN              30000        (111) 222-3333
```

Note that the row is so long that it wrapped around to the next line. Also, the column names and column data do not line up. *Names* and *Companies* and *Street Addresses* are usually too long to fit nicely into such a table. Therefore, we need a list format like this:

```
Number    1
Name      Ronald McDonald
Company   McDonald's
Street    123 Mac Attack
City      Memphis
State     TENN
ZIP       30000
Phone     (111) 222-3333
```

These two formats (table and list) are interchangeable by using two programs: **listtotable** and **tabletolist.** You can enter and keep a file in list format. When you want to use several commands, you can convert it to table format and pipe it into the regular commands for faster execution. For example:

```
$ listtotable < maillist | column Name Phone | justify

Name            Phone
---------------  ---------------
Ronald McDonald  (111) 222-3333
```

It is best, therefore, to remember that *Name* and *Phone* are column names. The information following them in the list is the first row of a table (that can be created by the **listtotable** command).

RULE 1. Use the editor first to create the list file. Type each column name followed by one tab (only one). Also enter the information for the first row (record).

RULE 2. Be sure to put a newline (blank line) as the first line of the file.

RULE 3. Be sure to put a blank line at the end of each row (record). In the previous example, after the *Phone*. This tells the program that it has reached the end of the row.

You can then save the file and use the **enter** program. Type:

```
$ enter maillist

Name            _
```

The **enter** program will respond with the first column name and a tab and wait for you to enter whatever you wish for *Name*. The underscore (_) shows where the cursor of your CRT will be waiting for you to input data.

RULE 4. Type in your data for the item. Use the return key to end the information for this item. If you type more than 80 or so characters your terminal will wrap around. That means your cursor will jump to the left side of the screen at the next line. You can continue to type and wrap around until you reach your editor line limit or hit the return key. Then **enter** will again give you the name of the next column head, a tab, and wait for your entry.

RULE 5. Exit the **enter** program when it has given you the first column name of a new record and is waiting for a response. At that time type a CTRL-d. That means hold down the CTRL key and strike the *d* key at the same time. The **enter** program will return you to the UNIX operating system.

For list-formatted files it is better to use the **enter** command than an editor. If you do your entry with a text editor, you must include all of the column names, in the same order and spelled correctly.

EXAMPLE

To add a line to the *maillist* file, type:

```
$ enter maillist

Number          2
Name            Chiquita  Banana
Company         Standard Brands
Street          ^
Company         United Brands
Street          Uno Avenido de la Reforma
City            San Jose
State           Costa Rica
ZIP             123456789
Phone           1234

Name            <CTRL-d>
$
```

Note we made an error entering *Company* and did not realize it until we were at

Street. We typed caret (^) which reprompted us for *Company*, which we reentered. **enter** then went on to prompt us for *Company* again. Now you can see the file with a **cat** command:

```
$ cat maillist

Number        1
Name          Ronald McDonald
Company       McDonald's
Street        123 Mac Attack
City          Memphis
State         TENN
ZIP           30000
Phone         (111) 222-3333

Number        2
Name          Chiquita  Banana
Company       United Brands
Street        Uno Avenido de la Reforma
City          San Jose
State         Costa Rica
ZIP           123456789
Phone         1234
```

Note that the last row (actually eight lines and the bottom newline) is the one we entered. Just hit the return key if you have no data to put after a prompt. Now for a table example. If you wanted to add a line to the *inventory* file you could type:

```
$ enter inventory

Item#     Amount    Cost     Value    Description
-------   -------   -------  -------  ---------------
_
```

Then start typing your rows. Remember to insert tabs between columns.

```
8   123   5.98    0   widget
9   29    15.50   0   another widget
^d
```

Note the control-d represented here by: ^d. The inventory file now looks like this:

```
$ cat inventory

Item#     Amount    Cost     Value    Description
-------   -------   -------  -------  ---------------
1         3         5.00     0        rubber gloves
2         100       0.50     0        test tubes
3         5         8.00     0        clamps
4         23        1.98     0        plates
5         99        2.45     0        cleaning cloth
6         89        14.75    0        bunsen burners
7         5         175      0        scales
8         123       5.98     0        widget
9         29        15.50    0        another widget
```

Note that the last two lines are the ones we entered.

NAME
explode - produces table of subparts and their count for a part

SYNOPSIS
explode   Part Amount [table]

DESCRIPTION
explode takes a part number or name and looks it up in a part table to find all of its subparts. It then finds the subparts of those subparts, and so forth. It also multiplies the number of parts times the subpart counts at each interaction so that the final subpart table lists all of the subparts of the original part and the total number of subparts needed to make the part.

explode can be used to generate a list of all items needed to make a product. The cost of these subparts, times the count, gives the value which can be totaled to arrive at the total cost of the product. Also the items can be ordered.

EXAMPLE
If you had a *parttable,* like this:

```
$ cat parttable
Part    Subpart Count
----    ------- ------
10001   10010   3
10001   10020   4
10010   10100   2
10020   10100   5
```

and you wanted to find the subpart list and count for two part 10001s, you would type:

```
$ explode 10001 2
Part    Amount
----    ------
10001       2
10010       6
10020       8
10100      52
```

Note that both 10010 and 10020 have 10100 as a subpart, but **explode** uses **subtotal** to combine the 10100 subparts into one row. The table is also sorted.

SEE ALSO
bom

SOURCE
```
: %W% SCCS Information

# explode - finds all subparts of a part

USAGE='usage: explode Part Amount [ table ]
where: Part = part number, Amount = quantity, table = partlist'
EUSAGE=1
OK=0
TRUE=0
FALSE=255

# get fast access method
```

/rdb™ Release 4.0

```
case "$1" in
-*)     METHOD=$1
        shift
        ;;
esac

# need three or more variable

if test "$#" -lt 2
then
        echo "$USAGE" 1>&2
        exit $EUSAGE
fi

PART=$1
AMOUNT=$2
TABLE=${3-parttable}

TMP=/tmp/$$explode
TMP1=/tmp/$$1explode
TMP2=/tmp/$$2explode
trap 'rm -f /tmp/$$* ; trap 0 ; exit $OK' 0 1 2 3 15

# get column names from table, assume first through third
exec 0< $TABLE
OLDIFS="$IFS"
IFS=":$IFS"
read Part Subpart Count
IFS="$OLDIFS"

# build first key file
cat <<END > $TMP1
$Part   Amount
----    ------
$PART   $AMOUNT
END

# get headline from table
cp $TMP1 $TMP

# look till no more subparts
while test 2 -lt 'wc -l < $TMP1'
do
        # find subparts and compute amount
        jointable $TMP1 $TABLE |
        compute "Amount *= $Count" |
        column $Subpart Amount |
        rename $Subpart $Part > $TMP2

        # append to new part list
        tail +3 < $TMP2 >> $TMP

        # rename file for next loop
        mv $TMP2 $TMP1
done

sorttable < $TMP | subtotal $Part Amount

exit $OK
```

NAME
fd   - tests for functional dependency of columns

SYNOPSIS
fd   determinecolumn dependcolumn < table

DESCRIPTION
fd tests whether the first column determines the second column. Or in other words, the second column depends upon the first column. A column in a table is functionally dependent upon another column when for each value in the first column, there is only one value in the second column. This helps you to determine if a table is normalized. (See Normalization below).

EXAMPLE
First let's look at our inventory table:

```
$ cat inventory

Item   Amount   Cost   Value   Description
----   ------   ----   -----   --------------
   1        3     50     150   rubber gloves
   2      100      5     500   test tubes
   3        5     80     400   clamps
   4       23     19     437   plates
   5       99     24    2376   cleaning cloth
   6       89    147   13083   bunsen burners
   7        5    175     875   scales
```

Note that the first column, *Item,* is the key column for the table. It is supposed to functionally determine all of the other columns. Each value in *Item* is unique so each value determines, or is the key, to its row and all of the column values on it.

But *Cost* does not functionally depend on *Amount* because there are two 5 values in *Amount* and each has a different value for *Cost* associated with it (on the same row or line). The common sense (technically called the semantics) of the table is that knowing the amount of items we have in inventory does not tell us how much they cost.

Now let's see if **fd** can find the dependencies.

```
$ fd Item Cost < inventory
true
```

That is right, because *Item* is the key column.

```
$ fd Amount Cost < inventory
false
```

Right again, **fd.**

NORMALIZATION
A key column should aways functionally determine all of the other columns in the table. But nonkey columns should not be dependent upon each other.

If there is too little data in the table, there may be a phony dependency. Be sure your table has lots of data before testing.

To normalize your tables, you need to check for functional dependencies. When functional dependency is found with nonkey columns, the columns should be projected and uniqued to form a second table. Then the functionally dependent column, but not the determining column, should be removed from the first table.

```
$ column column1 column2 < table | uniq > newtable
$ column `sed 1q table | sed s/column2//` < table > tmp
$ mv tmp table
```

In the second table the column that determines the other column is the key for that table. If you need to recreate the original first table, you can join the two new tables with the **jointable** program.

```
$ jointable -j column1 table newtable > oldtable
```

Normalization, or simplification, is an important process. Normalized files are smaller and are easier to maintain.

SOURCE
```
: %W% SCCS ID Information

: 'fd - tests to see if a column is functionally depandant on another'

USAGE='usage: fd column1 column2 < table
    to test if column2 is functionally dependant on column1
    or column1 determines column2'
EUSAGE=1

TMP=/tmp/$$`basename fd`
trap 'rm -f /tmp/$$*' 0 1 2 3 15

if test "$#" -ne 2
then
    echo $USAGE >&2
    exit $EUSAGE
fi

column $* | sorttable | uniq > $TMP
if test `wc -l < $TMP` -eq `column $1 < $TMP | uniq | wc -l`
then
    echo true
    exit 0
else
    echo false
    exit 1
fi
```

NAME
filesize   - returns the number of characters in a file

SYNOPSIS
filesize   filename ...

DESCRIPTION
filesize displays the number of bytes in the files listed on its command line. It is much faster than the UNIX **wc** command because it gets the number from the inode table, with a **stat()** system call, rather than counting the bytes in the file.

If you ask for one file, you get a single number sent to *standard output.* It can be assigned to a shell variable. With more than one *filename* it produces a table of sizes.

EXAMPLE
```
$ filesize filesize.1
532
$ filesize ascii.1 filesize.1
  Offset Filename
-------- --------
     464 ascii.1
     532 filesize.1
```

NAME
fillform - fill a tax from with adjusted trial balance data

SYNOPSIS
fillform form

DESCRIPTION
fillform will fill in a tax form, *1120* corporate, *1120S* S corporation *C* schedule C, or partnership tax form.

EXAMPLE
```
$ fillform 1120S
$ sed 10q 1120S
Taxline   Amount   Description
-------   ------   -------------------------------------
101a      13500    Sales
101b          0    Returns and Allowances
101c      13500    Net Sales
102           0    Cost of Goods Sold
102-A1    20000    Beginning Inventory
102-A2     3601    Misc Merchandise
102-A3     2100    Salaries and Wages
102-A4        0    Other Costs
```

SEE ALSO
calculate

SOURCE
```
: fillform - fills in a blank tax form and creates a filled tax form
:       use this as a template
USAGE='usage: fillform form'

FORM=$1
FORMIN=$1.blank
FORMOUT=$1.filled

if [ "$#" -ne 1 ]
then
        echo 'usage: fillform taxform
        where taxform is C or 1120 or 1120S'
        exit 1
fi

if [ ! -r "$FORMIN" ]
then
        echo "$FORMIN does not exist in this directory."
        exit 2
fi

tail +3 < profit |
cat adjustedtrial - |
sorttable Taxline |
subtotal Taxline Debit Credit |
jointable -a1 -j Taxline $FORMIN - |
compute 'if (Debit != 0) Amount = sprintf ("%7.0f", Debit) ;\
        if (Credit != 0) Amount = sprintf ("%7.0f", Credit) ;\
        if (Amount == "") Amount = sprintf ("%7.0f", 0) ; ' |
column Taxline Amount Description > $FORMOUT
```

NAME
fixtotable   - converts fixed length format to /rdb table format

SYNOPSIS
fixtotable   column [= n1,n2] ... < fixtdb

DESCRIPTION
fixtotable converts databases from fixed length format to variable length **/rdb** format by selecting *n2* bytes of data from *fixtdb*, beginning at the *n1* position for each *column* name specified. Tabs are inserted between columns and **compress** is used to remove leading and trailing blanks. Header records are generated from the column names. Column names which do not specify start position (*n1*) and field width (*n2*) are considered empty columns, and appear as such in the output. Blank records are removed.

EXAMPLE
For example, let's look at a file named *journal*:

```
1       10      20      30
----+----|----+----|----+----|
820102101    25000
820102211.1       25000
820103150.1  10000
820103101         5000
820103211.2       5000
820104130    30000
```

The first six bytes are the date field; the next six bytes, starting at position 7 are the account number field; the next seven bytes, starting at position 13 are the credit field; and the last seven bytes, starting at position 20 are the debit field. Let's yank the account number and the credit and debit fields from this file and make a new table with a new field for the description:

```
$ fixtotable Account=7,6 Debit=13,7 Credit=20,7 Description < journal
Account   Debit   Credit   Description
-------   -----   ------   -----------
101       25000
211.1             25000
150.1     10000
101       5000
211.2             5000
130       30000
```

SEE ALSO
compress tabletofix

NAME

foot   - foot or subtotal Debits and Credit of ledger

SYNOPSIS

foot

DESCRIPTION

foot will subtotal the accounts in the *ledger*.

EXAMPLE

```
$ foot
$ cat footed
Account  Date    Debit   Credit   Ref      Short    Description
-------  ------  -----   ------   -------  -------  -------------------
1010     851231           1758             cash
1010     851231  5137                      cash
-------  ------  -----   ------   -------  -------  -------------------
1010             5137    1758

3010                      1601    deposit  sales
-------  ------  -----   ------   -------  -------  -------------------
3010             0        1601

3080     850125           250     c1459    royalty  book fees
-------  ------  -----   ------   -------  -------  -------------------
3080             0        250

3100     850118           3286    c101     income   sales
-------  ------  -----   ------   -------  -------  -------------------
3100             0        3286

4020             1601             check    merch
-------  ------  -----   ------   -------  -------  -------------------
4020             1601     0

4370     850101  2                r        parking  parking at clients
-------  ------  -----   ------   -------  -------  -------------------
4370             2        0

4380     850103  15               c115     travel   shuttle bus
4380     850104  13               v        travel   meal
4380     850105  13               c116     travel   meal
4380     850106  114              r        travel   hotel
-------  ------  -----   ------   -------  -------  -------------------
4380             155      0
```

SOURCE

```
: foot subtotals each account debits and credits and subtracts smallest

subtotal -1 Account Debit Credit < ledger > footed
```

NAME
getjournal   - copies journals for sales, pur, pay systems

SYNOPSIS
getjournal   journalname

DESCRIPTION
getjournal will copy, total, and adjust journals from other parts of the business system. These subsidiary journals are created automatically by the operations of sales, purchasing, and other departments. It also gets the inventory value for the *journaladjust*.

EXAMPLE
```
$ getjournal journaldeposit
Date       Amount    Account   Ref      Description
-------    -------   -------   -------  -------------------------
891231     13500.00  sales     deposit  from sales/deposit
```

SEE ALSO
consolidate

SOURCE
```
: %W% SCCS ID information
: 'getjournal knows where to get each journal and how to reformat it'

USAGE='usage: getjournal date journalname ...'

JOURNALS="journallast journalincome journalexpense journaladjust"
JOURNALS="$JOURNALS journaldeposit journalcheck journalinventory"
INVDEBIT=1110
INVCREDIT=4080
DATE=$1

export DATE
shift

if test "$#" -eq 0
then
        DATE='todaysdate'
        export DATE
        set $JOURNALS
fi

while test -n "$1"
do
case $1 in
journallast)      J=jl ;;
journalincome)    J=ji ;;
journalexpense)            J=je ;;
journaladjust)    J=ja ;;
journaldeposit)            J=../sales/deposit ;;
journalcheck)     J=../pur/check ;;
journalinventory) J=../inv/inventory ;;
journalpay)       J=../pay/journalpay ;;
esac

if check < $J
then
        cp $J $1
fi
```

```
case $1 in
journaldeposit)
        total Amount < $J |
        column Date Amount Account Ref Description |
        compute "Date=\"$DATE\";Account=\"sales\";Ref=\"deposit\";\
                Description=\"from sales/deposit\";" > $1
        ;;
journalcheck)
        total Amount < $J |
        column Date Amount Account Ref Description |
        compute "Date=\"$DATE\";Account=\"merch\";Ref=\"check\";\
                Description=\"from pur/check\";" > $1
        ;;
journalpay)
        rename Gross Amount < $J |
        total Amount |
        column Date Amount Account Ref Description |
        compute "Date=\"$DATE\";Account=\"wages\";Ref=\"payroll\";\
                Description=\"from pay/journalpay\";" > $1
        ;;
journalinventory)
        INVENTORY=`compute 'Value = Onhand * Cost' < $J |
        column Value |
        total Value |
        tail -1 |
        sed 's/^ *//'`

        compute "Account == $INVDEBIT && Name ~ /End/ \
                    { Debit = $INVENTORY }
                  Account == $INVCREDIT \
                    {Credit = $INVENTORY }" < ja > journaladjust
        ;;
esac
shift
done
```

NAME

 gregorian   - convert column of dates for math and format change

SYNOPSIS

 gregorian   [-c -e -u] [Column ...] < tableorlist

DESCRIPTION

 gregorian will convert Julian dates in one or more columns to Gregorian. It is used along with **julian** to be able to:

1. add days to a date
2. subtract days from a date
3. subtract two dates to find the number of days between them
4. change the format of a date

Gregorian dates are the ones we are used to seeing (861231). Julian dates are some huge integer number of days like 1752836. Julian dates can be added to and subtracted from each other to find the number of days between two dates.

To perform math on dates, first covert to Julian with the **julian** program, then use the **compute** program to add or subtract or find the difference, and finally convert the date back to Gregorian with the **gregorian** program.

To convert a date, simply pipe **julian** and **gregorian** together with the **julian** program having the option for the input format and the **gregorian** program having the output format.

OPTIONS

 The options specify the format of the date.

-c 861231 is *computer* date format that can be sorted on and selected on because it is in correct numerical sequence. It is the default, when you do not specify the date format.

-e 31/12/86 is *european* format day / month / year.

-u 12/31/86 is *us* format month / day / year.

EXAMPLE

Adding Days

Suppose we have a file with a date column like this:

```
$ cat journal
Date    Account Debit   Credit  Description
------  ------- -----   ------  ----------------------------------
861222  101     25000           cash from loan
861222  211.1           25000   loan number #378-14 Bank Amerigold
861223  150.1   10000           test equipment from Zarkoff
861223  101             5000    cash payment
861223  211.2           5000    note payable to Zarkoff Equipment
861224  130     30000           inventory - parts from CCPSC
861224  201.1           15000   accounts payable to CCPSC
861224  101             15000   cash payment to CCPSC for parts
```

Now for some reason we want to add 45 days to each of the dates. First let us see what **julian** does:

```
$ julian Date < journal
```

```
Date    Account Debit    Credit  Description
------  ------- -----    ------  ----------------------------------
1752827 101     25000            cash from loan
1752827 211.1            25000   loan number #378-14 Bank Amerigold
1752828 150.1   10000            test equipment from Zarkoff
1752828 101              5000    cash payment
1752828 211.2            5000    note payable to Zarkoff Equipment
1752829 130     30000            inventory - parts from CCPSC
1752829 201.1            15000   accounts payable to CCPSC
1752829 101              15000   cash payment to CCPSC for parts
```

Now the *Date* is a Julian date. Note we gave no option because computer format is the default.

Lets add 45 days.

```
$ julian Date < journal | compute 'Date += 45' | gregorian Date
Date    Account Debit    Credit  Description
------  ------- -----    ------  ----------------------------------
870205  101     25000            cash from loan
870205  211.1            25000   loan number #378-14 Bank Amerigold
870206  150.1   10000            test equipment from Zarkoff
870206  101              5000    cash payment
870206  211.2            5000    note payable to Zarkoff Equipment
870207  130     30000            inventory - parts from CCPSC
870207  201.1            15000   accounts payable to CCPSC
870207  101              15000   cash payment to CCPSC for parts
```

Wow, look at that! All of the dates are 45 days into the future. Kind of like a time machine.

Date Conversion.
Suppose you want US dates.

```
$ julian Date < journal | gregorian -u Date | justify Date
Date     Account Debit    Credit  Description
-------- ------- -----    ------  ----------------------------------
12/22/86 101     25000            cash from loan
12/22/86 211.1            25000   loan number #378-14 Bank Amerigold
12/23/86 150.1   10000            test equipment from Zarkoff
12/23/86 101              5000    cash payment
12/23/86 211.2            5000    note payable to Zarkoff Equipment
12/24/86 130     30000            inventory - parts from CCPSC
12/24/86 201.1            15000   accounts payable to CCPSC
12/24/86 101              15000   cash payment to CCPSC for parts
```

Since these dates are eight characters wide, **justify** was used to line things up.

NAME

hashkey - returns the hash offset for key strings

SYNOPSIS

hashkey rows keystring ...

DESCRIPTION

hashkey adds the ASCII value of each character in the *keystrings* (except blanks) and returns the modulo of *rows*. This is for computing the hash offset into hash index table for the hash fast access method. It is used by **append** to update the hash index table.

EXAMPLE

Here we convert several characters.

```
$ hashkey 11 ABCD
2
$ hashkey 29 abcdefg
4
```

SEE ALSO

append

NAME
headoff - removes the head from both table and list files

SYNOPSIS
headoff < tableorlist

DESCRIPTION
headoff allows you to strip off the header of either a table or a list file. Tables have a two line column head and list files have only a single line consisting of a single newline character.

The UNIX **tail +3** command does the same thing for a table and **tail +2** for a list. **headoff** is used by **union** to put together files. Only the first file keeps its head.

EXAMPLE
If you had a table, and you wanted to knock its head off, you could type:

```
$ headoff < inventory
    1         3      50       150     rubber gloves
    2       100       5       500     test tubes
    3         5      80       400     clamps
    4        23      19       437     plates
    5        99      24      2376     cleaning cloth
    6        89     147     13083     bunsen burners
    7         5     175       875     scales
```

SEE ALSO
headon insertdash

NAME
headon - adds a /rdb head to a table

SYNOPSIS
headon < table

DESCRIPTION
headon allows you to insert a /**rdb** header on to a table. Tables have a two line column head. When you have a table without a /**rdb** head, perhaps created by another program, you can add a head to it. You can also do this in a pipe and send the new table on to other /**rdb** commands for processing.

EXAMPLE
If you want to treat the /*etc*/*passwd* file as a table for /**rdb** command processing, use **headon.**

```
$ tr ':' '          ' < /etc/passwd | headon | justify
1      2                   3     4     5                 6
------ -------------       ---   ---   ---------------   -------------
root   dVAYxSsJy10Fg       0     3     Super User        /
daemon                     1     12    background        /
bin    rVOhF49RpZXEY       2     2     binary programs   /bin
uucp                       5     1     UUCP              /usr/lib/uucp
lp                         71    2     Line Printer      /usr/spool/lp
guest                      100   100   Guest User        /usr/guest
rod                        0     0     Rod Manis         /usr/rod
```

The **tr** command translates the colon (:) field separator into a tab. The **justify** command lines up the variable length columns.

Be sure the first line of the table has no blank fields or **headon** will count the wrong number of fields.

SEE ALSO
headoff insertdash rmblank

SOURCE
```
: %W% SCCS ID Information

: 'headon - puts a /rdb headline and dashline on a table'

USAGE='usage: headon < table'
EUSAGE=1

read FIRST
OLDIFS=$IFS
IFS=' '
set $FIRST
IFS=$OLDIFS

if test -z "$FIRST"
then
      echo $USAGE 1>&2
      exit $EUSAGE
fi

COLUMN=1
HEAD="$COLUMN"
DASH=-
```

```
while test "$COLUMN" -lt $#
do
      COLUMN=`expr $COLUMN + 1`
      HEAD="$HEAD     $COLUMN"
      DASH="$DASH     -"
done

echo "$HEAD"
echo "$DASH"
echo "$FIRST"

cat
```

NAME
helpme - lists the help commands available

SYNOPSIS
helpme

DESCRIPTION
helpme lists the other help commands.

EXAMPLE
```
$ helpme
There are many help programs:
Command               Description
------------------    -----------------------------------------
"menu"                a menu with some commands
"rdb"                 a list of the available commands
"commands"            discription and syntax of all the commands
"whatis command"      description and syntax of command
"whatwill feature"    info on commands with that feature
"man command"         the manual page for that command
```

SOURCE
```
: %W% SCCS ID Information
: help lists the help features
cat <<END
Command               Description
------------------    -----------------------------------------
"menu"                a menu with some commands
"rdb"                 a list of the available commands
"commands"            discription and syntax of all the commands
"whatis command"      description and syntax of command
"whatwill feature"    info on commands with that feature
"man command"         the manual page for that command
END
```

NAME
   howmany   - displays the number of commands in a directory

SYNOPSIS
   howmany

DESCRIPTION
   howmany displays the number of the commands it finds in the **/rdb** *bin* directory.

EXAMPLES
```
$ howmany
   101
```

SOURCE
```
: %W% SCCS ID Information

: howmany will count the rdb commands

USAGE='usage: howmany'

ls `path howmany` | wc -w
```

NAME
income - create incomestatement from adjustedtrial

SYNOPSIS
income

DESCRIPTION
income produces the *incomestatement* from *adjustedtrial*.

EXAMPLE
```
$ income
$ cat incomestatement
     Makeapile, Inc.
     Income Statement
          1985

          13500    Sales
            250    Gross royalties
           3286    Other Income
-----   ------   -----------------------
          17036    Income
20000                Beginning Inventory
 3601                Misc Merchandise
 2100                Salaries and Wages
          22130    Ending Inventory
-----   ------   -----------------------
          -3571   Cost of Goods Sold
    0                Depreciation
    0                Depletion
    0                Amortization
    2                Business parking
   41                Business travel
  114                Business travel hotel
-----   ------   -----------------------
           -157   Expenses
-----   ------   -----------------------
          13308   Net Profit or Loss
```

SEE ALSO
balance

SOURCE
```
: income will produce incomestatement

TMP=income$$
trap 'rm -f $TMP; trap 0; exit 0;' 0 1 2 3 15

: first get the header from the header file income.head

cp income.head incomestatement

: get the body of the table

row 'Format ~ /I-/' < adjustedtrial > $TMP

: subtotal the major groups of accounts

subtotal -1 Format Debit Credit < $TMP |
compute 'Account < 1 && Format !~ /----/ \
     { Credit -= Debit ; Debit = "" ; Name = "TOTAL" ; }' |
compute 'Name ~ /TOTAL/ && Format ~ /I-I/ \
```

```
        { Name = "Income" } ' |
compute 'Name ~ /TOTAL/ && Format ~ /I-COGS/ \
        { Name = "Cost of Goods Sold" } ' |
compute 'Name ~ /TOTAL/ && Format ~ /I-E/ { Name = "Expenses" }' |
column Debit Credit Name |
column +3 >> incomestatement

: find profit account number

PROFITACCOUNT=`row 'Name ~ /Profit/' < chart |
column Account |
tail -1`

if test "$PROFITACCOUNT" = ""
then
        echo "No profit account named $PROFITACCOUNT in your chart."
        echo "Please add it to your chart of accounts file and rerun."
        exit 1
fi

: total

compute 'Credit -= Debit' < $TMP |
total Credit |
compute "Account=\"$PROFITACCOUNT\" ;\
        Format=\"B-LE\" ; Name=\"Retained Earnings (Profit)\" ;" |
tee profit

: append total

column Debit Credit Name < profit |
compute "Name=\"Net Profit or Loss\" ;" |
tail -2 >> incomestatement
```

NAME
index   - set up table for search

SYNOPSIS
index   [-m[bhirs]] [-x] [-h -s -l [2> location]] tableorlist [keycol ...] [< keytable]

DESCRIPTION

index will set up a table for the **search** program. The indexing that it does makes it possible for the **search** program to find a row in a table or list file faster. This is very important for large files.

Exactly what **index** does depends upon which method you choose. For some methods it will build another table, called a secondary index file, that the specified method requires. It is possible to **index** a single file for all five methods. Some of the methods can index all of the columns.

These fast access methods are *static*. If the table or list is changed, by a text editor, for example, it may have to be reindexed. Application programs may manipulate the table or list files and their secondary index to update them together. Forms packages should *dynamically* maintain these files.

There is a trick to allow you to index any or all of the columns in a file. Simply link **ln** the file to as many different names as you have columns to index. Then index each one.

OPTIONS
-m   Default method is sequential. See -ms as follows.

-mb   binary. The **index** command simply sorts the file on the specified key column. No secondary file is created. Since a file can only be sorted on one column, only one column can be indexed. You don't have to use **index** for the binary method, because you can use **sorttable** instead.

-mh   hash. **index** will build a secondary file, named *tableorlist.h,* and *hash* all of the keys column values and place them and their offsets to the file's rows into this hash secondary index file. This secondary file is named by adding a *.h* to the name of the file being indexed. It is, therefore, best to name your file with no more than 12 characters.

-mi   inverted or indexed. **index** builds a secondary file of keys and offsets and sorts on the keys. The secondary file is named *tableorlist.i.* The trick to index more than one column, previously discussed, will also work for the inverted method.

          If you plan on using the incomplete match feature of search (which works only with the inverted method), you must specifiy the -x flag, so that the secondary index will be sorted properly.

-mr   record number. **index** builds a secondary file named *tableorlist.r* which is one fixed length column of row (record) offsets.

-ms   sequential or linear. **index** does nothing in this case because **search** will simply look through the whole file. So don't bother indexing for the sequential method.

-h   No head line on output table.

-l   Output the starting and stopping location of the row and the offset entry in the secondary index file. These numbers are used by the **replace** and **lock** and **unlock** commands. The **seek** command uses this option to grab the locations. The locations are sent to file descriptor 2, and can be redirected by: 2> locationfile. There it can be saved until needed by your shell programs.

This option produces four integers. If there is no secondary index file, the start location will be zero (0).

-s   Only a single row is found. This speeds up some of the methods because they do not have to continue searching after they find the first match. The sequential method will on average run twice as fast. Hash, binary and inverted, a little faster. The record access method will not change, since it only finds one match anyway.

METHODS AND SUFFIXES

Here are the secondary files' suffixes that **index** adds to the file name it is indexing to give the name of the secondary index file it builds:

```
    Method and File Suffix

Method   Suffix   Example
-------  ------   -------
-b       none
-h       .h       inventory.h
-i       .i       inventory.i
-r       .r       inventory.r
-s       none
```

EXAMPLE

Let's look at the first ten lines of an accounts chart, named *chart:*

```
$ head chart
Account  Name
-------  --------------------
100      Assets
101      Cash
111      Accounts Receivable
111.1    Allowance for Bad Debt
115      Notes Receivable
120      Deposits
130      Parts Inventory
150      Equipment
```

Access to the data in *chart* can be sped up by indexing it and using the **search** command to find the row you want. To index *chart* using the binary (sorted) search method:

```
$ index -mb chart Account
```

index will quietly return when it finishes. You are now ready to use **search** to find *Account* number in the *chart* table.

SEE ALSO
search append delete replace update

NAME
insertdash   - insert dash line as second line in table

SYNOPSIS
insertdash   < table-without-dashline

DESCRIPTION
insertdash will put a dash line in as the second line of the table. It makes the dash line by copying the head line and turning every character in the first into a dash except the tabs. It is useful for files created by the system or non-UNIX programs that do not have the dash line. However, you will also need to convert field separators into tabs. You can use the UNIX **tr** or **sed** commands to do this.

EXAMPLE
insertdash assumes a table like this:

```
$ cat inventory

Item      Amount   Cost    Value    Description
   1           3     50      150    rubber gloves
```

After **insertdash** it would look like this:

```
$ insertdash < inventory

Item      Amount   Cost    Value    Description
----      ------   ----    -----    --------------
   1           3     50      150    rubber gloves
```

SEE ALSO
headoff headon

SOURCE
```
: %W% SCCS ID Information

: 'insertdash - puts a dash line as the second line in a table'

USAGE='usage: insertdash < table
        Assumes that table is 1 head line and rows without dash line.'

sed       '1h
          1p
          1g
          1s/[^    ]/-/g'
```

          /rdb™ Release 4.0

NAME

intersect - output table of rows that are in both input tables

SYNOPSIS

intersect table1 table2

DESCRIPTION

intersect is a shell script that uses the UNIX **sort** and **uniq** commands to perform a logical AND on two tables. It produces a new table consisting of only the rows that are in both of the input tables. The two input tables must have the same number of columns (called *union compatible*) and rows must match exactly to be considered the same.

EXAMPLE

Here we use **intersect** to find out if any of the entries in the car expense journal (*carexpense*) are already in the general journal (*journal*):

```
$ cat journal
Date     Amount  Account Ref     Description
-------  ------- ------- -------  -------------------------------
820107    14.00  meal    v        meal with jones
820114    81.80  insur   c        car insurance allstate
820119    81.72  vitamin c        sundown vitamins
820121    20.83  meal    v        meal with scott
820121  2500.00  keogh   c        keogh payment
820125    99.00  dues    v        dues to uni-ops unix conference
$ cat carexpense
Date     Amount  Account Ref     Description
-------  ------- ------- -------  -------------------------------
820113   101.62  car     v        car repairs
820114    81.80  insur   c        car insurance allstate
820114    93.00  car     c        car registration dmv
$ intersect journal carexpense
Date     Amount  Account Ref     Description
-------  ------- ------- -------  -------------------------------
820114    81.80  insur   c        car insurance allstate
```

Sure enough, the insurance expense was already posted to the general journal.

SEE ALSO

difference union jointable

SOURCE

```
: %W% SCCS ID Information
: 'intersect - produces table with rows that are be in two input tables'

USAGE='usage: intersect table1 table2'
EUSAGE=1

if  test $# -ne 2
then
        echo $USAGE 1>&2
        exit $EUSAGE
fi

: first output the head for the first file
sed 2q $1
(tail +3 $1 ; tail +3 $2 ) | sort | uniq -d
```

NAME
invoice - print invoice for sale order

SYNOPSIS
invoice

DESCRIPTION
invoice prompts for the number of a sales order and then prints an invoice for that order.

EXAMPLE
```
Please enter order number (or Return to exit): 1
                        Invoice
                        -------
Makeapile, Inc., 123 Bigbucks Blvd., Dallas, TX 12345, 1-800-SOF-WARE

Order Number   1
Date Ordered   850723
Date Shipped   0

Mailing Address for Customer Number  2
Customer Number 2
Mr. Thomas  Boomer  President

Ye Olde Thermonuclear Bombe Shoppe
54321 Blooy Road
Livermore, California    USA

Order     Number    Code     Backord     Qty     Price    Total    Name
-------   -------   -------   -------   -------   -------  -------   ----
1         1         rdb           10         1      1500  1500.00   /rdb

                                                    Gross  1500.00
                                                      Tax    75.00
                                                    Total  1575.00

Please enter order number (or Return to exit):
```

SEE ALSO
cstate

SOURCE
```
: invoice        prints a invoice from salesorder and item
: po             print purchase order
USAGE="usage: $0 [printer]"

# get printer name from argument 1, or PRINTER, or set to pg
PRINTER=${1:-$PRINTER}
PRINTER=${PRINTER:-pg}

MGETORDER='Please enter order number (or Return to exit): '

PROG=`basename $0`
case "$PROG" in
invoice)
      FILE=../sales/saleorder
      FORM=../sales/invoice.f
      ;;
po)
      FILE=../pur/purchaseorder
      FORM=../pur/po.f
      ;;
esac
```

```
        echo $CLEAR
        prompt "$MGETORDER"

        while read ORDER
        do
                if test "$ORDER" -lt 1
                then
                        exit 0
                fi
                echo "$ORDER" |
                        search -ms $FILE Number |
                        report $FORM |
                        $PRINTER
                echo
                prompt "$MGETORDER"
        done
```

NAME

jointable - joins two tables into one where keys match

SYNOPSIS

jointable [-a[1|2]] [-j[1|2] column]... -n -] table1 [table2]

DESCRIPTION

jointable will join two tables on a column common to each table (called a key column). The tables must each be sorted on the key column. The output is a new table with a row for each row in the tables that have matching values in the key columns. The columns of the new table are all the columns in the first table followed by all the columns in the second table except the key column is not repeated. This is called a *natural join*. An *equi-join* would repeat the key column.

There is a UNIX **join** command, but it does not know about **/rdb** head lines.

STRING VS. NUMERIC SORT

The biggest problem people have is joining tables that have been sorted *numerically* on the key columns (that is, the columns that the tables are going to be joined on). They use **sorttable** with the *-n* option (for numeric) to sort a table, then use **jointable. jointable** would expect to see a *string sort* and would fail to join the tables correctly. So we have added the *-n* option for symmetry with the UNIX **sort** program.

Remember that a string sort and a numeric sort are different. If you want to join two tables with numeric key columns, you must either use the **sorttable** command without the *-n* numeric sort option so that it will default to string sort, or if you use the *-n* option for **sorttable,** be sure to use it for **jointable.** Here is an example of a string and a numeric sort:

```
   Difference Sorts of Sorts
string              numeric
-------             -------
1                   1
10                  2
2                   10
20                  20
```

Can you see why? Numeric is the way we count and obviously correct. But string sort looks at the first character, then the second. Blank sorts ahead of 0, so *1* comes before *10*. More importantly *1* comes before *2* regardless of the characters to the right. That is why *10* comes before *2* followed by a space. This problem will show up as empty output from a **jointable,** when you know some of the rows should be joined.

If the columns had been right justified, they would sort correctly. Can you see why? Right justifying makes numeric and string sorts the same. The leading spaces help the string sort sort numbers correctly.

OPTIONS

-an   All of one of the files (1 or 2) is output, whether it matches or not. In addition to the normal output, **jointable,** with this option, will produce a line for each unpairable line in file *n,* where *n* is 1 or 2.

```
$ jointable -a1 ledger chart
```

will force out all of the ledger table rows regardless of whether there is a match of the ledger's *Account* column value with the chart's *Account* column value.

-jn column   Join on the *column* column in table number *n*. If *n* is missing, use the *column* column in each table. For example:

```
$ jointable -j1 Account -j2 account ledger chart
```

will join *ledger* and *chart* using the *Account column in ledger* and the *account* column in *chart*. If no columns are specified (with the -j option), the first column of each table is the default key column. Thus this option allows you to join on any column defined in either file, even when they have different names and locations.

-n   Numeric join. This means that table 1 and table 2 were sorted with the *-n* option. Remember that if you use *-n* in the **sorttable** command, than you must use *-n* in the **jointable** command.

—   Put the dash in place of the table that is being piped in. For example:

```
$ sorttable < journal | jointable - chart
```

means to sort the *journal* and then join it with the *chart* so that *journal* is on the left of the output table and *chart* is on the right.

Most of these options are about the same as for the UNIX **join** command.

[ ]   The brackets around *table2* mean that *table2* is optional in the sense that if it is missing from the command line, then **jointable** will use the standard input (< *file* or pipe) for the second table to join.

EXAMPLE

If you have a chart of accounts file, and a ledger file you can join them on account number to get account names:

```
$ head chart
Account       Name
-------       ----
100           Assets
101           Cash
111           Accounts Receivable
111.1         Allowance for Bad Debt
115           Notes Receivable
120           Deposits
130           Parts Inventory
 ...

$ cat ledger
Account    Date    Debit    Credit
-------    ----    -----    ------
101        820102           25000
101        820103            5000
101        820104  15000
130        820104  30000
150.1      820103  10000
201.1      820104  15000
211.1      820102           25000
211.2      820103            5000

$ jointable ledger chart
Account    Date    Debit    Credit    Name
-------    ----    -----    ------    ----
```

```
101        820102           25000   Cash
101        820103            5000   Cash
101        820104   15000           Cash
130        820104   30000           Parts Inventory
150.1      820103   10000           Test equipment
211.1      820102           25000   Notes Payable - BA
211.2      820103            5000   Notes Payable - Z Equip
```

Note that the *Name* column has been added to the columns of the *ledger* table and that the *Account* column was not repeated. Also note that only rows with matching *Account* column values are produced. If a table has several rows with repeated key values (see the three *101's* in the *Account* column), the joined table's rows are also repeated (see the three *Cash Name* column).

If you have a journal, sorted on *Account,* like this:

```
$ cat journal
  Date   Account  Debit   Credit
  ----   -------  -----   ------
820104   101              15000
820103   101               5000
820102   101      25000
820104   130      30000
820103   150.1    10000
820104   201.1            15000
820102   211.1            25000
820103   211.2             5000
```

You could join it with *chart* like this:

```
$ jointable -j Account journal chart
```

or another way, that has the same result (because chart's join column defaults to column 1):

```
$ jointable -j1 Account journal chart
  Date   Account  Debit   Credit   Name
  ----   -------  -----   ------   ----
820104   101              15000    Cash
820103   101               5000    Cash
820102   101      25000             Cash
820104   130      30000            Parts Inventory
820103   150.1    10000            Test equipment
820102   211.1            25000    Notes Payable - Bank of Amerigold
820103   211.2             5000    Notes Payable - Z Equipment
```

The *-a* option lets you see all of one table whether or not there is a match.

```
$ jointable -a1 ledger chart
Account    Date     Debit   Credit   Name
-------    ----     -----   ------   ----
101        820102           15000    Cash
101        820103            5000    Cash
101        820104   25000            Cash
130        820104   30000            Parts Inventory
150.1      820103   10000            Test equipment
201.1      820104   15000
211.1      820102   25000            Notes Payable - Bank of Amerigold
211.2      820103    5000            Notes Payable - Z Equipment
```

Note that Account *201.1* in the ledger shows up here, even though it is not in the *chart.* This shows us that *201.1* is an error. All account numbers should be in the chart of accounts. We should either add *201.1* to the chart of accounts or find the correct number in the chart of accounts and replace *201.1* in the *journal* with the correct account number.

If you pipe a file into a **jointable,** you can control which table it will be (1 or 2) by using the dash or minus (-) option.

```
$ sorttable Account < journal | jointable -j Account - chart

Date     Account  Debit   Credit   Name
----     -------  -----   ------   ----
820103   101               5000    Cash
820104   101               15000   Cash
820102   101      25000            Cash
820104   130      30000            Parts Inventory
820103   150.1    10000            Test equipment
820102   211.1             25000   Notes Payable - Bank of Amerigold
820103   211.2             5000    Notes Payable - Z Equipment
```

Note the - before chart. It says that the standard input file will be file 1 or on the left side of the table.

NAME
    julian   - convert column of dates for math and format change

SYNOPSIS
    julian   [-c -e -u] [Column ...] < tableorlist

DESCRIPTION
    julian will convert Gregorian dates in one or more columns to Julian.

SEE ALSO
    gregorian computedate todaydate

NAME
    justify   - left and right justifies the columns of a table

SYNOPSIS
    justify   [-e -l -r -c -t'c'] [column ...] < table

DESCRIPTION
    justify will right justify the columns containing only numbers and left justify the
    columns with any nonnumeric characters. It also lines up floating point numbers
    (numbers with decimal points) on their decimal points. **justify** makes the table
    look better since we are used to seeing numbers right justified. It also makes vari-
    able length character string columns of equal length by padding with spaces on the
    right. This will cause the columns on the right to line up correctly.

    However, the extra spaces inserted to make it look better increase the size of the
    table. It could easily double or triple the size of the table. This increased size not
    only takes up disk space, but takes longer to process. It is up to the user to decide
    whether appearance or size is more important.

OPTIONS
-e   expand the column to the next tab stop (file will be bigger). Ordinarily a
          column is only as wide as the widest data or column name.

You can override the default options (left justify character strings, right justify
numbers) by using these options.

-*l* left justify (that is the letter "ell", not the number one)
-*c* center
-*r* right justify

These options are sticky, meaning that if you follow an *l, c,* or *r* option with several
column names, each will be treated according to the option. For example: -*l*
Description Account will force both *Account* and *Description* to be left justified.

If you need a field separator other than tab, you can use this option.

-t'c'   use *c* as the column separator instead of tab, where *c* can be any ASCII
            character.

However, remember that you can no longer use the /**rdb** commands on a table
without tabs as column separators. See the **trim** command for a discussion of protecting special characters from the shell.

EXAMPLE
    One use of **justify** is to line up columns. Variable length character columns (like
    names and descriptions) destroy the line up of the columns. For example, notice
    how the variable length names cause the tabs to break at different points.

```
$ cat credit
Name     Credit
----     -------
Anderson 23.49
Ho  145.98
Johnson 1.15
```

    One solution is to move the variable length column to the last column.

```
$ column Credit Name < credit
Credit   Name
-------  ---------------
23.49    Anderson
145.98   Ho
1.15     Johnson
```

Another solution is to use justify to right pad the *Name* column and to line up the floating point number in the *Credit* column while we are at it.

```
$ justify < table
Name       Credit
----       ------
Anderson    23.49
Ho         145.98
Johnson      1.15
```

Remember that your file is now larger. All of those extra blank spaces may double or triple the size of your file. There is a price for beauty.

It is easier to enter the initial data into a table without the padding characters. Then you can use justify to pretty up the table.

When using the **listtotable** command to convert a list format file to a table, you may wish to use **justify** to make the resulting table readable.

SEE ALSO
trim

NAME
label   - for printing mailing labels from a mailing list

SYNOPSIS
label   < list

DESCRIPTION
label will print mailing labels from a mailing list in list format. It is obsolete since the **report** command can make labels more easily. However, this **label** program is being retained as an example of shell programming. **label** is a shell script so it can be easily changed by the user to handle different lists and labels.

EXAMPLE
If you had a file called *maillist* that looked like this:

```
$ cat maillist

Number    1
Name      Ronald McDonald
Company   McDonald's
Street    123 Mac Attack
City      Memphis
State     TENN
ZIP       30000
Phone     (111) 222-3333

Number    2
Name      Chiquita  Banana
Company   United Brands
Street    Uno Avenido de la Reforma
City      San Jose
State     Costa Rica
ZIP       123456789
Phone     1234
```

You could generate mailing labels that would look like this:

```
$ label < maillist

Ronald McDonald
McDonald's
123 Mac Attack
Memphis, TENN 30000

Chiquita  Banana
United Brands
Uno Avenido de la Reforma
San Jose, Costa Rica 123456789
```

SEE ALSO
letter report

SOURCE
```
: %W% SCCS ID Information

: 'label - reads in a mailist and print mailing labels'

USAGE='usage: label < maillist'

while read COLUMNNAME INFO
do
        case $COLUMNNAME in
        Name )
```

```
                        echo $INFO
                        ;;
        M/S )
                        MAILSTOP=$INFO
                        if `test "$INFO"`
                        then
                                echo Mailstop: $INFO
                        fi
                        ;;
        Division )
                        DIVISION=$INFO
                        if `test "$INFO"`
                        then
                                echo Division: $INFO
                        fi
                        ;;
        Company )
                        COMPANY=$INFO
                        if `test "$INFO"`
                        then
                                echo $INFO
                        fi
                        ;;
        Street )
                        echo $INFO
                        ;;
        City )
                        read State STATE
                        read Zip  ZIP
                        echo $INFO, $STATE $ZIP
                        if `test -z "$MAILSTOP"`
                        then
                                echo
                        fi
                        if `test -z "$DIVISION"`
                        then
                                echo
                        fi
                        if `test -z "$COMPANY"`
                        then
                                echo
                        fi
                        echo
                        ;;
        esac
done
```

NAME

length   - returns the length of its argument or input file

SYNOPSIS

length   [string] [< file]

DESCRIPTION

length ouputs the number of characters in its first argument or, if there is no argument, the *standard input*. It uses **wc -c** to do the counting.

Since only the first argument is counted, you must put quotes around all of the words on the command line to make them one argument.

EXAMPLE

Here we find the length of a string and a file.

```
$ length aA1
    3
$ length 'word1 word2'
   11
$ length < length.1
   698
```

Note that you need to put strings in quotes if they have spaces or tabs in them.

SOURCE

```
: %W% SCCS ID Information

: 'length - length of character string'

USAGE='usage: length [string] [ < file ]'

if test "$#" -eq 0
then
        wc -c
else
        echo "$1"\\c| wc -c
fi
```

NAME
letter   - prints form letters from a mailling list

SYNOPSIS
letter   letter.1 ... < maillist

DESCRIPTION
letter will print form letters from a standard letter and a mailing list. It is obsolete now since the **report** program is so much more powerful and easier to use, but is being retained for compatibility and as an example of shell programming.

letter is a shell script so it can be easily changed by the user to handle different lists and letters. You will probably want to copy the **letter** program from *rdb/bin/letter* to your local directory. Then you can modify it with a text editor to handle any special features of your mailing list and letters.

EXAMPLE
If you have a file called *maillist* that looked like this:

```
$ cat maillist
Name     Ronald McDonald
Company  McDonald's
Street   123 Mac Attack
City     Memphis
State    TENN
ZIP      30000
Phone    (111) 222-3333
Name     Chiquita  Banana
Company  United Brands
Street   Uno Avenido de la Reforma
City     San Jose
State    Costa Rica
ZIP      123456789
Phone    1234
```

And two parts of your letter in two separate files, called *letter.1* and *letter.2:*

```
$ cat letter.1
We have a new product that we want to sell to everyone at
$ cat letter.2
Please have everyone send us an order.  We will be very grateful.
Sincerely,
Mr. Marketing
Makeapile, Inc.
```

You could generate letters that would look like this:

```
$ letter letter.1 letter.2 < maillist
Ronald McDonald
McDonald's
123 Mac Attack
Memphis, TENN 30000

Dear Ronald McDonald:

We have a new product  that  we  want  to  sell  to  everyone  at
McDonald's.   Please  have  everyone send us an order.  We will be
very grateful.
Sincerely,
```

```
Mr. Marketing
Makeapile, Inc.
```

< There are spaces here to skip down to the bottom of the letter. They are removed here to save space. >

```
Chiquita  Banana
United Brands
Uno Avenido de la Reforma
San Jose, Costa Rica 123456789

Dear Chiquita  Banana:

We have a new product that we want to sell to everyone at  United
Brands.   Please have everyone send us an order.   We will be very
grateful.

Sincerely,
Mr. Marketing
Makeapile, Inc.
```

< There are spaces here to skip down to the bottom of the letter. They are removed here to save space. >

This sample letter program prints out the mailing name and address and a *Dear Name*. It then cats *letter.1,* echos the company name and finally cats *letter.2*. It writes all of its output to a temporary file *TMP* and then **nroff**'s the *TMP* file to the *standard out*. The **nroff** program causes the file to be reformated (left and right justified) for each company name length.

By studying the **letter** shell script and the UNIX shell's documentation, (**sh** or **csh),** you can do very fancy and complex form letters.

SEE ALSO
report label

SOURCE
```
: %W% SCCS ID Information

: 'letter - will writer a letter from a form letter and a mailing list
:        letter picks up letter1 letter2 etc from the argument list'

USAGE='usage: letter letter1 letter2 ... < maillist'

TMP=/tmp/$$letter
trap 'rm -f /tmp/$$*' 0 1 2 3 15

while read COLUMNNAME INFO
do
        case $COLUMNNAME in
        Name )
                name=$INFO
                echo > $TMP
                echo .nf >> $TMP
                echo $INFO >> $TMP
                ;;
        Company )
                COMPANY=$INFO
                echo $INFO >> $TMP
                ;;
        Street )
                echo $INFO >> $TMP
                ;;
        City )
                read State STATE
                read Zip  ZIP
```

```
                echo $INFO, $STATE $ZIP >> $TMP
                echo >> $TMP
                echo >> $TMP
                echo Dear $name: >> $TMP
                echo .fi >> $TMP
                echo >> $TMP
                cat $1 >> $TMP
                echo $COMPANY. >> $TMP
                cat $2 >> $TMP
                echo >> $TMP
                echo >> $TMP
                nroff $TMP
                ;;
        esac
   done
```

NAME
like   - finds names that sound like similar name

SYNOPSIS
like   similar-name file [name-column]

DESCRIPTION
like converts a name to Knuth's soundex code and looks it up in the *.x* secondary index file of a name. To work, you must have run the **soundex** command first, to create the soundex file.

EXAMPLE
See **soundex** for examples.

SEE ALSO
soundex

SOURCE
```
: like - finds names that sound like a name using soundex codes
USAGE='usage: like similar-name file [ name-column ]'
EUSAGE=1

if test "$#" -lt 2
then
        echo $USAGE
        exit $EUSAGE
fi

NAME="${3:-Name}"

echo "$1" |
headon |
soundex |
tee tmp.x |
column Soundex |
tail -1 |
search -mb -x $2.x Soundex |
column $NAME |
sorttable |
uniq |
tee tmp.uniq |
search -mi -x $2 $NAME
```

NAME
listtosh - converts list format to shell variable

SYNOPSIS
listtosh < list

DESCRIPTION
listtosh converts a list format (column(tab)data) to a shell variable format (VARIABLE='value') for grabbing a record into a shell program.

EXAMPLE
```
$ cat maillist
Number   1
Name     Ronald McDonald
Company  McDonald's
Street   123 Mac Attack
City     Menphis
State    TENN
ZIP      30000
Phone    (111) 222-3333

Number   2
Name     Chiquita Banana
Company  United Brands
Street   Uno Avenito De La Revolution
City     San Jose
State    Costa Rica
ZIP      123456789
Phone    1234

$ eval `row 'Number == 2' < maillist | listtosh`
Number='2'
Name='Chiquita Banana'
Company='United Brands'
Street='Uno Avenito De La Revolution'
City='San Jose'
State='Costa Rica'
ZIP='123456789'
Phone='1234'

$ echo "$Name's phone number is $Phone."
Chiquita Banana's phone number is 1234.
```


SEE ALSO
  tabletolist

SOURCE
```
: listtosh turns list format into var = value shell format

sed    's/      /="/
       /./s/$/"/'
```

NAME
   listtotable   - for converting from list to table format

SYNOPSIS
   listtotable   [-e -l] < listfile

DESCRIPTION
   listtotable converts a file in list format into a file in table format. Some **/rdb** programs need to see files in table format so the conversion is necessary.

   In addition, table-formatted files are processed faster than list-formatted files. Anytime you send a list-formatted file through a pipe of two or more programs, even if they can handle list format, convert them to table format so that the programs in the pipe will run two or three times faster on average. The reason that table-formatted files run so much faster is that a list file is often two or three times larger than a table because of the repeated column names. Therefore, when handling list-formatted files, the programs have to process two or three times as many characters.

OPTION
-e   Expand each column to next tab stop. Ordinarily table columns heads are only as wide as list column heads.

-l   No head line in the list file. A head line for a list file is a newline (blank head line as described below). This option makes it possible to convert and sometimes use the older list-formatted files. They did not use the leading newline as is now required in the list-formatted file. It was not easy to determine a list from a table format, so we now require a newline as the first character. You don't have this option on any other command. Only **listtotable** is smart enough to know that it has a list formatted file without the head line. Actually, it is not so smart. It assumes that its input file is list-formatted. It does no checking, so if you input a table, you will get a mess.

LIST AND TABLE FORMAT RULES
   List format looks like this:

```
$ cat maillist
Number   1
Name     Ronald McDonald
Company  McDonald's
Street   123 Mac Attack
City     Memphis
State    TENN
ZIP      30000
Phone    (111) 222-3333

Number   2
Name     Chiquita  Banana
Company  United Brands
Street   Uno Avenido de la Reforma
City     San Jose
State    Costa Rica
ZIP      123456789
Phone    1234

  . . .
```

   Remember there are three rules for list format and three for table (see the tutorial chapter on *Entry)*.

List rules:

1. First character is a newline which makes the file look like the first line is blank. Be sure that there are no unseen spaces, tabs or nonprinting characters on the first line or things will get quite messed up.

2. Two columns separated by a tab. The first column is the *column* name and the second column is the *column* values.

3. A newline (blank line) after each *row* (record).

Table rules:

1. A single tab between each column in a row and a newline at the end.

2. Name of the column at the top of the column, in the first line of the file.

3. A dash line as the second line in the file.

EXAMPLE

You could convert the *maillist* (list-formatted file) to a table format like this:

```
$ listtotable < maillist
Number  Name      Company  Street   City     State    ZIP      Phone
-------  -------  -------  -------  -------  -------  -------  -------
1         Ronald McDonald  McDonald's         123 Mac Attack    Memphis
TENN    30000     (111) 222-3333
2         Chiquita  Banana  United Brands      Uno Avenito De La
Revolution          San Jose Costa Rica        123456789          1234
```

When you look at this messy table you can see the need for list format. The information in each column is often too wide for the screen and *wraps around* to the next line.

SEE ALSO
tabletolist

NAME
lock   - locks a record or field of a file

SYNOPSIS
lock   filename processid from to indexfrom indexto

DESCRIPTION
lock locks a record or file by writing a row into a common lock file. */tmp/Lfilename* contains one line for each locked record or field. The line contains the process ID of the process (program) that locked it, and the begin (from) and end (to) of the bytes to be locked. Also the index begin and end bytes to be locked. When a process attempts to lock a string of bytes that is already locked, **lock** returns an error condition. This status code ($?) can be tested with the **test** command.

EXAMPLE
Let us use **lock** on the *inventory* table:

```
$ cat inventory

Item   Amount  Cost  Value  Description
----   ------  ----  -----  -------------
   1        3    50    150  rubber gloves
   2      100     5    500  test tubes
   3        5    80    400  clamps
   4       23    19    437  plates
   5       99    24   2376  cleaning cloth
   6       89   147  13083  bunsen burners
   7        5   175    875  scales
```

First we use **seek** to locate the record and return the offset and size.

```
$ LOCATION=`echo 5 | seek -mb inventory Item`
$ echo $LOCATION
207 245 0 8
```

This means that the record is offset 207 bytes into the file and that it is 38 bytes long, ending at byte 245. The 0 and 8 mean that there is no secondary index file.

Now we can call **lock** to lock the record:

```
$ lock inventory $$ $LOCATION
```

Note that we use the *$LOCATION* shell variable to supply the two values, *from* and *to*. We also use the automatic shell variable double dollar ($$) to put the process ID on the command line.

Let's see what the lock file looks like:

```
$ cat /tmp/Linventory
207 245 0 8
```

SEE ALSO
unlock

SOURCE
```
: %W% SCCS ID Information

: 'lock - locks an area, usually a record, of a file'
```

```
USAGE='usage: lock filename pid from to indexfrom indexto'·
EUSAGE=1

LOCKSET=0
ELOCKED=2

umask 000

case "$#" in
6)
     LOCKROW="$2     $3      $4                 $5$6"
     LOCKFILE=/tmp/L$1
     TMP=/tmp/$$lock

     if test -s $LOCKFILE
     then
             echo "$LOCKROW" >> $LOCKFILE
             exec 0< $LOCKFILE
             while read PID FROM TO XFROM XTO
             do
                     if test "$LOCKROW" = "$PID$FROM$TO$XFROM$XTO"
                     then
                             exit $LOCKSET
                     elif test "$3" -ge "$FROM" -a "$3" -lt "$TO"\
                             -o "$4" -gt "$FROM" -a "$4" -le "$TO"
                     then
                             sed "/$LOCKROW/d" < $LOCKFILE > $TMP
                             mv $TMP $LOCKFILE
                             exit $ELOCKED
                     fi
             done

             # own lock gone means lock file updated with sed mv
             exit $ELOCKED

     else
             echo "$LOCKROW" > $LOCKFILE
             exit $LOCKSET
     fi
     ;;
*)
     echo $USAGE 1>&2
     exit $EUSAGE
     ;;
esac
```

NAME
lowercase   - returns the lowercase of its argument or input file

SYNOPSIS
lowercase   [string ...] [< file]

DESCRIPTION
lowercase converts to lower case every letter in its arguments or, if there are no arguments, the standard input. It uses **tr,** the UNIX character translate command, to do the converting.

EXAMPLE
Here we convert to lower case a string and a file.

```
$ lowercase BIG WORDS
big words
$ cat CAPITALS
THESE ARE ALL CAPS.
$ lowercase < CAPITALS
these are all caps.
```

SEE ALSO
cap uppercase

SOURCE
```
: %W% SCCS ID Information

: 'lowercase - converts characters to lowercase'

USAGE='usage: lowercase [string ...] [< file]'

if test "$#" -eq 0
then
        tr '[A-Z]' '[a-z]'
else
        echo "$*" | tr '[A-Z]' '[a-z]'
fi
```

NAME
makecatalog   - print catalog from inventory table

SYNOPSIS
makecatalog

DESCRIPTION
makecatalog creates a catalog, really a price list or order form, from the *inventory* file.

EXAMPLE
```
$ makecatalog
$ cat catalog
Code       Qty          Price    Total      Name
-----      -------      -------  -------    ----------------
rdb          _____x     1500    =$_____   /rdb software
act          _____x     1500    =$_____   /act software
docrdb       _____x       50    =$_____   /rdb manual
docact       _____x       50    =$_____   /act manual
binder       _____x       20    =$_____   binders
f1           _____x        5    =$_____   floppy 2s2d
f2           _____x        8    =$_____   floppy 2s4d
tape         _____x       15    =$_____   tape 1600bpi
-----      -------      -------  -------    ----------------
                                 _____   Total
                                 _____   - Discount
                                 _____   Net
                                 _____   - Sales Tax
                                 _____   Amount Due
```

SOURCE
```
: 'makecatalog - creates a catalog from the inventory file'

column Code Qty Price Total Name < inventory |
compute 'Qty = "_____x"; Total = "=$_____";' > catalog


echo " -----       -------     -------   -------                  ----------------
                                 _____   Total
                                 _____   - Discount
                                 _____   Net
                                 _____   - Sales Tax
                                 _____   Amount Due" >> catalog
```

NAME
    maximum   - displays the maximum value in each column selected

SYNOPSIS
    maximum   [-l] [column ...] < table

DESCRIPTION
    maximum displays the highest value of each column selected. If no columns are listed, all of the columns will be calculated and displayed.

OPTIONS
    -l   option will cause the entire file to be listed also.

EXAMPLE
    See **total.**

NAME

    mean   - displays the mean (average) of each column selected

SYNOPSIS

    mean   [-l] [column ...] < table

DESCRIPTION

    mean displays the average (total / rows) value of each column selected. If no columns are listed, all of the columns will be calculated and displayed. Blank lines are treated as zero. If that is not what you want, you can use **rmblanks** or **compress -b** to remove blank lines. Blank values are also treated as zero.

OPTIONS

    -l   option will cause the entire file to be listed also.

EXAMPLE

    See **total.**

NAME
menu   - root menu with some UNIX commands

SYNOPSIS
menu

DESCRIPTION
menu displays a table of commands that you can execute by simply typing a number or a name. Menus are useful for inexperienced users. They can be set up by more experienced users very easily. **menu** is a shell script that simply echos the **menu** table of choices, then waits for the user to type in a number or name. Then **menu** uses a shell case statement to execute a command or series of commands for each choice. To set up your own menus, simply copy the **menu** shell command from the /*rdb*/*bin* into your directory and edit it. You should change its name to *Menu* or *Menu.something*. There is a sample local **menu,** named **Menu** in /*rdb*/*demo*.

EXAMPLE
```
$ menu
                        UNIX MENU
  Number   Name      For
  -------  -------   --------------------------------------------------
       0   exit      leave menu or return to higher menu
       1   Menu      goto another local menu (if any)
       2   sh        get unix shell
       3   vi        edit a file
       4   mail      read mail
       5   send      send mail to someone
       6   cal       see your calendar
       7   who       see who is on the system
       8   ls        list the files in this directory
       9   cat       display a file on the screen
      10   rdb       display rdb commands
Please enter a number or name for the action you wish or DEL to exit:
_
```

The underline at the bottom is the cursor. **menu** is waiting for you to type your choice of number or name. Numbers are quicker to type, but names are more mnemonic and help you learn how to do things at the shell level.

Setting Up Your Own Menus
You can nicely automate your operations with menus. If you have naive users who might have trouble learning or remembering the UNIX or /**rdb** commands, you can set up menus for them. Also, when you have an operation in which a few commands are repeatedly executed, they can put them into a menu for simple choice.

You can put your menus in the directories in which they will be used or in your *$HOME*/*bin* or other *bin* directories.

To start, go to the directory of your choice and copy the /**rdb** *menu* to your directory:

```
$ cp /rdb/bin/menu Menu
```

or

```
$ cp /rdb/demo/Menu .
```

You may have a different path to your **/rdb** directory. Type:

```
$ path menu
/usr/rdb/bin
```

to find its path on your system. We suggest the convention of using the name **Menu** with the capital *M* so that it will appear at the top of your list of files when you do a **ls** command. Therefore it won't get so easily lost among the other files in the directory. You can then name submenus: *Menu.other* where other is something that suggests the kinds of commands the menu covers.

Now edit the Menu command. If you use vi, type:

```
$ vi Menu
```

As you study the code, you will find that it is very easy to create your own directory.

Menu is in two parts. Part one is the menu table:

```
        cat <<SCREEN
$CLEAR                          UNIX MENU
Number   Name     For
-------  -------  --------------------------
     0   exit     leave menu or return to higher menu
     1   Menu     goto another local menu (if any)
     2   sh       get unix shell
     3   vi       edit a file
     4   mail     read mail
     5   send     send mail to someone
     6   cal      see your calendar
     7   who      see who is on the system
     8   ls       list the files in this directory
     9   cat      display a file on the screen
    10   rdb      display rdb commands
Please enter a number or name for the action you wish or DEL to exit:

SCREEN
```

The **cat** command will simply send to the screen everything after the command and before the line that begins with *SCREEN,* including the *Please enter a number* ... line. The *$CLEAR* on the first line will be replaced by a sequence of characters that will clear the terminal. The *$CLEAR* shell variable should be set by the following command in the **menu** or in the *.profile* file of the user:

```
$ CLEAR='termput cl'
```

or on System 5 Release 2 and higher:

```
$ CLEAR='tput clear'
```

The second part of Menu is a large **case** statement that you can edit to do what you want. Here is a sample:

```
        read ANSWER COMMENT

        case $ANSWER in

        0|exit)   exit 0 ;;
        1|Menu)   Menu ;;
        2|sh)     sh ;;
        3|vi)
                  echo 'Which file or files do you wish to edit'
                  read ANSWER COMMENT
                  vi $ANSWER $COMMENT
                  ;;
        4|mail)   mail ;;
```

```
      5|send)
                  echo 'Please enter login name of person to send mail to'
                  read ANSWER COMMENT
                  echo 'Type you letter, and end by typing Ctrl-d'
                  mail $ANSWER
                  ;;
      6|cal)      (cd ; calendar) ;;
      7|who)      who ;;
      8|ls)       ls ;;
      9|cat)
                  echo 'Please enter the name of the file you wish to see'
                  read ANSWER COMMENT
                  cat $ANSWER
                  ;;
     10|rdb)      menu.rdb ;;
      *)          echo 'Sorry, but that number or name is not recognized.' ;;
      esac
```

The **read** command waits for the user to enter his or her choice. The first word typed is assigned to the *ANSWER* shell variable. If the user types any more words, they will be assigned to *COMMENT,* which might be used in your commands.

Next is the **case** statement that looks at the *$ANSWER* to decide which command to execute. Note that the number and name are separated by a vertical bar character (|) to mean *or:*

```
0|exit)           exit 0 ;;
```

This line will be selected if the user types either 0 or **exit.** The **exit** command is then executed. The double semicolons (;;) are required to show the end of the commands for this **case** statement. You can type in any command or series of commands that you could type at your terminal or in a shell script after each **case** choice. The **esac** at the bottom is case spelled backwards and is required to end the whole **case** statement.

The *) will catch any pattern that does not match earlier patterns. In this case a message is displayed. The number (#) symbol starts a comment. The shell will ignore the rest of the line after the sharp symbol. So you can add comments, which we recommend.

You have great power to do things as a result of the user selecting a choice. Of course you will need to match the name and number in your menu table with the patterns in the **case** statement. It is easy to edit one, and forget to edit the other.

PORTABILITY

   menu uses a shell variable called *CLEAR*. Different UNIX systems have different ways of clearing the screen.

```
CLEAR='termput cl'    # All UNIX Systems with /etc/termcap
CLEAR='tput clear'    # UNIX System V, Release 2
CLEAR='clear'         # Berkeley UNIX
```

You will have to figure out how to do this on your system. You should put the proper assignment for your terminal in your *.profile* file in your home directory. Using the shell variable to clear the screen is much faster than executing a command each time.

SEE ALSO

   UNIX **sh case** statement and shell programming.

SOURCE

```
: %W% SCCS ID Information

: 'menu is the root of your personal menus'

USAGE='usage: menu'

ANSWER=""

while true
do
        if test "$ANSWER" = ""
        then
        cat <<SCREEN
$CLEAR                              UNIX MENU
Number  Name    For
-------  ------  ------------------------------------
    0     exit    leave menu or return to higher menu
    1     Menu    goto another local menu (if any)
    2     sh      get unix shell
    3     vi      edit a file
    4     mail    read mail
    5     send    send mail to someone
    6     cal     see your calendar
    7     who     see who is on the system
    8     ls      list the files in this directory
    9     cat     display a file on the screen
   10     rdb     display rdb commands

Please enter a number or name for the action you wish or DEL to exit:

SCREEN

        read ANSWER COMMENT
        fi
                        .
        case $ANSWER in

        0|exit) exit 0 ;;
        1|Menu) Menu ;;
        2|sh)   sh ;;
        3|vi)
                echo 'Which file or files do you wish to edit'
                read ANSWER COMMENT
                vi $ANSWER $COMMENT
                ;;
        4|mail) mail ;;
        5|send)
                echo 'Please enter login name of person to send mail to'
                read ANSWER COMMENT
                echo 'Type you letter, and end by typing Ctrl-d'
                mail $ANSWER
                ;;
        6|cal)  (cd ; calendar) ;;
        7|who)  who ;;
        8|ls)   ls ;;
        9|cat)
                echo 'Please enter the name of the file you wish to see'
                read ANSWER COMMENT
                cat $ANSWER
                ;;
        10|rdb) menu.rdb ;;
        *)      echo 'Sorry, but that number or name is not recognized.' ;;
        esac

        echo '
Hit the Return key when you are ready to see the menu again.
        read ANSWER
done
```

NAME
    minimum   - displays the minimum of each column selected

SYNOPSIS
    minimum   [-l] [column ...] < table

DESCRIPTION
    minimum displays the lowest value of each column selected. If no columns are listed, all of the columns will be calculated and displayed. Blank lines will count as zero.

OPTIONS
    -l   option will cause the entire file to be listed also.

EXAMPLE
    See **total.**

NAME

not   - logical not reverses return status of command

SYNOPSIS

not   command ...

DESCRIPTION

not converts a zero (0) return status to 255, and any nonzero return status to 0. True becomes false and vice versa. This is used to test a command for not true or false.

EXAMPLE

Here we see what that **not** reverses the return code of **true** and **false.**

```
$ true ; echo $?
0
$ not true ; echo $?
255
```

SOURCE

```
: %W% SCCS Information

: not - logical not reverses return code of command

USAGE='usage: not command ...'
EUSAGE=1


if test "$#" -lt 1
then
        echo $USAGE 1>&2
        exit $EUSAGE
fi

if eval $*
then
        exit 255
else
        exit 0
fi
```

NAME
number - insert a column row number in a table or list

SYNOPSIS
number < tableorlist

DESCRIPTION
number will create a new column with the row numbers of the table prepended to the table, or as the first field in a list.

If you use **Number,** instead of **number,** the column head will be capitalized, that is, the name of the command will be the name of the column. The way you call it is the way the column name will print. You can also use the **rename** command to change the column name.

EXAMPLE
If you need to number each row, use the number command:

```
$ cat inventory
Item#   Amount   Cost    Value   Description
-------  -------  -------  -------  ---------------
     1       3    5.00    15.00   rubber gloves
     2     100    0.50    50.00   test tubes
     3       5    8.00    40.00   clamps
     4      23    1.98    45.54   plates
     5      99    2.45   242.55   cleaning cloth
     6      89   14.75  1312.75   bunsen burners
     7       5  175.00   875.00   scales

$ Number < inventory
Number   Item#   Amount   Cost    Value   Description
-------  -------  -------  -------  -------  ---------------
     1       1       3    5.00    15.00   rubber gloves
     2       2     100    0.50    50.00   test tubes
     3       3       5    8.00    40.00   clamps
     4       4      23    1.98    45.54   plates
     5       5      99    2.45   242.55   cleaning cloth
     6       6      89   14.75  1312.75   bunsen burners
     7       7       5  175.00   875.00   scales
```

Note that the first column is the new number column.

If you want the number column in a different position, use **column** to move it. If you want to change the name of the number column to something else, use **rename.**

NAME

pad   - adds extra spaces at end of last column

SYNOPSIS

pad   [-number] < tableorlist

DESCRIPTION

pad adds extra spaces to the end of the last column of each record in the input table or list file. It is useful for setting up a file that will be updated by the **update** command. **update** will put an edited record back into the file in the same place it was taken out. If the user adds characters while editing the record, it will not fit. The **replace** command will look for trailing and leading spaces to trim off to fit the record back in. But if it does not find enough room, it will append the record to the end of the file. Padding gives each record a fixed number of extra spaces to be trimmed as needed.

The traditional solution is to use fixed length records and fields. To do this, one should use **justify** to pad the file. But that often increases the file by two or three times. That makes a much larger and slower file to process. **pad** gives you the power to control how much larger each record will be.

DEFAULT

-number is the number of spaces that will be added to the last row. The default is 70 spaces.

EXAMPLE

If you had a *maillist* file, and you wanted to pad it, type:

```
$ pad < maillist > tmp
```

To **see** the results, pipe it to see:

```
$ pad < maillist | see
$
Number^J1$
Name^JRonald McDonald$
Company^JMcDonald's$
Street^J123 Mac Attack$
City^JMenphis$
State^JTENN$
ZIP^J30000$
Phone^J(111) 222-3333                                    $
$
Number^J2$
Name^JChachita Banana$
Company^JUnited Brands$
Street^JUno Avenito De La Revolution$
City^JSan Jose$
State^JEl Salvadore$
ZIP^J123456789$
Phone^J1234                                              $
$
```

Note the dollar signs, signifying the end of the line, way out to the right of the last column, *Phone*. Those are the default extra spaces that have been added. On such a small record that is probably far too many.

TECHNICAL

Also note that *Phone* had a value in it. If there is a value in the last column already, it will over write the spaces. If the value is longer than the spaces, the value will be written, but no spaces added. It is recommended that you have a last column named *Comment* or *Remarks that is a catch all* for both comments and padding.

SEE ALSO

replace

NAME
padstring   - returns string with blanks to fill a field

SYNOPSIS
padstring   [-]size string

DESCRIPTION
padstring adds blanks to a string so that it will be the desired length. It is useful for screen and report writing where you want everything to line up. This requires fixed length fields.

A *-size* means to left justify the string in the field, that is, to put the padding blanks to the right of the string.

EXAMPLE
First, let's pad a simple string.

```
$ padstring 10 string
   string
```

Now we can use this in a **report** program form file to make fixed length fields. An ordinary form will have the files to the right of a field moving all around.

```
$ report form < mailtable
Name  : Ronald McDonald          Company: McDonald's
Street: 123 Mac Attack
City  : Menphis          State  : TENN      ZIP: 30000
Phone : (111) 222-3333

Name  : Chiquita Banana          Company: United Brands
Street: Uno Avenito De La Revolution
City  : San Jose          State  : Costa Rica      ZIP: 123456789
Phone : 1234
```

But if we edit the *form* file to include the **padstring** command, then we will get a fixed form.

```
$ cat form
Name  : <!padstring -17 '<Name>'!> Company: <Company>
Street: <Street>
City  : <!padstring -17 '<City>'!> State  : <State>      ZIP: <ZIP>
Phone : <Phone>

$ report form < mailtable
Name  : Ronald McDonald   Company: McDonald's
Street: 123 Mac Attack
City  : Menphis          State  : TENN      ZIP: 30000
Phone : (111) 222-3333

Name  : Chiquita Banana   Company: United Brands
Street: Uno Avenito De La Revolution
City  : San Jose          State  : Costa Rica      ZIP: 123456789
Phone : 1234
```

Note that *State* has not been done yet, and therefore *ZIP* moves back and forth. But *Company* and *State* stay lined up correctly. If **padstring** is too long a name, link (UNIX **ln** command) it with a shorter name.

SEE ALSO
screen, report

NAME

paste   - outputs two or more tables sides by side

SYNOPSIS

paste   table1 table2 [...]

DESCRIPTION

paste displays the tables named side by side. There is a command in UNIX system III and higher with the same name and function, but most other UNIX systems do not have it. **paste** uses the UNIX **pr** command to list the tables side by side:

```
$ pr -m -t -s table1 table2 [...]
```

paste differs from **jointable** in that **jointable** looks for matching values in key columns and only puts out rows where a match is found. **paste** does not care what it is pasting together. You can get some interesting garbage with **paste.**

You can also do a kind of visual **diff** in which you can see, perhaps an old and new file, lined up side by side. You could do this with two list files, but be careful, because the output will generally not be acceptable by other **/rdb** programs.

EXAMPLE

If you had taken a table and projected (**column**) it into two tables, you could put them back together with **paste.**

```
$ column Item Value < inventory > tmp1
$ cat tmp1
 Item   Value
 -----   -----
    1     150
    2     500
    3     400
    4     437
    5    2376
    6   13083
    7     875
$ column Cost Amount Description < inventory > tmp2
$ cat tmp2
Cost   Amount   Description
----   ------   --------------
  50       3    rubber gloves
   5     100    test tubes
  80       5    clamps
  19      23    plates
  24      99    cleaning cloth
 147      89    bunsen burners
 175       5    scales
```

Now, perhaps after some work, you could put them back together, in a different order, with **paste.**

```
$ paste tmp1 tmp2
Item    Value   Cost   Amount   Description
-----   -----   ----   ------   --------------
    1     150     50       3    rubber gloves
    2     500      5     100    test tubes
    3     400     80       5    clamps
    4     437     19      23    plates
    5    2376     24      99    cleaning cloth
```

```
6   13083    147     89   bunsen burners
7     875    175      5   scales
```

This is not an efficient way to do column commands, which could all be done with one column command instead of two. But it is a good way to put tables together if **jointable** is inappropriate. If you had wanted to use **jointable** here, you should **project** the *Item* column in both tables.

SOURCE

```
: %W% SCCS ID Information

: 'paste outputs the named files side by side'

USAGE='usage: paste table1 table2 [ ... ]'
EUSAGE=1

if  test "$#" -lt 2
then
      echo $USAGE 1>&2
      exit $EUSAGE
fi

pr -m -t -s $*
```

NAME
path   - finds the full path of a command

SYNOPSIS
path   [command ...]

DESCRIPTION
path will find the directory path to a command if it is in one of the directories in your shell *PATH* environment variable. A path means two things in UNIX. 1. It means the lists of directories that one must go through to find a file or program. 2. It means a list of directories to be searched by the shell to find an executable program that matches the command typed in.

The **path** program will look through the directories in your PATH (meaning 2) to find the **path** (meaning 1) of the command. If **path** cannot find the command or if the command is not executable, **path** returns nothing.

EXAMPLE
If you type:

```
$ path column
/usr/rdb/bin
```

and get this result, then the **column** command is in */usr/rdb/bin.*

SOURCE
```
: %W% SCCS Information
: 'path returns the path to a executible command'

USAGE='usage: path command'
EOK=0
EUSAGE=1
ENOFIND=2

: test for a command in our argument list
if test "$#" -lt 1
then
        echo $USAGE 1>&2
        exit $EUSAGE
fi

: parse the PATH variable into words
COMMAND=$1
OLDIFS=$IFS
IFS=:
set $PATH
IFS=$OLDIFS

: look for the command in the path directories
for DIR in $*
do
        if test -r $DIR/$COMMAND
        then
                echo $DIR
                exit $EOK
        fi
done

exit $NOFIND
```

NAME
　　precision　　　　　　- displays the precision of each column selected

SYNOPSIS
　　precision　　　　　　[-l] [column ...] < table

DESCRIPTION
　　precision displays the maximum number of digits to the right of the decimal point of each column selected. If no columns are listed, all of the numeric columns will be calculated and displayed.

OPTIONS
　　-l option will cause the entire table to be listed also.

EXAMPLE
　　See **total.**

NAME
project   - outputs selected projects (same as project)

SYNOPSIS
project   [project ...] < tableorlist

DESCRIPTION
project is just another name for **column. column** and **project** are linked, with the **ln** command, to the same program file.

SEE ALSO
column

SOURCE
```
: project.sh - input table and output only selected columns

read HEAD

if test -z "$HEAD"
then
        (echo; cat) | listtotable | $0 $* | tabletolist
        exit 0
fi

read DASH

for ARG
do
        C=1
        for I in $HEAD
        do
                if test "$I" = "$ARG"
                then
                        COL="$COL,\$$C"
                        shift
                fi
        C=`expr "$C" + 1`
        done
done

COL=`expr "$COL" : ',\(.*\)'`

(echo "$HEAD"; echo "$DASH"; cat) |
awk "BEGIN {FS=OFS=\"      \";} {print $COL;}"
```

NAME
  prompt   - like echo but no newline

SYNOPSIS
  prompt   string ...

DESCRIPTION
  prompt solves the problem of the change in syntax for the UNIX **echo** command. Old echo used -*n* to mean no newline at the end of the string. The new UNIX systems require *c*. **prompt** looks for a shell variable called *ECHONOCR*. If the variable is missing or not equal to -*n* than you get the new form, else the old -*n* form. Since this is usually used for prompting the user, the name is **prompt.** Nice, uh?

EXAMPLE
```
$ prompt "Please enter your name: "
Please enter your name: _
```

  To change to the old system, put this line in your *.profile*.

```
$ ECHONOCR=-n
```

SEE ALSO
  chr

SOURCE
```
: %W% SCCS Information

: prompt echos a string without a new line
:        it knows about the change from echo -n to echo \\c
: you must put the following in your .profile to make this work
# if your systems echo requires -n for no cr, else do not set
# ECHONOCR=-n

USAGE='usage: prompt string ...'
EUSAGE=1

if test "$ECHONOCR" = -n
then
        echo -n "$*"
else
        echo "$*\c"
fi
```

NAME

rdb   - lists all /rdb programs in *rdb*/*bin* directory

SYNOPSIS

rdb

DESCRIPTION

rdb will find the *rdb*/*bin* directory in your *PATH*. It will then list all of the commands in that directory.

EXAMPLE

If you type:

```
$ rdb
```

The current list of /**rdb** programs will follow.

BUGS

rdb uses the UNIX **ls** command. On some systems you get a long list and on others you get columns. Edit the **rdb** shell script for the listing format you prefer, if it does not come automatically.

SEE ALSO

helpme

SOURCE

```
: %W% SCCS ID Information

: 'rdb will list the /rdb bin'

USAGE='usage: rdb'

ls 'path rdb' | pr -5 -t
```

NAME

record   - finds and outputs record from table

SYNOPSIS

record   [-h] number < table'

DESCRIPTION

record searches through a table for the record number you specify on the command line. If you give it the *-h* option, no head line will be output.

EXAMPLE

To get record number 3 from the *inventory* table:

```
$ record 3 < inventory
Item    Amount  Cost   Value   Description
----    ------  ----   -----   --------------
   3         5    80     400   clamps
```

The following shell script uses **record** and **read** to find specific values in a table. The **read** command uses the head line of *inventory* to assign values to each column name.

```
$ cat describe
: describe - gives the description for an item in inventory
USAGE='usage: describe Item < table'

record $1 < inventory |
(       read HEAD
        read DASH
        read $HEAD
        echo "Item $Item is $Description"
)
$ describe 1 < inventory
Item 1 is rubber gloves
```

The *-h* option gets a single record without a head:

```
$ record -h 1 < inventory
   1         4    50     150    rubber gloves
```

SEE ALSO

row search

SOURCE

```
: %W% SCCS Information
: record - outputs the record number you request
USAGE='usage: record number < table'

case $# in
1)      LINE='expr $1 + 1'
        NEXT='expr $1 + 2'
        case "$LINE" in
        1)
                sed     "${NEXT}q" ;;
        *)
                sed     "3,${LINE}d
                        ${NEXT}q" ;;
        esac ;;
*)      echo $USAGE
        exit 1 ;;
esac
```

NAME
rename - change column name in head line

SYNOPSIS
rename [oldcolumn newcolumn ...] < tableorlist

DESCRIPTION
rename will change a column name to a new name. You can change as many as you want in one pass with pairs of old and new column names. The first of the pair is taken to be the old column name, which is looked up in the head line of the table, and replaced with the second column name of the pair.

EXAMPLE
If you need to change a column name, you could simply edit it in a text editor. Or you can use the **rename** program:

```
$ cat inventory
Item#   Amount     Cost     Value   Description
-----   ------    -----   -------   --------------
    1        3     5.00     15.00   rubber gloves
    2      100     0.50     50.00   test tubes
    3        5     8.00     40.00   clamps
    4       23     1.98     45.54   plates
    5       99     2.45    242.55   cleaning cloth
    6       89    14.75   1312.75   bunsen burners
    7        5   175.00    875.00   scales
$ rename Amount Qty Description Name < inventory
Item#    Qty     Cost     Value   Name
-----    ---    ------   -------   --------------
    1        3     5.00     15.00   rubber gloves
    2      100     0.50     50.00   test tubes
    3        5     8.00     40.00   clamps
    4       23     1.98     45.54   plates
    5       99     2.45    242.55   cleaning cloth
    6       89    14.75   1312.75   bunsen burners
    7        5   175.00    875.00   scales
```

Note that the two columns *Amount* and *Description* have had their names changed. If you have a list-formatted file, you can also rename the column names. For example, if you have a *maillist* file:

```
$ cat maillist

Number    1
Name      Ronald McDonald
Company   McDonald's
Street    123 Mac Attack
City      Memphis
State     TENN
ZIP       30000
Phone     (111) 222-3333

Number    2
Name      Chiquita  Banana
Company   United Brands
Street    Uno Avenido de la Reforma
City      San Jose
State     Costa Rica
ZIP       123456789
Phone     1234
```

You can change names by typing

```
$ rename Number Num ZIP Zip < maillist
```

```
Num        1
Name       Ronald McDonald
Company    McDonald's
Street     123 Mac Attack
City       Memphis
State      TENN
Zip        30000
Phone      (111) 222-3333

Num        2
Name       Chiquita  Banana
Company    United Brands
Street     Uno Avenido de la Reforma
City       San Jose
State      Costa Rica
Zip        123456789
Phone      1234
```

Note that *Number* and *ZIP* are now *Num* and *Zip*.

NAME

replace - put a record into a file at specified location

SYNOPSIS

replace [-a] [-m[bhirs] tableorlist from to [xfrom xto] < intableorlist

DESCRIPTION

replace puts the single input record in the input table or list file into the output file at the location specified. It will not put in a record larger than the size of *to* minus *from*. **replace** will add spaces to the *last* column of records that are smaller than the size of the input record.

The **update** command remembers the location and size of the record it takes out of a file and passes it on to **replace** so that only the correct sized file goes back into the file.

OPTION

-a   Do not append the record to the end of the file. The ordinary mode is to append if the record is too big to fit back into the location. This option allows you to prevent appending. If you want a binary file to stay sorted, you will either have to resort it or not allow appending.

-m[bhirs]   See **index** for the fast access method options.

EXAMPLE

If you had a table with a single record in it and you wanted to replace it in another file, you might type:

```
$ replace bigfile 1421 1487 0 8 < recordtable
```

Using a small table like *inventory* let's see what happens.

```
$ cat inventory
Item   Amount   Cost   Value   Description
----   ------   ----   -----   --------------
   1        3     50     150   rubber gloves
   2      100      5     500   test tubes
   3        5     80     400   clamps
   4       23     19     437   plates
   5       99     24    2376   cleaning cloth
   6       89    147   13083   bunsen burners
   7        5    175     875   scales
```

First, let's get the record out with the **seek** program and save the offset in the **LOCATION** shell variable.

```
$ LOCATION=`echo 5 | seek -mr -o tmpfile inventory Item`
$ echo $LOCATION
207 245 54 62
$ cat inventory
Item   Amount   Cost   Value   Description
----   ------   ----   -----   --------------
   5       99     24    2376   cleaning cloth
```

Here we use the record fast access method. We can see *LOCATION* and *tmpfile*.

Now let's edit the *tmpfile* so we can see a change. Let's change the 99 to 199, and ignore the problem of recomputing the *Value* column for now.

```
Item   Amount   Cost   Value   Description
----   ------   ----   -----   --------------
```

```
    5      199     24    2376   cleaning cloth
```

Now we can replace the record:

```
$ replace -mr inventory $LOCATION < tmpfile
$ cat inventory
Item   Amount   Cost   Value   Description
----   ------   ----   -----   --------------
   1        3     50     150   rubber gloves
   2      100      5     500   test tubes
   3        5     80     400   clamps
   4       23     19     437   plates
   5      199     24    2376   cleaning cloth
   6       89    147   13083   bunsen burners
   7        5    175     875   scales
```

You can see that row 5 has been updated, because it now has 199 in it.

NAME
    report   - writes reports using a form and a table

SYNOPSIS
    report   form < tableorlist

DESCRIPTION
    report will produce reports, form letters, mailing labels, invoices, and so forth, for each row (line) in the input table or list file according to a form you lay out. You use a text editor to fill out the form as you want the report to look. You insert column names from the table or list file, in angle brackets (< >), where you want the data to be inserted into the report.

You can even call shell commands from the **report** form, and their output will be printed on the **report** at that point. And you can insert information from the input table, into the commands before they are called. This is therefore a very powerful extension to UNIX shell programming.

report mostly replaces the older label and letter sample shell programs. But they are retained as examples of a shell programming approach.

FORM SYNTAX

regular text	Any characters in your form that don't match the symbols below, will be printed as they are
<column name>	angle brackets (greater than and less than symbols) indicate that data from the column of the current row of the input is to be inserted in place of the name.
<!command!>	angle brackets and exclamation points indicate that the command is to be executed by the shell. Any output will appear in its place in the report.
<!cmd <col>!>	This is an insert within a command. The data from the table will replace <col> and then the command will be executed. Each row of the table will give the command a new string to operate on.

If a column name is not recognized, then the *<column name>* will simply be printed as if it were normal text. This allows you to use the angle brackets in your form, if you wish. As long as they don't match a column name they will not be

/rdb™ Release 4.0   **369** replaced. Also it will help you debug your form. If the data from the table is not replacing *<column name>*, then *column name* does not exactly match the column name in the table. Check for spelling errors, upper and lower case discrepancies, embedded blanks, and nonprinting characters.

EXAMPLE

If you have a file called *maillist* that looked like this:

```
$ cat maillist

Name      Ronald McDonald
Company   McDonald's
Street    123 Mac Attack
City      Memphis
State     TENN
ZIP       30000
Phone     (111) 222-3333

Name      Chiquita Banana
Company   United Brands
Street    Uno Avenido de la Reforma
City      San Jose
State     Costa Rica
ZIP       123456789
Phone     1234
```

You would use an editor to develop a form like the following:

```
<Name>
<Company>
<Street>
< City >, <State>  <ZIP>

Hi <  Name >:

The date and time is <!date!>

We are also sending this letter to:

<! column Name City < mailtable | row 'Name != "<Name>"' | justify !>
Bye <! echo <Name> !>
```

Note that we have used all three types of inserts: column name, command, and command insert. Now with these two files ready, you only need to type:

```
$ report form < maillist

Ronald McDonald
McDonald's
123 Mac Attack
Memphis, TENN  30000

Hi Ronald McDonald:

The date and time is Wed Aug 19 01:58:19 PST 1983

We are also sending this letter to:

Name             City
---------------  -------
Chiquita Banana  San Jose

Bye Ronald McDonald


Chiquita Banana
United Brands
Uno Avenido de la Reforma
San Jose, Costa Rica  123456789

Hi Chiquita Banana:

The date and time is Wed Aug 19 01:58:40 PST 1983

We are also sending this letter to:
```

```
Name            City
--------------- -------
Ronald McDonald Memphis
Bye Chiquita  Banana
```

Some users have noted that the shell escape places an extra line in the output. If you don't want the extra line say something like:

```
<! echo -n `date` !>
```

for older systems, and

```
<! echo `date`\\c !>
```

for system V.

NAME
reportwriter　　　　- sample program to produce standard reports

SYNOPSIS
reportwriter

DESCRIPTION
reportwriter is a sample shell program that produces a sample standard report. It uses **splittable** to divide the table into page-sized tables. It shows several tricks for using UNIX shell programming and **/rdb** tools to put together reports.

EXAMPLE
Here is what the sample produces (with the middle of each page replaced with ... to keep the listing short):

```
$ reportwriter
         Prices of Computers that ran UNIX(TM) in 1983
            From Urban Software of New York City
                Report Date: 9 Feb 1985

   Price  Company                         City
   -----  -------                         ----
          Advanced Micro Devices          Santa Clara
          Alcyon Corporation              San Diego
          American Telephone & Telegraph
          BASIS Microcomputer GmbH        D-4400 Muenster
          Corvus Systems                  San Jose
          David Computers Inc.            Kitchener
          Digital Computers Ltd.          Tokyo 102
          Heurikon Corp.                  Madison
    ...
          Western Digital                 Irvine
          Western Electric Corp.
    4.2   Venturcom/IBM PC                Cambridge
    ...
   13.9   Victory Computer Systems, Inc.  San Jose


        Page 1
(formfeed)
```

SOURCE
```
: %W% SCCS Information

: reportwriter is a sample shell script to write standard reports
:     it uses splittable to break up the table and adds headers and footers
:     simply copy this file to your directory and edit for each report
:     be sure to rename your copy and make executable: chmod +x yourreport

USAGE='usage: reportwriter'

TABLE=report$$

: you can edit this number to fit your page between header and footer

NUMBER=-50

: the next two lines gets todays date

set `date`
DATE="$3 $2 $6"

: edit the next line to start on a different page number
```

```
PAGE=1

: preprocess the data in the table

total -l Price < unixprice > $TABLE

: split table into page sized tables

splittable $NUMBER $TABLE

: loop printing each page from header, splittable and footer

for I in $TABLE[a-z][a-z]
do
echo "
     Prices of Computers that ran UNIX(TM) in 1983
         From Urban Software of New York City
                                    Report Date: $DATE

"
cat  $I
echo "


                                        Page $PAGE
\f
"
PAGE=`expr $PAGE + 1`
done

: be sure to remove the split tables

rm $TABLE $TABLE[a-z][a-z]
```

NAME
rmblank - removes blank rows from the input table

SYNOPSIS
rmblank < table

DESCRIPTION
rmblank deletes all input rows that consist of only blanks and tabs (white space). The programs **delete** and **replace** can blank out records. They can be used in transaction processing where the files are too large to process and several users are updating them. At a quiet time the files can be compacted and reindexed.

Be sure to reindex any file that is processed by either **rmblank** or **compress.**

EXAMPLE
First we have the inventory file:

```
$ cat inventory
Item    Amount  Cost    Value   Description
----    ------  ----    -----   --------------
   1         3    50       150   rubber gloves
   2       100     5       500   test tubes
   3         5    80       400   clamps
   4        23    19       437   plates
   5        99    24      2376   cleaning cloth
   6        89   147     13083   bunsen burners
   7         5   175       875   scales
```

Then we delete record four:

```
$ echo 4 | delete inventory Item
$ cat inventory
Item    Amount  Cost    Value   Description
----    ------  ----    -----   --------------
   1         3    50       150   rubber gloves
   2       100     5       500   test tubes
   3         5    80       400   clamps

   5        99    24      2376   cleaning cloth
   6        89   147     13083   bunsen burners
   7         5   175       875   scales
$ see < inventory
Item^IAmount^ICost^IValue^IDescription   $
----^I------^I----^I-----^I--------------$
   1^I     3^I  50^I  150^Irubber gloves$
   2^I   100^I   5^I  500^Itest tubes$
   3^I     5^I  80^I  400^Iclamps$
    ^I      ^I    ^I     ^I       $
   5^I    99^I  24^I 2376^Icleaning cloth$
   6^I    89^I 147^I13083^Ibunsen burners$
   7^I     5^I 175^I  875^Iscales$
```

Now we can remove that blank line.

```
$ rmblank < inventory
Item    Amount  Cost    Value   Description
----    ------  ----    -----   --------------
   1         3    50       150   rubber gloves
   2       100     5       500   test tubes
   3         5    80       400   clamps
   5        99    24      2376   cleaning cloth
   6        89   147     13083   bunsen burners
```

```
    7       5   175     875   scales
```

Remember to reindex the file after running **rmblank** on it.

SEE ALSO
compress delete replace

SOURCE
```
: %W% SCCS Information

: rmblank - removes all blanked out lines
:    delete and replace blank out lines

USAGE="usage: rmblank < filein > fileout"
EUSAGE=1

: remove all records that have only spaces and tabs in them

sed '/^[     ]*$/d'
```

NAME

rmcore   - remove all core files to free up space on the disk

SYNOPSIS

rmcore

DESCRIPTION

rmcore searches for files named *core* in the current directory, and all following directories. When it finds a file named *core,* **rmcore** removes it.

Run this command first when disk space gets small or runs out. **rmcore** starts at the directory you are in and goes down the file tree. If you are super user, you can issue this command at the root (/) and clean the whole system.

rmcore uses the UNIX **find** command.

EXAMPLE

```
$ rmcore
./core
```

SOURCE

```
: %W% SCCS Information

: rmcore will remove all files named core starting in the current
:       directory and preceeding down the directory tree

USAGE='usage: rmcore'

find . -name core -print -a -exec rm {} \;
```

NAME

row   - makes new table where rows match logical condition

SYNOPSIS

row   'column condition column-or-value ...' < table

DESCRIPTION

row makes a new table from the input table. The new table consists of only those rows that meet the logical condition specified. **row** uses the UNIX **awk** program which gives it great power for specifying the logical condition.

Several conditional expressions can be combined by *and* (&&) and *or* (||). Since the logical conditions are represented by special characters, they must be enclosed by single quotes ('). These single quotes protect the condition from being changed by the shell. If you have special characters within a column name, enclose the whole column name in double quotes (").

EXAMPLE

First a simple example. If you have an *inventory* table like this:

```
$ cat inventory
Item   Onhand  Cost   Value   Description
----   ------  ----   -----   -----------
  1        3     5      15    rubber gloves
  2      100     1     100    test tubes
  3        5     8      40    clamps
  4       23     2      51    plates
  5       99     2      97    cleaning cloth
  6       89    18    1602    bunsen burners
  7        5   175     875    scales
```

To make a table of all of the parts that cost more that $5 dollars, type:

```
$ row 'Cost > 5' < inventory
Item   Onhand  Cost   Value   Description
----   ------  ----   -----   -----------
  3        5     8      40    clamps
  6       89    18    1602    bunsen burners
  7        5   175     875    scales
```

Now a more complex example. If you want a table of all the burners and all of the items that we have less than 10 of, type:

```
$ row 'Description ~ /burner/ || Onhand < 10' < inventory
Item   Onhand  Cost   Value   Description
----   ------  ----   -----   -----------
  1        3     5      15    rubber gloves
  3        5     8      40    clamps
  6       89    18    1602    bunsen burners
  7        5   175     875    scales
```

The ~ */burner/* is a search for the string *burner* anywhere in the column. The double pipe (||) means *or*.

COLUMN NAMES

The **row, compute** and **validate** commands recognize column names as upper and lower case letters, digits, and the underscore (_). The regular expression is: [A-Za-z0-9_]. If you have any other characters in your column names, put single or double quotes around them. The recognized strings are compared with the head line of the table. Only if a match is found will the string be converted to the $1,

$2... column positions that **awk** needs.

AWK'S RESERVED WORDS

The following words are recognized by **awk. awk** is the big batch UNIX spreadsheet program that does all of the work for **row, compute** and **validate.** If you name any of your columns with any of these reserved names, and then try to use them in a query, these programs will turn them into column positions and **awk** will not see them. It is best to avoid these names as column heads or simply capitalize the first letter of each of your column names. Sorry about this inconvenience, but awk makes up by giving us enormous power.

This list also indicates the many functions you have with **awk.** However, do not rely on the following descriptions. Use your UNIX documentation for complete and accurate definitions of **awk** functions on your system.

NOTE: this list of **awk** functions and reserved words comes from UNIX System V. Earlier versions of UNIX do not have all of these functions.

Reserved Words	Description
BEGIN	pattern that matches before first input record
END	pattern that matches after last input record
break	get out of for or while loop
continue	goto next iteration of for or while loop
else	used in "if then else expression"
exit	leave program entirely as if end of input
exp	raise number to a power
for	for (expression ; condition ; expression) statement
getline	get next input line
if	if (condition) statement [else statement]
in	for (variable in array) statement
index	index (string1, string2)
int	truncate argument to integer
length	returns current line length, or length of argument
log	returns log (to base 2) of argument
next	skip to next record and reexecute all commands
print	outputs variables
printf	printf ("format", variable, ...)
split	split (string, arrayname, separator)
sprintf	sprintf ("format", variable, ...)
sqrt	returns square root of argument
substr	substr (string, start, number)
while	while (condition) statement

SOURCE

```
: row.sh - input table or list and output only selected rows

read HEAD

if test -z "$HEAD"
then
        (echo; cat) | listtotable | $0 $* | tabletolist
        exit 0
```

```
        fi

        read DASH
        echo $HEAD
        echo $DASH

        C=1
        for I in $HEAD
        do
                COL="$COL $I=\$$C;"
                C=`expr "$C" + 1`
        done

        if test -n "$COL"
        then
                echo awk "BEGIN {FS=OFS=\"         \";} {$COL} $1 {print;}"
                awk "BEGIN {FS=OFS=\"     \";} {$COL} $1 {print;}"
        fi
```

NAME

sale   - enter saleorder and item, update customer

SYNOPSIS

sale

DESCRIPTION

sale enters a sales order *saleorder* and items *saleitem* and can update the customer information file *customer*. The customer comes in or calls and the order taker can add a new customer or check old information. Then the order information and item information is added.

EXAMPLE

The program is interactive allowing you to confirm each action. First it asks for customer number. If you give it a number, it looks the number up in the *customer* file. If the customer is found, information is displayed for you to confirm. If you do not have the customer number, you can search with the slash string option or enter the question mark to get into the customer file. There you can search for the customer or add a new customer.

```
$CLEAR
MakeaPile, Inc.                saleorder
Enter Customer Number (? for new, /string search, Return to exit) 1
Vendor Number 1
Mr. Luke  Skywalker   CEO

Rebel Enterprises
123 Lea Street
Space Port City, Far Side  123456789  Tatooy

Code     Qty
-------  -------
rdb      1
Order    Number   Code     Backord      Qty     Price    Total   Name
-------  -------  -------  -------   -------  -------  -------  -------
1        1        rdb         10        1      1500  1500.00  /rdb
Number   Cust     Date     Shipped    Gross      Tax    Total
------   ----     -------  -------   -------  -------  -------
1        2        850723   0         1500.00    75.00  1575.00

Is this correct? (y, n) y
$ cat saleorder
Number  Cust   Date    Shipped   Gross       Tax      Total
------  ----   ------- -------   -------   -------   -------
     1     2   850723  860525    1500.00     75.00   1575.00
     2     2   850724  860525    3000.00    150.00   3150.00
     3     3   850902  860525   22500.00   1125.00  23625.00
     4     3   850902  0        36000.00   1800.00  37800.00
     5     3   850902  0        21000.00   1050.00  22050.00
$ cat saleitem
 Order   Number  Code    Backord      Qty    Price    Total    Name
-------  ------- ------- -------   ------- -------   -------   ----
     1        1  rdb        10         1      1500   1500.00   /rdb
     2        1  rdb        10         2      1500   3000.00   /rdb
     3        1  rdb        10         5      1500   7500.00   /rdb
     3        2  act        10        10      1500  15000.00   /act
     4        1  rdb        10         5      1500   7500.00   /rdb
     4        2  rdb        10        19      1500  28500.00   /rdb
     5        1  rdb        10         5      1500   7500.00   /rdb
     5        2  act        10         9      1500  13500.00   /act
```

Once you enter the correct customer number, you are given a table of items to enter. You type in *Code* and *Qty* and the program looks up the other information in the inventory. You can verify that the information is correct and make sure that you have enough in inventory to satisfy the order. You continue entering items until through. A carriage return will indicate you are finished, and the program will calculate the totals for the order, including tax.

This program uses the **cursor** and **termput** programs to move about the screen.

SEE ALSO
invoice postar

SOURCE
```
: 'sale          enter a sales order'
: 'purchase      enter a purchase order'

PROGRAM=`basename $0`
USAGE='usage: $PROGRAM'
TMP=$PROGRAM$$
TMP1=$PROGRAM1$$

SALE=sale
PURCHASE=purchase
MPROGNAME="$PROGRAM: This program must be named $SALE or $PURCHASE"

case $PROGRAM in
sale)
        ORDERFILE=saleorder
        ITEM=saleitem
        NAME=Customer
        NUMBER=Cust
        FILE=customer
        SCREEN=customer.s
        SCREEN='ve customer'
        ;;
purchase)
        ORDERFILE=purchaseorder
        ITEM=purchaseitem
        NAME=Vendor
        NUMBER=Vendor
        FILE=vendor
        SCREEN='ve vendor'
        ;;
*)      prompt "$MPROGRAM"
        exit 1
        ;;
esac
BLANKLINE="                                                              "
MGETNUMBER="$COMPANY                    $ORDERFILE
Enter $NAME Number (? for new, /string search, Return to exit)"
: while user is scratching head, do overhead work, set variable, etc.

: test for correct
MCORRECT='Is this correct? (y, n) '

MCODEQTY='Code    Qty
-------         -------'

TAXRATE=.05

: get $FILE number

echo $CLEAR ; prompt "$MGETNUMBER"

L0=`cursor 0 0`
L11=`cursor 11 0`
L13=`cursor 13 0`
L14=`cursor 14 0`
```

```
L16='cursor 16 0'
L22='cursor 22 0'

while read CVNUMBER
do

case $CVNUMBER in
"")     # NULL is CR want to leave
        rm -f $TMP $TMP1
        exit 0
        ;;
/*)     # search requested
        CVNUMBER='echo $CVNUMBER | sed 's/.//''
        (sed 2q $FILE ; grep "$CVNUMBER" $FILE) | report mail.f
        prompt "Hit Return key when ready to continue"
        read CVNUMBER
        echo $CLEAR ; echo "$MGETNUMBER"
        continue
        ;;
\?)     # new or unknown
        $SCREEN
        prompt $CLEAR ; prompt "$MGETNUMBER"
        continue
        ;;
*)      # number supplied
        if (sed 2q $FILE ; grep "^$CVNUMBER     " $FILE 2> /dev/null)| report mail.f
        then
                prompt "$L22$MCORRECT"
                read ANSWER
                prompt "$L22$BLANKLINE"
                case $ANSWER in
                Y*|y*)    ;;
                *)
                        prompt "$CLEAR$MGETNUMBER"
                        continue
                        ;;
                esac
        else
                prompt $CLEAR
                prompt "$L22Can not find that number. "
                prompt "$L0$MGETNUMBER"
                continue
        fi
        ;;
esac

: get next order number

ORDER='cat nextorder' ; expr 'expr "$ORDER" + 1' > nextorder

: get $ITEM info

echo "$L11$MCODEQTY"

sed 2q $ITEM > $TMP1
SEQNUMBER=1

while read CODE QTY
do
        case $CODE in
        "")       break ;;
        esac

        prompt "$L14"
        echo $CODE | search -ms ../inv/inventory Code |
        column Order Number Code Onhand Qty Price Total Name |
        compute "Qty = \"$QTY\"; Total = sprintf (\"%7.2f\", (Price * Qty));\
                Order = \"$ORDER\" ; Number = \"$SEQNUMBER\"; " | tee $TMP

        prompt "$L22$MCORRECT"
        read ANSWER
```

```
        prompt "$L22$BLANKLINE"
        case "$ANSWER" in
        y|yes|j|ja)
                tail -1  $TMP >> $TMP1
                SEQNUMBER=`expr $SEQNUMBER + 1`
                ;;
        esac

        echo "$L13$BLANKLINE" "$L16$BLANKLINE" "$L11$MCODEQTY"
done

: compute order

cat $TMP1

set `total Total < $TMP1 | tail -1`
GROSS=$1

(sed 2q $ORDERFILE ;
: Number         $SEQNUMBER         Date      Shipped  Gross   Tax        Total
echo "$ORDER     $SEQNUMBER         `todaysdate`       0       $GROSS     00") |
compute "Tax = sprintf (\"%7.2f\", (\"$TAXRATE\" * Gross)) ;\
Total = sprintf (\"%7.2f\", (Gross + Tax));\
Gross = sprintf (\"%7.2f\", Gross)" |
tee $TMP

prompt "$L22$MCORRECT"
read CORRECT
prompt "$L22$BLANKLINE"
if test "$CORRECT" = y
then
: write out $ORDERFILE row

tail +3 $TMP  >> $ORDERFILE
compute 'Onhand = 0' < $TMP1 | tail +3 >> $ITEM


else
: handle not ok
fi

prompt $CLEAR ; prompt "$MGETNUMBER"

done

rm -f $TMP $TMP1
```

NAME

schema - lists the database dictionary from table

SYNOPSIS

schema tableorlist ...

DESCRIPTION

schema outputs a schema, or a database dictionary, from a list of table and list files. In other database systems the user has to define the schema prior to database creation. In **/rdb,** schemas are derived from the data tables, which have already been created with a text editor.

EXAMPLE

```
$ schema inventory maillist | justify
Table       Field   Name
---------   -----   -----------
inventory     1     Item
inventory     2     Amount
inventory     3     Cost
inventory     4     Value
inventory     5     Description
maillist      1     Number
maillist      2     Name
maillist      3     Company
maillist      4     Street
maillist      5     City
maillist      6     State
maillist      7     ZIP
maillist      8     Phone
```

The **schema** shell program can be modified to give widths of columns, datatypes, and so on.

SEE ALSO

datatype precision width

SOURCE

```
: %W% SCCS Information
: schema  -  produces a database dictionary from a list of tables

USAGE='usage: schema tableorlist...'

echo "Table       Field       Name"
echo "-----       -----       ----"

for I in $*
do
        if tableorlist < $I > /dev/null
        then
                cat < $I
        else
                listtotable < $I
        fi |
        sed 1q |
        awk "BEGIN { OFS=\"   \";}
                {
                for (i=1; i<=NF; i++)
                print \"$I\",i,\$i ;
                }"
done
```

NAME

    screen   - converts form into screen input shell program

SYNOPSIS

    screen   < form > shellprogram

DESCRIPTION

    screen reads in a form file and outputs a UNIX shell program that will paint the screen and read in the users input. Since it is a shell program, you can edit it to do validations, read data and put it on the screen, and so on.

    The form file is in the same format as described for the **report** program.

    The shell program, that is output, is simple. It will work as is to read user data input at the screen and produce a standard table. It uses the **cursor** program to move to the screen input fields.

    This program has many uses. It can be used as a form entry to a table. With editing it can have its output appended to a table. It can put up a simple form for the user to enter data into a pipe. It can be edited to read in data and display on the screen. Validations can be added to check the user input. It can be embedded in another shell program for screen form input.

    Commands can be entered in the screen form file or in the program.

SETUP STEPS

    1. Fill in screen form file with a text editor.
    2. Run screen program to input form file and output shell program.
    3. Run the shell program to input data and output table.
    4. Edit shell program to validate, lock records, and so forth.

    See the **update** shell program for an advanced example of what you can do.

EXAMPLE

    A simple form looks like this:

```
$ cat mail.f
                         Mail List Entry Form
                <!date!>

Name  : <Name>         Company: <Company>
Street: <Street>
City  : <City>          State  : <State>      ZIP: <ZIP>
Phone : <Phone>
```

    Everything will go to the screen except what is in angle brackets (<>) which are variables to be input. In angle bracket-exclamation marks <*!date!*> are commands to execute when the program is running.

```
$ screen < mail.f > mail.s
$ cat mail.s
: paint crt screen
exec 3>&1 1>&2
cat <<SCREEN
${CLEAR}                        Mail List Entry Form


Name  :                Company:
Street:
```

```
City  :                 State  :              ZIP:
Phone :

SCREEN

: read user input
cursor  1 23 ; date;
cursor  3  8 ; read Name;
cursor  3 36 ; read Company;
cursor  4  8 ; read Street;
cursor  5  8 ; read City;
cursor  5 36 ; read State;
cursor  5 55 ; read ZIP;
cursor  6  8 ; read Phone;

: output table head
exec 1>&3
echo "Name  Company  Street  City  State  ZIP  Phone"
echo "----  -------  ------  ----  -----  ---  -----"
: append row
echo "$Name $Company $Street $City $State $ZIP $Phone"
```

This shell progam is in three parts. First, the *paint crt screen* section will put the form on the screen after clearing the screen. Second, the *read user input* section will move the cursor to each input field and wait for the user to enter a string of characters which will be assigned to the column variables. Third, the *output table head* section will write out a table in the standard form to the standard out.

The **exec** commands sends the screen output to the screen through the third file descriptor, *standard error output,* so that the screen program can be used in a pipe. For example, the table can be piped onto another program. *Standard error output* is usually unbuffered, which should speed up output to the screen and it is usually connected to the screen.

You must make the *mail.s* program executable with the **chmod** comand.

```
$ chmod +x mail.s
```

Then you can run it and input the data.

```
$ mail.s > mail.t
                   Mail List Entry Form
              Wed Sep  4 14:09:30 EDT 1985
Name  : Hi Ho            Company:
Street: 1st St.
City  : LA               State  : CA         ZIP: 90024
Phone : 213-555-1212

$ cat mail.t

Name    Company   Street    City    State    ZIP    Phone
----    -------   ------    ----    -----    ---    -----
Hi Ho   HH Inc.   1st St.   LA      CA       90024  213-555-1212
```

The table output can be directed to a file or pipe. Here it was directed into a table, *mail.t,* which could be used alone or appended to a table with the **append** command.

NAME

search   - set up table for search

SYNOPSIS

search   [-m[bhirs]] [-h -s -n -x +x] [-l [2> location]] tableorlist [keycolumn ...] [< keytable]

DESCRIPTION

search finds a row quickly. It searches the table or list file you specify for a row in which the value of one of the columns (the key column) matches the key you supply. The key's value must match exactly the string in the file's key column, unless one of the -*x* or +*x* options is used. The table or list file must have been previously indexed with the **index** command. If the table or list file is not large, say under several hundred rows or records, it is probably not worth the effort to index it. In that case use **row.**

search can be used in several ways. Since it takes the key values from the *standard input,* you can input the keys three ways: (1) interactively (type them in at the terminal), (2) from a file using the < *file* form, and (3) from a pipe (|). (See Examples). Therefore, it is easy to use on line or in a shell program. For example, the **domain** command shell script uses it to speed up its searches. If you use a pipe, you can think of a stream of keys going into **search** and a stream of matching rows coming out. Think of it as a highspeed join in which one table is only keys. The output is only the rows of the other table that match.

If you are not sure which method to use, you can try them all on your bigfile. Use the UNIX **time** command to find out how long each method takes. Pick the one that seems to be the best for your application. Another program, **timesearch,** will run each **search** on the sample **unixtable** in the demo directory. Since **timesearch** is a shell script, you can modify it to time the different methods for your own file.

Exactly what **search** does depends upon which method you choose. For some methods it first searches another table called a secondary index file that was built by the **index** program. In one case, sequential, search looks at every row.

If you change a table or list file, such as add a new row or delete an old one, you will have to reindex it. If you develop application programs you can have them update secondary index files to handle dynamic file processing.

METHODS

-m   *m* stands for fast access method. The letter that follows it indicates which method. When no letter follows, *sequential* is the default fast access method.

-mb   binary. A binary search first looks at the middle record of the file. If the key column value is greater than the key that **search** is looking for, **search** will look at the record one quarter of the way through the file. **search** will continue to divide the part of the file it looks at in half, until the row is found, or not. **search** requires that you sort a file on the key column. So the **index** command simply sorts on key columns. A binary search takes log(2) n accesses.

Accesses   Records   Number

| -------- | ------- | ------ |
10	thousand	1,000
20	million	1,000,000
30	billion	1,000,000,000
40	trillion	1,000,000,000,000

Binary is a good method for tables that must stay sorted on their key column anyway.

-mh hash. A hash search computes an address from the key and looks into a secondary file at that address. If the key matches, it gets the address of the row you want in the main file and puts it out. If the address **search** hashes to is empty (value of 0), then the key does not match and the row is not in the file. If there is another key there that happens to hash to the same address, called a *collision,* then search will keep looking at subsequent entries in the secondary table until **search** finds a match, or finds an empty or deleted (-1) entry. A hash search usually takes two disk accesses when the hash table is half full. This is why we set up hash tables twice as large as the number of records we are hashing. As the data table grows, it should be reindexed to keep the hash speed down. Hash is a good method for tables that must remain static, that is, not change much over time.

-mi inverted or indexed. An inverted search uses a secondary file that must have been created by the **index** program. This index file has two columns. One is the key column from the table. This column has been sorted by the index program so that **search** can do a binary search of it to find the key that **search** is looking for. If *search* finds the key, it will look at the adjacent offset column for the address of the row in the big table. With this address, **search** retrieves the row in a single disk read. The inverted method takes a little longer than binary, but sorting the index file is much faster than sorting the big file. Sorts are not too bad. The best algorithms can sort a table in log(2) n time.

-mr record number. A record search simply retrieves the row requested. If you enter a 5, you will get the fifth row in the file. **search** uses a secondary file that is fixed length and has the offset for each record in the big table. The record method is a faster way to get to the record if you know its number. But you must keep it in that order or reindex it. The **replace** program can move a row to the end and update the secondary index to point to the new location.

-ms sequential or linear. A sequential search looks at each record in the big table. It is not a fast access method, although it may still be faster than **row.** It is provided as a benchmark for timing other methods. If your file is not big enough to make the other access methods worthwhile, just use sequential **search** or **row** and save yourself the overhead of the **index** program. Sequential can search multiple key columns, and any column can be searched. The sequential method is better than the UNIX **grep** program because sequential looks at a single column, while **grep** scans the whole row for a pattern match.

OTHER OPTIONS:

-h no table head line is output. Normally the head line of the big table is output. This option allows you to suppress it and only get the rows you are looking for.

-l   asks for the location of the record and also the location of the index record in the index table. This location, in the form: *from to xfrom xto,* can be used by **replace, lock** and **unlock. search** sends this location to the *standard error output,* to separate it from the output table. **seek** uses this option to find the location and output the record into another file at the same time. **seek** is a shell program, so you can see an example of how this is done. Turning on this option also turns on the *-s* option because we only allow you to lock and/or replace one record at a time. Therefore, you will have to have unique keys in your file or some will never be found.

-s   only a single row is searched for. This will speed up the search because it can quit when the first match is found, and not have to keep looking through the file.

-x   partial match and upper or lower case insensitive (like Berkeley look).

+x   exact match (normal ignores blanks).

EXAMPLES

If you have a file called inventory that looks like this:

```
$ cat inventory
Item    Amount  Cost    Value   Description
----    ------  ----    -----   -----------
   1         3    50      150   rubber gloves
   2       100     5      500   test tubes
   3         5    80      400   clamps
   4        23    19      437   plates
   5        99    24     2376   cleaning cloth
   6        89   147    13083   bunsen burners
   7         5   175      875   scales
```

and if you have indexed the *Description* column with the **index** command, (see **index),** then you have several ways to find rows.

1. Interactively type in key values and the rows found will be printed out immediately.

For example, type:

```
$ search -mh inventory Description
```

The program will respond with the head line of the inventory table. Now you can type names, in this example *scales,* and if a match is found, you will get back a row:

```
Item    Amount  Cost    Value   Description
----    ------  ----    -----   --------------
scales
   7         5   175      875   scales
```

2. Input a table or list file.

If you have a file with a column of key values, like this:

```
$ cat description
Description
-----------
scales
clamps
```

you can input this table and get a table of matching rows out:

```
$ search -mh inventory Description < description
Item   Amount   Cost   Value   Description
----   ------   ----   -----   --------------
   7        5    175     875    scales
   3        5     80     400    clamps
```

3. Input keys through a UNIX pipe.

```
$ column Description < sometable | search -mh inventory | column Value
Value
-----
  875
  400
```

If you wanted to justify a table like this, just add another pipe and the **justify** program.

You can use the **echo** command to send a key value to **search** like this:

```
$ echo scales | search -mh inventory Description
Item   Amount   Cost   Value   Description
----   ------   ----   -----   --------------
   7        5    175     875    scales
```

In shell programming, you can capture the output of a program or a pipe by putting it within two backquote (') symbols. The backquote (') symbol is called an *acute accent,* or *back single quote,* or an *accent grave* in French and is different than the single quote (') which is also called the apostrophe. If you are not familiar with it, then look around your ASCII keyboard.

In a shell script you can set a variable like this:

```
$ RECORD=`echo key | search -mh -h bigtable column`
$ echo "$RECORD"
7   5   175    875    scales
```

Now the *RECORD* variable is equal to the matching row in the table. Note the *-h* is important to keep the head line from being sent to *RECORD*.

SEARCH VS. SELECT

search is important for application programs, written in shell scripts, or C programming language, or other code. It can be used interactively, but **row** is much more powerful, because it can look for combinations of logical conditions, regular expressions, and conditions such as *greater than,* while **search** needs a key (either exact or partial). But for pulling a row out of a big table from a program, **search** may speed things up enough to be worthwhile. In summary, **search** is for high speed access with keys, and **row** is slower, but can retrieve rows that match complex logical conditions and regular expressions.

SEE ALSO

index seek replace append delete update

NAME
    searchtree   - looks for goal string node in tree table

SYNOPSIS
    searchtree   [-m[bhirs]] table root goal column1 column2

DESCRIPTION
    searchtree will search through a tree, represented by a table, to find a matching string. It returns a shell status code of true or false depending upon whether it finds the goal string.

-m[*bhirs*]   is the fast access method to use. The default is sequential (-ms). See **search** for descriptions of each method. These can be used to speed up your tree searches. *table* is the tree table to be searched. *root* is a string that is the root of the tree, or starting point of the search. *goal* is the string that you are trying to find. It may be in the table and a simple grep will find it, but you want to know if it can be reached by a path from the root string. *column1* is the column in which the root is found. It is the parent column. *column2* is the goal, or child column.

searchtree is a breadth first search that uses the **search** fast access methods to find all of the children at each level of a tree. This is the kind of search often done in artificial intelligence programs. However, **searchtree** uses secondary storage, so that it will work on very large databases. It is a shell program, so that it can be modified to serve many kinds of searches. For example, you can add a message like *yes/no* or *true/false*. You can also add shell code to print out a path. You might want to use heuristics to guide the search at each level and side effects to update data or print messages along the way.

This kind of searching is also employed by PROLOG. However, PROLOG must have its database in memory which limits the size of the database it can handle. Secondly, PROLOG uses depth first searching which requires it to backtrack.

EXAMPLE
    Imagine the tree represented by the following table:

```
$ cat isa
Name      Isa
----      ---
barbara   human
bill      human
evan      human
rod       human
human     primate
primate   mammal
cat       mammal
dog       mammal
mammal    animal
bird      animal
fish      animal
animal    lifeform
plant     lifeform
```

Remember that all trees, in fact all graphs, can be listed as tables where the nodes (vertices) that are connected by a line (arcs) are on each row. A directional graph is handled by having one column be *From* and another be *To*.

```
$ searchtree isa rod lifeform Name Isa
```

```
$ echo $?
0
```

Since **searchtree** only returns a status code, it can be used as a test condition. Your shell program could have a statement like this:

```
$ cat hello
prompt "What is your name: "
read NAME
if searchtree isa $NAME lifeform Name Isa
then
        echo "So, I am talking to a lifeform."
else
        echo "So, I am talking to another machine."
fi
$ hello
What is your name: rod
So, I am talking to a lifeform.
```

The result of the search of the tree was tested by the **if** statement and used to decide which message to print.

SEE ALSO
search

SOURCE

```
: %W% SCCS Information

: searchtree - looks for string node in tree table
:         it is a breath first search by using the
:         fast access methods to find all of the children at
:         each level or pass
:         add sort and uniq if the table is huge and several paths
:         produce many matches of identical nodes at several levels

USAGE='usage: searchtree [-m[bhirs]] table root goal column1 column2'
EUSAGE=1
TRUE=0
FALSE=255

case "$1" in
-*)     METHOD=$1
        shift
        ;;
esac

if test "$#" -lt 5
then
        echo $USAGE 1>&2
        exit $EUSAGE
fi

TABLE=$1
ROOT=$2
GOAL=$3
COLUMN1=$4
COLUMN2=$5

TMP=/tmp/$$is
TMP1=/tmp/$$1is
trap 'rm -f $TMP $TMP1 ; trap 0 ; exit $EXIT' 0 1 2 3 15

echo $ROOT > $TMP

until grep "^$GOAL\$" < $TMP > /dev/null
do
        search $METHOD $TABLE $COLUMN1 < $TMP |
```

```
        column $COLUMN2 |
        tail +3 > $TMP1
#       sort | uniq > $TMP1

        mv $TMP1 $TMP

        if test 0 = "`wc -l < $TMP`"
        then
                EXIT=$FALSE
                exit $EXIT
        fi

done

EXIT=$TRUE
exit $EXIT
```

NAME

    see   - displays nonprinting as well as printing characters

SYNOPSIS

    see   < tableorlist

DESCRIPTION

    see allows you to *see* nonprinting characters, by converting them to *ˆsome-printing-character*. It is essentially the same as the Berkeley UNIX **see** or **cat -v.** But since, AT&T is not going to add the *-v* option to **cat, see** is provided here for UNIX System V.

    see is very useful for seeing if you have gotten your tabs into your tables or lists. Tabs print out as *ˆI* because they are also obtained by typing control-I (hold down the control key (CTRL) while pressing the letter *i* key). **see** is also helpful for finding nonprinting characters.

EXAMPLE

    If you had a table, and you wanted to see if the tabs were in correctly, you could type:

```
$ see < badtable
DateˆIAccountˆIDebitˆICreditˆIDescription$
------ˆI-------ˆI-------ˆI-------ˆI------------------------$
820102ˆI101ˆI25000ˆIˆIcash from loan$
820102ˆI211.1ˆIˆI25000ˆIloan number #378-14 Bank Amerigold$
820103ˆI150.1   10000ˆIˆItest equipment from Zarkoff$
820103ˆI101ˆIˆI5000ˆIcash payment$
820103ˆI211.2ˆIˆI5000ˆInote payable to Zarkoff Equipment$
820104ˆI130ˆI30000ˆIˆIinventory - parts from CCPSC$
820104ˆI201.1ˆIˆI15000ˆIaccounts payable to CCPSC$
820104ˆI101ˆIˆI15000ˆIcash payment to CCPSC for parts$
```

TECHNICAL

    see assumes ASCII characters. Negative characters and characters with values greater than 127 have 128 added. Then characters with values less than ASCII ' ' (blank or space) have ASCII 'A' added to them so that they will map to the upper case characters.

For example:

From	To
NUL	ˆ@
TAB	ˆI
FF	ˆL

NAME
seek   - returns the beginning and ending offset of a row

SYNOPSIS
seek   [-m[bihrs]] [-o outfile] tableorlist [keycol...] < file

DESCRIPTION
seek returns the byte address of the beginning of a record in the *tableorlist* file, and the byte end of the record. It uses the **search** command with the *-l* location option.

The offset and size integers returned can be used by the **replace** program to write a new record. They are also used by the **lock** and **unlock** programs to set and remove record locks.

OPTIONS
-m[bhirs]

Fast access methods. See **search.**

-o

Output the record found to the **outfile.**

EXAMPLE
Let's use **seek** on the *inventory* table:

```
$ cat inventory
Item   Amount   Cost   Value   Description
----   ------   ----   -----   --------------
   1        3     50     150   rubber gloves
   2      100      5     500   test tubes
   3        5     80     400   clamps
   4       23     19     437   plates
   5       99     24    2376   cleaning cloth
   6       89    147   13083   bunsen burners
   7        5    175     875   scales
```

seek will now find row 5.

```
$ echo 5 | seek -mb inventory Item
207 245      0      8
```

This means that the record is 207 bytes into the file and that it is 38 bytes long, ending at byte 245.

Here are commands that will extract and blank a row, and then write back into the *inventory* table on top of the original row.

```
$ LOCATION=`echo 5 | seek -mb -o tmp inventory Item`
```

The *-o tmp* option to **seek** will cause the record with key equal to 5 to be placed into the the *tmp* file.

```
$ echo tmp
Item   Amount   Cost   Value   Description
----   ------   ----   -----   --------------
   5       99     24    2376   cleaning cloth
$ blank < tmp | replace inventory $LOCATION
$ cat inventory
Item   Amount   Cost   Value   Description
----   ------   ----   -----   --------------
```

```
1      3     50    150    rubber gloves
2    100      5    500    test tubes
3      5     80    400    clamps
4     23     19    437    plates

6     89    147  13083    bunsen burners
7      5    175    875    scales
```

SEE ALSO
search index lock unlock replace

SOURCE

```
: %W% SCCS ID Information

: seek - returns the start and stop bytes of record and index

USAGE='usage: seek [-m[bihrs]] [-o outfile ] tableorlist keycolumn < keytable'
EUSAGE=1

if test "$#" -eq 0
then
    echo $USAGE 1>&2
    exit $EUSAGE
fi

while test -n "$1"
do
    case $1 in
    -o)     shift
            OUTFILE=$1
            ;;
    -*)     OPTION="$OPTION $1"
            ;;
    *)      if test -z "$TABLE"
            then
                    TABLE="$1"
            else
                    KEYCOLUMNS="$KEYCOLUMNS $1"
            fi
            ;;
    esac
    shift
done

(search $OPTION -l $TABLE $KEYCOLUMNS 1> ${OUTFILE-/dev/null} ) 2>&1
```

NAME

select   - outputs selected rows

SYNOPSIS

select   'column condition column-or-value' < table

DESCRIPTION

select will produce a new file consisting of the rows of the input table that match the logical condition specified. **select** is linked, **ln,** to the **row** program. Therefore, it is simply another name for **row.** It is included for those users who prefer the name **select** (which is a relational theory name) to **row.** However, it conflicts with the Korn shell which also has a **select** command. We strongly recommend you use **row** instead.

EXAMPLE

See **row.**

SOURCE

```
: select.sh - input table or list and output only selected rows

read HEAD

if test -z "$HEAD"
then
        (echo; cat) | listtotable | $0 $* | tabletolist
        exit 0
fi

read DASH
echo $HEAD
echo $DASH

C=1
for I in $HEAD
do
        COL="$COL $I=\$$C;"
        C=`expr "$C" + 1`
done

if test -n "$COL"
then
        echo awk "BEGIN {FS=OFS=\"        \";} {$COL} $1 {print;}"
        awk "BEGIN {FS=OFS=\"      \";} {$COL} $1 {print;}"
fi
```

NAME
sorttable - sorts a table by one or more columns

SYNOPSIS
sorttable [sort options] [columnname ...] < tableorlist

DESCRIPTION
sorttable will sort a table using the UNIX **sort** command. **sorttable** knows about the column name and dash head lines. It passes all the options you give it on to **sort.** See **sort** in the UNIX Programmer's Manual for the options. However, with **sorttable,** you use the column names rather than column numbers as in **sort.** **Sorttable** also tells sort to use tabs as field (column) separators, instead of *white space* (blanks and tabs).

Note we have bent to user pressure and now **sorttable** will sort on each column named, and not on a range of columns starting with the first column and ending with the second as **sort** does. Now you have to name each column you want to sort on.

sorttable will completely sort by the first column you name. If there are any duplicate values in that column, it will go to the second column and sort on those values. **sorttable** will continue across the named columns until it finds unique values. If you sort a ledger on Account and Date, Account will be completely sorted, and within each account, Date will be sorted.

If no columns are named, the table will be sorted left to right all the way across.

OPTIONS
See your UNIX system's user's manual for the **sort** command.

EXAMPLE
If you had an inventory like this:

```
$ cat inventory
Item#    Amount    Cost    Value   Description
-------  -------   ------- ------- ---------------
    1        3       5.00   15.00  rubber gloves
    2      100       0.50   50.00  test tubes
    3        5       8.00   40.00  clamps
    4       23       1.98   45.54  plates
    5       99       2.45  242.55  cleaning cloth
    6       89      14.75 1312.75  bunsen burners
    7        5     175.00  875.00  scales
```

and you wanted to see the inventory sorted with the highest *Cost* items on top, you would type:

```
$ sorttable -n -r Cost < inventory
Item#    Amount    Cost    Value   Description
-------  -------   ------- ------- ---------------
    7        5     175.00  875.00  scales
    6       89      14.75 1312.75  bunsen burners
    3        5       8.00   40.00  clamps
    1        3       5.00   15.00  rubber gloves
    5       99       2.45  242.55  cleaning cloth
    4       23       1.98   45.54  plates
    2      100       0.50   50.00  test tubes
```

Note that the *Cost* column is in reverse order (the *-r* option) and that it was treated as a number (-*n* option) instead of a character string.

If you use the **sorttable** command a lot, you should carefully study the UNIX manual pages for **sort.** For example, you can control which columns are used to sort on. If you name several columns, **sort** will see each column's numbers proceeded by a +. The + means start sorting on this column, the minus (-) means stop on the next column. To see this, use the -*D* (debug) option for **sorttable.** (By the way, it is because **sort** has a -*d* option that we use a capital -*D* for the debug option for the /**rdb** commands).

```
$ sorttable -D Cost Description < inventory
    Item   Onhand     Cost    Value   Description
   ------- -------   -------  ------- ----------------
sorttable: command executed: sort -t'
      2      100       1       100    test tubes
      4       23       2        51    plates
      5       99       3       297    cleaning cloth
      1        3       5        15    rubber gloves
      3        5       8        40    clamps
      6       89      18      1602    bunsen burners
      7        5     175       875    scales
```

The line beginning with **sort** is the line passed to UNIX with a system call. Note the +1 -2, and so on. That tells the **sort** command to sort on columns 2 and 4 (where the first column is 0). Thus **sorttable** correctly turns the column names you type into a **sort** command by looking up the column names in the table head line and converting them to column numbers for the UNIX **sort** command. People are often confused by **sort** because it does not behave the way one would expect. Study its documentation in your UNIX system's user's manual.

NAME
    soundex - converts names into soundex codes

SYNOPSIS
    soundex < file > file.x ; index -mb file.x Soundex

DESCRIPTION
    soundex creates a secondary index to a file using Knuth's soundex code. It is used
    by the **like** command to find a name that sounds like another name.

    You must input the file and output a file with the same name with an *.x* appended.
    Then **index** the file.x file on the *Soundex* column for high speed search.

EXAMPLE
If you have a file with many names
```
$ sed 10q name
Name
----
Abraham
Abraham
Ackerman
Actor
Adams
Adams
Adams
Adams
```

Use **soundex** to create the secondary index file.
```
$ soundex < name > name.x ; index -mb name.x Soundex
$ sed 10q name.x
Name         Soundex
-            -------
Avila        A140
Avila        A140
Avila        A140
Abraham      A160
Abraham      A160
Aissen       A220
Ajeska       A220
Augustine    A223
```

Now you can use the **like** command to find a name.
```
$ like Manis name
Name
-
Mann
Mann
Means
Mink
Monahan
Moniz
Mooney
Mooney
Munoz
Munoz
```

Gee, that is so much fun, let's do another one.
```
$ like Schaffer name
Name
-
```

```
Schaeffer
Schaffer
Schiffrin
```

SEE ALSO
like

SOURCE
```
: soundex - computes codes to index a file
:        assumes first column is the name column
USAGE='usage: soundex < file > file.x ; index -mb file.x Soundex'
EUSAGE=1

if test "$#" -gt 0
then
        echo $USAGE
        exit $EUSAGE
fi

awk -F"  " 'NR == 1 {print $1 "Soundex"}
NR == 2 {print $1 "-------"}
NR > 2 {Name = sprintf("%s",substr($1,1,1))
for (i=2; i < length($1); i++) {
s = substr($1,i,1)
if (s == "b" || s == "f" || s == "v")
        Name = sprintf("%s%d",Name,1)
if (s == "c" || s == "g" || s == "k" || s == "q" || s == "s" || s == "x" || s == "z")
        Name = sprintf("%s%d",Name,2)
if (s == "d" || s == "t")
        Name = sprintf("%s%d",Name,3)
if (s == "l")
        Name = sprintf("%s%d",Name,4)
if (s == "m" || s == "n")
        Name = sprintf("%s%d",Name,5)
if (s == "r")
        Name = sprintf("%s%d",Name,6)
}
Name = sprintf("%s000",Name); Name = substr(Name,1,4); print $1 "" Name}'
```

NAME
   splittable   - divide table into smaller tables

SYNOPSIS
   splittable   [-n] table

DESCRIPTION
   splittable will take in a table and break it into several smaller tables with head
   lines on the top. *n* (in -n) is the number of rows for each smaller table (not counting the two head lines). This command is most useful for report writing because it
   splits tables into page-sized tables.

   splittable uses the UNIX **split** command, so read its UNIX manual page for
   details. Both programs create file names ending with aa, ab ... zz. This give 676
   (26 x 26) possible files.

EXAMPLE
   Here is an example using a very short table:

```
$ cat inventory

Item#   Amount  Cost    Value   Description
-----   ------  ----    -----   --------------
  1        3     50       150   rubber gloves
  2      100      5       500   test tubes
  3        5     80       400   clamps
  4       23     19       437   plates
  5       99     24      2376   cleaning cloth
  6       89    147     13083   bunsen burners
  7        5    175       875   scales

$ splittable -4 inventory
```

   Since inventory only has seven lines we are using the -n option set to 4 to get at
   most four lines in each split table.

```
$ ls inventory*
inventory
inventoryaa
inventoryab
```

   The **ls** command shows us that we now have two new files ending in *aa* and *ab* as
   a result of the **splittable** command.

```
$ cat inventoryaa
Item#   Amount  Cost    Value   Description
-----   ------  ----    -----   --------------
  1        3     50       150   rubber gloves
  2      100      5       500   test tubes
  3        5     80       400   clamps
  4       23     19       437   plates

$ cat inventoryab
Item#   Amount  Cost    Value   Description
-----   ------  ----    -----   --------------
  5       99     24      2376   cleaning cloth
  6       89    147     13083   bunsen burners
  7        5    175       875   scales
```

SOURCE
```
 : %W% SCCS Information

 : splittable -   takes a table and breaks it into many tables putting the
```

```
:                   header on each

USAGE='usage: splittable [-n] table'
EUSAGE=1

HEAD=/tmp/$$splith
ROWS=/tmp/$$splitr

trap 'rm -f /tmp/$$*' 0 1 2 3 15

case "$#" in
2)      NUMBER=$1
        TABLE=$2
        ;;
1)      NUMBER=50
        TABLE=$1
        ;;
0)      echo $USAGE 1>&2
        exit $EUSAGE
        ;;
esac

sed 2q $TABLE > $HEAD
tail +3 $TABLE > $ROWS
split $NUMBER $ROWS $TABLE

for I in $TABLE[a-z][a-z]
do
        cat $HEAD $I > $ROWS
        mv $ROWS $I
done
```

NAME
substitute   - replace old string with new string in files

SYNOPSIS
substitute   oldstring newstring file ...

DESCRIPTION
substitute will replace *oldstring* with *newstring* in all files listed. Since it uses **sed,** be sure to protect with backslash (\) all **sed** special characters: * ^ $ and \

EXAMPLE
```
$ cat inventory
 Item   Amount   Cost   Value   Description
 -----  ------   ----   -----   --------------
    1        3     50     150   rubber gloves
    2      100      5     500   test tubes
    3        5     80     400   clamps
    4       23     19     437   plates
    5       99     24    2376   cleaning cloth
    6       89    147   13083   bunsen burners
    7        5    175     875   scales
$ substitute 'rubber' 'latex' file
$ cat inventory
 Item   Amount   Cost   Value   Description
 -----  ------   ----   -----   --------------
    1        3     50     150   latex gloves
    2      100      5     500   test tubes
    3        5     80     400   clamps
    4       23     19     437   plates
    5       99     24    2376   cleaning cloth
    6       89    147   13083   bunsen burners
    7        5    175     875   scales
```

Note that row one has changed.

SOURCE
```
: %W% SCCS Information
: substitute old string for new string using sed in each file

USAGE='usage: substitute oldstring newstring file ...'
EUSAGE=1

if test "$#" -lt 3
then
     echo $USAGE 1>&2
     exit $EUSAGE
fi

TMP=/tmp/$$substitute

FROM=$1
shift
TO=$1
shift

for I in $*
do
     echo $I
     sed "s/$FROM/$TO/g" < $I > $TMP
     mv $TMP $I
done
```

NAME
subtotal - outputs the subtotal of columns in a table

SYNOPSIS
subtotal [-l] [break-column column ...] < table

DESCRIPTION
subtotal computes the subtotals in one or more numeric columns using a *break column*. As long as the value in the *break column* remains the same, the values in the other columns are accumulated. When the value in the *break column* changes, the values accumulated since the last break are printed out.

If no columns are specified, then the first column, or leftmost column of the table is the *break column*. All of the rest of the columns to the right will be subtotaled on each break in the first column.

OPTIONS
-l   list whole table, not just subtotals.

EXAMPLE
There are two forms of output. One produces only the subtotals. If you wanted to see the daily subtotals of your *journal,* you can type:

```
$ subtotal Date Debit Credit < journal
Date    Account  Debit   Credit  Description
------  -------  -----   ------  ---------------------------------
891222           25000   25000
891223           10000   10000
891224           30000   30000
```

With the *-l* option, you can see the whole table:

```
$ subtotal -l Date Debit Credit < journal
Date    Account  Debit   Credit  Description
------  -------  -----   ------  ---------------------------------
891222  101      25000           cash from loan
891222  211.1            25000   loan number #378-14 Bank Amerigold
------  -------  -----   ------  ---------------------------------
891222           25000   25000

891223  150.1    10000           test equipment from Zarkoff
891223  101               5000   cash payment
891223  211.2             5000   note payable to Zarkoff Equipment
------  -------  -----   ------  ---------------------------------
891223           10000   10000

891224  130      30000           inventory - parts from CCPSC
891224  201.1            15000   accounts payable to CCPSC
891224  101              15000   cash payment to CCPSC for parts
------  -------  -----   ------  ---------------------------------
891224           30000   30000
```

This lets you see each row as well as the subtotals. This could help you find out when you got out of balance.

NAME
tableorlist   - reports whether the file has a table or list format

SYNOPSIS
tableorlist   [tableorlist...] [< tableorlist]

DESCRIPTION
tableorlist prints *table* or *list* depending upon the format of the input file. If the first character of the file is a newline, it is a list (status code 1); otherwise, it is a table (status code 0).

EXAMPLE
```
$ tableorlist inventory
table
$ echo $?
0
```

The *$?* is the shell status set on program exit.

SOURCE
```
: %W% SCCS ID Information
: tableorlist - decides if a file is a table or list by first byte

USAGE='usage: tableorlist < tableorlist'

case "$#" in
0|1)
        if test "$#" = "1"
        then
                exec 0 < $1
        fi
        read HEADLINE
        if test "$HEADLINE" = ""
        then
                echo list
                exit 1
        else
                echo table
                exit 0
        fi
        ;;
*)
        echo "Type      File"
        echo "----      ----"
        for FILE in $*
        do
                exec 0 < $FILE
                read HEADLINE
                if test "$HEADLINE" = ""
                then
                        echo "list      $FILE"
                else
                        echo "table     $FILE"
                fi
        done
        exit 0
        ;;
esac
```

NAME
    tabletofact   - converts table format to prolog fact file format

SYNOPSIS
    tabletofact   table ... > prologfactfile

DESCRIPTION

tabletofact will convert one or more tables into a file of facts in predicate calculus functor form that can be input to the **prolog** interpreter. **prolog** facts are in the form: *parent(sally,fred)*. Which means *sally is the parent of fred.*

prolog is an artificial intelligence language that makes possible *programming in logic*. It was picked by the Japanese for their fifth generation computer system.

There are facts, rules, and questions in **prolog.** If you build a database of facts and rules, you can ask questions and get answers. If a question you ask does not have a corresponding fact in the database, **prolog** will look through its rule file to see if other facts might logically deduce the fact requested.

EXAMPLE

Suppose we have these simple tables:

```
$ cat parent
Parent   Child
-------  -------
Sally    Fred
Mike     Fred
Fred     Jane
$ cat female
Name
----
Jane
Sally
$ cat male
Name
----
Fred
Mike
$ tabletofact parent female male > fact
$ cat fact
parent(Sally,Fred).
parent(Mike,Fred).
parent(Fred,Jane).
female(Jane).
female(Sally).
male(Fred).
male(Mike).
```

Now **prolog** can use its **consult** command to read in this file. If **prolog** had rules about father, mother, grandparent, and so on, then it could answer questions like: *mother(sally,fred)?* That fact is not in the database, but can be deduced from rules like: *mother(X,Y) if parent(X,Y) and female(X).*

SEE ALSO
tabletorule

SOURCE
```
: %W% SCCS Information
```

```
: tabletofact - takes an /rdb table and makes a prolog fact file

USAGE='usage: tabletofact table ... > prologfile'
EUSAGE=1

if test "$#" -eq 0
then
        echo $USAGE
        exit $EUSAGE
fi

for FILE
do
        sed     "1,2d
                s/      /,/g
                s/.*/$FILE(&)./" $FILE
done
```

NAME

    tabletofix   - converts /rdb table format to fixed length format

SYNOPSIS

    tabletofix   column=n [r] ... < tableorlist

DESCRIPTION

    tabletofix converts databases from variable length **rdb** format to fixed length for-
mat by projecting (**column**) the named columns from *tableorlist* and doing whatever is necessary (padding with blanks or truncating) to make the width of each
column exactly *n* characters wide. If the letter *r* is used with the width
specification, columns are padded with leading blanks (right justification); otherwise, columns are padded with trailing blanks. The header records, along with all
tabs and blank records, are removed.

EXAMPLE

    For example, we might have a table named *journal* which looks like this:

```
$ see journal
Date^IAccount^IDebit^ICredit^IDescription$
----^I-------^I ----^I -----^I----------$
820102^I101^I25000^I^Icash from loan$
820102^I211.1^I^I25000^Iloan number #378-14 Bank Amerigold$
820103^I150.1^I10000^I^Itest equipment from Zarkoff$
820103^I101^I5000^I^Icash payment$
820103^I211.2^I^I5000^Inote payable to Zarkoff Equipment$
820104^I130^I30000^I^Iinventory - parts from CCPSC$
```

(The *^I*s indicate tabs, and the *$* symbol indicates the newline at the end of each
record.) Let's generate a fixed length field database from the *journal* table. We'll
use the *Date* and *Account* columns and give them a width of six bytes each, and
the *Credit* and *Debit* fields, which we will right justify with a width of seven bytes
each:

```
$ tabletofix Date=6 Account=6 Debit=7r Credit=7r < journal > newjournal
$ see newjournal

820102101    25000        $
820102211.1          25000$
820103150.1  10000        $
820103101            5000$
820103211.2          5000$
820104130    30000        $
```

SEE ALSO

    fixtotable column see

NAME
tabletolist   - converts a file from table to list format

SYNOPSIS
tabletolist   [-l] < table

DESCRIPTION
tabletolist will convert a file in table format into a file in list format.

OPTION
-l

> No newline (blank head line) for the list file output. This is for compatibility with the older list format and for other uses. Be careful. If you create a file like this, **/rdb** commands cannot read them correctly.

EXAMPLE
You might have a file in table format like this:

```
$ cat mailtable
Number  Name       Company Street  City    State   ZIP     Phone
------- -------    ------- ------- ------- ------- ------- -------
1          Ronald McDonald  McDonald's         123 Mac Attack    Memphis
TENN    30000    (111) 222-3333
2          Chiquita  Banana United Brands      Uno Avenito De La
Revolution           San Jose Costa Rica       123456789         1234
```

This shows the need for a list format. The information in each column is often too wide for the screen. So it *wraps around* to the next line. You could convert it to list format like this:

```
$ tabletolist < mailtable

Number    1
Name      Ronald McDonald
Company   McDonald's
Street    123 Mac Attack
City      Memphis
State     TENN
ZIP       30000
Phone     (111) 222-3333

Number    2
Name      Chiquita  Banana
Company   United Brands
Street    Uno Avenido de la Reforma
City      San Jose
State     Costa Rica
ZIP       123456789
Phone     1234

  . . .
```

NAME
    tabletom4   - converts table format to m4 define file format

SYNOPSIS
    tabletom4   < table > definefile

DESCRIPTION

    tabletom4 will convert a two column table into a file of define statements that can be input to the **m4** macroprocessor. Define macros are in the form: *define(old,new)*. **m4** can do many things including word-for-word substitution. It can be used for language translation (in a stiff, inflexible way) and for other conversions of databases.

    The *definefile* produced is required by the **translate** command. Only words that have a corresponding translation in the second column will be put in the *definefile*. In this way you can use the file before you have all of the translations entered.

EXAMPLE

    Suppose we have a simple translation table:

```
$ cat ed.t
English Deutch
------- -------
I       Ich
love    liebe
you     dich
widgit

$ tabletom4 < ed.t > ed
$ cat ed
define(I,Ich)
define(love,liebe)
define(you,dich)
```

    Note that *widgit* did not get converted because it did not have a translation string in the second column of the table. This *ed* file can now be used by **m4** or **translate**

```
$ cat text
I love you.

$ m4 ed text
Ich liebe dich.
```

SEE ALSO
    translate

SOURCE
```
: %W% SCCS Information

: tabletom4 - takes an /rdb table and makes a m4 file

USAGE='usage: tabletom4  < table > m4file'

sed     "1,2d
        /        $/d
        s/       /,/g
        s/^/define(/
        s/\$/)/"
```

NAME

tabletorule   - converts table format to prolog rule file format

SYNOPSIS

tabletorule   table ... > prologrulefile

DESCRIPTION

tabletorule will convert one or more tables into a file of rules in predicate calculus implication form that can be input to the Prolog interpreter. Prolog rules are in the form: *mother(X,Y) :- female(X), parent(X,Y)*. Which means *X is the mother of Y, if X is female and X is the parent of Y*.

Prolog is an artificial intelligence language that makes possible *programming in logic*. There are facts, rules, and questions in Prolog. If you build a database of facts and rules, you can ask questions and get answers. If a question you ask does not have a corresponding fact in the database, Prolog will look through its rule file to see if other facts might logically deduce the fact requested.

EXAMPLE

Suppose we have these simple tables:

```
$ cat parent
Parent   Child
-------  -------
Sally    Fred
Mike     Fred
Fred     Jane
$ cat female
Name
----
Jane
Sally
$ cat male
Name
----
Fred
Mike
$ cat ruletable
True     If
-------  ------------------------
mother(X,Y)       female(X), parent(X,Y)
$ tabletorule ruletable > rule
$ cat rule
mother(X,Y) :- female(X), parent(X,Y).
```

Now Prolog can use its **consult** command to read in this file. Prolog could then answer questions like: *mother(sally,fred)?*

SEE ALSO
tabletofact

SOURCE

```
: %W% SCCS Information

: tabletorule - takes an /rdb table and makes a prolog rule file

USAGE='usage: tabletorule table ... > prologfile'
EUSAGE=1
```

```
if test "$#" -eq 0
then
        echo $USAGE
        exit $EUSAGE
fi

for FILE
do
        sed     '1,2d
                s/       / :- /
                s/$/./'  $FILE
done
```

NAME
tabletosed   - converts table format to m4 sed file format

SYNOPSIS
tabletosed   < table > sedfile

DESCRIPTION
tabletosed will convert a two-column table into a file of **sed** statements that can be input to the **sed** stream editor. **sed** macros are in the form:

```
s/old/new/g
```

sed can do many things including word for word substitution. The *sedfile* produced is used by the **translate** command. It can be used for language translation (in a stiff, inflexible way) and for other conversions of databases.

EXAMPLE
Suppose we have a simple translation table:

```
$ cat ed.t

English  Deutch
-------  -------
I        Ich
love     liebe
you      dich
widgit
$ tabletosed < ed.t > ed.sed.1
$ cat sed.1
s/I/Ich/g
s/love/liebe/g
s/you/dich/g
```

We can now use the *ed.sed.1* file with **sed** or **translate.**

```
$ cat text
I love you.

$ sed -f ed.sed.1 text
Ich liebe dich.
```

It can also be used for form letters.

SEE ALSO
translate

SOURCE
```
: %W% SCCS Information

: tabletosed takes an /rdb table and makes and m4 sed file
:        Note that first column must be single word for m4
:        Note also that the second column must have a string to be used

USAGE='usage: tabletosed < table > sedfile'

OLDIFS=$IFS
IFS='

: delete headline
: delete rows without a string in the second column
: delete rows with spaces in first column
: converte tabs to slash
```

```
: put the new lines into sed format

sed     '1,2d
        /        $/d
        /^.* .*  /d
        s:       :/:
        s:.*:s/&/g:'
```

NAME
tabletostruct   - convert table to C language struct (record)

SYNOPSIS
tabletostruct   tag name

DESCRIPTION
tabletostruct converts a standard /rdb table into a C language struct declaration. **struct** is the C record format. This command is useful for writing table driven code. The tables, used by your programs, can also be manipulated by the database and your users, or nonprogrammer developers (engineers, experts, managers, operators). Then the application tables can be converted to **struct** and compiled into the C code for high speed access. However, once compiled, changing the tables no longer affects the program until it is recompiled. Therefore, you get maximum speed at the price of recompiling the system and losing the flexibility of being able to modify the tables during execution.

ARGUMENTS
tag   is the struct tag for declaring other variables
name   is the struct name to reference the structure values

EXAMPLE
Here we start with a simple table, convert it to **struct,** make it an include file (.h is a header file), compile it into a simple program that prints out each field.

```
$ cat table
A   B   C
-   -   -
1   2   3
$ tabletostruct Table table < table > table.h
$ cat table.h
struct Table
{
char *A;
char *B;
char *C;
}   table [] =
{ "1","2","3" }
;
$ cat Makefile
printtable:printtable.o
 cc -o printtable printtable.o

$ cat printtable.c
#include"table.h"

main ()
{
 printf ("A=%s0, table[0].A);
 printf ("B=%s0, table[0].B);
 printf ("C=%s0, table[0].C);
}
$ make
 cc -O -c printtable.c
 cc -o printtable printtable.o
$ printtable
A=1
B=2
C=3
```

Note that the **struct** is an array and that we have to give a subscript for each row we want. We can also put the **tabletostruct** into the *makefile* to futher automate the compilation.

```
$ cat Makefile
printtable:table.h printtable.o
 cc -o printtable printtable.o

table.h:table
 tabletostruct Table table < table > table.h
```

This says that the printable program depends upon *table.h* being up to date, and *table.h* depends upon *table* being up to date. If you modify *table* since the last compile, the *tabletostruct* command will be reexecuted.

SEE ALSO
listtotable tabletolist

NAME

tabletotbl   - converts /rdb table format to UNIX tbl/nroff format

SYNOPSIS

tabletotbl   < tablefile > tblfile

DESCRIPTION

tabletotbl will convert a /**rdb** table to a UNIX **tbl** format. **tbl** is a UNIX program that formats tables for the **nroff/troff** formatting and typesetting programs. See the UNIX documentation for **tbl, nroff,** and **troff.**

EXAMPLE

Suppose we have a journal table:

```
$ cat journal
Date    Account  Debit   Credit   Description
------  -------  -----   ------   -------------------------------
861222  101      25000            cash from loan
861222  211.1             25000   loan number #378-14 Bank Amerigold
861223  150.1    10000            test equipment from Zarkoff
861223  101                5000   cash payment
861223  211.2              5000   note payable to Zarkoff Equipment
861224  130      30000            inventory - parts from CCPSC
861224  201.1             15000   accounts payable to CCPSC
861224  101               15000   cash payment to CCPSC for parts

$ tabletotbl < journal
.TS
 r n r r l.
Date    Account  Debit   Credit   Description
------  -------  -----   ------   -------------------------------
861222  101      25000            cash from loan
861222  211.1             25000   loan number #378-14 Bank Amerigold
861223  150.1    10000            test equipment from Zarkoff
861223  101                5000   cash payment
861223  211.2              5000   note payable to Zarkoff Equipment
861224  130      30000            inventory - parts from CCPSC
861224  201.1             15000   accounts payable to CCPSC
861224  101               15000   cash payment to CCPSC for parts
.TE
```

This can be sent on to **tbl** and **nroff,** or inserted into text that will be sent to them.

```
$ tabletotbl < journal | tbl | nroff
```

SOURCE

```
: %W% SCCS ID Information

# tabletotbl - converts a /rdb table to UNIX tbl for nroff/troff

USAGE='usage: tabletotbl < tablefile > tblfile'

TMP=/tmp/$$tabletotbl
trap 'rm -f /tmp/$$*' 0 1 2 3 15

cat > $TMP

# find the type of each column for justification

TYPE="`datatype < $TMP | tail -1`"

for I in $TYPE
do
     case "$I" in
```

```
        -1)    LIST="$LIST l"    ;;
        0)     LIST="$LIST r"    ;;
        *)     LIST="$LIST n"    ;;
        esac
done

# output tbl

echo ".TS"
echo "$LIST."
cat $TMP
echo ".TE"

rm $TMP
```

NAME

tax   - compute tax from income and tax table

SYNOPSIS

tax   income < taxtable

DESCRIPTION

tax will take taxable *income* from the first argument and a taxtable as *standard input* and put the computed tax to the *standard output*. **tax** returns the computed tax rounded off to the nearest dollar.

EXAMPLE

The user must create the tax table and it must be in the three column format shown in the following example. This is the federal income tax for single taxpayers for 1983 (Schedule X):

```
$ cat X83
income     tax   percent
------     ---   -------
  2300       0       11
  3400     121       12
  4400     251       15
  6500     566       15
  8500     866       17
 10800    1257       19
 12900    1656       21
 15000    2097       24
 18200    2865       28
 23500    4349       32
 28800    6045       36
 34100    7953       40
 41500   10913       45
 55300   17123       50
```

If your taxable income is $20,000, you would key in the following:

```
$ tax 20000 < X83
   3369
```

The 3369 on the next line is your computed tax.

You can also catch the output in a shell variable like this:

```
$ TAX='tax 20000 < X83'
$ echo $TAX
$ 3369
```

Note the use of the back quote (`) which tells the UNIX shell to execute the enclosed command and put the resulting string onto the line so that it will be assigned to the variable on the left of the equal sign. The echo command is used to see the value assigned to the tax string variable.

You can then use the *TAX* shell variable to input the tax into a table:

```
$ compute "line == 35 { value = $TAX }" < form1040
```

Note the use of the double quotes (") instead of the single quote ('), because we want the shell to substitute the value of tax where we have typed $TAX. To quote something within double quotes ("), we must use single quotes ('). If we used the same quotes within those quotes, the effect is to start and stop the quotes, not to nest the quotes. This produces unpredictable results.

NAME

termput - get terminal capability from /etc/termcap file

SYNOPSIS

termput capability

DESCRIPTION

termput is used by a shell program to get control of the terminal screen. You can do reverse video, blinking, and so on. Whatever capabilities your terminal has can be defined in the */etc/termcap* file. Hopefully, it is set up right for you. A two letter capability code is followed by a string of characters that, when sent to the terminal screen, will turn on or off that capability.

termput searches the */etc/termcap* file for a terminal capability. **termput** is like the UNIX System 5, Release 2 **tput** command, except **termput** uses the */etc/termcap* file so that it is compatible with all UNIX systems that have **vi. tput** uses the *terminfo* system which is not portable to other UNIX systems. The termcap idea was invented by Bill Joy when he wrote the **vi** text editor. It enables the editor to work with the hundreds of different computer terminals. Each terminal's capabilities are entered into the */etc/termcap* file that comes with almost all UNIX systems today.

CAPABILITIES

The capabilities are two letter codes that are defined in your UNIX manual under *termcap*. Here are some examples:

cl   clear the terminal screen
cm   cursor movement - see below
so   start standout mode like reverse video
se   end standout mode

Cursor movement is more complicated. The row and column you want must be edited into the cursor movement command string. **cm** just gives you the format of the cursor movement string. See the **cursor** command for details.

EXAMPLE

Here we convert several characters.

```
$ termput cl
(clear screen)
$ termput se
(reverse video)
$ termput so
(normal video)
$
```

SETUP

For screen handling, it is much faster to set up shell variables with the capability strings and to use them in your shell programs, than to execute **termput** each time. To set up these shell variables put them in your *.profile* in your *$HOME* directory.

```
AE='termput ae'        # end alternate character set - graphics
AS='termput as'        ·# start alternate character set - graphics
```

```
CLEAR=`termput cl`      # use in here files
ECLEAR="$CLEAR# ECLEAR="-n $CLEAR"   # use in echo commands - other UNIX
CURSOR=`termput cm`     # cursor movement - for the cursor command
MB=`termput mb`         # start blinking mode
ME=`termput me`         # turn off all attributes
SE=`termput se`         # end stand out mode
SO=`termput so`         # start stand out mode
UE=`termput ue`         # end underline mode
US=`termput us`         # start underline mode
export CLEAR CURSOR AE AS MB ME SE SO SE UE US
```

Once this is set up, you can put the shell variables in your shell program. If you want a message to stand out, you can use the *$SO* and *$SE* pair.

```
$ echo "${SO} LOGOFF NOW ${SE}"
```
LOGOFF NOW

SEE ALSO
clear cursor screen

SOURCE
```
: %W% SCCS Information

: 'termput - put terminal strings from /etc/tercap file'
: '               like tput in system V release 2, but portable'

USAGE='usage: termput feature'
EUSAGE=1

if test "$#" -lt 1
then
                echo $USAGE 1>&2
                exit $EUSAGE
fi

# /etc/termcap example
# cpc|pc|PC|IBM pc:\
#                   :al=\EI:cd=\E[J:ce=\E[K:cl=\E[0;0H\E[2J:\
#                   :cm=\E[%2;%2H:co#80:dl=\EL:\
#                   :if=/usr/lib/tabset/std:\
#                   :li#25:nd=\E[C:\
#                   :ku=\E[A:kl=\E[D:kr=\E[C:kd=\E[B:kh=\E[H:\
#                   :k0=\ED:k1=\E;:k2=\E<:k3=\E=:k4=\E>:k5=\E?:\
#                   :k6=\E@:k7=\EA:k8=\EB:k9=\EC:\
#                   :pt:sr=\EM:se=\E[m:so=\E[7m:\
#                   :sf=\ED:up=\E[A:us=\E[4m:

# get the entry from TERMCAP variable or cut out of /etc/termcap
if test -n "$TERMCAP"
then
                echo "$TERMCAP"
else
                sed                                         "1,/$TERM|/d
                                                            /:\$/q" < /etc/termcap
fi |
grep ":$1=" |
sed                     "s/.*:$1=//
                        s/:.*//
                        s/\\\\\E//g"
```

NAME

testall   - tests all /rdb programs in demo directory

SYNOPSIS

testall   [> testall.new]

DESCRIPTION

testall runs most of the /**rdb** programs with the files in the *demo* directory. It outputs the results to compare with *testall.old* in the demo directory *rdb/demo/testall.old*. **testall** should be run in the demo directory, because the test files are there and you can use **diff** to see if the *testall.new* file is different than *testall.old* file. This testing is done when the /**rdb** database is installed on new computers and when code is changed. The **diff** command will quickly show if the output is changed. Naturally the dates will be different. Other differences suggest that the programs may not all be working right.

EXAMPLE

First go to the demo directory. Assuming the path is */usr/rdb/demo:*

```
$ cd /usr/rdb/demo
$ testall > testall.new
$ diff testall.old testall.new
```

The **diff** command will show if there is any different output then the *testall.old.* After careful checking, if differences are correct:

```
$ mv testall.new testall.old
or
$ rm testall.new
```

to save space, because these files are large.

NAME
testsearch   - tests the fast access methods in demo directory

SYNOPSIS
testsearch

DESCRIPTION
testsearch will run and time the **index** and **search** commands. **testsearch** is a shell script that currently tests the *unixtable* and *unixlist* files in the *rdb/demo* directory. You might edit the **testsearch** script to time the search of a big file you are working with.

EXAMPLE
First go to the demo directory.

```
$ cd rdb/demo
$ testsearch
```

The results come to your screen.

SEE ALSO
timesearch testall

SOURCE
```
: %W% SCCS ID Information

: testsearch - uses unixtable to test index and search programs
:          WARNING: must be run in demo directory

USAGE='usage: testsearch'

echo     "index and search"
echo
echo     "first make unixlist"
echo
echo     "tabletolist < unixtable > unixlist"
echo
tabletolist < unixtable > unixlist

for i in b h i s
do
        echo
        echo "index -m$i unixtable Company City"
        index -m$i unixtable Company City
        echo "search -m$i unixtable < CompanyCity"
        search -m$i unixtable < CompanyCity
        echo
        echo "index -m$i unixlist Company City"
        index -m$i unixlist Company City
        echo "search -m$i unixlist < CompanyCity"
        search -m$i unixlist < CompanyCity
done

echo
echo "index -mr unixtable"
index -mr unixtable
echo "search -mr unixtable < 1, 47 and 87"
search -mr unixtable <<EOF
1
47
87
```

```
EOF

echo
echo "index -mr unixlist"
index -mr unixlist
echo "search -mr unixlist < 1, 47 and 87"
search -mr unixlist <<EOF
1
47
87
EOF

rm unixtable.? unixlist*

echo End Test of index and search
```

NAME

timesearch   - times the fast access methods in demo directory

SYNOPSIS

timesearch   [> timesearch.new]

DESCRIPTION

timesearch will run and time the **index** and **search** commands on a file. **timesearch** is in the *rdb/demo* directory and not in bin because it is written to test just the *unixtable* and *unixlist* files there. Its purpose is to find out which is the *best* fast access method to use in a particular situation. Theory often fails us when working with access methods. A sequential search by the select command may often be better than one of the fast access methods when the indexing overhead is considered.

timesearch is a shell script that currently tests the *unixtable and unixlist* files in *rdb/demo*. You might edit the *timesearch* script to search a big file you want to test.

EXAMPLE

First go to the demo directory. *$RDBPATH* is the path to your **/rdb** directory.

```
$ cd $RDBPATH/rdb/demo
$ timesearch
```

The output is the output of the **index** and **search** commands and the output of the UNIX **time** command that is used to time the programs.

SEE ALSO

testsearch testall

SOURCE

```
: %W% SCCS ID Information

: timesearch - times the execution of each of teh search methods
:         WARNING: must be run in demo directory

USAGE='usage: timesearch'

echo index -mr unixtable
time index -mr unixtable
echo search -mr unixtable \<\<
time search -mr unixtable <<EOF
1
70
EOF

for i in b i h s
do
        echo index -m$i unixtable Company
        time index -m$i unixtable Company
        echo search -m$i unixtable \< Company
        time search -m$i unixtable < Company
done
```

NAME
   todaysdate   - output the current date in the format: 840415

SYNOPSIS
   todaysdate

DESCRIPTION
   todaysdate displays the current date in the form: *891022*. This is the best format for entering data in a column because it will sort correctly.

EXAMPLE
```
$ todaysdate
890401
```

SEE ALSO
   julian gregorian computedate

NAME
total   - sums up each column selected and displays

SYNOPSIS
total   [-l] [column ...] < table

DESCRIPTION
total adds up the values in each column selected and displays them. If no columns are listed, all of the columns will be totaled.

Several other commands behave just like total except the value they produce is not a total but: **datatype, maximum, minimum, mean, precision, width, length,** and so on. The all use the same program but decide what to print depending upon the name used to call it.

OPTIONS
-l option will cause the entire table to be listed.

EXAMPLE
There are two formats. Without the -*l*, total just gives the head lines and the total line:

```
$ total Debit Credit < journal
Date    Account   Debit   Credit   Description
----    -------   -----   ------   -----------
                  65000    65000
```

However, if you wish to see the whole table like a report:

```
$ total -l Debit Credit < ledger
Account     Date     Debit    Credit
-------    -------   -------   -------
101        890102    25000
101        890103               5000
101        890104              15000
130        890104    30000
150.1      890103    10000
201.1      890104              15000
211.1      890102              25000
211.2      890103               5000
-------    -------   -------   -------
                     65000     65000
```

NAME
translate - word for word substitution using translation files

SYNOPSIS
translate language < text > translatedtext

DESCRIPTION
translate will do word for word replacement in an input file. It uses both **m4** for which it needs a definefile that can be produced by **tabletom4,** and **sed** for which it needs sed files that can be produced by **tabletosed.**

The definefile must be named: *language,* for example, *ed* for English to Deutsch (German), and the preprocess sedfile: *language.sed.1* and the postprocess sedfile: *language.sed.2*

Define statements that can be input to the **m4** macroprocessor are define macros in the form: *define(old,new).* It can be used for language translation (in a stiff, inflexible way) and for other conversions of databases. You can do a large language translation, if you are willing to type in a dictionary, or to get one machine readable.

We translated this manual and the tutorial into German using this system. We used **word** to find all of the words and was surprised to discover that there are only a little more than 2,000 different words. We must know more, we just did not use them all. Then we typed in the German words from a dictionary. Took about 30 hours. Ugh. Then converted the table to defines with **tabletom4.** We handled a few sticky problems with the pre and post **sed** processors. Then used **translate** to do the word-for-word substitution. It was not good German. Some sentences made no sense. But most were ok and acceptable to the German users who were very happy not have to struggle through the English version.

EXAMPLE
Suppose we have a simple translation table:

```
$ cat ed.t
English Deutsch
------- -------
I       Ich
love    liebe
you     dich
widgit
$ tabletom4 < ed.t > ed
$ cat ed
define(I,Ich)
define(love,liebe)
define(you,dich)
```

Note that *widgit* did not get converted because it did no have a translation in the table. This **ed** file (English to Deutsch) can now be used with **translate.**

```
$ cat text
I love you.

$ translate ed text
Ich liebe dich.
```

This program was also used in a biomedical expert system.

The idea is to convert each word into its value after looking them up in a table.

This is something the Lisp language does a lot of.

```
Var      Value
-------  -------
age      42
weight   80
 ...
```

It can also be used for form letters.

SEE ALSO
tabletom4 tabletosed translate word

SOURCE
```
: %W% SCCS Information

: translate converts from one language to another

USAGE='usage: translate langtolang < textfile'
EUSAGE=1

TMP=/tmp/$$translate
TMP1=/tmp/$$1translate

trap 'rm -f /tmp/$$*' 0 1 2 3 15

if test "$#" -lt 1
then
        echo $USAGE 1>&2
        exit $EUSAGE
fi

LANGUAGE=$1
shift

: preprocess if a sed.1 file

if test -r "$LANGUAGE.sed.1"
then
        sed -f $LANGUAGE.sed.1 > $TMP
else
        cat > $TMP
fi

: use m4 for word for word substitution

if test -r "$LANGUAGE"
then
        m4 $LANGUAGE $TMP > $TMP1
else
        mv $TMP $TMP1
fi

: postprocess if a sed.2 file

if test -r "$LANGUAGE.sed.2"
then
        sed -f $LANGUAGE.sed.2 $TMP1
else
        cat $TMP1
fi
```

NAME
trim   - squeezes a table for printing

SYNOPSIS
trim   [-[l|n|ln] col...][-r[n] col...][-t'c']...< table

DESCRIPTION
trim allows you to print a wide table with the minimum width for each column. **WARNING: trim** removes all tabs in order to reduce the extra space created by tabs. Therefore, you cannot input a trimmed table to any of the **/rdb** commands (including **trim** itself). **trim** replaces the tabs with a single space.

trim without any options will do the best it can to squeeze your table, without losing any information. It will make each column as wide as its widest column name or data. **trim** also allows you to reduce a column, even if it has to throw away characters, if you tell it to.

Note that **trim** will trim all columns even if some are listed with the options. Most other **/rdb** commands, such as **justify,** will only affect the columns listed, unless none are listed, in which case they do the same thing to all of them.

OPTIONS
n   is number of characters remaining after the trim.

-n column ...   will return only n characters from the left of column.

-ln column ...   will return only n characters from the left of column
                     (that is, the letter ell, not the number one).

-rn column ...   will return only n characters from the right of column.

You can also force trim to use a character other than blank as a field separator. For example, you may want to keep the tab so that the table can be used by other **/rdb** commands.

-tc   will use character 'c' as the column separator.

Remember that with UNIX, special characters like tab and the vertical bar (|) or the pipe symbol, are specially treated by the shell. So to protect them use a single quote or a backslash (for single character). For example: *-t' '* or *-t* where you type the tab key between the single quotes or after the backslash is the proper way to get the tab past the shell and to the program. Another example: **-t'|'** or **-t\|** for the vertical bar. Sorry for all this special character business, but it does add lots of power in a few keystrokes.

Only columns listed will be affected. All others will be normally trimmed. The options are *sticky,* meaning that you can follow an option with as many column names as you wish, and they will all be treated as specified by the leading option.

EXAMPLE
If you have a table like this:

```
$ cat inventory
   Item    Amount    Cost    Value    Description
```

```
   1       3      5.00     15.00   rubber gloves
   2     100      0.50     50.00   test tubes
   3       5      8.00     40.00   clamps
   4      23      1.98     45.54   plates
   5      99      2.45    242.55   cleaning cloth
   6      89     14.75   1312.75   bunsen burners
   7       5    175.00    875.00   scales
```

you can trim it simply by typing:

```
$ trim < inventory
 Item Amount Cost  Value   Description
 ---- ------ ----- ------- --------------
   1    3      5.00    15.00 rubber gloves
   2   100     0.50    50.00 test tubes
   3    5      8.00    40.00 clamps
   4   23      1.98    45.54 plates
   5   99      2.45   242.55 cleaning cloth
   6   89     14.75  1312.75 bunsen burners
   7    5    175.00   875.00 scales
```

Note that the length of the column names *Item* and *Amount* determined the width of their columns, but with the other columns, the data determined the width.

You might want to see the output table with the **see** command:

```
$ trim < inventory | see
Item  Amount     Cost    Value  Description       $
----  ------    -----  ------- --------------    $
   1       3     5.00    15.00  rubber gloves     $
   2     100     0.50    50.00  test tubes        $
   3       5     8.00    40.00  clamps            $
   4      23     1.98    45.54  plates            $
   5      99     2.45   242.55  cleaning cloth    $
   6      89    14.75  1312.75  bunsen burners    $
   7       5   175.00   875.00  scales            $
```

Note that there are no tabs (^I). This table is only for printing. Don't input or pipe into another /**rdb** command unless you use the *-t* option which will retain the tab as a column separator.

We can further squeeze the table with the *-n, -ln* and *-rn* options.

```
$ trim -1 Item < inventory
I   Amount     Cost    Value  Description
-   ------    -----  ------- --------------
1       3     5.00    15.00  rubber gloves
2     100     0.50    50.00  test tubes
3       5     8.00    40.00  clamps
4      23     1.98    45.54  plates
5      99     2.45   242.55  cleaning cloth
6      89    14.75  1312.75  bunsen burners
7       5   175.00   875.00  scales
```

Note that the *Item* column has been reduced to one character by the *-1* option. It had to throw away all but the *I* of the column name *Item*. Note that the other columns were normally trimmed. Since the options are *sticky* you can name several columns after one option:

```
$ trim -5 Item Amount Cost Description < inventory
Item  Amoun    Cost    Value  Descr
----- -----   -----  ------- -----
1         3    5.00    15.00  rubbe
2       100    0.50    50.00  test
3         5    8.00    40.00  clamp
4        23    1.98    45.54  plate
```

```
5        99    2.45    242.55   clean
6        89   14.75   1312.75   bunse
7         5     175    875.00   scale
```

Note that all of the columns named were printed out five characters wide.

-n and *-ln* options are the same. We can also use the *-rn* option to get both the n right characters of a column and to line up numbers on the right.

```
$ trim -r3 Amount < inventory
Item   Amo     Cost      Value   Description
----   ---    -----    -------   ---------------
1        3     5.00      15.00   rubber gloves
2      100     0.50      50.00   test tubes
3        5     8.00      40.00   clamps
4       23     1.98      45.54   plates
5       99     2.45     242.55   cleaning cloth
6       89    14.75    1312.75   bunsen burners
7        5   175.00     875.00   scales
```

Note that the *Amount* column name has been reduced to *Amo*. Also, the column is right justified as a result of taking the right three characters of each field in the column.

A complex trim might be done like this:

```
$ trim -1 Item -r3 Amount -r5 Cost -17 Value Description < inventory
I   Amo    Cost      Value   Descrip
-   ---   -----    -------   -------
1     3    5.00      15.00   rubber
2   100    0.50      50.00   test tu
3     5    8.00      40.00   clamps
4    23    1.98      45.54   plates
5    99    2.45     242.55   cleanin
6    89   14.75    1312.75   bunsen
7     5   175.0     875.00   scales
```

We have squeezed this table a lot.

We have been working with an unjustified table. What if the table had been justified? First let's justify the table.

```
$ justify < inventory > tmp ; mv tmp inventory
```

Now inventory is justified.

```
$ cat inventory
    Item    Amount      Cost     Value   Description
-------   -------   -------   -------   ---------------
      1         3      5.00     15.00   rubber gloves
      2       100      0.50     50.00   test tubes
      3         5      8.00     40.00   clamps
      4        23      1.98     45.54   plates
      5        99      2.45    242.55   cleaning cloth
      6        89     14.75   1312.75   bunsen burners
      7         5    175.00    875.00   scales
```

Now, if we trim:

```
$ trim < inventory
Item Amount Cost   Value   Description
---- ------ ------ ------- ---------------
             5.0   15.00 rubber gloves
       10    0.5   50.00 test tubes
             8.0   40.00 clamps
        2    1.9   45.54 plates
        9    2.4  242.55 cleaning cloth
        8   14.7 1312.75 bunsen burners
            175.0  875.00 scales
```

This mess results from getting the leading (left) characters in the right justified columns: *Item, Amount* and *Cost.* Since these leading characters are blanks (spaces), we have lost our meaningful data. One way to fix this is to tell trim that the columns are right justified, like this:

```
$ trim -r Item Amount Cost < inventory
Item   Amount    Cost     Value   Description
----   ------    ------   -------  --------------
   1        3     5.00     15.00   rubber gloves
   2      100     0.50     50.00   test tubes
   3        5     8.00     40.00   clamps
   4       23     1.98     45.54   plates
   5       99     2.45    242.55   cleaning cloth
   6       89    14.75   1312.75   bunsen burners
   7        5   175.00    875.00   scales
```

You can also compress the file before piping it into **trim.** For further compression:

```
$ trim -r1 Item -r3 Amount -r6 Cost -l11 Description < inventory
I Amo   Cost   Value Description
- ---   ----   ----- -----------
1   3   5.00   15.00 rubber glov
2 100   0.50   50.00 test tubes
3   5   8.00   40.00 clamps
4  23   1.98   45.54 plates
5  99   2.45  242.55 cleaning cl
6  89  14.75 1312.75 bunsen burn
7   5 175.00  875.00 scales
```

NAME
trimblank　　　　　　- removes leading and trailing blanks for a string

SYNOPSIS
trimblank　　　　　　[string] [< file]'

DESCRIPTION
trimblank strips off spaces from the front and back of a string. It is useful in shell programming when you may get a string that is padded (justified) with spaces, and need them cleaned off to use the string.

EXAMPLE
```
$ echo         '    here is the good stuff       '
    here is the good stuff
$ trimblank '    here is the good stuff       '
here is the good stuff
```

Note that when you echo the single quote (') protected string, you get it back, but that **trimblank** compresses it for you.

SOURCE
```
: %W% SCCS ID Information

: trimblank - removes leading and trailing blanks for a string

USAGE='usage: trimblank [string] [ < file ]'

if test "$#" -eq 0
then
        sed       's/^ *//
                  s/ *$//'
else
        echo "$*"|sed     's/^ *//
                          s/ *$//'
fi
```

NAME

    tset   - returns the termcap entry for the TERM terminal

SYNOPSIS

    tset   [TERM]

DESCRIPTION

tset duplicates the Berkeley program by the same name. It finds the termcap entry in the */etc/termcap* file, and can be used to assign that entry to *TERMCAP*.

EXAMPLE
```
$ echo $TERM
pc
$ tset
:al=\EI:cd=\E[J:ce=\E[K:cl=\E[0;0H\E[2J:\
:cm=\E[%i%2;%2H:co#80:dl=\EL:\
:li#25:nd=\E[C:pt:sr=\EM:up=\E[A:\
:ku=\E[A:kl=\E[D:kr=\E[C:kd=\E[B:kh=\E[H:\
:k0=\ED:k1=\E;:k2=\E<:k3=\E=:k4=\E>:k5=\E?:\
:k6=\E@:k7=\EA:k8=\EB:k9=\EC:\
:se=\E[m:so=\E[7m:us=\E[4m:\
:if=/usr/lib/tabset/std:\
:sf=\ED:
$ TERMCAP=`tset`
```

The *TERM* variable had been set in the *.profile* to the *pc* terminal. **tset** returns the termcap entery for the *pc*. This can be used in your *profile* to assign to the shell variable *TERMCAP* and therefore to speed up screen programs.

SOURCE
```
: %W% SCCS Information

: 'tset - outputs the /etc/termcap terminal capatilities'

USAGE='usage: tset [ TERM ]'
EUSAGE=1

if test "$#" -eq 1
then
        TERM=$1
        export TERM
fi

# /etc/termcap example
# cpc|pc|PC|IBM pc:\
#       :al=\EI:cd=\E[J:ce=\E[K:cl=\E[0;0H\E[2J:\
#       :cm=\E[%2;%2H:co#80:dl=\EL:\
#       :if=/usr/lib/tabset/std:\
#       :li#25:nd=\E[C:\
#       :ku=\E[A:kl=\E[D:kr=\E[C:kd=\E[B:kh=\E[H:\
#       :k0=\ED:k1=\E;:k2=\E<:k3=\E=:k4=\E>:k5=\E?:\
#       :k6=\E@:k7=\EA:k8=\EB:k9=\EC:\
#       :pt:sr=\EM:se=\E[m:so=\E[7m:\
#       :sf=\ED:up=\E[A:us=\E[4m:

sed     "1,/$TERM|/d
        /:\$/q" < /etc/termcap
```

NAME
union   - appends tables together

SYNOPSIS
union   tableorlist ... [-] [< tableorlist]

DESCRIPTION

union produces a new table or list consisting of all the rows in the first input table or list followed by the rows of the second and so on. Think of it as the *concatenation* of the two tables or lists. The input tables or lists must have the same number of columns. (Called *union* compatible). It is best that the columns have the same name and the same type of data.

The - tells where in the list of files the standard input is to go. This gives you the freedom to use **union** in a pipe and to put the input file anywhere in the output.

EXAMPLE

```
$ cat journal

   Date    Amount   Account   Ref   Description
   ----    ------   -------   ---   -----------
   820107   14.00   meal      v     meal with jones
   820119   81.72   vitamin   c     sundown vitamins
   820121   20.83   meal      v     meal with scott
   820121 2500.00   keogh     c     keogh payment
   820125   99.00   dues      v     dues to uni-ops

$ cat carexpense

   Date    Amount   Account   Ref   Description
   ----    ------   -------   ---   -----------
   820113  101.62   car       v     car repairs
   820114   81.80   insur     c     car insurance allstate
   820114   93.00   car       c     car registration dmv

$ union journal carexpense

   Date    Amount   Account   Ref   Description
   ----    ------   -------   ---   -----------
   820107   14.00   meal      v     meal with jones
   820119   81.72   vitamin   c     sundown vitamins
   820121   20.83   meal      v     meal with scott
   820121 2500.00   keogh     c     keogh payment
   820125   99.00   dues      v     dues to uni-ops
   820113  101.62   car       v     car repairs
   820114   81.80   insur     c     car insurance allstate
   820114   93.00   car       c     car registration dmv
```

A more complicated example would be:

```
$ echo journal | union - carexpense
```

which would have the same output as above, but shows you how it can be used in a pipe.

SOURCE

```
: %W% SCCS Information

: 'union - concatenates two or more tables or lists'

USAGE='usage: union tableorlist ... [ - < tableorlist ]'
EUSAGE=1

if test "$#" -lt 1
```

```
then
        echo $USAGE 1>&2
        exit $EUSAGE
fi

cat $1
shift

for FILE in $*
do
        if test "$FILE" = "-"
        then
                sed 1,2d
        else
                sed 1,2d < $FILE
        fi
done
```

NAME
uniondict   - combines three tables into translate dictionary

SYNOPSIS
uniondict   langtolang > definefile

DESCRIPTION
uniondict makes an **m4** *definefile* out of three tables. *langtolang* is a two letter code like *ed* for English to German. It expects one table of lower case letters like *ed.low* and one all capital letters like *ed.allcap* and builds its own table with first letter caps. Finally dictionary uses **tabletom4** to create a *definefile* for **m4.**

EXAMPLE
```
$ uniondict ed
```

If the two precursor files are there, then there should be a new file named *ed* that is needed by the **translate** command.

SEE ALSO
tabletom4 translate word

SOURCE
```
: %W% SCCS ID Information

: uniondict - makes an m4 define file out of three tables
:        it expects one lower case like ed.low
:        and one all caps like ed.allcap and
:        builds its own table with first letter caps.
:        finally dictionary uses tabletom4 to create define table

USAGE='usage: uniondict langtolang'
EUSAGE=1

if test "$#" -le 0
then
        echo $USAGE 1>&2
        exit $EUSAGE
fi

LANG=$1
cap < $LANG.low |
union $LANG.allcap - $LANG.low |
tabletom4 > $LANG
```

NAME
unlock   - unlocks a record or field of a file

SYNOPSIS
unlock   tableorlist processid from to indexfrom indexto

DESCRIPTION
unlock unlocks a record or file by removing a row from a common unlock file. */tmp/Lfilename* contains one line for each locked record or field with the process ID of the process (program) that locked it, the begin (from) and end (to) of the bytes to be locked, and the secondary index file begin and end bytes.

EXAMPLE
Let us use **unlock** on the *inventory* table:

```
$ cat inventory
Item  Amount  Cost  Value  Description
----  ------  ----  -----  --------------
   1       3    50    150  rubber gloves
   2     100     5    500  test tubes
   3       5    80    400  clamps
   4      23    19    437  plates
   5      99    24   2376  cleaning cloth
   6      89   147  13083  bunsen burners
   7       5   175    875  scales
```

First we use **seek** to locate the record and return the offset and size.

```
$ LOCATION='echo 5 | seek -mb inventory Item'
$ echo $LOCATION
207 245 0 8
```

This means that the record is 207 bytes into the file and that it is 38 bytes long (ends at byte 245). Now we can call **unlock** to unlock the record:

```
$ unlock inventory $$ $LOCATION
```

Note that we use the *$LOCATION* shell variable to supply the location. We also use the automatic shell variable double-dollar ($$) to put the process ID on the command line.

Let's see what the lock file looks like:

```
$ cat /tmp/Linventory
cat: cannot open /tmp/Linventory
```

unlock will remove the whole file if the last lock line has been removed.

SEE ALSO
See **lock** for locking examples.

SOURCE
```
: %W% SCCS ID Information

: unlock - removes lock on area, usually a record, of a file

USAGE='usage: unlock filename processid from to indexfrom indexto'
EUSAGE=1

UNLOCKED=0
```

```
ENOREAD=2

case "$#" in
6)
    LOCKFILE=/tmp/L$1
    TMP=/tmp/$$unlock
    LOCKROW="$2     $3      $4              $5$6"

    if test ! -r $LOCKFILE
    then
            exit ENOREAD
    fi

    sed "/$LOCKROW/d" < $LOCKFILE > $TMP
    if test -s $TMP
    then
            mv $TMP $LOCKFILE
    else
            rm $LOCKFILE $TMP
    fi
    exit $UNLOCKED
    ;;
*)
    echo $USAGE 1>&2
    exit $EUSAGE
    ;;
esac
```

NAME

update   - displays and edits records in any sized file

SYNOPSIS

update   [-l -m[bhirs] -v] tableorlist [keycolumn...]

DESCRIPTION

update allows you to find a record, display it and *update* it. It has several ways to find a record: by moving up and down in the file, by record number, and by a character string pattern in a record, and fast access method search.

update allows you to edit, with your favorite editor, the record you find. To lock out other users who might be looking at your file, a blank record can be written back into the file. When you finish editing, **update** puts your new record into the file. If the new record is smaller than the old record because you deleted some characters, space characters are added to the end of the last column to pad out the record. If the new record is larger than the old record, trailing and leading spaces are trimmed from the columns. If **update** cannot find enough blank spaces to trim, it will not replace the record but will append it to the end of the table and update the fast access method indexes.

You then have several options. You can reedit the record. You can append the record to the end of the file using **enter** and delete the current record. You can also pad each record with extra spaces so that there will be room when you do updates. To do padding, use the **pad** program.

The importance of updating in place is that it does not interfere with the fast access methods in which indexes or sorts assume that the records don't move. As long as you don't change the key columns, the fast access methods should be able to find the records.

Also, **update** can handle any sized file, whereas the text editors and word processors mostly cannot handle files of more than a few hundred thousand characters.

OPTIONS

-l   No lock. Do not lock record by blanking out the record in the file while updating. This is much faster. But use only when you are the only person updating the file. When you have multi-users, you have to blank the record to keep others from making changes to the record while you are, and then clobbering your changes.

-m   Fast access method. See **index** for these options.

-v   Verbose. Print info on what is going on as you update a record. Shows you the steps and shows you what is taking time on your system.

Getting In and Out

Type:

```
$ update tableorlist
```

update will prompt you with:

```
> _
```

The underline represents the cursor. To exit you have three choices:

```
> CTRL-d
```

means hold down the CTRL key and press the *d* key.

```
> quit
```

or simply the letter *q*. **update** only looks at the first character of the one word commands.

Finally, the DEL or CTRL-c keys will kill the program as it does other UNIX commands (except the **vi** editor).

HELP MENU

Type:

```
> help
```

to get a menu of the commands. Just the single letter *h* will do.

Command	Description	update [-l -m[bhirs] -l] file
CTRL-d	exit, hold down CTRL key and press *d* (see quit below)
Return key	display next record
number	display record number you enter (number = 1,29,...)
+number	move forward the number of records in the file
-number	move backwards the number of records in the file
/pattern	find next record with pattern
=key	find records with matching key equal to what you type
!command	execute the unix command while still in update
!enter file	enter new records at end of the file
(You need only type the first letter of the commands below)	
delete	delete the current record
m[bhirs] [col]	set up fast access method for key column b=binary, h=hash, i=index, r=record, s=sequential
lock	lock update record by blanking (toggle, true)
search key	find records with matching key
help	help list displayed (this help list)
quit	quit (also cntl-d)
update	update current record, allows you to edit, replace
verbose	report internal actions (toggle, false)

FINDING A RECORD

There are several ways to find the record you want.

update displays the first record in the file when it comes up. It knows about tables and lists. To move forward to the next record, simply hit the RETURN key:

```
> <RETURN KEY>
```

You can move forward any number of records with a plus sign and a number:

```
> +5
```

or back with a minus:

```
> -16
```

You can also select a specific record number:

```
> 57
```

will give you record number 57. Record numbers are displayed with each record.

PATTERN SEARCH

If you try to go beyond the last record or before the first record, **update** will tell you.

You can also search for a record that has a specific character string by typing the slash key followed by the pattern as you would do in the vi editor:

```
> /Ronald
```

update searches forward starting with the next record, then wraps around and goes to the first record in the file and continues till it finds a match or returns to the current record.

FAST ACCESS METHODS

You can turn on the fast access methods two way.

1. On the command line that calls the **update** program:

```
$ update -mh inventory Description
```

2. With the **update** program by invoking the *m* command:

```
> mh Description
```

Both ways tell **update** which method to use and which column is the key column.

Once invoked, you can search with either the = or *s* commands:

```
> =keyvalue
> s keyvalue
```

UPDATING

To **update** the current record simply type:

```
> update
```

Just the letter *u* will do. The sequence, starting from UNIX, is:

1. update file name.

2. Find the record you want by record number, pattern, or fast access.

3. Type *u* for update.

4. The update program copies the record to a file with a header so that it is a one record table or list.

5. It replaces the record with a blank copy of the record to hold the place and lock out other users.

6. It copies the temporary record file to a backup in case you mess up.

7. It calls the editor (either vi or $EDITOR from your environment).

8. You edit the record while in your editor.

9. When you exit your editor, it writes the record onto the file, adding or removing trailing spaces to make it fit. If it doesn't fit, it gives you the option of reediting or appending.

You can also validate a record before leaving the editor by typing:

```
:!validate file.v < file
```

See the validate command for details.

OTHER USEFUL COMMANDS

If you need to see the current record again because it has run off the screen, simply type the period or dot key:

```
> .
```

To execute UNIX shell commands, type the exclamation point and the command:

```
> !ls
```

This is also how you can enter new records (append to the end):

```
> !enter thisfilename
```

When you leave the enter command, you will be back in **update.** You can also index the file, such as:

```
> !index -mi filename keycolumn
```

which will create a *filename.i* file for the fast access methods search command. You have to set up the *.v* validation file. See the validate command.

PADDING

When you set up a file that you intend to update, you will probably want to pad it, that is, add extra space characters to each record. Then you can add characters to a record and **update** will trim off the space characters to fit it back into the file. See the **pad** command for details.

SEE ALSO
update.sh

NAME

update.inv   - multi-user update with screen form and record locking

SYNOPSIS

update.inv

DESCRIPTION

update.inv is a sample shell program that demonstrates several features of **/rdb: multiuser, fast access, screen form input, record locking,** etc. It updates an inventory file named *inv* that is in the *rdb/demo* directory. Use it to see how to use the UNIX shell to tie **/rdb** and UNIX programs together for high speed, multiuser, large file applications.

You will have to set the *TERM* shell variable to the correct name of your terminal in the */etc/termcap* file. To make the reverse video and underlining work, you will have to set up shell variable assignments in your *.profile* file in your home directory.

EXAMPLE

cd to the *rdb/demo* directory, set *.profile*, and run **update.inv:**

```
$ cd rdb/demo
$ . .profile
$ update.inv
Makeapile, Inc.           Inventory Update        Tue Sep 17, 1989

Item Number: _____        (or hit Return key to exit.)

Item        Cost      Value      Description
----        ----      -----      -----------

Amount Onhand: _____
```

We can not show the full screen capabilities on paper. Try the program for yourself and study the program source which is in shell programming language.

SEE ALSO

seek search lock replace unlock

SOURCE

```
: %W% SCCS ID Information

: update.inv - updates the inv table with form entry and record locking

USAGE='usage: update.inv'

  MSEEKING="${MS}Seeking record.$ME  "
  MLOCKING="${MS}Locking record.$ME  "
  MREADING="${MS}Reading record.$ME  "
MREPLACING="${MS}Replacing record.$ME"
MUNLOCKING="${MS}Unlocking record.$ME"
    MBLANK='
while :
do
: paint crt screen
exec 3>&1 1>&2
cat <<SCREEN
${CLEAR}Makeapile, Inc.           Inventory Update
```

```
    Item Number: $SO      $SE         (or hit Return key to exit.)

    Item        Cost     Value    Description
    ----        ----     -----    -----------


    Amount Onhand: $SO         $SE



$MB$MESSAGE$ME
SCREEN

cursor 0 60 ; set 'date' ; echo $1 $2 $3, $6

MESSAGE=

: read user input
cursor  2 13 ; echo "$SO\c" ; read Item; echo "$SE\c"

if test -z "$Item"
then
        echo "$CLEAR"
        exit 0
fi

: seek Item in inv
cursor 12 0 ; echo "$MSEEKING"

LOCATION='echo "$Item" | seek -mb -o tmp inv Item'

if test -z "$LOCATION"
then
        MESSAGE="Item $Item not found."
        continue
fi

: lock record
: lock command adds line to lock file /tmp/Lfilename
cursor 12 0 ; echo "$MLOCKING"

if lock inv $$ $LOCATION
then
        cursor 12 0 ; echo "$MREADING"
else
        MESSAGE="That record is already locked."
        continue
fi

: we could also write a blank record into the file
: blank < tmp | replace inv $LOCATION

: replace the record if this program abnormally exits
: trap "replace inv $LOCATION < tmp" 1 2 3 15

: read record
exec 4<&0 0< tmp
read    HEAD
read    DASH
read    $HEAD
cursor 12 0 ; echo "$MBLANK"

: display record
cursor  6  0 ; echo $Item;
cursor  6 12 ; echo $Cost;
cursor  6 23 ; echo $Value;
cursor  6 34 ; echo $Description;
cursor  8 15 ; echo "$SO$Amount$SE";

: read new Amount
exec 0<&4
```

```
cursor  8 15 ; echo "$SO\c" ; read A ; echo "$SE\c"
Amount=${A:-$Amount}

: output table
cursor 12 0 ; echo "$MREPLACING"
exec 1>&3
cat <<TABLE  | replace inv $LOCATION
$HEAD
$DASH
$Item    $Amount $Cost    $Value   $Description
TABLE

trap 0

: unlock record

cursor 12 0 ; echo "$MUNLOCKING"
unlock inv $$ $LOCATION
cursor 12 0 ; echo "$MBLANK"
done
```

NAME
    update.sh   - updates table with blank record locking

SYNOPSIS
    update.sh   -m[bhirs] tableorlist keycolumn

DESCRIPTION
    update.sh is a shell program that demonstrates record locking by blanking out the record to be edited. It uses fast access methods to quickly get the record you want and puts it into a temporary file. Then it calls the editor that you have assigned to the shell variable *EDITOR,* or **vi.** You are then in the editor, free to edit it. When you are through, the record is replaced in the file.

    Study the code of the **update.sh** shell program for ideas on how to do your own shell programs. After writing your own, you can create a menu program to make it easy to execute them.

EXAMPLE
    Here we convert several characters.

```
$ update.sh -mb inv Item
Enter unique record key or just the Return key to exit:
1
<you are now in vi until you type:>
:wq
Enter unique record key or just the Return key to exit:

$
```

SEE ALSO
    update replace seek lock unlock

SOURCE
```
: %W% SCCS ID Information

: update.sh will search for a record, write it to a tmp file,
:       null out or space out the old record, call an editor to edit it,
:       and replace the old record

USAGE='usage: update.sh -m[bihrs] tableorlist keycolumn < key'
EUSAGE=1

MTABS='Somehow you removed or added a tab while editing.
Can not replace the record, because it would corrupt the file.
You may request the record again and reedit.'

KEYREQUIRED='keycolumn is required when fast access method is given'

TMP=/tmp/$$update
TMP1=/tmp/$$1update

: handle arguments

if test "$#" -lt 1
then
        echo $USAGE 1>&2
        exit $EUSAGE
fi

: test for fast access method
```

```
for I in $*
do
        case "$I" in
        -D*)    DEBUG="$I"
                ;;
        -m*)    METHOD="$I"
                ;;
        *)      if test "$FILE" = ""
                then
                        FILE="$I"
                else
                        KEYCOLUMN="$KEYCOLUMN $I"
                fi
                ;;
        esac
done

: test that there are keycolumns

if test "$#" = ""
then
        echo $KEYREQUIRED 1>&2
        echo $USAGE 1>&2
        echo $EUSAGE
fi

: get key and update record

while true
do

        echo 'Enter unique record key or just the Return key to exit:'

        read KEY

        if test "$KEY" = ""
        then
                exit 0
        fi

        : search for the record and null out old record

        trap 'rm $TMP $TMP1; trap 0; exit' 1 2 3 15

        LOCATION="`echo "$KEY" | seek $METHOD -o $TMP $FILE $KEYCOLUMN`"

        : make an extra copy of the record in case of failure

        cp $TMP $TMP1

        trap "trap 0; replace $FILE $LOCATION < $TMP1; rm $TMP; exit 1" 0 1 2 3 15
        : lock record by writing a blank record back into the file

        blank < $TMP  | replace $METHOD $FILE $LOCATION

        : edit the tmp record

        ${EDITOR=vi} $TMP

        : write the tmp record to the file

        if check < $TMP
        then
                replace $FILE $LOCATION $SIZE < $TMP
        else
                echo "$MTABS" 1>&2
                replace $FILE $LOCATION < $TMP1
        fi
done
```

NAME

uppercase   - returns the upper case of its argument or input file

SYNOPSIS

uppercase   [string ...] [< file]

DESCRIPTION

uppercase converts to capitals every letter in its first argument or, if there is no argument, the *standard input*. It uses the UNIX **tr** character translation program to do the converting.

EXAMPLE

Here we convert to upper case a string and a file.

```
$ uppercase little words
LITTLE WORDS
$ cat lowers
these are all lowercase.
$ uppercase < lowers
THESE ARE ALL LOWERCASE.
```

SEE ALSO

cap lowercase

SOURCE

```
: %W% SCCS ID Information

: 'uppercase - converts characters to uppercase'

USAGE='usage: uppercase [string ...] [< file]'

if test "$#" -eq 0
then
        tr '[a-z]' '[A-Z]'
else
        echo "$*" | tr '[a-z]' '[A-Z]'
fi
```

NAME

validate - finds invalid data and prints messages

SYNOPSIS

validate 'pattern { action } ...' < tableorlist

DESCRIPTION

validate will check your tables and lists for invalid data. It will also print out messages of your choosing and show you the line that caused the error. It is almost identical to **row** and **compute. validate** passes your commands on to **awk** after converting your column names to *$1, $2,* and so on, which is how **awk** refers to columns.

Pattern is a logical condition that would be invalid, such as values that are negative and should not be, or greater than they should be. *Action* is what to do about it. Usually the *action* is to print out a message.

EXAMPLE

First a simple example. You might have an *inventory* table like this:

```
$ cat badinventory
Item#   Onhand  Cost    Value   Description
-----   ------  ----    -----   --------------
    1        3    50      150   rubber gloves
    2      100     X      500   test tubes
    3       -5    80     -400   clamps
    4       23    19      437   plates
    5      -99    24    -2376   cleaning cloth
    6       89   147    13083   bunsen burners
    7        5   175      875   scales
```

There are several invalid values that have gotten into this table. You might want to check that no *Onhand* items are less than zero. You can type this command:

```
$ validate 'Onhand < 0 {print "negative Onhand in line " NR}' < badinventory
Item#   Onhand  Cost    Value   Description
-----   ------  ----    -----   --------------
    1        3    50      150   rubber gloves
    2      100     X      500   test tubes
negative Onhand in line 3
    3       -5    80     -400   clamps
    4       23    19      437   plates
negative Onhand in line 5
    5      -99    24    -2376   cleaning cloth
    6       89   147    13083   bunsen burners
    7        5   175      875   scales
```

The *NR* means number of record or row. It is an **awk** built-in variable. **awk** will replace it with the line number of the line it is processing. You can also put the command into a file and call it something like *validateinv*. It is now a shell program that can be run regularly.

Now a complex example. You can put many tests and messages in one validation file. For example, more can be added to the *validateinv* program.

```
$ cat validateinv
echo validating badinventory

validate '{if (Onhand < 0 ) print "negative Onhand in line " NR; \
        if (Value < 0 ) print "negative Value in line " NR; \
        if (Cost ~ /[A-Za-z]/) print "letter in Cost in line " NR; }' \
        < badinventory
```

To validate just type:

```
$ validateinv
validating badinventory
Item#    Onhand   Cost     Value    Description
-----    ------   ----     -----    --------------
   1         3     50       150     rubber gloves
letter in Cost in line 2
   2       100      X       500     test tubes
negative Onhand in line 3
negative Value in line 3
   3        -5     80      -400     clamps
   4        23     19       437     plates
negative Onhand in line 5
negative Value in line 5
   5       -99     24     -2376     cleaning cloth
   6        89    147     13083     bunsen burners
   7         5    175       875.    scales
```

You can validate while still in the **vi** editor by typing:

```
:!validateinv
```

You will see the error lines and you can fix them while still in the editor. Or direct the output of **validate** to a file, bring it into the editor and correct the errors and remove the error lines as you go. To make it easier to find those error lines in the editor, you could have all error lines contain a string that is easy to find like: *ERROR*. Then in **vi** you can type */ERROR* to move down to the next error line.

If you only want to see the error lines, use the **row** command.

LOGICAL CONDITIONS

For syntax and possibilities see **row, compute,** and UNIX **awk.**

NAME
ve   - visually edit a database table

SYNOPSIS
ve   [table [-n[n] -fc -mc -i -s [file] -h [file] -a [file] -v [file]]][-b]

DESCRIPTION
ve is a multi-user database table editor which defines rows or *records* as containing a fixed number of columns or *fields*. Fields are defined as text which is delimited by an exclusive *column separation character*. Normally, the first two rows in
a **ve** table are *header records* which describe the column layout of the table. Each
field in the first header record contains the name of the column; columns in the
second header record are dashes (-). **ve** with no arguments will display a menu of
on-line **ve** help topics and instructions.

OPTIONS
The *table* argument in the command line refers to the name of the table. When
table is specified, any other arguments must follow it. If it does not exist, **ve** will
create the necessary header records from a screen file or a header table.

-b   Use the terminal's highlighting capability. If specified, **ve** will do its best to
        emphasize nondata text and on-line help file keywords by displaying them
        at high intensity. This may produce odd results if */etc/termcap* entries for a
        particular terminal are incorrect or missing, or if your terminal type is set
        incorrectly.

-n*n*   Use automatic record numbering. **ve** assumes that data in the first column
        of each record is a unique number, and keeps track of the largest numbered
        record in the table. As new records are added to the table, this number is
        incremented and stored in the first column of the new record. When *n* is
        specified, **ve** begins numbering records at *n*. For example, *-n2001* means
        use automatic record numbering and begin the numbers at 2001.

-f*c*   Use the character *c* to delimit columns instead of the TAB (default). With
        the exception of the screen file, all files associated with the **ve** table *must*
        use the same column separation character.

-m*c*   Enter **ve** in *c* mode, where *c* is *i* for *i*nsert mode, *n* for *n*ext mode, and / for
        search mode. **ve** will return to this mode following each successful *write*.

-i   Initialize the table. **ve** maintains a private sequential index of all of the
        records in a table, so that it can keep track of records in use and records
        which have been deleted during an edit session. It also uses this index to
        clean up the table when the edit session is over. If the table is modified by a
        program other than **ve**, then the **-i** switch must be used during the next **ve**
        edit session to reinitialize the private index. You can use this index for fast
        searching by record number if each record has a number and no records are
        ever deleted.

If there are files in the directory that follow the **ve** naming convention *data-c*,
where *-c* is a file option switch (**-s, -h, -a, -v**), they will be incorporated automatically in the command line before the the argument list is processed. Files which

are not named according to this convention must be specified on the command line each time they are used and will override the inclusion of any default names in the command line.

-s *file*   If *file* is specified, **ve** will use the screen file named *file*. The screen file is created with any text editor to resemble the desired screen display. As such, the entire screen file should not exceed 23 lines. **ve** scans the screen file for column names enclosed in <>'s and will display data in those columns between the <>'s. Both brackets must be on the same line. If the screen file is used to initialize the table, all column names must be listed; otherwise, excluded column names also exclude data in those columns from viewing, searching, and modification. Data in columns whose names are preceded by *!* in the screen file are displayed and can be searched but cannot be modified.

-h *file*   The **-h** switch specifies that the header records are in a separate file (*file* or *data-h* if not specified). When a header table is included in the command line, **ve** assumes that the first two records in the table are actual data. The header table can be created by **ve** only when the table is being initialized with a screen file.

-a *file*   If the audit table does not exist, **ve** will create an audit table named *file* (or *data-a* if *file* is not specified).

          ve audits tables by recording each addition, modification and deletion made and stores this information in the audit table. The audit table looks like the table, with the addition of two columns in the beginning of each record, the *time stamp* column and the *modification code* column.

          The first column of each row in the table must be a unique number in order for rows to be tracked accurately. **ve** manages these numbers and assigns new ones to rows which are added. If the table already exists, **ve** begins record numbering at the largest record number in the table plus 1; for new tables, **ve** begins record numbering at 1.

          Each time a record is added (code *a*), changed (code *c*), or deleted (code *d*), **ve** will record the date and time, the modification code, and the record number in the audit table. When a record is changed or deleted, the data in the record prior to modification is stored in the audit table.

-v *file*   If the validation table does not exist, the **-v** switch will create the validation table named *file* (or *data-v* if *file* is not specified). Then **ve** uses itself to edit the new validation table so that the user can enter validation requirements for desired columns before editing the table.

When a validation table is included in the command line, **ve** checks the data as it is entered into columns, which are specified in the validation table, to make sure they meet certain requirements.

The first header record of the validation table must have a *name* column, a *character* column, a *length* column, and a *table look-up* column, in that order. The first column in a validation table record is the name of a column from the table which is being subjected to validation.

The second column of each validation table record lists the valid characters and/or ranges of characters for data in the table column. Each character or range must be separated by a comma (,). Ranges or characters which are preceded by *!* exclude that range or character from the valid list. For example, the validation string *a-z,!y,1-9,#,., ,,* means that all lower case characters with the exception of *y* are valid, as are numbers from 1-9, pound symbols, periods, blanks, and commas. A simple way of specifying anything but numbers is *!0-9*.

The third column of the validation table describes column length limits and is indicated by the *<,>,=* and *!* symbols. The first three are specified with a number and mean *less than number*, *greater than number*, and *equal to number*. The *!*, when used in conjunction with one of the other three, means that data can also be zero length. For example, *!,=5* specifies data for columns which, if not blank, must be exactly 5 in length. *>10,<28* specifies that the length of the data in this column must be at least 11 and not more than 27 characters in length.

The fourth column in the validation table lists the name of the table in which **ve** should look to make a comparison between the data entered and the data in the table. When the name of the table is preceded by *!*, data entered in the column must *not* be in the table; otherwise it *must* be in the table. Lookup tables are created from **ve** tables with the *vindex* command. They are named after the column you are vindexing, which is called the *key column*. If the name of the key column is longer than 11 characters, the name of the table will be truncated to 11 characters. Blanks in the key column name are converted to '_'. For example, the specification *!name* tells **ve** to check the data against a table comprised of all text located in a column named *name*; if the data is *not* found in the table, then it passes table look-up validation.

COMMANDS

Table 1 on page 457 is a list of **ve** edit commands. **ve** uses two modes when editing a table: *command mode* and *insert mode*. Commands which switch **ve** from command to insert mode are indicated by '<ESC>'; the ESC key switches **ve** from insert to command mode.

The *c* and *d* commands require *targets*. Targets are destinations for the command (*c*hange or *d*elete) being executed. For example, the command *dfa* means *delete text from the cursor up to and including the first 'a' character encountered*. In this case the target command is *f*. In Table 1, commands which may be used as targets for the *c* and *d* commands are indicated by (t).

Some commands recognize a number which indicates how many times it should execute. For example, the command *5l* means *move right 5 characters*. The command *3rP* means *replace the next 3 characters with the character 'P'*. Counts may also be used with targets: the command *c2w* means *change the next 2 words*. Commands which recognize counts are indicated in the Table 1 by (c).

Table 2 lists two other kinds of **ve** commands — *colon* commands and CTRL-*key* commands, all of which map directly to commands in Table 1. Colon commands are provided for users familiar with **vi**. CTRL-key commands allow the user to define command macros by specifying the CTRL-key character and the command(s) from Table 1 which should be executed each time the CTRL-key is hit. These definitions, or *macros* are defined in a **/rdb**-formatted file named *.verc* located in the user's home directory. If there is no *.verc* file, then the default CTRL-key commands apply. If the user is in insert mode when a CTRL-key is hit, **ve** will attempt to restore that mode following successful execution of the macro.

Table 1: ve Commands

Command	Description	Command	Description
A*text*<ESC>	append *text* at field end	R<ESC>	replace
a*text*<ESC>	append *text* after cursor	r*x*	replace with *x*
B	back field (c)	S	redraw the screen
b	back word (t,c)	s<ESC>	substitute text (c)
C<ESC>	change to field end	t	Table display
c<ESC>	change to target	u	undo last command
D	delete to field end	v	validation display
d	delete to target	W	write record
dd	delete record	w	next word (t,c)
e	end of word (t,c)	x	delete character (c)
F*x*	find *x* left (t,c)	Y	yank current record
f*x*	find *x* right (t,c)	y	yank current field
G	go to last record (c)	ZZ	write record & quit
H	first field	z	field display
h	left character (t,c)	;	repeat F/f cmd (t)
I*text*<ESC>	insert *text* at field start	^	start of field (t)
i*text*<ESC>	insert *text* before cursor	$	end of field (t)
j	down field (c)	/*text*<ESC>	search for text
k	up field (c)	/<ESC>	repeat search
L	last field	-	get preceding record
l	right character (t,c)	%	execute the shell
m	mark search field	!	shell escape
M	unmark search field	!!	repeat shell escape
n	get next record	>	scroll field left
O*text*<ESC>	open new record	<	scroll field right
o*text*<ESC>	open new field	#	help file(s) display
P	put yanked record	RETURN	next field (c)
p	put yanked field	TAB	next field (c)
q	quit **ve**	SPACE	right character(t,c)

Table 2: Colon and CTRL-key Commands

colon		CTRL-key	
command	maps to	command	maps to
:h[*elp*]	#	CTRL-a	#
:n[*ext*]	n	CTRL-r	S
:o[*pen*]	O	CTRL-t	t
:q[*uit*]	q	CTRL-q	ZZ
:s[*hell*]	%	CTRL-s	%
:w[*rite*]	W	CTRL-w	W
:!*cmd*	!*cmd*	CTRL-v	v
:!!	!!	CTRL-d	ddn

SEE ALSO
  vindex(1)

NAME

vilock   - locks a table before vi and unlocks afterwards

SYNOPSIS

vilock   tableorlist

DESCRIPTION

vilock keeps others from editing the same file you are. **vilock** will change the name of the table to *LOCKtable,* a temporary file that will only last as long as you are doing the edit. Then it will execute the program **vi** *LOCKtable.* When you finish editing, **vilock** will move **mv** *LOCKtable* back to its original name. If anyone else tries to edit the table while you have it in **vilock,** they will get a message that it is locked or missing.

EXAMPLE

```
$ vilock inventory
```

will put you in the editor, with a file named *LOCKinventory.*

When you finally finish with the file and get out of the editor, **vilock** will **mv** *LOCKinventory* back to *inventory.* If you list your directory again, you will now see the *inventory* file.

SOURCE

```
: %W% SCCS ID Information
: vilock locks a file by moving it to another name.  It then calls
:          vi so you can edit it.  When you return from vi, it moves the
:          file back to its old name.  If anyone trys to vilock it while
:          you have it, they will get a message: file locked.

USAGE='usage: vilock textfile'
EUSAGE=1
LOCKED="$1 is locked"
ELOCKED=2
NOFIND="$1 is unreadable, not in the directory, or non-existant."
ENOFIND=3

if test "$#" -lt 1
then
        echo $USAGE 1>&2
        exit $EUSAGE
fi

TMP=/tmp/$$$1
if test -f "$1" -a -r "$1"
then
        mv $1 $TMP
        trap "mv $TMP $1" 0 1 2 3 15
        vi $TMP
elif ls /tmp/[0-9]*$1 # 2> /dev/null 1> /dev/null
then
        echo $LOCKED
        exit $ELOCKED
else
        echo $NOFIND
        exit $ENOFIND
fi
```

NAME
　vindex　- create and display ve look-up tables

SYNOPSIS
　vindex　table [key-column [: decode-column] ...]]

DESCRIPTION
　vindex creates and displays tables comprised of columns in **ve** tables. These tables are used by **ve** when validating column entries. The required *table* argument specifies the *name* of the **ve** table.

　When no options are specified, **vindex** displays the contents of all existing column tables associated with *table*.

　For each *key-column* argument specified, **vindex** collects the text from that column and stores it in two files which are prefixed by the name of the *key-column* and are suffixed by *-A* and *-B*. If the *key-column* name exceeds 14 characters, the table name prefix is truncated to 14 characters. *Key-column* names which contain blanks must be surrounded by double quotes (") in the **vindex** command line: blanks are converted to underscore (_) in the table name. These files are referred to in the fourth column of **ve** validation files by the table name prefix.

　When the colon (:) argument follows a key-column name, the column name following this argument is assumed to be the name of a *decode-column*. As key-column text is collected in the table the associated decode-column text is linked to it as a cross-reference.

EXAMPLE
　The following **vindex** command will create a look-up table for the *key-columns: Snumber* and *State* in a table named *personnel,* and cross-reference the information in the *Snumber* column with the text in the *Employee decode-column:*

```
$ vindex personnel "Snumber" : Employee State
```

　The resulting table names are *Snumber* and *State*.

SEE ALSO
　ve

NAME

whatis   - displays the command description and syntax

SYNOPSIS

whatis   command

DESCRIPTION

whatis displays the description and syntax of the command selected. It is similar
to the **whatis** command of the Berkeley enhancements except it handles **/rdb** and
also gives the syntax.

EXAMPLE

```
$ whatis column
    column      - display columns of a table in any order
    column      column ... < tableorlist

$ whatis whatis
    whatis      - displays the command description and syntax
    whatis      command
```

SOURCE

```
: %W% SCCS ID Information

: whatis - displays the description and syntax for a command

USAGE='usage: whatis command'

DIR=`path whatis`

for COMMAND in $*
do
        grep "^$COMMAND  " $DIR/../lib/Commands
done

: for Berkeley UNIXs

if test -r /usr/man/whatis
then
        grep "^ *$1[ ]" /usr/man/whatis
fi
```

NAME
whatwill - displays the commands with function in description

SYNOPSIS
whatwill function

DESCRIPTION
whatwill displays the description and syntax of the command which will perform the function selected, like the permuted index of the UNIX User's Manual. **whatwill** is like the Berkeley Enhancement command **appropos.** It is similar to the **whatis** command, except it looks for the function anywhere in the name of the command, the description, and the syntax. So if you ask for **total,** you will get both **total** and **subtotal.**

This is like an automatic key word index.

EXAMPLE
```
$ whatwill column
     column      - display columns of a table in any order
     column      column ... < table

$ whatwill total
     subtotal    - outputs the subtotal of columns in a table
     subtotal    [ -l ][ break-column column ...] < table
     total       - sums up each column selected and displays
     total       [ -l ][ column ... ] < table
```

SEE ALSO
whatis

SOURCE
```
: %W% SCCS ID Information

: whatwill - displays the description and syntax for a command

USAGE='usage: whatwill keyword'
DIR='path whatwill'

for COMMAND in $*
do
        grep "$COMMAND" $DIR/../lib/Commands
done

: for Berkeley UNIXs

if test -r /usr/man/whatwill
then
      grep "$1" /usr/man/whatwill
fi
```

NAME

widest   - outputs the length of widest column in a table

SYNOPSIS

widest   < table'

DESCRIPTION

widest inputs a table and outputs another table with the number of characters of the widest field in each column.

EXAMPLE

```
$ widest < inventory
Item    Amount   Cost    Value   Description
----    ------   ----    -----   --------------
4       6        4       5       14
```

This can be used for formatting, and so on. **/rdb** does not require a schema because it gets the parameters of the tables from the tables themselves.

SOURCE

```
: %W% SCCS ID Information

: 'widest outputs the length of widest column'

USAGE='usage: widest < table'
EUSAGE=1

awk 'NR <= 2 {print}
{n=split($0,field,"        ");
for (i=1; i<=n; i++) {
        x=length(field[i]);
        if (x > width[i]) width[i]=x
        }
}
END {for (i=1; i<n; i++) printf("%s\t",width[i]);
        printf("%s",width[n]);
        printf("\n")
        }'
```

NAME
 width - displays the width of each column selected

SYNOPSIS
 width [-l] [column ...] < table

DESCRIPTION
 width displays the maximum length of each column selected. If no columns are
 listed, all of the columns will be calculated and displayed.

OPTIONS
 -l option will cause the entire file to be listed also.

EXAMPLE
 See **total.**

NAME
word   - converts text file into list of unique words

SYNOPSIS
word   < text > table

DESCRIPTION
word will input any text file and produce a long list of unique words. It can be used for language translation and for other conversions of databases by using the **translate** command.

EXAMPLE
Lets find the words in the description paragraph above which has been saved in a file called *words*.

```
$ word < words
It
a
and
any
bases
be
by
can
command
conversions
data
file
for
in
(...)
words
```

SEE ALSO
translate

SOURCE
```
: word extracts a list of each word in a text file
USAGE='usage: word < text > wordlist'

tr -cs '[A-Z][a-z]' '[\012*]' |
sort |
uniq
```

NAME

yourprog   - one line description of yourprog goes here

SYNOPSIS

yourprog   syntax goes here

DESCRIPTION

Description of your program goes here.

OPTIONS

List and describe all of the options (-o flags) here.

EXAMPLE

Please show examples of yourprog here.

SECTION

If you need subsections, you can use .SS

SEE ALSO

List other related programs here. Your Name

SOURCE

Include the source if you wish.

DISCUSSION

Discuss the source, the algorithms and special tricks you used.

SOURCE

```
: %W% SCCS Information

: yourprog - a description of the command
:         any futher comments about the command
:         this is a sample program for you to copy and modify

: edit the line below to represent the syntax of your program

USAGE="usage: yourprog -o arg ... [ oparg ... ] < filein > fileout"

: the above is standard, below is optional

: if you have abnormal exit status codes, define them here

: error - bad syntax or usage

EUSAGE=1

: error - other errors messages and return codes with increasing numbers

MOTHER='Error: other error message.'
EOTHER=2

: if you are going to use temporary files, inclúde a line for each

TMP=/usr/tmp/$$yourprog
TMP1=/usr/tmp/$$1yourprog
```

```
: be sure to trap interrupts and remove the temporary files

trap "rm -f /usr/tmp/$$*" 0 1 2 3 15

: if you have required options, you can test for them here
: be sure to send error messages to standard error

if test "$#" -lt 1
then
        echo $USAGE 1>&2
        exit $EUSAGE
fi

: here is a crude sample of argument parsing

for ARG in $*
do
        case $ARG in
        -a)     OPTIONA=true ;;
        -o)     OPTIONO=true ;;
        *)      OPARG="$OPARG $ARG" ;;
        esac
done

: finally the program code simply echos the name of this program

echo yourprog
```

Bibliography

AMSBURY, WAYNE, *Data Structures: From Arrays to Priority Queues.* Wadsworth Publishing Company, 1985. Illustrated review of fast access methods.

BECKER, RICHARD A., AND JOHN M. CHAMBERS, *S: An Interactive Environment for Data Analysis and Graphics.* Wadsworth, Inc., 1984. Tutorial and manual for the S statistical and graphics package from AT&T.

CHEN, P. P., *The entity-relationship model: Toward a unified view of data.* ACM Transactions on Database Systems, 1976, Volume 1, 9-36. The classic article that introduced the entity-relationship database model.

———, *Entity-Relationship Approach to Systems Analysis and Design.* North-Holland Publishing Company, 1980. A book of articles by researcher studing the entity-relationship model.

CODD, E. F., *A Relational Model of Data for Large Shared Data Banks.* Communications of the ACM, June 1970, 377-87. The classic article that introduced the relational database model.

———, *Relational Database: A Practical Foundation for Productivity.* Communications of the ACM, February 1982, 109-117. 1981 ACM Turing Award Lecture with definition of "relationally complete."

COX, BRAD J., *Object Oriented Programming, An Evolutionary Approach.* Reading, MA: Addison-Wesley, 1986. Introduces enhancements to the C language for object oriented programming. Also much wisdom about software applications development.

DATE, C. J., *An Introduction to Database Systems (3rd ed.),* Reading, MA: Addison-Wesley, 1981. Textbook with good coverage of relational and other database models.

———, *An Introduction to Database Systems, Volume II.* Reading, MA: Addison-Wesley, 1982. Covers several advanced issues in database theory.

FEIGENBAUM, EDWARD, AND P. MCCORDUCK, *The Fifth Generation.* Michael Joseph, 1983. An influential and very readable review of Japan's Fifth Generation computer project and a plea for a western response.

FORSYTH, RICHARD, *BEAGLE: a Darwinian approach to pattern recognition.* Kybernetes, 1981. Describes software that lets the best classification rules win.

————, ed., *Expert Systems: Principles and Case Studies.* Chapman and Hall, 1984. Collection of articles on the practical side of expert system development.

GRAY, PETER, *Logic, Algebra, and Databases.* New York, NY: Halsted Press, a division of John Wiley & Sons, 1984. Ties together relational database with logic programming and Prolog.

JACKSON, PETER, *Introduction to Expert Systems.* Reading, MA: Addison-Wesley Publishing Company, 1986. Review of expert systems and theory.

KERNIGHAN, BRIAN, AND ROB PIKE, *The UNIX^{TM} Programming Environment.* Englewood Cliffs, NJ: Prentice-Hall, 1985. Several chapters on shell programming and a lex/yacc application.

KERNIGHAN, BRIAN, *AWK.* 1987. Introduction to **awk** by one of its creators.

KERSCHBERG, LARRY, *Expert Database Systems: Proceedings From the First International Workshop.* Benjamin/Cummings Publishing Company, 1986. Many papers on combining expert systems with database management systems, the next important step.

KIM, WON, *Relational Database Systems.* Computing Surveys, September 1979, 185. Review of the implementation of the relational model in several systems.

KOCHAN, STEPHEN G., AND PATRICK H. WOOD, *UNIX^{TM} Shell Programming.* Hayden Book Company, 1985. UNIX shell programming basics.

MAIER, DAVID, *The Theory of Relational Databases.* Computer Science Press, 1983. Heavy mathematical treatment of relational database theory.

MANIS, ROD, AND MARC H. MEYER, *The UNIX^{TM} Shell Programming Language.* Indianapolis, IN: Howard W. Sams and Co., Inc., 1986. Complete survey of UNIX shell programming tools and techniques with many examples.

MICHALSKI, R. S., AND R. L. CHILAUSKY, *Learning by being told and learning from examples.* International Journal of Policy Analysis and Information Systems, 1980. Describes an AI program that learns to classify soya-bean diseases.

PRATA, STEPHEN, *Advanced UNIX^{TM} — A Programmers Guide.* Indianapolis, IN: Howard W. Sams and Co., Inc., 1985. More advanced than the many introductory UNIX books, covers shell and C programming environment.

QUILLIAN, J. R., *Induction over Large Databases.* Report HPP-79-14, Stanford University, 1979. Describes an AI program that builds its own decision tree from a database considered as examples.

————, *Semantic memory.* Semantic Information Processing (Minsky, M., ed.) MIT Press, 1968, 227-70. Original semantic network article.

SOWA, J. F., *Conceptual Structures: Information Processing in Mind and Machine.* Reading, MA: Addison-Wesley, 1984. Excellent presentation of the manipulation of concepts by operations on conceptual networks.

TSICHRITZIS, DIONYSIOS C., AND FREDERICK H. LOCHOVSKY, *Data Models.* Englewood Cliffs, NJ: Prentice-Hall, Inc., 1982. In depth discussion of eleven data models: relational, and so on.

ULLMAN, JEFFREY D., *Database Systems (2nd ed.),* Computer Science Press, 1982. Up-to-date practical and theoretical review of database ideas.

WINSTON, ALAN, *4GL Faceoff: A look at Fourth-Generation Languages.* UNIX/World, July 1986, 34-41.

Index

YES—I'd like\rdb for my UNIX system

Cut out this form and fill
in all necessary information.
Then enclose this form
in an envelope and mail to:

Please send me pricing information for **\rdb** for my **UNIX**
system. I understand that **\rdb** runs on *all* UNIX based
computers, micro to mainframe, and most UNIX derivitives
(XENIX, Microport System V/AT, 4.3 BSD, AIX, ULTRIX, etc.).
Prices for **\rdb** vary by size of system from $795 to $2,495.

Robinson Schaffer Wright
711 California Street
Santa Cruz, CA 95060
(408) 429-6229

My computer is _____, it runs the following
version of UNIX _____, and supports _____users.

Name_____
Firm/Department_____
City_____State_____Zip_____
Daytime telephone number(_____) _____ _____

NOTE: Prices subject to change without notice.

YES—I'd like /rdb and/or MKS Toolkit for DOS
for my PC-DOS or MS-DOS system

The MKS Toolkit provides over 100 UNIX like commands and is required to take
advantage of /rdb in a DOS environment (version 2.0 and later releases).

Cut out this form and fill
in all necessary information.
Then enclose this form with
your check or money order
only in an envelope and
mail to:

Please send the items checked below. PAYMENT ENCLOSED
(check or money order *only*). Robinson Schaffer Wright
will pay all shipping and handling charges.

_____/rdb and MKS Toolkit for DOS—$275
_____/rdb for DOS only. I have MKS Toolkit—$139
_____MKS Toolkit for DOS only (I don't need /rdb yet)—$139
California residents please add 7% sales tax

Robinson Schaffer Wright
711 California Street
Santa Cruz, CA 95060
(408) 429-6229

Name_____
Firm/Department_____
City_____State_____Zip_____
Daytime telephone number (_____) _____ _____

NOTE: Prices subject to change without notice.